TABLE OF CONTENTS

LIST OF HANDS-ON EXERCISES

ABOUT THE AUTHOR

HOWARD MASSEY has been professionally involved in the world of synthesizers for over a decade. He is a composer, record producer, and recording engineer, in addition to his activities as a session synthesizer programmer and synthesizer instructor.

Currently Project Director of the Public Access Synthesizer Studio in New York, he has been teaching the intricacies of the Yamaha DX7 to novice and experienced musicians alike, both in formal workshops and through private instruction, since 1983. Additionally, he has organized and taught seminars on MIDI and on programmable analog synthesis.

As a composer, he has written numerous television and film themes, ambient electronic soundtracks for holography exhibitions, and a hit single for Herb Alpert! As a producer/engineer/programmer, he has worked with a broad spectrum of popular recording artists: from Kraftwerk to Spandau Ballet; from Roy Buchanan to Sham 69, and the list goes on and on... Born in New York City, he was resident in London, England for some four years before returning to the U.S. in late 1982. He presently lives in Huntington, Long Island.

The Complete DX7 is his first book.

FOREWORD

The success of Yamaha's DX7 is one of those enigmas that makes perfect sense—sort of. The instrument is currently the best-selling synthesizer of all time, yet it is also one of the least user-friendly machines on the market. Its sound is so popular that it is precariously close to cliche-hood, yet the majority of people playing the instrument find it so difficult to program that an entire cottage industry has sprung up dedicated to selling DX patches and DX programming aids. Even now, three years after its release, people are having a hard time learning their way around it, yet there's no end in sight to the momentum of its popularity.

If you have one of those love/hate relationships with the instrument—you know, you love its sound but you curse a lot because you don't know an operator from a rate scale—then Howard's book should help clear up the confusion.

Some bald-headed wise old monk probably said something like, "The path to knowledge is a difficult one, "at one time or another, and that certainly applies to knowledge about the DX7. Learning its ins and outs won't be easy, but it's not impossible. This book may not reveal the hidden paths to truth, justice, and the American way, but it goes a long way towards unlocking the secrets of the DX7.

Dominic Milano
Editor,
Keyboard Magazine

AUTHORS NOTE: After receiving this foreword from Dominic, I shelved my plans to add a seventeeth chapter, tentatively entitled "Truth, Justice, and the American Way".

ACKNOWLEDGEMENTS

I am very indebted to many people for having made this book possible, for having provided encouragement, and for having put up with me during the time I was chained to my word processor writing it!

First and foremost, a thank you from the bottom of my heart to my patient, supportive, and loving wife, Linda Law, for helping me to retain a three-dimensional perspective on things. Secondly, I'd like to specifically express my appreciation to the following people for easing this new author through his first book:

I am very grateful for the assistance provided by all the staff of PASS (the Public Access Synthesizer Studio), particularly Daniel Shklair, Judith Bruk, and Executive Director Gerald Lindahl, and to my long-standing and close friend Bob Styles (alias Traf Tragen), who has helped me virtually every step of the way. On the technical side, thanks to Eric Braun for his invaluable aid and moral support, to Dominic Milano and Ted Greenwald of Keyboard Magazine, to Mark Koenig, Phil Moon, and Steve Demmings of Yamaha, and to Bob Lawson, George McCormick and Howie Rosenberg, who helped keep my orphaned computer running (and provided selfless assistance when it wasn't!).

Special mention must go to Dr. John Chowning, without whom the DX7 would not have been possible, and to my dear mother and father, without whom I would not have been possible. Sincere thanks also to Barrie Edwards, Dan Earley, Kendall Minter, Denis Kellman, Andrew Glassner, Michael Assante, Larry Tucker, Dave Crombie, Craig Anderton, Juli Davidson, Patty Stotter, Steve Parr, my brother Richard Massey, Marvin and Estelle Tolkin, David and Deli Snow, Burt Rashbaum, and particularly to Al Gorgoni for providing the original impetus for this book.

Last, but by no means least, let me publicly thank the hundreds of DX7 students I've taught during these past three years - with each new student I, too, learned something new about the instrument. Thank you for continually prodding me further, whether you knew it or not!

Howard Massey
June 1986

INTRODUCTION

In 1983 the Yamaha Corporation released upon a largely unsuspecting public a synthesizer that would change the course of modern music. This machine, of course, was the model **DX7**, and, for the first time ever, digital audio synthesis was made available to the musician at a reasonable price.

Prior to the unveiling of the DX7, the only two digital synthesizers commonly in use were the Fairlight Computer Musical Instrument and the Synclavier - and both of these formidable machines had list prices in excess of $30,000 and were obviously out of the financial reach of most musicians. Furthermore, both of these systems offered literally thousands of controls, commands, and configurations, making them far too complicated and not nearly enough "user-friendly" for most of their intended market.

The DX7 changed all that. Its list price was a very modest $1,995, and when you bought the machine you also received, as a bonus, data cartridges containing no less than 128 very attractive and usable sounds. Contemporary musicians took to this device like the proverbial ducks took to water. In no time at all it seemed as if every keyboard player owned one despite the fact that for nearly a year in most major cities you couldn't find one for love or money (in an industry where list price rarely has any real meaning, the DX7 was actually sold everywhere at its list price, NONDIS-COUNTED, for more than a year after its introduction). In New York City, for example, only one of the major music retailers was able to get DX7s at all, and the waiting list at one time was actually more than eight months!

In any event, by hook or by crook (or, much to Yamaha's dismay, by gray market), in what seemed to be no time at all, DX7s abounded, in every recording studio, in every rehearsal hall, in every keyboardist's living room... if the machines reproduced **themselves**, they couldn't have done much better.

There was a problem, however. Due to the very sketchy documentation originally provided by Yamaha, combined with the fact that the DX7 used a synthesis system never before seen, nobody seemed to know how to actually work the darned things! Oh, people found the on/off switch and the output jack, alright, but short of endlessly using the 128 cartridge sounds (the "presets"), people were not generally using the machine to anywhere near its actually vast capabilities.

As of this writing, some three years later, the situation has not really improved appreciably. An upgraded version of the preliminary manual has been released by Yamaha, and a book or two have made appearances, but all of these seem to be of limited value to the average user. The difficulty lies in the fact that, first of all, the DX7 at first glance **seems** unassuming and many people have trouble accepting the idea that so very many controls and parameters are actually available to the user. Secondly, the system used by the DX7 and its later cousins (the DX9, DX1, DX5, DX21, DX27, DX100, TX7, and TX rack), called *digital* FM, is so radically different from previously used systems, that people have had problems assimilating and utilizing its many unique features. Digital FM (short for "frequency modulation") demands that you **analyze** the sounds you work with to a far greater degree than was previously required. It is difficult, if not impossible, to use by musicians who have not taken the time and trouble to familiarize themselves with basic acoustic principles and audio theory. Thirdly, because this is a purely *digital* system, some small degree of computer literacy is required in order to fully understand the workings of the system. And, lastly, those 128 presets, for the most part, really *do* sound good, reducing the incentives for people to learn to make their own sounds or even modify pre-existing ones. Commercial enterprises have sprung up, allowing users who don't feel confident programming their own machines to purchase ready-made sounds. The sum of all of the above means that, even today, most DX7 owners are no closer to knowing how to use their machines then they were three years ago when the instrument first appeared.

And that's where this tutorial comes in. This book is dedicated to the principle that it makes no sense to spend $2,000 on a machine that you basically only know how to turn on and off! Computers such as the DX7 have become a big part of most people's lives but it's important not to lose sight of the fact that **we** are still the computer's master. Yamaha has taken the time and trouble to provide DX7 owners with a phenomenally large array of tools to control the actions of the machine, and we are wasting a lot of the instrument's potential if we don't thoroughly familiarize ourselves with them.

Like most musicians, my first exposure to synthesizers came with the MiniMoog back in the early 1970's. It seemed to me that the only way to *really* master that machine (which was absolutely primitive compared to the DX7), was to lock myself in a room with it for a month or so and wrestle with it (all of this figuratively, of course - for those of you with a mental picture of a man with a beard emerging from a room with a MiniMoog in a headlock, forget it!). Ten years later, with a decade of experience as a session synthesist, session programmer, clinician, consultant, salesman, and teacher behind me, this seemed again the only way to master the DX7. And that's pretty much what I did, with the advantage that by now I knew enough people in the industry to annoy with endless questions and to receive invaluable feedback and instruction from. When I felt confident enough to actually impart this information to others, the opportunity arose to organize and teach a course in the operation of this machine at the Public Access Synthesizer Studio in New York (PASS), where I am currently serving as Project Director. At the urging of several students, I began in late 1985 to put the full course curriculum in writing, and this book is the ultimate result of that effort.

Here then, is the plan of action: We will begin, first of all, with a grounding in basic audio theory. I strongly recommend that all readers at least peruse, if not digest Chapter One thoroughly. Even if you feel knowledgable in this topic, you should read this chapter anyway, as the terminology and jargon covered therein will be used throughout the entire book. Secondly, we will cover in depth the actual digital FM system used by the DX7, including a description of ALL the switches and controls available on the machine, with practical exercises in their use offered throughout. Next, we will offer a discussion of MIDI, the standardized digital interface used by the DX7 and all other modern synthesizers. Following the MIDI chapter, we will cover several advanced DX7 programming techniques, and offer an examination of other DX7-like devices made by Yamaha. Finally, the Appendices will provide several important references and listings of DX7-compatible MIDI devices.

Most of the time while reading this book you will probably find it necessary to have a DX7 within easy reach. The enclosed sound sheet contains examples of sounds you should be hearing at various points as you do the exercises included here. We recommend that you immediately copy this onto a cassette for ease of use, and so it will also be helpful to have a cassette player handy. As this book is based upon the actual course taught at the Public Access Synthesizer Studio, it is meant to be very much a "hands-on" experience. I suggest you therefore prepare your hands for some serious synthesizer tweaking!

Throughout, I have attempted to make things as non-technical as possible. The emphasis is on *use* of the machine above all. It is the author's sincere hope that the information gleaned here will spark the creation of many, many sounds never before heard on this planet of ours!

Howard Massey
June 1986

CHAPTER ONE:
BASIC AUDIO THEORY

What Is A Synthesizer?

A synthesizer, by definition, is any kind of machine or device that can create sounds without the benefit of any kind of physical motion. This is what differentiates electronic instruments from acoustic instruments. The one thing that is common to all acoustic instruments is that the sound they create always originates as something physically vibrating, be it a string, a reed, or a skin. We should probably extend our definition somewhat and add that a true synthesizer should allow the operator some degree of control over how the sound is shaped and created. If we don't make this disclaimer then we would have to allow instruments such as the home organ and toy-like devices such as the smaller Casio machines to share in the glory! These instruments do create their sounds electronically and not physically but they allow no significant controls to the user.

Within this broad definition there are two different types of synthesizers: analog and digital. These two breeds are as different as the proverbial apples and oranges in the way they operate. Basically, analog synthesizers create their sounds by manipulating electrical voltages whereas digital synthesizers are essentially computers which evolve sounds by manipulating numbers.

Numbers?? How can we hear numbers? Allow me, if you will, to answer your rhetorical question with another question: How can we hear voltages? Before we jump right in with a discussion of digital (which after all is the system the Yamaha DX7 uses) it will be helpful to gain a rudimentary understanding of how analog systems work.

What Is Analog?

The word "analog" itself simply means "like" or "similar to". The best way to understand how analog systems work is to examine how a very common home analog system, like the standard record player, operates.

If you are not a Tibetan monk sitting on top of a mountain, you probably own or at least have at some time used a common garden variety stereo system with record player. Odds are you slap a record on weekly, daily, or maybe even hourly (!) without ever thinking about what is physically occurring, and that's fine, because it creates jobs for people like me!

Let's examine the process: First of all, as you know, the needle is bouncing around in the groove of the record, so we start with actual physical motion. The purpose of the cartridge in your tone arm is to "listen" to that physical movement and convert it into an electrical signal. But it's not just any kind of arbitrary electrical signal; it is an ANALOG electrical signal, because it will perfectly emulate the physical motion of the needle bouncing around. In other words, whenever the needle bounces up and down, say a hundred times in a particular second, the electrical signal will wobble, or "bounce", you guessed it, a hundred times per second! This is the basic process of creating an ANALOG. You essentially are converting energy from one form to another, but you preserve the movements of that energy through the conversion.

Okay, let's continue on with our tracing of the journey as Bruce Springsteen's voice travels from the grooves of his latest platinum offering to your eager ears. The cartridge sends it's electrical signal down the wires of your tone arm and out the record player into your amplifier (or receiver, if it happens to have a radio attached), where the sound is simply amplified, or in plain English, made louder. If the amplifier is a good one, that's about all it will do, and if it's not such a good one it may add various kinds of distortions to the sound, but we won't concern ourselves with that. This amplified signal then travels out of your amplifier/receiver down the speaker wires to your speakers (or head-phones, which really are no different from small speakers).

A speaker is just a box with two magnets inside it. One of the magnets is actually an electromagnet and it is mounted firmly on the back wall of your speaker box and the other magnet is sort of suspended in mid-air nearby, attached to a paper cone. The electromagnet is going to be receiving the electrical signal from the speaker wire and will alternately become magnetized and demagnetized as the electrical signal moves forward and backward (remember, this electrical signal is an ANALOG of the original needle movements). As this fixed electromagnet goes through its paces it will alternately attract and repel the floating speaker. Because the floating speaker is attached to a paper cone, these small movements back and forth will translate themselves into larger movements of the cone, which will cause air to be pushed back and forth.

This movement of air eventually reaches our ear, and our eardrum is designed to sympathetically vibrate accordingly. These internal vibrations are transmitted to our inner ear where a series of physiological events transform these movements back into an electrical signal. This electrical signal travels through your nerve fibers and up into your brain where you finally perceive all of these various convolutions as a sound: At last, Brooooooooooce!!

Let's review what's happened: Our signal has undergone four separate transformations. We started as physical motion (the needle bouncing around), converted to analog electrical (inside the cartridge), converted to analog magnetic (inside the speaker), back to physical (the movements of the speaker cone), and once again back to electrical (in our inner ear). We can trace back still further if we like, to the recording process itself. The sound actually began with Brooooooce himself singing into a microphone in a recording studio somewhere in Hackensack or thereabouts. So the sound obviously began life as physical motion, air being moved by Brooooce's vocal chords. The purpose of the microphone was similar to that of the record player cartridge; to convert physical movement into an analog electrical movement. This electrical signal (containing of course the same type of movements as the original physical source) travels down wires into a mixing console where it is processed in a number of ways and then enters a tape recorder. The record head of the tape recorder converts this electrical signal yet again to a magnetic signal which can be encoded on tape. The tape is played back and the playback head converts it back again to electrical! (Stick with it, we're nearly done...) In the cutting room, this electrical signal from the tape playback is fed to a cutting lathe which then reconverts it back to the physical motion of a needle cutting a groove in a lacquer plate. This lacquer plate will eventually form the template for the record you finally purchase and play.

It's fairly complicated, but the point is that the original sound in every case undergoes many conversions before you finally get to hear and enjoy it. The important thing to understand is that all of these conversions are ANALOG, that is, the original qualities of the sound are in all cases preserved as nearly as possible. When you analyze things this way, it's really pretty amazing that your records actually sound **something** like the original performance!!

So where has all this gotten us, in terms of synthesizers? Well, analog synthesizers work in a very similar fashion to a record player except that they start at step two, not one. Instead of beginning life as a physical motion, analog synthesizer sounds actually **begin** as an electrical signal. This signal will still have to travel down some wires into and through an amplifier and into some speakers in order for us to hear it. The difference then is solely that the sound **originates** as an electrical signal of some kind.

What Is Digital?

Back, finally, to our original question; how can we hear numbers?? (Some of you might rightfully be annoyed that I'm presuming you asked this question where in fact I have no way of knowing if you did or not. Sorry, but you'll just have to allow me some poetic license) When somebody uses the word "digital" a little light bulb should switch on over your head and you should immediately think "computer" because these words are virtually synonymous. A digital synthesizer, as mentioned earlier, is a computer that can create sounds by manipulating numbers, typically at very high speeds. Although in a perverted way we could define human beings as the ultimate computers, we still do not have the ability to hear numbers. But we have seen that by using various conversion processes we **can** hear voltages. Therefore, digital synthesizers need to be able to convert the numbers they generate into voltages so that we can perceive them as sounds, and this is accomplished by using a clever little microchip called a digital-to-analog converter, or "DAC" for short. All digital synthesizers contain a DAC; otherwise we couldn't hear the sounds they create. How does this DAC convert numbers into voltages? Well, let's presume, for example, that our computer is generating the following numbers:

0,2,4,6,8,6,4,2,0,-2,-4,-6,-8,-6,-4,-2

and let's say that it keeps generating these same numbers over and over again. This stream of numbers is fed in "real time", that is, as it happens, to the DAC, which then outputs an electrical voltage that undergoes the same movements as the numbers, that is, an ANALOG voltage. What we would derive from this particular stream of numbers would be a smooth, steadily changing voltage which alternated back and forth at whatever rate of speed the computer was sending the numbers. If the computer all of a sudden decided to output a bunch of very large numbers very quickly, we would get a spike in the voltage. In other words, the DAC is "looking" at the numbers fed to it and "graphing" them out electrically. **(See Figure 1-1.)**

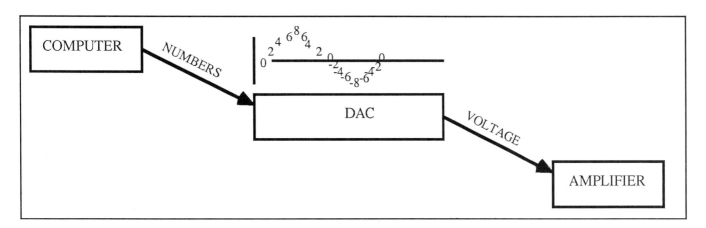

Figure 1-1

Digital synthesizers generate sounds using one of two different methods: additive synthesis and frequency modulation (or FM) synthesis. Until Yamaha introduced the DX7 in 1983, only the former method was commercially available (except to those users of the Synclavier, which incorporates some FM within it's general additive system). These two methods are substantially different and we will present brief summaries of their operations and differences at the end of this chapter. However, now that you've been sufficiently dazzled by the concepts presented above, it's really time to take a step backwards and talk about sound in general, not specifically as applied to synthesizers.

What Is A Sound?

We can define a sound as anything that our brain perceives as a direct result of air moving our eardrum. Sounds obviously can come in an enormous variety, from the sweet tones of a violin to a jackhammer, from the hum of a motor to a crack of lightning, from a swallow to a cough. We can categorize sounds as being musical or nonmusical, loud or soft, gentle or harsh. In all instances, however, we can only perceive sounds if air has somehow been moved (by the originating object itself or by a loudspeaker emulating the movement of the originating object). Furthermore, this movement of air must occur in a fairly regular ("periodic") back-and-forth manner, or in "waves".

No matter how many different sounds there can be (and the number is certainly infinite), there are surprisingly only three ways of describing a sound and for the purpose of this book we will refer to these as the THREE PARAMETERS OF SOUND.

The Three Parameters of Sound:

1) Volume
2) Pitch (or lack of pitch)
3) Tonal quality

ALL sounds, regardless of their origin, can be described with these parameters and these parameters only. Every sound has a particular loudness, or volume (the two terms are not technically synonymous, but for the purposes of this book we will assume that they are). Every sound has a particular pitch, and every sound has a particular kind of tonal quality. What's more, EVERY sound ALWAYS has all three of these qualities. There is no sound that has a particular volume and pitch, but no particular tonal quality. There is no sound that has a particular tonal quality and pitch but no particular volume. Furthermore, (and this is an extremely important point), as a rule, all three of these parameters typically CHANGE over the duration of the sound. **Understanding these principles is really the key to understanding audio synthesis of any type**.

We have seen that the synthesizer by definition will normally allow us a certain degree of control over shaping the sound we create. That means that we need to be able to control each of these three parameters if we are to be in the driver's seat. All synthesizers worthy of the title, be they analog or digital, will allow you these controls to some extent. The DX7 will allow us particularly fine control, but the point is that **everything** we will be doing from here on in will relate back to these **same three parameters**.

Jargon:

Every type of specialization has a jargon associated with it, and the area of audio synthesis is certainly no exception. Jargon sometimes serves merely as an ego device, in order to keep "outsiders" outside, but sometimes jargon exists to make definitions more precise. Synthesizer jargon is largely a mix of these two, but the purpose of this book is to make all of you outsiders "insiders" and so wherever possible we will identify jargon as such and give you "plain English" translations. Besides, once you know the jargon, you'll not only be able to impress your friends but you'll be able to make them feel like "outsiders" too! (and the circle goes 'round and 'round...)

Synthesists refer to "volume" as **amplitude**; they refer to "pitch" as **frequency**; and they refer to "tonal quality" as **timbre**. The first two are technical terms and the third is a musical term, but all three are universally used.

The Oscilloscope:

For the purposes of this chapter nothing could be more useful than a device called an "oscilloscope". An oscilloscope is basically a television-type receiver into which we can feed an audio signal; in short, it enables us to literally look at a sound. Unfortunately oscilloscopes are rather too large and expensive to be packaged inside this book and so we will have to make do with the following diagrams and a good sense of imagination: **(See Figure 1-2.)**

The oscilloscope plots the sound fed into it on a graph superimposed on a TV screen. It measures the amplitude, or volume, of the sound over time; basically we are looking at the way a sound changes volume over time, and typically over very short periods of time (usually a second, a tenth of a second, or even a hundreth of a second).

Amplitude:

The height of the wave is its AMPLITUDE. A car horn at a distance of two inches (very loud!!) might look like this: **(See Figure 1-3.)**

whereas the same car horn (i.e., same pitch and tonal quality) at a distance of two hundred feet (much quieter) might look like this: **(See Figure 1-4.)**

Note that nothing about the wave, except it's height, changes.

The amplitude or volume of a sound is normally measured in "decibels", or "db" for short. A single decibel is roughly the smallest unit of volume change that the human ear can detect, and sounds louder than about 180 decibels generally cause physical pain and/or damage (keep that in mind next time you are tempted to stick your head inside a PA bin at a rock concert!!)

It should be obvious that **all** sounds **always** change amplitude during their duration; after all, no one has yet invented a perpetual sound that lasts forever. Furthermore, **every** sound **always** eventually changes to an amplitude of 0 db (in plain English, every sound eventually ends!).

Frequency:

The substitution of the word **"frequency"** for "pitch" is actually a very logical one, as the pitch of the sound is represented on the oscilloscope by how frequently the wave reoccurs. In other words, the more waves we have within a given time period, the higher the pitch, or frequency, of the sound. Each time a musical sound goes up an octave, its frequency doubles; that is, we have twice as many waves occurring in the same time period. The sound of a piano playing Middle C might look on an oscilloscope like this: **(See Figure 1-5.)**

whereas the same piano playing C above Middle C might look like this: **(See Figure 1-6.)**

Of course in these particular examples we are presuming that the piano plays these notes at the same volume both times. Each time a musical sound goes down an octave, it's frequency is halved, so the same piano now playing C below Middle C would look like this: **(See Figure 1-7.)**

Notice that regardless of the height or shape of the wave, we always observe "hills" and "valleys", that is, an up portion followed by a down portion which is the direct inverse of the up portion. If you take the up portion, or "hill", and flip it upside down, it will look just like the "valley". This makes perfect sense in light of the fact, as we stated earlier, that sound always travels in repeating waves. We call one "hill" plus one "valley" a **cycle**, since they are always inseparable. If we then measure how many cycles occur in every second of the sound's duration, we can then make an accurate accounting as to the sound's FREQUENCY. **(See Figure 1-8.)**

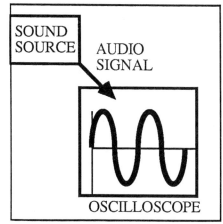

Figure 1-2

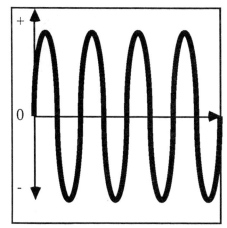

Figure 1-3

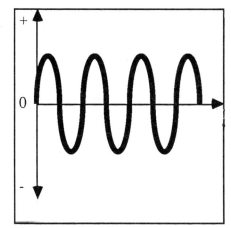

Figure 1-4

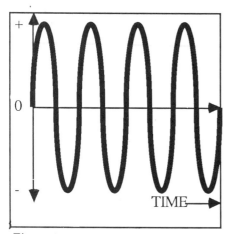

Figure 1-5

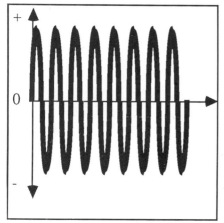

Figure 1-6

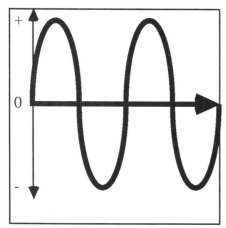

Figure 1-7

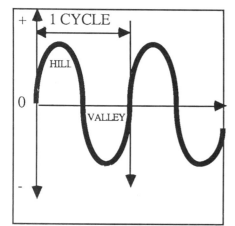

Figure 1-8

The unit of measurement used to describe frequency is the "Hertz", or **Hz** for short. A sound that generates, for example, exactly one cycle of waves per second is said to have a frequency of one Hertz. Therefore, if we speak, of a sound having a frequency of, say, 100 Hz, what we are saying in plain English is that this sound generates one hundred complete wave cycles per second. A shorthand term for describing 1000 Hertz is the "KiloHertz", or kHz for short.

Human beings have a particularly wide range of perceiving different frequencies. We can typically hear sounds having frequencies as low as 20 Hz, and as high as 20,000 Hz (20 kHz). That is not to say that sounds don't exist above and below these frequencies - they do, but most humans cannot hear them. Sounds within the range of human hearing are said to be in the **audible** range, and this is generally taken to be in the 20 to 20,000 Hz area. Sounds below the audible range are called **subsonic** and these are frequencies which we can sometimes feel, but generally not hear. When you listen to most kinds of music at high volumes (such as at a live rock concert) you will often experience the phenomenon of feeling your chest pounding. This is caused by subsonic range vibrations which actually are making your body vibrate. Sounds also exist above the audible range, and these are termed **supersonic**. Many animals are able to hear subsonic and/or supersonic frequencies. This is the way dog whistles work, for example. When you blow into the dog whistle you hear nothing but your dog certainly does. (Maybe it even sounds like Broooce to them! Sorry about that...)

In any event, most synthesizers will allow you to work with not only *audible* frequencies but with *subsonic* and *supersonic* ones as well. The need for this may not seem obvious now but will become more clear as we delve further into the operation of our DX7. Bear in mind, again, that the frequency of most sounds generally changes somewhat (often only slightly) during the duration of the sound.

Timbre:

This is the tricky one of the three to understand. Amplitude and frequency, after all, are pretty straightforward: it's very easy to conceptualize these terms from everyday experiences. But when it comes to tonal quality, or timbre, well, it all seems so subjective...

Fortunately, everything in audio theory is logical and highly mathematical (this is, after all, why computers are so good at synthesizing sounds). We have seen that both amplitude and frequency can easily be measured in real numbers and, believe it or not, so too can timbres.

Let's explore this with a simple example. Suppose you walk into a room and you have somebody play, say, "A" above Middle C on a piano that just happens to be sitting in a corner. This particular piano has just been tuned so you can be certain that the note you are hearing has a frequency of 440 Hz ("A440" is used as a reference tuning for most instruments and it simply means that the A above Middle C is tuned until it sends out a basic frequency of 440 cycles per second).

Okay, now you're hearing this note and suddenly (like a Hitchcock movie!) the lights go out. Before you can do anything about it, somebody else walks in, this time with a flute, and begins playing the same note. Right on the heels of the flutist is someone else with a guitar, and then another musician with a saxophone, and one after another they all begin playing the same note, A440. Let's take this improbable scenario one step further and add that all four of these musicians are so adept at their particular instruments that each one is playing their A440 at exactly the same volume.

So here you are in this darkened room listening to first a piano, then a flute, then a guitar, and then a saxophone, all playing exactly the same note (same frequency) at exactly the same volume (same amplitude). Even if our musicians try to get tricky and begin playing their A440's out of order, it's pretty obvious that neither you nor anyone else is going to be fooled. It's easy to tell the difference between a piano and a flute and a guitar and a saxophone, even with the lights out. Why is this? Because every instrument has a characteristic TIMBRE.

How do we define the characteristic timbre of a sound? There are no units of measurement as there were with amplitude and frequency but instead we will see that timbre is in fact frequency-related. When the bizarre example we just gave was presented, we told you a little white lie, and that LWL (technical jargon for Little White Lie) was that each instrument was playing a frequency of 440 Hz. In fact no acoustic instrument can create a sound that consists of only one frequency. To explain this more clearly, let's examine further just what happened when our pianist played his A above Middle C: the string in question began vibrating as soon as it was hit with the piano hammer. These string vibrations, first time around, looked like this: **(See Figure 1-9.)**

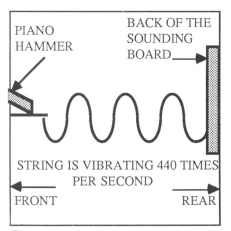

Figure 1-9

As you can see, the string begins moving back and forth, 440 times per second. So far, so good. But what happens when the string vibrations reach the back of the sounding board? Well, now the string begins rebounding back towards the front of the board, again 440 times per second. But don't forget that the original movements continue throughout, and so the patterns crisscross, causing a simultaneous vibration of twice the frequency, or 880 times per second. **(See Figure 1-10.)**

This process repeats itself when the string once again reaches the front board, now causing a third vibration of 1320 times per second, and yet again at the other end, causing a fourth vibration of 1760 times per second, and on and on until eventually the string runs out of energy and stops vibrating altogether (in other words, when the amplitude drops to 0). These secondary vibrations are called the OVERTONES of the sound, and it is the **type** and **quantity** of these overtones that determines a sound's TIMBRE.

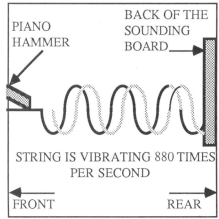

Figure 1-10

The initial frequency we started our string vibrating at (440 Hz in this example) is called the FUNDAMENTAL frequency. Overtones such as those described above whose frequencies are simply whole number multiples of the fundamental are called **harmonic overtones**, or **HARMONICS** for short. Thus, the second harmonic of any sound will always be the octave of that sound (remember, every time you go up an octave you double the frequency). So too will the fourth harmonic be double that of the second, and the eighth double that of the fourth. In other words, the second, fourth, eighth, sixteenth, and thirty-second harmonics (we rarely hear beyond this point, for reasons which will soon become apparent) are all OCTAVES of the fundamental frequency.

But what about the other harmonics? Well, as luck would have it, the entire western musical system is based upon these overtones, which all are pleasing musical intervals of the fundamental. For example, the third harmonic is a musical fifth higher than the second, and the fourth harmonic is a musical fourth higher than the third. These relationships are important to be aware of when working with an FM system such as that provided by the DX7.

When we heard that first A440 coming from the piano in the darkened room, what we were in fact hearing was a composite of many different frequencies blended together in a particular way, as follows:

Harmonic	Relationship	Frequency(Hz)
First	Fundamental	440
Second	Octave (8va)	880
Third	Fifth (8va)	1320
Fourth	Octave (16va)	1760
Fifth	Third(16va)	2200

etc., etc. In fact, we were hearing these additional overtones right up until the point where we couldn't hear any more! If you keep multiplying 440 on and on eventually you'll hit the number 20,000 and, remember, unless your name is Fido, you probably can't hear anything above that frequency anyway. Unless your fundamental is an extremely low note it's rare that you will be able to hear anything higher than the thirtieth or perhaps thirty-second harmonic.

The important point to remember is that anytime you hear any natural sound at all (and most electronic sounds), you are **never** hearing just a single frequency, but instead a composite sound composed of **many** frequencies blended together in a particular way. It is the type of blend which tells your brain what kind of *timbre* you are hearing.

I'm afraid we now have to complicate matters a bit further again as we inform you that in all likelihood when we heard our phantom pianist play the A440 we also probably heard a certain amount of, let's see, 3215.7 Hz as well. Also probably a certain amount of 602 Hz, and, um, 14,987.6 Hz too. These numbers obviously have no mathematical relationship at all to our fundamental of 440 but nonetheless they were probably there due to the physical abnormalities of the instruments. These oddball overtones are called DISHARMONICS (or ENHARMONICS) and are always present to some degree in all acoustically (and often electronically) generated sounds.

It is the relative amounts of harmonics versus disharmonics that determines whether we consider a sound to be MUSICAL or NONMUSICAL. Musical sounds, such as our piano, flute, guitar, or saxophone would produce would certainly have much higher proportions of harmonics than disharmonics, but those sounds produced by jackhammers, coughing, wind, or motors humming will generally contain proportionally more disharmonics. The speaking voice has more disharmonics than the singing voice. A classical guitar will contain more harmonics than an electric guitar through a fuzz pedal. Generally, any sound which has a determinable pitch is considered musical and will usually have a basically harmonic overtone content, whereas sounds with no discernable pitch (most percussive sounds, for example) will have a greater **disharmonic** content.

To finally get to the point, the reason we were able to tell the difference between our four phantom instruments (even in the dark) was because each instrument had a particular OVERTONE CONTENT; that is, each one had a certain amount of each particular harmonic and also certain amounts of particular disharmonics. These relative amounts not only allow us to tell the difference between different instruments but also between different types of the same instrument and even two supposedly "identical" instruments. When listening to pianos, the overtone content will allow us, for example, to distinguish between a 9' Steinway and a 6' Steinway; or between a Steinway grand and a Steinway upright; or between a Steinway upright and a Baldwin upright; or even between two Baldwin uprights manufactured the same day, standing side by side!

If all of this weren't mind-boggling enough, let's again remind you that timbre, as with the other two parameters of sound, ALWAYS changes, and usually quite drastically, over the duration of the sound. A very common experiment in college-level electronic music courses is to have students record the sound of a single piano note on tape and then splice out just the very beginning (or "attack") of the sound. When you listen back, your piano sounds nothing at all like a piano; in fact, it sounds much closer to an organ. The acoustic piano is one instrument which has undergone severe scrutiny by acoustic scientists and has been proven to generate one of the most complex sounds in existence. During the few seconds that we hear a single piano note, researchers have discovered that literally thousands of timbral changes occur. Take this along with the amplitude and frequency changes which are simultaneously occurring and you will realize why - advertising claims notwithstanding - no manufacturer has yet produced a synthesizer that comes even close to recreating the sound of a real acoustic piano. No computer exists yet which can make all of these calculations quickly enough to actually reproduce this very complicated series of events.

We have seen that when we observe a sound on an oscilloscope, the height of the wave tells us of its amplitude, and the number of waves occurring per second tells us of its frequency. How can we tell anything about its timbre? The timbre of a sound will be reflected in the SHAPE of the wave on the oscilloscope. Sounds which are smooth and gentle will have smooth and gentle shapes, such as this: **(See Figure 1-11.)**

On the other hand, sounds which are harsh and raspy will have jittery and fairly irregular shapes, such as this: **(See Figure 1-12.)**

The oscilloscope cannot provide us with as accurate a means of defining the timbral parameter as it it does amplitude and frequency, but, as we see, it does help give us a clue as to the tonal quality of the sound we are observing; and, perhaps more importantly, in the way this tonal quality changes over the duration of the sound.

It cannot be stressed enough that a clear understanding of these three parameters, what they mean, what they are, and what they contribute to a sound, is **vital** in the understanding of how **any** synthesizer works. REFER TO THIS CHAPTER often as you work your way through the rest of this book because it is all too easy to get wrapped up in the technicalities of synthesis and to lose sight of the fact that at **all** times you are manipulating one of these three parameters!

AND NOW, BACK TO SYNTHESIZERS:

We began this chapter with a brief discussion of analog synthesizers and their system of creating sounds. Analog synthesis is often referred to as SUB-TRACTIVE SYNTHESIS because the electronic components responsible for generating the original signal (the oscillators) present complex timbres at the outset. These complex timbres then pass through filtering devices that are used to remove undesired overtones. Hence the term "subtractive" since we always create sounds in analog synthesizers by REMOVING overtones.

Digital synthesizers, on the other hand, can sometimes be capable of doing exactly the opposite, in which case they use the method of ADDITIVE SYN-THESIS. The additive digital synthesizer (such as the Synclavier or Fairlight) will allow us to specify a fundamental frequency and then direct it to add overtones of particular harmonics (and sometimes disharmonics) in particular quantities. This method allows us to literally build sounds from scratch. The DX7 is capable of some limited additive synthesis but this is not the main method used by it.

An additive synthesis system will typically also allow the user the option of SAMPLING sounds. "Sampling" means that we can literally feed into our computer any real sound, be it live on microphone or from tape or record, and the computer will do a high-speed analysis of the sound fed it, in terms of its amplitude, frequency, and timbre (and how these parameters change over time). Once this analysis is complete (a process that only takes a second or two) it is generally a simple matter for the computer to recreate the sound using its additive synthesis skills, and play it back for you at whatever pitch you desire. Instructions as to which pitch you wish to hear are usually relayed simply by playing the appropriate note on the keyboard. The original sound, of course, has to be fed into the computer as an electrical signal, and the internal device that converts this electrical signal into usable digital code (binary numbers) is the opposite of our old friend, the DAC: this is an Analog-To-Digital converter, or ADC for short. Essentially (and greatly simplified), if you plug an *ADC* into a *DAC*, you have the makings for a sampling system: **(See Figure 1-13.)**

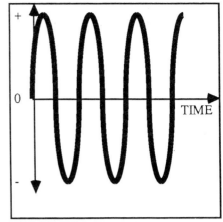

Figure 1-11

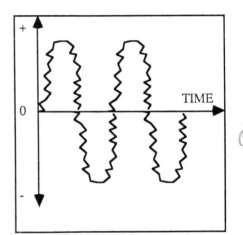

Figure 1-12

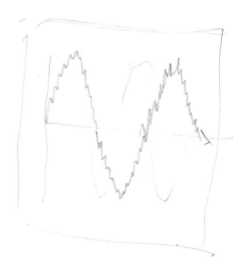

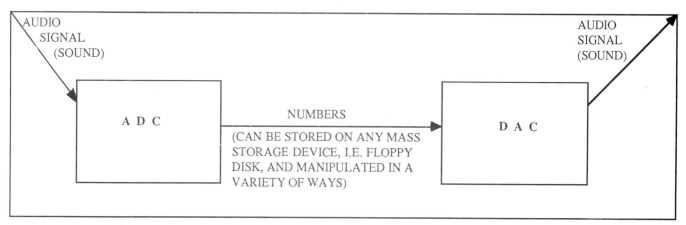

Figure 1-13

Although, as stated earlier, the DX7 does have some limited additive capabilities, it does not have an ADC capable of receiving audio input onboard and so you cannot sample sounds on a DX7, nor, as of this writing, on **any** of the Yamaha DX or TX devices. The main method of synthesis that our DX7 employs is something called Digital FM (short for Frequency Modulation). Instead of merely adding waves of different frequency and amplitude together, as additive synthesizers do, this system "collides" waves together. This means that we will not hear **both** of the colliding waves individually, but instead we hear the composite **result** of this collision. Of course, since we are talking about a digital, and not analog, system, there are no actual waves colliding at all. Instead, the microprocessor aboard the DX7 has been trained to quickly compute "What-would-happen-if" calculations. We abstractly give the computer input as to what kinds of waves we wish to theoretically collide, and the DX7 provides for us what would have been the result **if** these waves had actually existed.

This computer program was developed in the late 60's/early 70's by a team of computer scientists headed by Dr. John Chowning at Stanford University's Digital Music Lab. Back in the prehistoric (by synthesizer standards) days of the mid-70's the Yamaha Corporation quietly purchased the patent outright and spent nearly a decade developing and refining the system into the modern DX7. Although frequency modulation as a means of **modifying** sound has been a staple of analog synthesizers for many years, what sets our DX7 apart from all of its ancestors is that it incorporates FM **digitally** and as its primary basis for **generating** sounds. The DX7 system is proprietary and for any other manufacturer to use it (such as Synclavier) a royalty to Yamaha must be paid. For this reason, learning the DX7 system will be of little or no use to you when you encounter any other type of synthesizer. It's an amazing machine - and it lives in a world of its own!

Which Is Better - Analog or Digital?:

I'll bet a lot of you synthesizer owners out there skipped ahead to this section once you looked at the table of contents! I'm sorry to disappoint you but there unfortunately is no answer to this question. "Better" is too subjective a term, and what I might consider "better", you might consider "expletive deleted". The only statement that can fairly be made is that the two systems are qualitatively **different**.

Analog systems work with electrical signals which are notoriously unreliable and distorted. We don't notice changes in electrical signals in our daily lives because they are generally minute, but these small imperfections translate directly to true distortions when dealing with sound. Of course, you shouldn't think of the word "distortion" in a necessarily negative way because all acoustic instruments and sound sources **always** produce sound which is distorted somehow. There is no such thing in the real world as a perfect sound. Every Stradivarius has a flaw, and so too does every Stratocaster (even the vintage ones!). It is precisely these small and unpredictable distortions which lend a very "human", or "warm" sound to most good analog synthesizers.

On the other hand, digital machines don't suffer from the same kind of distortions. Because we are making sounds out of numbers, it doesn't matter what the temperature is, for example: the number 3 is still the number 3. It is not true to say that digital synthesizers cannot distort - they do - sometimes on purpose, sometimes not - but in general they will deliver much purer, cleaner sounds than analog. Some critics of digital sound use the term "sterile"; some critics of analog sound accuse it of being "muddy". The debate rages on...

Digital machines are newer and so have greater novelty value at the moment. The word "digital" itself is a buzzword. Analog synthesizers have been around since the 1920's, and their modern voltage-controlled versions since the 1950's. All too often the public confuses newer with better (talk to anyone who went out and purchased an 8-track cartridge player ten years ago). Digital is obviously here to stay, and the Yamaha digital FM systems are probably the most powerful and exciting synthesizers commercially available at the moment, but I for one do not believe that analog is ever going to be completely replaced. Fortunately, digital and analog synthesizers tend to complement one another - what one does well, the other doesn't, and vice-versa. For example, don't hold out too much hope for your DX7 to produce big, lush string ensemble sounds - even though you can get those easily from even the smallest analog systems. But on the other hand, don't expect to be able to get much of a Fender Rhodes sound from even the largest of analog systems - though your DX7 or DX9 can do that without even blinking.

In general, analog systems are very good at generating lush, warm, powerful sounds; whereas digital systems excel at clean, pure, crystalline sounds. They can emulate each other to a certain degree but each excels at something different. The best solution? Buy one of each!

You think I'm kidding, don't you? Before 1982, I would have been. Today, I'm not, thanks to the advent of MIDI. MIDI is a topic that will be covered in detail at the end of this book but for now we can just explain that MIDI is a language that allows different synthesizers - even radically different ones made by different manufacturers, to work together with each other and with most standard computers.

It's fairly obvious that digital synthesizers can communicate with computers (since they are, in fact, computers themselves), but how can **analog** systems "talk" to computers? The answer comes from DAC's cousin, *ADC*. The relatively low cost of this component has encouraged virtually all analog synthesizer manufacturers in recent years to include onboard computers in all their machines. These computers have nothing at all to do with the generation of sound (if they did, the systems wouldn't be analog any more) but they act instead as silent watchdogs, keeping track of where all the voltages are traveling, and how. Once a sound is set up on the analog machine, the ADC can convert all the various routings into a digital code which can then be stored in the memory of another digital device called a **"programmer"**. This programmer can then recall and re-set-up any sound in it's memory by simply routing all the analog voltages in the way that it remembered them as having been. The first so-called "programmable" analog synthesizer appeared in the late '70s (that's how new the technology is) and today all analog machines now are of this variety. Remember - even though these so-called "hybrid" synthesizers have computers on board, they are NOT digital synthesizers.

In any event, because today ALL synthesizers of every variety, digital and analog, have computers onboard, they all have the capability to communicate with one another and with central computer terminals. The standard for communications is MIDI. The applications are enormous. If you are seriously involved in synthesizers you will probably want to own both digital and analog systems, and then simply hook them together with a MIDI cable.

For now, though, let's just concentrate on the DX7 and learn how we can use this amazing machine to its fullest capablilities.

CHAPTER TWO:
THE FRONT PANEL AND
MODES OF OPERATION

Let's begin our discussion of the DX7 with an examination of the physical layout of the instrument. All of the operations of programming the machine are performed on the two sliders and forty-two membrane switches on the front panel, which is laid out as follows: **(See Figure 2-1.)**

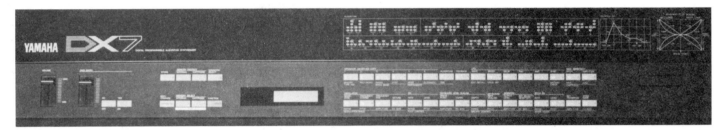

Figure 2-1

Going from left to right, here's what we see: First of all, the volume control slider - it's operation is fairly straightforward, but bear in mind that the DX7 outputs a pretty low level signal and so for best signal-to-noise ratio (that is, maximum DX7 sound and minimum noise), it is advisable to usually keep it at or near the top of its range (just be careful that your amp is initially set at a fairly low volume before you do this!).

Immediately to the right of the volume slider is a set of three controls; a slider and two switches, which are together labeled *Data Entry*. We will use these to send commands and numbers ("data") to the DX7 - in other words, this is the area where we will be able to "speak" to the computer. A more detailed discussion of the *Data Entry* section will follow later.

Next, we see a series of eight membrane switches, arranged in two rows of four each. The middle two switches in each row are green and the others are of various colors. These switches are actually color-coded and the reasons for the specific colors chosen will soon be apparent. The bottom four switches are referred to as *mode select* switches by Yamaha. These are used to determine the operation of the set of thirty-two membrane controls on the right side of the machine, and their operation will be covered in detail shortly.

The next thing we encounter is an LED/LCD display. LED stands for "Light Emitting Diode" and is the small electronic component giving us the red, one-or-two digit number on the left side of the display. The meaning of various LED numbers will be explained shortly. To the right of the LED is an LCD, or Liquid Crystal Display, similar to that seen on many digital watches. The DX7 LCD can display up to two lines of 16 "characters" - letters or numbers - each. Taken together, the LED/LCD display is the area where the computer "speaks" to us. In this area, our DX7 will be able to show us information about the sound we are currently using, and also to occasionally ask us questions or inform us of operations the machine is performing.

Finally, on the far right-hand side of the instrument are a series of thirty-two membrane switches. These controls perform a multitude of functions, depending on the most recent *mode select* switch (remember them?) pressed. Basically, the DX7 needed a whole lot more than just thirty-two main controls; it actually requires more than 168! The engineers at Yamaha no doubt felt that presenting the public with a machine with over 168 switches would not exactly help sales, and besides, providing all those switches would have been prohibitively expensive. Instead, using common digital design concepts, they gave us thirty-two switches, but made each of these switches a *multi-function* switch. In plain English, a multi-function device is simply one which can perform several different functions, depending on what "mode" the machine is in. The "mode" is simply a particular way that our computer can operate. This is determined by a special group of devices called - you guessed it - "mode select" switches.

Let's look at the thirty-two *multi-function* switches a little more closely: **(See Figure 2-2.)**

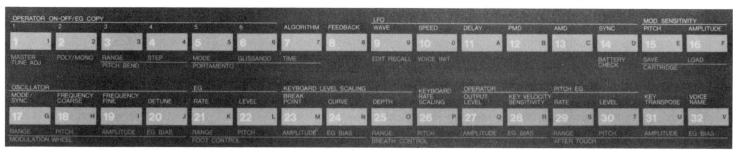

Figure 2-2

You'll notice that each membrane switch has something written **over** it in blue; something written **under** it in brown; a number written **on** it in white; and a small character (letter or number) lurking **inside** it in black!

The key to using these switches is to be certain at all times whether they are active for their *blue* functions, their *brown* functions, their *white* functions, or their *black* characters. Each switch can only be active for **one** of these things at any one time. Again, the controls which determine this are the mode select controls, the bottom row of the eight switches on the left-hand side of the front panel.

We mentioned earlier that the mode select switches are color-coded, and it should now start to become obvious how this works. The bottom left-hand switch, labeled "EDIT", is blue. Pressing this activates the thirty-two main switches for their "blue" functions, the "EDIT PARAMETERS". The bottom right-hand mode select switch, labeled "FUNCTION", is brown. Pressing **this** activates our thirty-two main switches for their "brown" functions, the "FUNCTION CONTROLS". Finally, beneath each of the two middle mode select switches (which are labeled "memory select" and are colored ordinary green) is a white bar, labeled "PLAY". Pressing either of these two activates the thirty-two main switches for their white numbers, and puts the machine in "PLAY" mode. The black characters inside the main switches are only used for naming sounds, and we will describe their use later in the book.

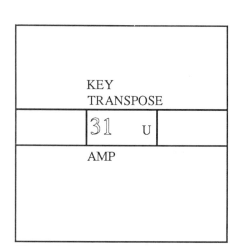

Figure 2-3

To summarize: the DX7 has three main *modes* of operation: EDIT, FUNCTION, and PLAY. Each time we enter a different mode, the thirty-two main switches become activated for a different function; their blue, brown, or white ones. For the purposes of this book, we will refer to these thirty-two switches according to their specific mode of operation: for example, "edit switch #31" means main switch number thirty-one, activated in EDIT mode (for this particular example, "Key Transpose"). **(See Figure 2-3.)**

Play Mode:

The simplest mode of operation is the one all DX7 owners become immediately familiar with: PLAY mode. This mode of operation allows us to access and hear the sounds contained, in the form of digital data, inside the memory of our machine or its memory cartridges (more about these later).

"Memory" is a term that requires some definition. Computers are able to "memorize" information by storing large amounts of binary numbers (zeroes and ones) representing this information in coded form within a series of electrical switches. Essentially, switches are quickly being turned on and off; wherever a switch is left on, the computer recognizes a "one" and wherever a switch is left off, the computer recognizes a "zero". Because a computer memory circuit typically contains many thousands, if not millions, of these switches, large amounts of encoded information can thus be stored. This information may be in the form of instructions to tell the computer what to do at all times (program instructions) or it may simply be "voice data", that is, numbers which will eventually be translated by the DAC into a particular sound. *Microprocessors* (logic circuits) inside the actual computer are able to utilize this data in memory to perform computing operations. The memory circuits inside the computer may be capable of keeping their switch positions intact if somehow electrical power can be supplied to them even though the computer itself is turned off. This protective auxiliary power is normally supplied by small batteries, called "back-up batteries" which usually have a long life - five years or more. Alternatively, the data stored in these switches can be stored "off-line" - outside the computer, in devices like tape, floppy disks, or special data cartridges. The computer can mechanically retrieve this data (**"read"** it) by many different means.

Our DX7, we know, is itself a full-fledged, card-carrying computer and it utilizes both internal and off-line data storage. These storage units are commonly lumped under the umbrella heading of *memory*. The DX7 thus has both *internal* and *external* memory. The internal memory is a large memory circuit inside the machine protected by a back-up battery, so it can "remember" data even though the DX7 itself may be off. The external memory can be in several different formats, but the most commonly used is that of *data cartridges*. The two mode-select switches which put the DX7 in PLAY mode allow us to specify whether we wish to access data stored in the *internal* memory or in *cartridge* memory. **(See Figure 2-4.)**

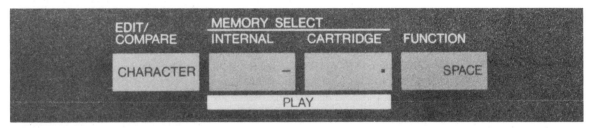

Figure 2-4

A good way to think of memory is to picture a hotel lobby. Behind the hotel desk we see a series of pigeon-holes, used to store messages and keys for guests. A "memory slot" is equivalent to one of these pigeon-holes, with one main difference. In our hotel lobby, any number of messages, or data, can be stored in each slot; but in our computer, only **one** "message", or piece of data, can be stored in a slot at any one time. If you tell the computer to put data into a particular slot, it will be happy to accomodate you (provided you followed the correct **storage** procedure) but it will also remove and throw away whatever "message" was previously in that slot. This means that you will have to be extremely careful when storing data in various memory slots because the computer will ALWAYS have to destroy whatever was previously in that slot - and it will do it automatically.

Figure 2-5

Figure 2-6

The internal memory of the DX7 has thirty-two slots, or pigeon-holes, in which to store data (actually, there are thirty-three, but we'll get to that thirty-third one later). We can access this information and hear the sounds the data will create (**"read"** the data), or we can replace it with new sound data, (**"write"** data) in the internal memory.

The cartridge memory which the DX7 uses comes in two different formats: *RAM* (for Random Access Memory) cartridges, and *ROM* (for Read Only Memory) cartridges. RAM cartridges work much like the internal memory - you can **read** the data stored in them and you can **write** new data to them. ROM cartridges are different, however, in that you can **only** read data stored in them. **You cannot write data on a ROM cartridge.**

In order to get data from a cartridge, we will need to insert it gently into the provided slot on the right side of the instrument. Always have the front label, the one that says "DX7 Voice ROM" or "DX7 Data RAM", facing you so you can read it without doing a headstand. This will insure that the cartridge is in the right way around. In NO event should you ever force a cartridge into the slot: if it doesn't go in easily, you're doing something wrong. **(See Figure 2-5.)**

When you purchase your DX7 you will normally receive two different ROM cartridges, numbered "one" and "two" if you've bought a Japanese machine, and "three" and "four" if you own an American machine. (It's easy to tell which you have: look in the back, near where the power cord is. If you see the words "100 volts", you've got a Japanese machine. If it says "120 volts", it's an American machine.) Each of these ROM cartridges contains 64 different sounds, organized in two sides of 32 each, the "A" side and "B" side. You choose which side you wish to access by flipping the small switch on the rear of the ROM cartridge: **(See Figure 2-6.)**

The "A/B" switch can be flipped at any time, whether the cartridge is seated in the machine or not.

The ROM cartridges contain sounds which are called *presets*, because they have been pre-programmed by someone employed by Yamaha. While many of these sounds are quite good and quite useful, we should not lose sight of the fact that these sounds did not come down from the heavens but were actually created by mere human beings. The fact that, for reasons described earlier, the DX7 is not the simplest of synthesizers to program, explains why an undue reliance has been placed on these 128 sounds by DX7 owners everywhere. We can easily, however, modify these presets to taste, or even create brand new "presets" from scratch with the multitude of controls provided on this instrument, and **that**, after all, is the reason for this book in the first place. If all that were involved in using a DX7 were calling up presets, people like myself would have to find a new line of work!

In any event, entering PLAY mode on our machine is a very simple operation: press either of the two green "memory select" *mode select* switches (the ones with the white "play" bar underneath) to activate our thirty-two main switches for their white numbers. These switches will now allow us to select and hear any of the thirty-two sounds stored in the internal memory, any of the thirty-two sounds stored in the RAM cartridge, or any of the thirty-two sounds stored on either side of the ROM cartridges.

Whenever we are using one of the three main modes of operation on our DX7, the top line of our LCD display tells us precisely which mode we are in. In *play* mode, the top line will always read either "INTERNAL VOICE" or "CARTRIDGE VOICE" depending on whether we are accessing the *internal* or *external* memory. In addition, the LED display will always output the *number* of the memory slot we are currently listening to. In these ways the computer is "communicating" with us and letting us know that it is correctly responding to the commands we have issued.

In order to actually hear the sound created by the data you read, you will need to not only select the mode but also to select the number with one of the thirty-two main switches. If you change modes from internal play to cartridge play, or vice-versa, you will need to press a number switch of some kind in order to be able to hear the sound. Until you hit this second switch, the previous sound stays in the DX7. Try it!!

EXERCISE 1

Playing back an internal sound: (See Figure 2-7.)

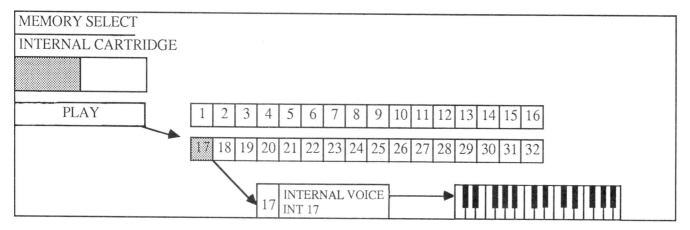

Figure 2-7

1) Press the internal memory play *mode select* switch.
2) Press any one of the thirty-two main switches.
3) OBSERVE: LED displays the number of the sound you have selected.
4) OBSERVE: Top line of LCD reads *INTERNAL VOICE*. Bottom line of LCD reads *INT*, followed by the **number** of the voice, followed by the **name** of the voice.
5) LISTEN: The sound you selected is there!
6) TRY: Selecting each of the thirty-two sounds stored in your DX7's internal memory.

EXERCISE 2

Playing back a cartridge sound: (See Figure 2-8.)

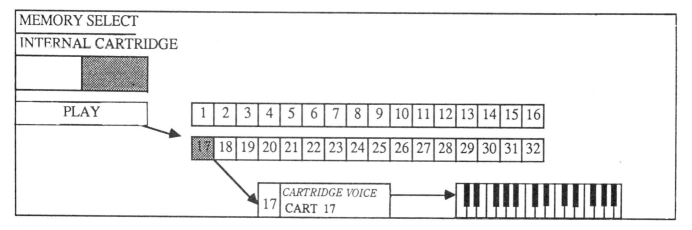

Figure 2-8

1) Insert a cartridge (ROM or RAM) into your DX7 cartridge slot. Press the cartridge memory play *mode select* switch.

2) Press any one of the thirty-two main switches.

3) OBSERVE: LED displays the number of the sound you have selected.

4) OBSERVE: Top line of LCD reads *CARTRIDGE VOICE*. Bottom line of LCD reads *CRT*, followed by the **number** of the voice, followed by the **name** of the voice.

5) LISTEN: The sound you selected is there!

6) NOTE: If you were previously playing *internal* voices and then went to this exercise, you had to follow **both** steps **1** and **2** above in order to actually see and hear the cartridge voice.

7) TRY: Selecting each of the thirty-two sounds stored on your RAM cartridge (if you're working with a brand new RAM cartridge there won't be anything there yet. Don't worry, there will be soon enough!). If you haven't already done so, TRY selecting each of the 128 *presets* stored on your two ROM cartridges (don't forget the A/B switches on the back of the cartridges!).

The Edit Buffer:

A couple of pages back, you may remember a somewhat teasing mention of a "thirty-third" internal memory slot. Where is this elusive bit of memory and how can we access it with only 32 switches? you may well now be asking. Here's a simple experiment to answer both questions at once:

EXERCISE 3

Discovering the edit buffer:

1) Put a ROM cartridge in your DX7.

2) Select *cartridge* play mode using the proper mode select switch.

3) Select a voice from the cartridge at random. Any one will do.

4) Play the keyboard. The sound you selected should be there.

5) Now **remove** the cartridge.

6) Play the keyboard again. LISTEN. Amazingly, the same sound is still in the machine even though you removed the cartridge!

What's going on here? We were able to hear the sound you selected because our DX7 **read** the data from the ROM cartridge. When the ROM cartridge was physically removed from the machine, however, somehow the DX7 was **still** able to access its data. Or was it?

The answer to this mystery is the presence of a wonderful little piece of DX7 memory called the *edit buffer*. This is our "thirty-third" internal memory slot and the way it works is this: Whenever you go into play mode and select a sound from **any** memory source, internal or external, the DX7 will **not** actually give you the sound. Instead, what our clever little computer does is - at very high speed - make a **copy** of the sound we've picked and puts that copy in the *edit buffer*.

You can think of the edit buffer as being a kind of scratch pad, a place where you can mess around with the sound to your heart's content, secure in the knowledge that at no time are you actually doing anything to the sound itself. The original is still residing securely in whatever memory slot it was stored in. The only thing you are altering is a **copy** of that sound.

ANYTIME YOU DO ANYTHING AT ALL ON THE DX7, YOU ARE ALWAYS WORKING IN THE EDIT BUFFER. **Always**. That means that you are **never ever** working with the sound you select, only a copy. This allows you to alter and modify sounds in your DX7 to any degree without ever altering the sounds themselves! In order to actually change the originals, you will have to go through a fairly complicated *store* procedure, something you are extremely unlikely to do by accident, since it involves hitting four different switches, in a particular order. See Chapter Eight for a detailed description of the *store* procedure.

The edit buffer is one of the most wonderful features on an already wonderful machine. It gives you the freedom to experiment and manipulate and it is automatically provided to you at all times. There is no way to bypass this feature, nor could there be any reason why you would particularly want to.

Function mode:

The function mode controls of the DX7 encompass what are known in jargon as *global commands*. This means that whatever function mode parameter you alter will affect **any and all** sounds that you happen to call up in the machine. For the most part, the function controls affect relatively minor things such as portamento, the physical controllers (like the two wheels on the side of the keyboard, known as *pitch bend* and *modulation wheels*, respectively), and copying data from memory to memory. They also affect some more important things like the overall tuning of the instrument and the MIDI communications interface.

When we refer to these controls as *global*, we are really saying that the function controls are not *voice-linked*; that is, these commands do not affect any sound in particular, and moreover that there is no way on the DX7 of accomplishing this. On later model Yamaha digital FM devices, like the TX rack units, function controls **are** voice-linked, that is, we can, for example, save one piano sound with a particular portamento effect, and, in a different memory slot, another with **no** portamento. We mustn't forget that the DX7 was the pioneer machine in this series and so in many respects still is a bit "old-fashioned", relative to its newer cousins. It is hoped that in the future Yamaha will issue software updates for the DX7 which will allow its function controls to be voice-linked.

Software. This is the first time this mysterious word has surfaced in this book and so we should offer a brief explanation to any of you who are not sure what the word means. After long and careful consideration, I have decided to tell the one and only formal joke I've ever heard regarding this subject:

Q: How many computer programmers does it take to change a light bulb?

A: None, it's a hardware problem!

Computer programmers earn their living by writing *software*, that is, instructions to a computer. Computers are actually incredibly stupid (but incredibly fast) devices. They need to be told **exactly** what to do at all times, and these very fine and precise instructions are what the software provides. Software should be differentiated from *hardware*, which are the actual nuts-and-bolts physical workings of the machine. Think about, for example, a home cassette deck. The casing, meters, tape drive, and switches on the panel are its *hardware* , but without *software*, in the form of magnetic instructions on a cassette tape, you won't hear a darned thing! The machine is, in effect, useless without a tape playing in it. Same with the DX7. If Yamaha's and Stanford's programmers had not developed software to tell the machine what to do at all times (for example, "when the 'internal memory select play switch is depressed along with a number switch, search and retrieve data stored in the associated internal memory slot"), all we would have for our $2,000 is a pile of switches, displays, and microprocessors attached to a keyboard which cannot make sounds. Not much good to most of us...

In any event, back to the *function controls*. Not only are they not voice-linked but they are never reset, under any conditions. That means that once you alter a function control, it stays that way until you physically go back and un-alter it, even if the DX7 has been turned off in the interim. That's because the back-up battery in the instrument which is protecting its memory slots is **also** protecting the current function control settings. This could be a good thing, but most of the time it's just a pain in the proverbial expletive deleted.

Let's see how this works. Chapter 13 contains a detailed explanation of **all** the function controls but for now let's just work with one, the Master Tune Adjust control.

The function control parameters, as you no doubt remember, are colored *brown* and are located underneath each of the thirty-two main switches. Underneath switch #1 we see the words "MASTER TUNE ADJ", written in brown. Eureka! In order to activate this switch for its tuning capabilities, we will, of course, first have to press the FUNCTION *mode select* switch. Once this is accomplished, we can **change** the overall tuning of the machine by simply entering data into the computer, in this case by moving the *data entry* slider:

EXERCISE 4:

Adjusting the master tuning: (See Figure 2-9.)

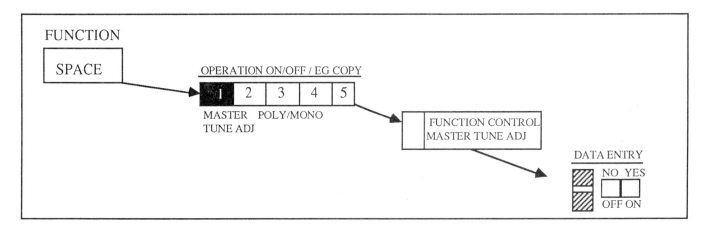

Figure 2-9

1) If you're not too happy with the sound currently in your machine, CALL UP a new one by entering *play mode* and selecting a voice either from your machine's internal memory or from a cartridge.
2) Enter *function mode* by pressing the function *mode select* switch.
3) Press switch #1.
4) OBSERVE: LED does **not** change. The red number currently displayed is the **number** of the sound you are listening to, regardless of whether it came from the internal or the cartridge memory.
5 OBSERVE: Top line of LCD reads *FUNCTION CONTROL* (this is the main mode you are in). Bottom line of LCD reads MASTER TUNE ADJ (the function parameter you have selected).
6) MOVE the data entry *slider*. As you are doing so, play a note on the keyboard and LISTEN to the pitch change. Now play a chord. NOTE that all the notes change precisely the same way. The RANGE of the data entry slider is about plus or minus a semitone (that is, a half-step). NOTE that the data entry *switches* (the "yes"/"no" buttons) have no effect at all on the tuning.
7) CALL UP a different sound by reentering *play* mode and selecting a new number from the main switches. Play the keyboard and NOTE that this new sound is tuned to the same reference as the previous one. This is because all function controls are *global* commands.

There is no reference tone easily accessible on the DX7 to tell us whether or not the machine is in standard concert tuning, that is Middle A = A440. Yamaha tells us that the DX7 will be at this concert tuning if the data entry slider is moved to the halfway point. That's all well and good except that as you've probably noticed there is no indent of any kind to tell us when we are **at** the halfway point. All we can do is approximate, by eye. So, if the master tuning is adjusted with the data entry slider set at approximately halfway, your DX7 will be approximately at concert tuning. (It's actually a very fine point and it will in fact be **very** close if the slider is set anywhere near the middle mark.) In general, though, it's better to tune your DX7 to someone else's instrument than vice-versa, simply because of this lack of reference.

Another anomaly of the function controls is that when leaving function mode and re-entering play mode, the data entry slider remains active for the last function control you were using. This can be particularly problematic if you are not aware of it! For example, suppose you're playing a concert with your DX7, and hours before you're due to go on stage you and your group do a sound check. Because your guitar player has a tin ear, tuning is always a sore point. After much ado, everyone is finally in tune; you've set the tuning of your DX7 at about the halfway point so you're sure you and everyone else is in tune, so you've gone back to *play* mode and selected the first sound you'll be using.

Right, so you go off and have dinner with your friends, confident that tonight, at last!, the band will at least be in tune. You return to the gig, and, a minute before you're due to start the set, some bozo comes over to you and your just-tuned DX7 and says, "Hey, what a neat machine! What does this little gizmo do?", as he proceeds to move the data entry slider up and down. You may not realize it now but your DX7 has just been put completely out of tune, because the last function control you were using was MASTER TUNE ADJUST. Even though your machine was in *play* mode, the data entry slider was therefore still controlling the tuning!

Let's try it ourselves: Redo Exercise 4 above, and this time, after you've selected your new sound (step 7), move the data entry slider. Play a few notes as you do so and observe that the slider is indeed changing the tuning of the machine **even though you are no longer in function mode**.

Yamaha's logic behind doing this (and this was done purposefully, though not vindictively) was that this would hopefully make the DX7 more useful in live performance situations - that there would be times you would want to rapidly change a function control without having to reenter function mode. This, of course, assumes that you've taken the care to select the proper function mode you'll need to change, **last**, before going to *play* mode. While this may be useful to some, my personal feeling is that Yamaha would have been better off to have left this idea in the circular file. Just be aware of it, so you don't get caught short.

Finally, whenever you return the DX7 to *function* mode from any of the other main modes, our smart microprocessor will always automatically call up the function parameter you were working with last. This **is** a useful feature in that you can at least always be reminded of your last operation in this mode. If you've been assiduously doing the exercises in this book, your DX7 should be in *play* mode at the moment. If you now press the *function* mode select switch, your LCD should be showing you the MASTER TUNE ADJ parameter because that was the last function parameter we were using.

Although I don't advise it just yet, inveterate skipper-aheaders can refer to Chapter 13 for a detailed explanation of all the *function controls*.

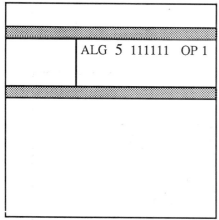

ALG 5 111111 OP 1

Figure 2-10

Edit mode:

The parameters activated in *edit mode* are those things which actually make a sound on our DX7 a sound. In other words, we can select "E.PIANO 1" (the Fender Rhodes sound) from our ROM cartridge and a moment later select "FLUTE 1". Obviously, everything sounds totally different. Why is this? Because each of the two sounds has totally different EDIT parameters. EDIT parameters are **not** global commands; they are very much *voice-specific*.

In the other modes we have discussed, we have observed that the top line of our LCD constantly informs us of **which** mode we are in, and the same is true of EDIT mode, although not in such an obvious way. Press the edit switch on your DX7. The top line of your LCD should look like this: **(See Figure 2-10.)**

Looks like hieroglyphics at this point, doesn't it? We will see in Chapter Four exactly what "ALG", "111111" and "OP" mean, but for now let's just state that WHENEVER you select *edit* mode, this is what will appear on the top line of your LCD. Yamaha could have simply put the words "Edit Mode" or "Edit Control" up there, but the thought was that, while manipulating EDIT parameters, you will want to have some basic information about the sound available to you continuously. Limited by the size of the LCD display, they chose to give us these mysterious (but not for much longer!) symbols instead - and they do prove useful most of the time.

Let's try using one of the simpler *edit parameters* to see how it works. The bulk of this book will be devoted to explaining in detail all of these controls but we can jump right in with something called "Key Transpose".

All of the keys on the DX7 are, to the central microprocessor, numbered; that's, after all, the only way a computer can think. The bottom "C" on the keyboard is called C1, and the uppermost "C" is C6, with all the other keys in between similarly designated. Middle "C", then, would be C3: **(See Figure 2-11.)**

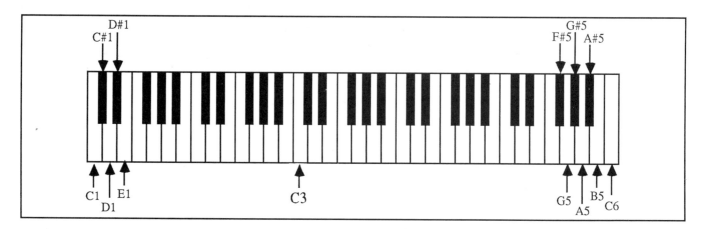

Figure 2-11

The "Key Transpose" *edit parameters* allows us to shift the tuning of the entire sound (not **all** sounds, just the particular one you are EDITING - remember, these are *voice-specific* commands, not global ones) to any interval you would like, within a range of four whole octaves!

This parameter is located above main switch #31, in blue, and, of course, in order to activate this switch for this parameter, we will have to press the EDIT *mode select* switch. Having done that, we will be able to enter data **directly from the keyboard** (not to confuse you, but this is the **only** EDIT parameter that does **not** accept data from the data entry section! Sorry 'bout that!). Let's do it with the "E.PIANO 1" (Fender Rhodes) preset (ROM 1A-11 if you have a Japanese machine, and ROM 3A-8 if you have an American one).

EXERCISE 5:

Key transposition: (See Figure 2-12.)

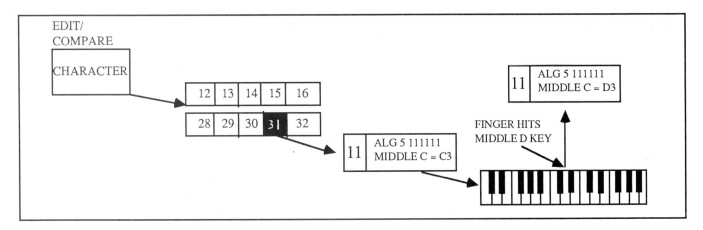

Figure 2-12

1) Insert ROM cartridge 1 (or 3) into the provided slot.

2) Put your DX7 in cartridge PLAY mode by pressing the "cartridge" *memory select* switch.

3) CALL UP the "E.PIANO 1" sound by pressing main switch 11 (if you're using ROM 1) or 8 (if you're using ROM 3).

4) OBSERVE LCD confirming that you are in CARTRIDGE PLAY mode and that you have "E.PIANO 1" in the *edit buffer*. Play a scale on the keyboard to confirm it to your own ears! (AUDIO CUE 5A).

5) Put your DX7 in EDIT mode by pressing the EDIT *mode select* switch.

6) Select the "Key Transpose" parameter by pressing main switch #31.

7) OBSERVE no change in the LED; it should still read "11" or "8"(depending upon whether you used ROM 1 or ROM 3).

8) OBSERVE top line of LCD shows "ALG 5 111111". This is an indication that we are in EDIT mode. Bottom line of LCD reads "Middle C = C3". This tells us the obvious, that Middle C on our keyboard has been numbered C3 by the computer. We can, however, CHANGE the value of Middle C and make it equal to ANY OTHER NOTE, within a range of five octaves, by following this procedure:

9) Press "D" above Middle "C" on your keyboard.

10) OBSERVE that the bottom line of the LCD now reads "Middle C = D3"!

11) LISTEN: Play the same scale as in step 4 above, and NOTE that the entire sound has been raised, or transposed up, a full tone! (AUDIO CUE 5B).

12) DO IT AGAIN: Since you are **already** in EDIT mode, there is no need to press the EDIT *mode* select switch again. Simply press switch # 31 again and press any other note on the keyboard. The first note you press will **not** make a sound: this is because it is simply **entering** data into the computer. OBSERVE that whatever note you press, **within** the range C1-C5, is immediately entered into the bottom line of the LCD. You can now play the keyboard to your heart's content and NOTE that the sound has indeed been TRANSPOSED. Entering a note **above** "C5" will simply result in a "Middle C = C5" entry as these notes are not recognized as valid transpositions.

This is a wonderful tool that will, in effect, allow you to be a musical idiot while pretending proficiency! No insult whatever is intended, as I firmly place **myself** in that category. The clever use of the KEY TRANSPOSE parameter will allow you to play any song in any key at all INSTANTLY, as long as you can play it in the key of C (for those of you reading this out there who are not musically inclined, the key of C is the one with no black notes in it; by far the easiest). It also means that the next time your singer wants to try "Born To Run" (back to Bruce again) in the key of F# minor, you, the DX7ist in the band, can do it a lot more easier than those poor primitive folks with the guitar or bass in hand, who have to first try and remember which fret F# is again! (No insult intended here either, I have no idea which fret it is myself!)

Remember, our friend the *edit buffer* has allowed us to fool around with this sound and change the value of Middle C several times **without actually altering the sound itself!** To restore the "E.PIANO 1" sound back to its original tuning, all you have to do is re-enter PLAY mode with the *mode select* switch, and CALL UP the sound once again. I'll pause here while you try it and prove to yourself that you have not in fact altered "E.PIANO 1" in any permanent way...

Back so soon? Good... hopefully the *edit buffer* has saved yet another DX7 owner from a fate worse than death! The only tricky thing about the KEY TRANSPOSE parameter is that if you use it a lot, you may end up with a memory full of sounds which are all in different keys. We'll see later how we can help matters by cataloging sounds intelligently.

Before you move on, it will probably be a good idea to spend a little time reviewing this chapter with your DX7 close at hand in order to get thoroughly comfortable with the concept of selecting different modes and activating the main switches for the parameter you wish to adjust. So far, we've only examined two, the "Master Tune" *function* parameter, and the "Key Transpose" *edit* parameter. You can experiment with others as you like - there is no way to harm the machine by doing so - but at this point most of the other parameters may make little or no sense. When you feel comfortable with the front panel and the modes of operation, read on, as we examine just how the DX7 **makes** sounds.

SWITCHES AND CONTROLS COVERED IN CHAPTER TWO:

SWITCH	PARAMETER	COMMENTS
INTERNAL PLAY Memory Select	Sets DX7 to play mode; calls up internal voices	Main mode select switch
CARTRIDGE PLAY Memory Select	Sets DX7 to play mode; calls up cartridge voices	Main mode select switch
ROM CARTRIDGE A/B	Selects 'A' or 'B' side of ROM cartridge	
FUNCTION mode select	Sets DX7 to FUNCTION mode	Main mode select switch
Function 1	Master tune adjust	
EDIT mode select	Sets DX7 to EDIT mode	Main mode select switch
Edit 31	Key transposition	Range C1-C5

CHAPTER THREE: THE OPERATOR

The heart of the DX7 is a device called the *OPERATOR*. This is a software component* which contains everything necessary to produce a sound, and it is laid out like this: **(See Figure 3-1.)**

The *sound source* of the DX7 is the box in the middle, labeled "OSCILLA-TOR". Before we talk about what the oscillator is and does, we should first define "sound source". In every acoustic instrument we have learned that the sound must originate from something physically vibrating, and that "something", be it a string, a reed, or a skin, is the *sound source* . In an analog synthesizer, the sound source would be an electronic component, called an *oscillator*, which generates a periodic moving, or "oscillating" *electrical* signal. But in a digital synthesizer such as the DX7 we have learned that our sound source must be a device which regularly - periodically - generates NUMBERS. And that is precisely what the oscillator inside the operator does - it is specifically a *digital oscillator*, which means that it is a number generator. This is where our sound begins life.

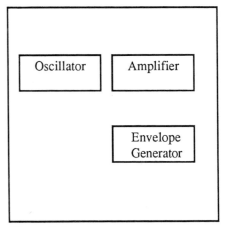

Figure 3-1

Inside the OPERATOR we have two other components which will process the numbers generated by the oscillator, and they are, respectively, the *amplifier* (specifically, a *digital* amplifier), and the *envelope generator* (again, a **digital** envelope generator). As the arrows in the diagram illustrate, the oscillator sends its signal (which are actually high-speed streams of numbers, ones and zeroes) into the amplifier, which exists for the purpose of increasing or decreasing these numbers. This will ultimately serve to increase or decrease the amount of overall signal leaving the OPERATOR, and this signal may eventually be converted by the DAC into an audible sound. If that turns out to be the case, then our *digital amplifier* will be acting the same as your stereo amplifier at home; that is, it will serve to make the sound louder or softer.

How does this work? Well, let's suppose that our oscillator is repeatedly sending the following stream of numbers to our amplifier:

0, 2, 4, 6, 8, 10, 8, 6, 4, 2, 0, -2, -4, -6, -8, -10, -8, -6, -4, -2

The amplifier may be instructed (by us, naturally) to multiply all of these numbers by a factor of ten, changing them to:

0, 20, 40, 60, 80, 100, 80, 60, 40, 20, 0, -20, -40, -60, -80, -100, -80, -60, -40, -20

or it might multiply them by a **tenth**, changing them to:

0, .2, .4, .6, .8, 1.0, .8, .6, .4, .2, 0, -.2, -.4, -.6, -.8, -1.0, -.8, -.6, -.4, -.2

In the first instance, of course, we **increased** the value of these numbers, and in the second instance we greatly **decreased** their value. Sending larger numbers to the DAC would result in a wave of higher amplitude, hence more volume. Sending smaller numbers to the DAC would result in the opposite, less volume.

* this means that the operator doesn't actually exist physically, just theoretically. The best thing you can do is forget I just said that!

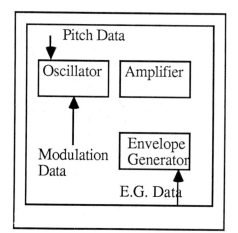

Figure 3-2

The function of the amplifier, then, would seem to be that of controlling the **volume** of the sound we hear coming from our DX7 and this is sometimes, but not always, true. This is another mysterious statement we will be explaining shortly. In any event, remember that volume, like the other two parameters of sound, ALWAYS changes over time and you will understand why our amplifier needs to constantly receive instructions from the *envelope generator*.

An envelope generator is a device in a synthesizer which allows the user to effect a **change over time** to one or more of the three parameters of sound. Again, the DX7 being a digital synthesizer, our envelope generator is a digital device; that is, it is issuing software instructions to the amplifier. Essentially, what it is doing is telling the amplifier **how much** to change the numbers being fed it by the oscillator, and when to make these changes. If we could translate these commands into something resembling English, it is as if the envelope generator (or *EG* for short) is continually barking at the amplifier, "get louder! now get softer! slowly!! more slowly!! now louder again! faster!!!".

Of course there is no evidence that the EG has the personality and charm of a Marine Drill Instructor, but somehow it wouldn't surprise me... since it issues commands **constantly** and receives absolute obedience from the amplifier it is controlling.

And this is actually all there is to the OPERATOR, just these three components: *oscillator*, *amplifier*, and *envelope generator*. The catch is that there would be no point in having them at **all** if we, the human beings in charge, could not tell them what to do, and we accomplish that via the DATA INPUTS.

Data Inputs:

There are three basic types of instructions, or commands, we need to send the operator, and they are set up as follows: **(See Figure 3-2.)**

First of all, the EG is telling the amplifier what to do, but how does it know **what** to tell the amplifier? It does because we give it instructions, via the *EG DATA INPUT*, and it then passes these commands on. We will be devoting an entire chapter later (Chapter Nine) to the operation of the EG and the data we input to it, but for now just be aware that this input exists.

Secondly, we need to give instructions to the oscillator; specifically, to tell it what *frequency* to run at and what type of *timbre* to emulate. These commands are routed via the *PITCH DATA INPUT* and the *MODULATION DATA INPUT*, respectively. BOTH of these commands are routed **directly** to the *oscillator*. Keeping in mind that our digital oscillator is in fact a number generator, we can see that the *modulation data* tells it what sequence of numbers to generate (as the changes in the stream of numbers will be interpreted by the DAC into waveshape changes) and the *pitch data* tells it how quickly to generate these numbers repeatedly (as the speed with which the pattern is repeated will be interpreted by the DAC into waves generated per second, or frequency).

We must, at all times, send the operator both *EG data* and *pitch data*. Otherwise, our amplifier would not know how much signal to pass and our oscillator would not know how often to repeat its numbers. However, it is not at all necessary to send *modulation data* to the operator. If no instructions are sent to this input then the oscillator will simply generate a predetermined stream of numbers which will have the effect of causing the DAC to generate a pure fundamental frequency, **with no overtones.**

In Chapter One we pointed out that no acoustic sound exists which does not have overtones to some degree. However, our DX7, not being an acoustic instrument, can generate a particular kind of wave, called a sine wave, which consists solely of fundamental frequency. The sine wave, then, is the only sound in existence which has no overtones. If our operator receives no instructions via the *modulation data input*, the only kind of wave it can generate is a sine wave.

The timbre of a sound, you will remember, is reflected in the wave **shape**, and if you look at a sine wave on an oscilloscope, it looks like this: **(See Figure 3-3.)**

Note that the sine wave is smooth and gentle, alternating between positive and negative movements. It's easy to see how our digital oscillator can generate this wave: all it has to do is send the DAC a regular stream of numbers which start at zero, slowly get bigger, just as slowly return to zero, and then go negative the same way, i.e.:

0, 2, 4, 6, 8, 10, 8, 6, 4, 2, 0, -2, -4, -6, -8, -10, -8, -6, -4, -2

or

0, 5000, 10000, 15000, 10000, 5000, 0, -5000, -10000, -15000, -10000, -5000,

Of course, the wave generated by the second example would be much louder than the one in the first example, but they would both have the same **shape**, (that is, *timbre*), like this: **(See Figure 3-4.)**

Remember that what the DAC is doing is "graphing out" the numbers it receives!

In succeeding chapters we will talk about specific ways of entering data into these inputs - but for now, just be sure you understand WHAT these inputs are and HOW the numbers entered there will affect the sound.

Prepare yourself for a shock time:

With this single component, the OPERATOR, the DX7 provides us with a very elegant system which allows us to completely shape and control the sound we generate. Relating back to the three parameters of sound (as we often will), we can see how this works: The EG data input allows us to control the **volume**, or amplitude of the sound, and to change it over time. The pitch data input allows us to determine the **pitch**, or frequency of the sound; and the modulation data input allows us to specify the timbre we wish to hear. It's very complete, and it's very neatly packaged.

Now comes the shocker: The DX7 actually provides us with **SIX** operators, all of which are completely independent of one another! That means that each one of our six operators has its **own** oscillator, its **own** amplifier, and its **own** EG; and furthermore, that we can input completely different sets of instructions to each regarding amplitude, frequency, and timbre. This may seem a bit mind-boggling but it is this fact which explains the enormous range of sounds that can be coaxed from this one instrument. Other Yamaha digital FM machines provide varying numbers of operators, from the four available on the DX9, DX27, and DX100, to the forty-eight (!) available on the TX816 rack.

The Output Signal: Carriers and Modulators:

By issuing commands to each operator through its data inputs, we have shaped a signal which will eventually contribute to the final sound we hear. The end result of all of these manipulations is that we derive some kind of *output* signal **from** the operators. Be sure that you clearly understand the difference between *input* signals and *output* signals: **(See Figure 3-5.)**

Now that we've got some an *output* from our operator, what will we do with it? The answer is that we have **two** options at our disposal and we will have to pick one or the other.

The first option is obvious: we can send the output signal to the DAC, in which case we will be able to hear the sound: **(See Figure 3-6.)**

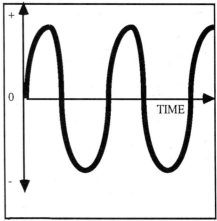

Figure 3-3

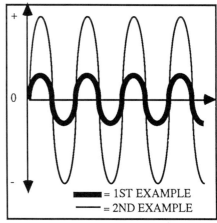

= 1ST EXAMPLE
= 2ND EXAMPLE

Figure 3-4

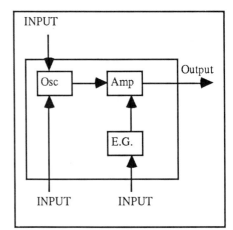

Figure 3-5

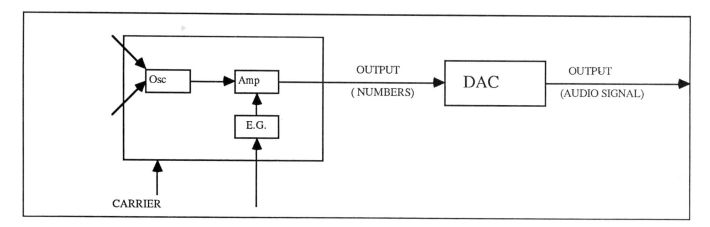

Figure 3-6

If we decide to do this with a particular operator, then digital FM jargon dictates that we call this operator a *CARRIER*. A *carrier*, by definition, is **any operator whose output goes to the DAC**.

On the other hand, we can decide **not** to send the output to the DAC but instead directly to the *modulation data input* of another operator! **(See Figure 3-7.)**

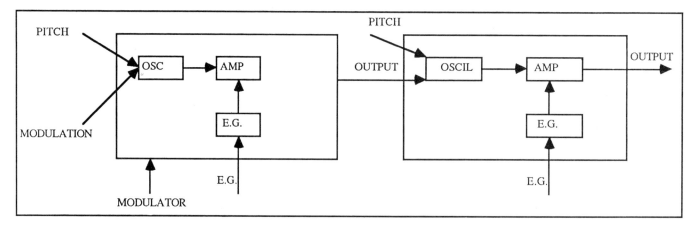

Figure 3-7

If we decide to follow this second option, then the operator in question is called a *MODULATOR*. A *modulator*, by definition, is **any operator whose output goes to the modulation input of another operator**.

THERE IS NO DIFFERENCE WHATSOEVER BETWEEN A CARRIER AND A MODULATOR APART FROM WHERE THEIR OUTPUT IS SENT!!

Why would we want to plug one operator into another like this? The fact is, this happens to be the **only** way that modulation data can be inputted to an operator. The sole reason for the *modulator's* existence, then, is to permit the carrier to generate complex timbres because **if no modulation data is present, the only wave that can be produced by an operator is a *sine wave*.** We will see shortly that while sine waves have their uses, it is easy to get sick of them rather quickly. To summarize: CARRIERS produce the actual sounds, and the timbres that they produce are determined by the actions of the MODULATORS. This one sentence pretty nearly summarizes the whole system of *digital FM synthesis*.

The only question remaining is, how do we know which operators are being used as CARRIERS and which ones are being used as MODULATORS? Furthermore, how do we know which MODULATORS are plugged into which CARRIERS? The answer to that question is the *ALGORITHMS*.

Algorithms:

An *algorithm* is a computer term referring to a mathematical way of solving a problem. On the DX7, the *algorithm* is **a means of configuring operators in order to generate a particular sound.**

We are provided with thirty-two different algorithms on this instrument and, as no one at Yamaha expected users to memorize each of them, diagrams illustrating these thirty-two configurations are located on the front panel of the DX7 itself: **(See Figure 3-8.)**

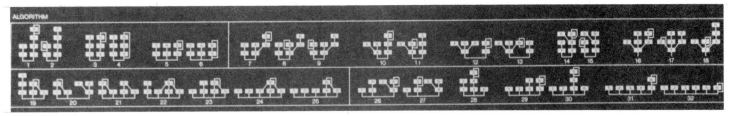

Figure 3-8

The diagrams themselves are extremely simple to understand and interpret, once you learn this basic principle: **whichever operators are being used as CARRIERS are always on the *bottom* row**. Those operators being used as modulators are stacked above the carriers, and vertical lines will always be present to indicate which modulators are plugged into which carriers. All six operators are simply numbered one through six for purposes of identification (they are all actually identical). **(See Figure 3-9.)**

The above is a diagram of Algorithm #5 (check the front panel of your DX7 to confirm this). As you can see, in this configuration, operators 1, 3, and 5 are being used as CARRIERS, and operators 2, 4, and 6 as MODULATORS. Furthermore, we see that operator 2 is modulating operator 1, 4 is modulating 3, and 6 is modulating 5.

Let's take a look at another algorithm, the simplest one of all, algorithm #32: **(See Figure 3-10.)**

In this configuration, all six operators are on the bottom row. That tells you that all six are being used as CARRIERS. Therefore, if we select this algorithm for a particular sound, we know that we can derive up to six different pitches (simultaneously, from one key!) at six different volumes, but that ALL SIX TIMBRES WILL BE IDENTICAL SINE WAVES. Contrast this with algorithm #5, which we examined above. Choosing **that** algorithm would allow us to generate a sound with up to three different pitches (again, from one key) at three different volumes, but with THREE DIFFERENT COMPLEX TIMBRES, since each CARRIER has its **own** MODULATOR attached. Let's examine a few more algorithms: **(See Figure 3-11.)**

This algorithm (#16) has only one CARRIER, operator 1, receiving modulation data from five separate modulators, operators 2 through 6. Moreover, MODULATOR 4 is actually modulating MODULATOR 3 as 6 is 5! The reasons for this may not yet be apparent but we will be covering these so-called "stacked" algorithms in depth later on. Sometimes, the opposite may occur, with more than one CARRIER being modulated by a single MODULATOR: **(See Figure 3-12.)**

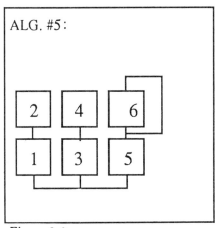

ALG. #5:

Figure 3-9

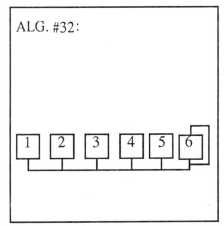

ALG. #32:

Figure 3-10

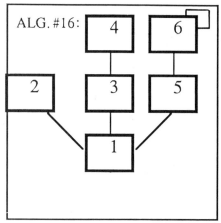

Figure 3-11

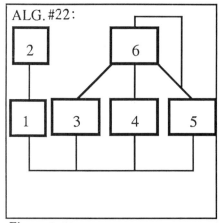

Figure 3-12

This algorithm (#22) has CARRIER 1 being modulated by MODULATOR 2; as well as CARRIERs 3, 4, and 5 all being modulated by MODULATOR 6. This means that using this configuration will allow us to generate one complex timbre of any pitch and volume (from the *system* of operators 1 and 2) and apparently three other sounds of varying pitch and volume but SIMILAR TIMBRE from the *system* of operators 3, 4, 5, and 6 since all the CARRIERS here are receiving modulation data from the same MODULATOR (operator 6). We'll learn later on that this isn't exactly the case, but you get the picture... The important point is that whenever you select an algorithm, you are simply telling the DX7 how you want it to **configure** the various operators - which ones are to be used as CARRIERS, which as MODULATORS, and where the modulation signals should be routed.

Probably the most common question I am asked by DX7 owners is, "how do I know which algorithm is best for a particular sound?"; or, more precisely, "which algorithm is the best for a string/brass/flute/woodwind/Star Wars sound?". The answer, unfortunately, is that there is no answer. Most algorithms will work for most sounds most of the time. Why then do we have so many available?

What the software engineers at Yamaha have done is provided us with just about any configuration you could possibly need for **specific** effects. We will examine many of these effects in the pages to come. The process of selecting the "best" algorithm for a particular sound is a fairly inexact one. What you will have to do is **eliminate** particular algorithms which appear to be unworkable for your specific application and create a shortlist of algorithms which look as though they **might** work. Then it's just a matter of making an educated guess and just choosing one. If it turns out, after tweaking your sound for a while, that you've made the wrong choice - no problem. **The DX7 allows you to change algorithms at any point!** Furthermore, if you do change algorithms, the **only** thing that will be changed is the configuration - **none** of your data entries will be lost. As we get further into the actual programming operations of the machine we will explain further the various criteria for selecting or eliminating particular algorithms in specific situations.

CHAPTER FOUR: VOICE INITIALIZATION

There are two basic methods of generating a sound on the DX7. First of all, you can create a sound "from scratch" by manipulating the voice-specific *edit* parameters in various ways and sending data inputs to the six operators. Alternatively, you can work with one of the *preset* sounds, the ones on your ROM cartridge, or presets you get from other DX7 owners on RAM cartridges, and modify one of these sounds to meet your special needs.

There is no secret to the fact that the latter method is the one used by most DX7 owners most of the time; it's easier to start with a sound that's close to what you need and simply tweak it till you're satisfied with the result. However, the cruel fact of the matter is that it is impossible to **purposefully** make changes to a sound in the DX7 unless you have a clear idea of how the sound was created in the first place. I wholeheartedly endorse the concept of modifying preexisting sounds on the DX7 in order to accomplish a particular result. But given this unfortunate fact of life, plus the idea that there will be times when there is no preset available that will be even close to what you want, we **do** need to learn how to create sounds "from scratch" on this instrument.

There is a wonderfully fast and simple procedure available on the DX7 which allows us to *reset* the edit buffer (just the edit buffer! which means that we won't actually be doing **anything** to any of the sounds already in memory) to a beginning stage - putting the machine in neutral, as it were. This procedure is called *VOICE INITIALIZATION* and it enables the DX7 user to establish a completely controllable and completely predictable environment in which to begin generating a sound.

Before we actually *initialize* our DX7, we should preview what will occur. First of all, and perhaps most importantly, whatever sound happens to currently be in the edit buffer (that is, whatever sound you are currently hearing), will disappear and be replaced by a single *sine wave*. Second of all, the DX7 will automatically place you in *edit mode*, allowing you to begin changing these parameters. Thirdly, each one of the various edit parameters will immediately have a number plugged into it - and that particular number we call a *DEFAULT* setting. *Default* is simply a computer term for a condition that exists when the computer is first turned on. The DX7 does not actually default on power-up because the back-up battery prevents it from doing so and instead keeps the most recent data in the edit buffer. This is the reason why you always hear the last sound you were playing whenever you first turn on the DX7, and why the LCD display always shows you the most recent mode and parameter you were using. The way to defeat all this and to get the DX7 to default itself instead, is by using the VOICE INITIALIZATION procedure.

A glance at your front panel will show you that function switch #10 (that is, main switch #10, in function mode) reads "VOICE INIT": **(See Figure 4-1.)**

Pressing this switch will inform the computer that we wish to *initialize*. Remember, initializing will **not** change any of the sounds currently in memory in any way, shape or form! The presence of the *edit buffer* ensures that. With this safely in mind, let's do it:

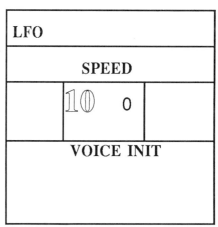

Figure 4-1

Exercise 6

Voice initialization:

1) No matter what mode your DX7 is currently in, or what sound is in the edit buffer, press the FUNCTION *mode select* switch, and then main switch #10.
2) OBSERVE: LED has same number as was previously there.
3) OBSERVE: Top line of LCD reads "FUNCTION CONTROL"; bottom line reads "VOICE INIT?"
4) NOTE: Our DX7 is asking us a question. Depending on the parameter we select, this may be a yes-no question, as this one is; or it may be an on-off question; or it may not ask a question at all and simply require that we enter a number. Since this particular parameter requires a yes-no answer.
5) Press the "yes" button in the data entry section.
6) OBSERVE: Bottom line of LCD now asks "ARE YOU SURE?". The DX7 is asking for confirmation that you want to pursue this procedure. Since we do,
7) Press the "yes" button in the data entry section once again.
8) OBSERVE: The LCD tells us that we are now in *Edit mode*; the top line reads "ALG x 111111" and perhaps "OP x" as well. The bottom line may have any edit parameter displayed.
9) LISTEN: Play the keyboard. No matter what sound you had in the DX7 previously, you should now hear only a single clear tone (AUDIO CUE 6A). This tone is a sine wave.
10) NOTE that as you play different keys on the keyboard, the sine wave plays different pitches, and that you can play chords of up to sixteen notes at any one time.

What's happened here? Let's examine this procedure, step by step. First of all, we had to put the DX7 into *function* mode in order to start the initialization. This makes sense since you can initialize at **any time**, no matter what you are doing on the machine. Initializing doesn't harm the DX7 at all and you can do it as many times as you like and whenever you like. Since *function* controls are global commands, it's logical that this procedure come from that mode.

Why did the DX7 ask "ARE YOU SURE?"? This is actually a typical computer procedure. Whenever you direct a computer to undertake a severe change in course, like telling it to initialize itself, it will normally ask for confirmation that this is in fact what you want it to do. Initializing the DX7, while totally harmless, is a fairly drastic procedure. What you are in fact instructing the computer to do is change a great many things at once - **all** the edit parameters. After all, if you, for example, had the "E.PIANO 1" sound called up prior to initialization, we know that the reason we heard the sound of a Fender Rhodes is because all the edit parameters had particular numbers plugged into them. Immediately after initializing, the sound was changed COMPLETELY to just a single sine wave. The explanation is that all the parameters were changed **at once**.

After we reassured the DX7 that Voice Initialization was in fact what we wanted it to do, we were automatically taken **out** of *function* mode and put into edit mode. This is logical, because the DX7 knows that the only reason for initializing is to create a sound from scratch, and that presumably we will be altering one or more of these edit parameters in order to concoct something more interesting than just a single sine wave.

Our instrument now has a particular set of *default* numbers plugged into all of its edit parameters. What are these numbers? Well, most of them are zeroes: most things on the machine are simply turned off. We will be taking note of the various defaults as we encounter them in this book, or for those of you who can't wait, you can turn to Appendix B. The important thing to understand is that **every time you initialize, all of the edit parameters default exactly the same way**. This means you can initialize your DX7 today, tomorrow, or next year, and **all** the edit parameters will have exactly the same default numbers entered into them as they do now. This is what we mean when we talk about giving ourselves a completely controlled environment - you can predict in advance precisely which parameters will have what values because **everytime** they will reset themselves the same way. This is the beauty of using Voice Initialization when creating a sound from nothing - you know just what's going on in the machine at all times.

We can now begin to make some sense of the odd messages on the top line of our LCD. When manipulating edit parameters, probably the most important thing you need to know is which *algorithm* you are working in. In edit mode, the upper left hand corner of the LCD will always show you which one you're using, and as we can see, right now the DX7 tells us "ALG 1". This is the *default* for the algorithm select parameter. **Whenever you initialize, the DX7 puts you into algorithm 1, whether you want to be there or not.**

OK, let's suppose you don't want to be in algorithm # 1. We can tell the computer that we wish to change algorithms simply by pressing edit switch 7, which is labeled "ALGORITHM", and is your *algorithm select* switch. **(See Figure 4-2.)**

Let's do it:

Exercise 7

Changing the algorithm:

1) If your DX7 isn't still set from the end of Exercise 6, *initialize* it by redoing that exercise now.
2) Check to see that you are in *edit mode* . If you have successfully initialized, that's just where you should be!
3) Press main switch 7. (Since we are already in *edit mode* , it will activate for its "ALGORITHM" parameter.
4) OBSERVE: Top line of LCD should currently read "ALG 1 111111". The bottom line of LCD should read "ALGORITHM SELECT".
5) NOTE: This is a parameter which does not require a yes-no nor on-off answer. Instead we are being asked to enter a number from 1 to 32 (since there are only 32 different algorithms). We can do this in the *data entry* section by using the "yes" - "no" switches, which will act to increment or decrement the current number by ones, or by using the data entry slider, which will simply increase or decrease the current number quickly. Therefore,
6) Press the data entry "yes" button once. As you do so, OBSERVE the top line of the LCD. You should see the "ALG 1" change to an "ALG 2". Now press the "no" button and OBSERVE the "ALG 2" change back to "ALG 1".
7) Now move the data entry slider. As you do so, OBSERVE the "ALG" number change rapidly or slowly, up or down, depending on how you move the slider. If the slider was at or near its top position when you began this step, OBSERVE that as soon as you moved it to any slight degree, it immediately became activated and the LCD number "jumped" to a value corresponding to the position of the slider. This effect will be true of ALL parameters we seek to change with the data entry slider as it will always need some small degree of movement in order to become activated.
8) Hold down a note and LISTEN as you make these algorithm changes again (AUDIO CUE 7A). NOTE that the sound does **not** change *pitch* or *timbre*, but that it does occasionally change in *volume*, and that these changes occur in REAL TIME; that is, as you are moving the slider, you hear these changes occur simultaneously.

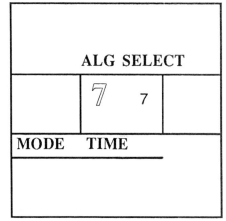

Figure 4-2

Each time you saw the "ALG" number change in the upper left-hand corner of the LCD, the DX7 was instantaneously reconfiguring the six operators according to the thirty-two diagrams on the machine. Note that no matter what you do, you CANNOT enter a number greater than 32 nor less than 1. That's because our DX7 has been instructed by the friendly folk at Yamaha that there are no more than these 32 algorithms available, and that they are numbered one through thirty-two. Again, bear in mind that changing the algorithm is something that you can do at any time - the computer really doesn't care how many times you change your mind, or when.

Why do we hear only a single sine wave when we initialize, and why does it sometimes change in volume, but not pitch or timbre, when we change algorithms? Again, the answer lies in the *default* settings being provided for us. Whenever we are in *edit mode*, the center of the LCD top line tells us the *status* of the operators; specifically which ones are **on** and which ones are **off**. This is referred to as the *operator status display*, and it consists of six "1"s or "0"s, in any combination. A "1" indicates that a particular operator is &on and a "0" indicates that it is **off**. Therefore, a display of, for example, "111000" would mean that operators 1, 2, and 3 were **on**, and that operators 4, 5, and 6 were *off*. Each of our six operators can be switched on or off like light bulbs, at will. This means that if you are not using a particular operator at a certain time, you don't have to see it or hear it at all; and conversely, if you want to hear a single operator or groups of operators, you can easily do so. The edit switches we use to turn operators on and off with are switches 1 through 6, happily labeled "OPERATOR ON-OFF". Each of these six switches is associated with a particular operator, i.e. switch 1 with operator 1, switch 2 with operator 2, etc., and each time you depress one of the switches the operator will flip on or off, depending on its current status.

Let's see how they work:

Exercise 8

Turning operators on and off:

1) *Initialize* your DX7 and leave it in algorithm #1.
2) OBSERVE the top line of the LCD, which reads "ALG 1 111111" and maybe "OP x".
3) Press main switch #1. Since we are already in *edit mode*, this switch is now activated for its "OPERATOR 1 ON/OFF" parameter.
4) OBSERVE the top line of the LCD. The center of the line, the **operator status display**, now reads "011111", indicating that operator 1 is now **off**.
5) Press main switch #1 again. OBSERVE that the operator status display now reads "111111" again, showing us that operator 1 is back **on** again.
6) Repeat steps 3, 4, and 5 above, this time using main switches 2, 3, 4, 5, and 6. OBSERVE that each of these switches controls an associated operator, and that *toggling* the switches (that is, pressing them repeatedly) turns them on or off.

Whenever you initialize, the *default* for the operator on-off status is **all operators on**. That's why, whenever you initialize, the top center line of the LCD will read "111111". So far, so good. But this still doesn't explain why we are only hearing a single sine wave and why the volume sometimes changes as we change algorithms. Well, let's see just what each of the six operators is contributing to the overall sound we are hearing:

Exercise 9

Listening to the individual operators:

1) *Initialize* your DX7 and turn off all six operators by pressing each of the "OPERATOR ON/OFF" switches (edit switches 1 through 6) **once**. (You may find that the quickest way to accomplish this is to **slide** your fingertip across the six switches. Go ahead, indulge yourself...)

2) OBSERVE the operator status display which should now read "000000".

3) Press main switch #1 once to change the operator status display to "100000". This indicates that the only operator we are hearing is operator 1.

4) LISTEN as you play a few notes. You should be hearing the same *sine* wave as before.

5) Now turn operator 1 **off** by pressing edit switch 1 again, and turn operator 2 on by pressing edit switch 2 once.

6) OBSERVE the operator status display which should now read "010000".

7) Play a few notes and LISTEN. No sound? Don't worry, your DX7 isn't broken.

8) Repeat this procedure for operators 3, 4, 5, and 6, LISTENing to each of them on their own in the same manner.

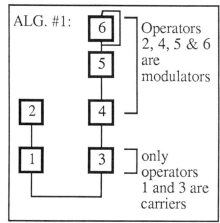

Figure 4-3

What conclusion can we reach? Obviously, we can only hear operator 1 for some reason. When we first initialized, the DX7 turned all six of its operators on, yet we now know that we were only hearing operator 1. Why should this be? Well, maybe the answer lies in the *algorithm*. We've found that the *default* for this parameter is algorithm 1. Aha! Maybe that's it: after all, in algorithm 1, four of our six operators are being used as MODULATORS, and remember, you can NEVER hear modulators, since they don't send any signal to the DAC. **(See Figure 4-3.)**

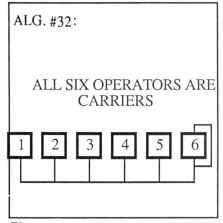

Figure 4-4

Well, let's see if our theory is correct. Repeat Exercise 9 above, but this time right after initializing, select algorithm #32 (if you don't remember how to do this, refer back to Exercise 7 earlier in this chapter). Algorithm #32 doesn't have any modulators, only carriers: **(See Figure 4-4.)**

If you've just redone Exercise 9 with algorithm #32 then you already know the bad news: we were wrong. Even though we now had all six operators sending their signal directly to the DAC, we still were only hearing operator 1. The real solution to this mystery lies in edit switch 27, labeled *output level*. **(See Figure 4-5.)**

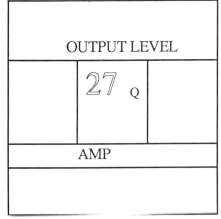

Figure 4-5

This switch allows us to independently control just how much signal leaves each of our six operators. This is the first parameter we have encountered which is *operator-specific*; that is, each operator can have a totally different output level if we so desire, and so for the first time we can explain away the "OP" that you may have occasionally noticed in the upper right-hand corner of the edit mode LCD display. Calling up such a parameter allows us the opportunity to view and/or change the setting for each operator individually. In order to cycle through the various operators we use the blue *Operator Select* switch at the upper right-hand corner of the eight switches to the left of the LED/LCD. **(See Figure 4-6.)**

When we call up the "output level" edit parameter, the DX7 will allow us to enter a number from 0 to 99. 0 is the **minimum** output level (equivalent to no output) and 99 is the **maximum** output for any operator, under all conditions. Let's try it out:

Figure 4-6

Exercise 10

The output level parameter:

1) *Initialize* the DX7 and select algorithm #32 by using the *algorithm select* switch (edit switch 7).

2) Turn off operators 2 through 6, using the *operator on/off* switches.

3) OBSERVE operator status display reads "100000".

4) Press main switch #27. Because we are already in *edit mode*, that switch is currently activated for its "OUTPUT LEVEL" function.

5) OBSERVE that LED does not change - it still displays the number of the last voice you called up on the machine. OBSERVE that the upper right-hand corner of LCD reads "OP 1": since operator 1 is currently the only operator turned on, that is the one we are viewing. OBSERVE that the bottom line of the LCD reads "OUTPUT LEVEL = 99". NOTE that 99 (maximum) is therefore the *default* value for the output level of operator 1 - in other words, whenever we initialize our DX7, operator 1 will automatically be given maximum output.

6) Play a few keys and LISTEN. NOTE the volume of the sine wave you are hearing.

7) Go to the data entry section, and using the yes-no buttons or the data entry slider, change the output level of operator 1 to 85. OBSERVE that as you do this the bottom line of the LCD changes to eventually read "OUTPUT LEVEL = 85".

8) Play a few keys and LISTEN. NOTE that the sine wave you are hearing is considerably lower in volume.

9) Change the output level of operator 1 to a new value of 0. Play a few keys and note that the sound is now gone altogether.

10) Restore the output level of operator 1 back to its default value of 99.

11) Turn operators 2 through 6 back on using the OPERATOR ON/OFF switches. OBSERVE that the operator status display now reads "111111" again. NOTE that the bottom line of the LCD still reads "OUTPUT LEVEL = 99", since we are still VIEWing operator 1. Let's look at operator 2 now:

12) VIEW operator 2 by pressing the blue "OPERATOR SELECT" switch once. OBSERVE as you do so that the "OP 1" in the upper right-hand corner of the LCD changes to "OP 2". OBSERVE that the default value for the output level of operator 2 is 0!

13) VIEW operator 3 by pressing the "OPERATOR SELECT" switch again. NOTE its default output level setting. Repeat this step for operators 4, 5, and 6, and NOTE their default output level values (they will all be 0 as well).

14) TRY turning various operators on and off selectively and changing their output levels, LISTENing as you do so. NOTE that the output level parameter **does not change in real time**, meaning that you do not hear the volume change occur as you are entering the new data. Instead, you must *retrigger* the operator by pressing the key on the keyboard a second time in order for that new data to be assimilated by the operator.

OUTPUT LEVEL IS IN FACT THE ONLY PARAMETER ON THE DX7 THAT DOES NOT CHANGE IN REAL TIME.

What have we learned from all this? The reason we were only hearing operator 1 even though all six operators were turned on, REGARDLESS OF ALGORITHM, is because when we initialize, operator 1 defaults to an output level of 99 (maximum volume) whereas the other five operators default to an output level of 0 (minimum volume). In other words, our clever little microprocessor has set things up so that, even though all six operators are initially on, we are only getting signal from one of them (operator 1). Having an operator on with an output level of zero is like switching your stereo amplifier on but turning the volume control to zero - it doesn't matter how good the record you have spinning is, you won't hear anything.*

OK, that answers one of the questions. What about an explanation for why the volume sometimes changes as we change algorithms? This is an easy one. Different algorithms, as you will observe from the diagrams on your machine, have different numbers of CARRIERS. The DX7 automatically adjusts the relative volume of each carrier, according to the algorithm, so that the total volume of the signal leaving the synthesizer remains more or less constant. That means that operator 1 in algorithm #16, for example, will have twice the volume of that same operator 1 in algorithm #3; three times the volume of the same operator 1 in algorithm #5; and six times the volume than if it were in algorithm #32. **(See Figure 4-7.)**

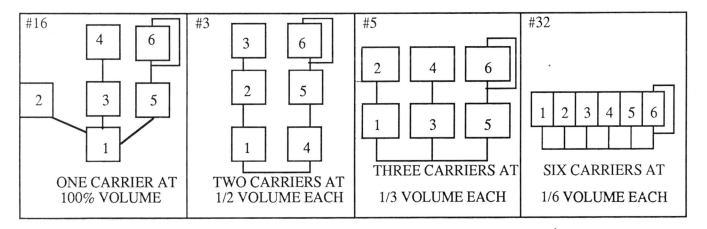

Figure 4-7

Since in the above exercises we now know that we were only hearing operator 1 after all, this explains the changes in volume as we selected various different algorithms.

We've just had our first exposure to the "OP" display in the upper right-hand corner of the edit mode LCD. This may not always be present, however. Put your DX7 into edit mode and call up the "algorithm select" parameter (edit switch 7). Note that the upper right-hand corner is now blank. The **absence** of an "OP" in the LCD tells us that we are viewing a parameter that is **not** operator-specific, such as "algorithm select" - after all, you can't put some operators in one algorithm and others in a different one at the same time - we can only work with one algorithm at a time and when we select a particular algorithm, all **six** operators are configured in that particular manner. Another non-operator-specific parameter that we have already worked with is "Key Transpose", which, of course, affects the entire sound and not just particular operators within the sound. To summarize, if you see that "OP" in the display, the DX7 is telling you that the parameter you have selected can be individually adjusted for each operator (in other words, it is *operator-specific*). If the "OP" isn't there, then the parameter you have selected affects **all** operators equally.

Of course, if your parameter **is** operator-specific, then you use the OPERA-TOR SELECT switch to both view and change individual operators. This switch is "intelligent" in that it always skips whichever operators are turned off. Therefore, if you have, for example, turned off operators 2, 4, and 6 with the OPERATOR ON/OFF switches 2, 4, and 6, then your status display would

* When you **store** a sound in the DX7's memory (either internal or RAM cartridge), the operator on-off statuses are **not** memorized: all operators will automatically be turned ON - even those you had turned OFF when programming the sound. Therefore, the only way to positively ensure that a sound will have particular operators inactive is to set those operator's OUTPUT LEVELS to 0 before storing.

read "101010" and pressing the OPERATOR SELECT switch would only allow you to view operators 1, 3, and 5. Those operators that were **off** would be passed over. Try it! If, on the other hand, operators 1 and 6 were the only operators switched on, the OPERATOR SELECT switch would only toggle between those two operators (try this, too). This provides you, the DX7 programmer, with a terrific time-saving feature, since you can selectively view and alter operators. It's a good idea in general to get in the habit of turning off whichever operators you are not working with at any particular time - this may save you from ever accidentally altering the **wrong** operator, and in any event will always make programming the machine go much faster (an important consideration in a place like a recording studio with a budget-conscious producer breathing down your neck!)

Let's continue now with a closer look at the workings of CARRIERS. Initialize your DX7, select algorithm #32, and read on…

SWITCHES AND CONTROLS COVERED IN CHAPTER FOUR:

SWITCH	PARAMETER	COMMENTS
Function 10	Voice initialization	Resets DX7 to defaults
Edit 7	Algorithm select	Range: 1 - 32
Edit 1 - 6	Operator on/off	
OPERATOR SELECT	View and/or change specific operations	Toggles only between operators switched <u>on</u>
Edit 27	Output level	Range: 0 - 99

CHAPTER FIVE: THE CARRIER

In this chapter we will be examining the actions of carriers alone: that is, operators sending output signals to the DAC that are not themselves receiving modulation data from *modulators*. As we have learned, the only kind of wave that such an operator can generate is a pure sine wave, containing no overtones. Sine waves are used in all types of digital synthesis (additive as well as FM) as building blocks from which to make complex sounds. While a single sine wave on its own is fairly uninteresting, combinations of sine waves of different frequency and amplitude can make for useful and realistic sounds. Combining sine waves together at a common output is essentially the way that *additive* digital systems (such as the Fairlight CMI or Synclavier) generate sounds, and, as has been mentioned, the DX7 is also capable of some limited additive capabilities. In this chapter we will examine these capabilities, and in the next chapter we will apply this information to the true DX7 sound generation system, *digital FM*.

We will be working exclusively with algorithm #32 in this chapter, and so although our six carriers will not yet be receiving any modulation data, we know that we will have to send them both *EG* and *pitch data*. The *EG data* is defaulted to a simple on-off configuration* when our instrument is initialized, so we won't be concerning ourselves with that just yet. However, the pitch input data is of great importance - so we'll start with the four switches that control this information: **(See Figure 5-1.)**

These switches (obviously all edit parameters) are, from left to right:

EDIT SWITCH #	PARAMETER
17	Mode/Sync
18	Frequency coarse
19	Frequency fine
20	Detune

All four of these switches are labeled on the DX7 under the somewhat misleading umbrella, "Oscillator" (look at the line above the blue edit parameter names). These are not actually the only data inputs to the oscillator, but they do comprise most of what determines the final pitch of the selected operator. Of course, it's fair to surmise that the keyboard also has something to do with it, but we'll soon see that that's not always the case.

Put your DX7 into edit mode (if its already in edit mode, **don't** hit the edit *mode select* switch again) and press main switch #17 (now activated for its *MODE/SYNC* function). In all probability, you will see the following display: **(See Figure 5-2.)**

If instead you see the words "FIXED FREQUENCY" in the bottom line of the LCD, simply press the "Yes" button in the *data entry* section and it will revert to the illustration above.

*that is, maximum volume immediately when a key is depressed and minimum volume immediately when it is released. See Chapter Nine for more information on this.

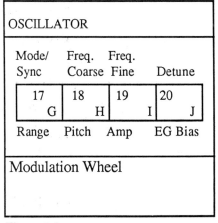

Figure 5-1

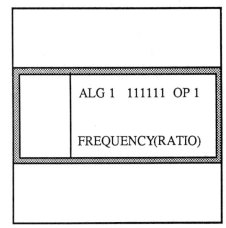

Figure 5-2

What do the words "FREQUENCY(RATIO)" mean? Obviously, our computer has no way of telling that a C# is a C# or that a G is a G on the keyboard: computers can only "think" in numbers. As we discovered in Chapter Two when we used the Key Transpose function control, all of the keys on our keyboard are in fact **numbered**, from C1 to C6. Each of these key numbers are associated in the computer's memory with a particular **frequency**, in Hz; for example, A3 (middle A) with 440. Whenever you press middle A, then, the computer quickly looks up a little table in its memory and generates the number 440. This number is called the *frequency number*. The next thing the DX7 will do is look up another number, called the *ratio number*, and it will automatically **multiply** the two. The end result of this calculation is the final frequency that we hear. Therefore the display "FREQUENCY(RATIO)" should be interpreted in the *algebraic* sense, with the parentheses indicating the multiplication function (remember, in high school algebra, when you wanted to multiply 2 by 2, you would write it out 2(2). Hopefully, you came up with 4 as the answer. If not, please return this book immediately for a refund!).

Where does this ratio number come from? From us, natch. How do we see what it is and/or change it? That's precisely what edit switches 18, 19, and 20 are for. Let's begin by finding out the default value for these switches. When you *initialize*, all six operators have the same default values for these parameters, so if we view one, we know what they all are. Let's do it:

EXERCISE 11

Default pitch data values:

1) INITIALIZE your DX7 and select algorithm #32. (if you're not sure how to do this, refer to Exercises 6 and 7 in the preceding chapter).
2) Using the operator on-off switches TURN OFF operators 2 through 6. OBSERVE that the operator status display in the LCD reads "100000".
3) Press main switch #17 (MODE/SYNC). NOTE that the "OP" in the upper right-hand corner is "OP 1". We are now only going to be able to view operator 1, since it is the only operator on. OBSERVE that the bottom line of LCD reads "FREQUENCY(RATIO)". This is the *default* value for this parameter for all operators.
4) Press main switch #18 (FREQ COARSE). OBSERVE that the bottom line of LCD reads "F COARSE = 1.00". This is the *default* value for this parameter for all operators.
5) Press main switch #19 (FREQ FINE). OBSERVE that the bottom line of LCD reads "F FINE = 1.00". This is the *default* value for this parameter for all operators.
6) Press main switch #20 (DETUNE). OBSERVE that the bottom line of LCD reads "OSC DETUNE = 0". This is the *default* value for this parameter for all operators.
7) If you are the disbelieving type (or if you were born in Missouri), TURN ON the other five operators and view these same four parameters for each of them in turn. NOTE that they have all defaulted to the same values as operator 1.

Before we find out how we can change this *ratio number*, we should stop and think about what the "FREQUENCY(RATIO)" mode really means. What the DX7 is actually telling us is that the operator in question will *track* (respond to), the notes we play on the keyboard. In plain English, this mode indicates that the operator will play different pitches as we play different notes. When we first initialized and listened to that single plain sine wave, we found that that was true; tinkling the notes to "Strangers In The Night" (I've decided to stop picking on Bruce) did in fact allow us to hear that melody. The other option to this parameter is called "FIXED FREQUENCY" and if we select that, then our operator will ignore the notes we play on the keyboard and will simply output a particular fixed frequency no matter what notes we play. We'll explore that other option shortly. The other operation of edit switch 17, the "SYNC" parameter is of little consequence and will be covered at the end of this chapter. For now, let's get a bit further into *FREQUENCY(RATIO)*.

Exercise 11 has shown us that the ratio number defaults to exactly 1.00, for every operator. This means that, no matter which operator we are listening to, if we play a middle "A", our DX7 will look up the *frequency number* 440 and **multiply** it by the *ratio number* 1.00, resulting in the output of a sine wave of exactly 440 Hz (440 x 1.00 = 440). Of course, we will be able to change the ratio number. Edit switch 18, FREQUENCY COARSE, allows us to change the ratio number by whole numbers. Multiplying a particular fundamental frequency by whole numbers, remember, gives us the *harmonic overtones* of that frequency. Therefore, this parameter will allow us to step through the *harmonic series* for any particular note:

EXERCISE 12:

Frequency coarse parameter:

1) INITIALIZE your DX7 and select algorithm #32. TURN OFF all operators except operator 1.("100000")

2) VIEWing operator 1 (which is automatic since it is the only operator ON), press edit switch 18 (FREQUENCY COARSE) and OBSERVE that the *ratio number* is at its default value of 1.00. Play a short, recognizable sequence of notes (if you don't know "Strangers In the Night" then most anything else will do) on the keyboard (AUDIO CUE 12A).

3) Using the "yes" button in the data entry section (which will act to increment this value in steps of whole numbers), CHANGE the *ratio number* to 2.00. OBSERVE that bottom line of LCD now reads "F COARSE = 2.00".

4) Play the same series of notes on the keyboard and LISTEN. Your melody has now been raised an octave! (AUDIO CUE 12B) Since the *ratio number* has been doubled, all the notes have gone to their second harmonic, which is an octave higher. For example, playing middle "A" on the keyboard now results in an output of 880 Hz (440 x 2.00 = 880).

5) Continue playing the same sequence of notes, and as you do so, CHANGE the value of the *ratio number* to 3.00. LISTEN and note that the notes have now been transposed up another musical fifth (to the third harmonic). (AUDIO CUE 12C) NOTE that this change occurred in *real time*, as you were playing the notes. Since we are not affecting output level, this parameter will change in real time.

6) Hold down a single key on the keyboard and use the "yes" button in order to slowly CHANGE the *ratio number* upward till you reach the maximum value of 31.00. LISTEN as you do so (AUDIO CUE 12D), and NOTE that all of the resulting transpositions are musically related to the original pitch; after all, we are stepping through the harmonic overtones. At the maximum value of 31.00, the DX7 is actually multiplying the notes you play by 31, and so if you are holding down a high note, it may well be supersonic at this point. NOTE that using the data entry slider will initiate the same changes as the "yes" button, but more rapidly.

7) Now reverse course and use the "no" button in order to slowly return the ratio number back to 1.00, LISTENing as you do so (AUDIO CUE 12E). NOTE that below 1.00, you can lower the ratio number to its minimum of 0.50, thereby lowering your note to an octave below where you started (remember, halving the frequency drops it an octave). NOTE once again that moving the *data entry* slider will change these values quickly, and also in *real time*, as before.

It may occur to some of you that the results we receive from this exercise are extremely similar to those we encountered from working with the Key Transpose parameter (Exercise 5, Chapter 2). How do they differ? The Key Transpose allowed us to transpose an entire sound, and, since it was an edit parameter, it was most definitely *voice-specific*. However, the Frequency Coarse parameter takes things a step further; it is *operator-specific*, so we are changing the tuning of particular operators within the total sound. This will allow us, by using *additive* synthesis methods, to actually create a complex composite sound out of several, differently pitched, simple waveshapes. Therefore, we're now ready to create our first real sound on the DX7:

EXERCISE 13

Creating a sound using additive synthesis:

1) INITIALIZE your DX7 and select algorithm #32. TURN OFF operators 2 through 6 (operator status = "100000").

2) VIEWing operator 1 (which is automatic since it is the only operator ON), press edit switch 18 (FREQUENCY COARSE) and OBSERVE that the *ratio number* is at its default value of 1.00. Play a few notes on the keyboard to confirm that operator 1 has output level, and press edit switch 27 (OUTPUT LEVEL) to visually confirm that fact.

3) TURN OFF operator 1 and TURN ON operator 2 only ("010000"). Since this is now the only operator on, the upper right-hand corner of LCD should read "OP 2". Play a few notes on the keyboard. You should not be hearing anything! Press switch 27 and OBSERVE that the output level of operator 2 is *defaulted* to 0. CHANGE the output level of operator 2 to 99. Play a few notes and LISTEN - it should be there!

4) Press edit switch 18 again and CHANGE the *ratio number* for operator 2 to 2.00. LISTEN and note that the operator is now an octave higher (second harmonic).

5) TURN ON operator 1 again ("110000"). Play a few notes and LISTEN. You should be hearing two sine waves playing together **in octaves** (AUDIO CUE 13A). The fact that we are hearing both sine waves mixed together at the same output gives the result of a single complex sound. This is the way that additive synthesis works.

6) TURN OFF operators 1 and 2 and TURN ON operator 3. Operator status display should read "001000". CHANGE the output level of operator 3 from its default of 0 to a new value of 99. CHANGE the ratio number for operator 3 to 3.00. Play a few notes and LISTEN. The operator is now playing every note at its third harmonic - an octave and a fifth higher!

7) Selectively TURNING ON and OFF operators 1, 2, and 3, LISTEN to the following combinations: operators 1 and 3 (AUDIO CUE 13B); operators 2 and 3 (AUDIO CUE 13C); and, finally, all three operators together (AUDIO CUE 13D). Starting to sound familiar? The Hammond organ creates its sound by combining together sine waves of various harmonic frequencies. Our DX7 is obviously able to simulate this method digitally.

8) TURN OFF operators 1, 2, and 3; and TURN ON operator 4 ("000100"). Set operator 4 to an output level of 99 and give it an F COARSE value of 4.00 (fourth harmonic = two octaves higher). Play a few notes on the keyboard to confirm this.

9) Using the same procedures, TURN ON operators 5 and 6 one at a time, setting both to an output level of 99 and setting the ratio number for operator 5 to 5.00 (the fifth harmonic) and operator 6 to 6.00 (the sixth harmonic). LISTEN to each operator independently as you do so.

10) Finally, TURN ON all six operators and LISTEN to the composite result (AUDIO CUE 13E).

11) EXPERIMENT by changing the ratio numbers for various operators to different harmonics and by altering the output levels of different operators in order to achieve different blends. NOTE that often even small changes to either of these parameters will induce large changes in the overall sound.

Congratulations!! We've now created our first musically useful sound from scratch. Doing organ sounds on the DX7 is particularly easy because these sounds are usually derived from simple sine waves. The trick is in combining several sine waves of different pitch and volume in order to create an interesting composite whole. In doing so, we have stumbled on one of the most important CARDINAL RULES of programming the DX7:

CARDINAL RULE 1: CHANGING THE OUTPUT LEVEL OF A CARRIER WILL ALWAYS RESULT IN A CHANGE IN VOLUME.

Throughout the course of this book, we will probably be repeating this so many times that you will be sick of hearing it! But this Cardinal Rule - and just a few others - is really the key to understanding how to program the DX7. Remember, we warned you way back in Chapter One that everything we do in programming synthesizers relates back to the three parameters of sound - and we've just learned how to control one of them.

The output level control, then, can be thought of as a *mixer*. This is the way that we can control the volume of various parts of our sound - if the operators in question are CARRIERS (we'll see in the next chapter that modulators don't respond the same way).

Okay, back to the various pitch data input controls. We've seen that the FREQUENCY COARSE control allows us to change the ratio number in whole number increments. But what if that's not what we need? Suppose, for example, that we want a ratio number of 1.25? Or 9.78?? Or any other **non-whole number** value? We can accomplish this with the FREQUENCY FINE control - edit switch 19. This parameter will always allow you to as much as nearly double whatever ratio number you currently have set, in fractions of whole numbers. Its range is determined by the value of the FREQUENCY COARSE control. For example, if F COARSE = 1.00, then the range of the F FINE control is 1.00 to 1.99, in increments of 0.01. On the other hand, if F COARSE = 2.00, then the range of the F FINE control is 2.00 to 2.98, in increments of 0.02. An F COARSE of 3.00 will yield an F FINE range of 3.00 to 5.97 in increments of 0.03, and so on. Try it!

EXERCISE 14

The frequency fine control:

1) INITIALIZE your DX7 and set it to algorithm #32. TURN OFF operators 2 through 6 ("100000"). Play a few notes and LISTEN. You should be hearing a single sine wave, coming from operator 1 only (AUDIO CUE 14A).
2) Press edit switch 19 (FREQUENCY FINE parameter), and, using the "yes-no" buttons or data entry slider, change the value of F FINE to 1.50.
3) Play a few notes on the keyboard and LISTEN. The operator is now playing a musical fifth higher than it was previously.* (AUDIO CUE 14B)

* For those of you who aren't sure why this should be, here's the explanation: The third harmonic (a ratio number of 3.00) is an octave and a fifth higher than the fundamental. Halving this (a ratio number of 1.50) will drop it back a full octave, yielding a frequency merely a musical fifth higher.

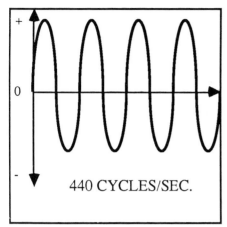

Figure 5-3

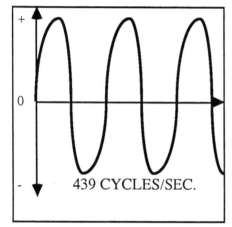

Figure 5-4

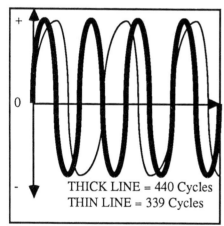

THICK LINE = 440 Cycles
THIN LINE = 339 Cycles

Figure 5-5

4) CHANGE the F FINE value to 1.99. Play a few notes and LISTEN. The operator is now playing nearly (but not quite) an octave higher than originally. (AUDIO CUE 14C)

5) Return the F FINE value to 1.00 and press edit switch 18 (FREQUENCY COARSE). CHANGE the F COARSE value to 2.00. Play a few notes and confirm that it is now a perfect full octave higher. (AUDIO CUE 14D)

6) Press edit switch 19 and CHANGE the F FINE value through its full range - 2.00 to 3.98. OBSERVE that it makes these changes in increments of 0.20. As you are doing so, play a few notes on the keyboard and LISTEN (AUDIO CUE 14E). NOTE that FREQUENCY FINE, like FREQUENCY COARSE, changes in *real time*.

7) EXPERIMENT by setting the F COARSE of operator 1 to various other values and then changing the F FINE value. Try doing the same with the other operators and listen to the composite result of setting more than one operator to various non-whole ratio numbers - the results will probably be more than a little cacophonous since we are blending *disharmonics* rather than *harmonics*. Bear in mind that the entire purpose of the FREQUENCY FINE parameter is to allow you to set an operator to a disharmonic frequency.

One byproduct of the FREQUENCY FINE control is that by using it at all, you will be changing the various FREQUENCY COARSE values available to you - they will no longer just be whole number values. Try changing one of the operators to a F FINE value of 1.63, for example. Now go back to the F COARSE control, and using the "yes" button, step through the various increments available. You'll be surprised to see that it does **not** offer you the values of 2.63, 3.63, or 4.63; but instead gives you the strange options of 3.26, 4.89, and 6.52. These values aren't quite so mysterious when you realize that 1.63 times 2.00 equals 3.26; that 1.63 times 3.00 equals 4.89; and that 1.63 times 4.00 equals 6.52. In any event, if it appears at any time that the F COARSE control is not giving you whole number values, simply go to the F FINE control and move the data entry slider down to its lowest position. That will drop the F FINE value to be exactly equal to the F COARSE value and things will operate normally.

The Detune Control

In order to understand the workings of this control, we need to discuss the acoustic phenomenon of *beating*. Whenever we hear two sounds simultaneously of nearly, but not exactly, the same frequency, we will encounter this effect. Let's suppose, for example, that we play A440 on a piano that's just been tuned. On an oscilloscope, the wave might look something like this: **(See Figure 5-3.)**

Now let's wheel another piano into the same room, and this one hasn't been tuned in quite a while, so **it's** middle A is actually at 439 Hz. On the oscilloscope, it would look like this: **(See Figure 5-4.)**

Let's get the two pianos next to each other, stretch our arms out, and play middle A on both pianos simultaneously. The oscilloscope would actually show a composite wave, but if we use our imagination we can theorize that the two waves together look something like this: **(See Figure 5-5.)**

As you can see, there are areas where the two waves cross each other and there are many more areas where they diverge. Because in our example the two waves differed in frequency by exactly one Hz, the amount of time between each cross-over point will be exactly one second. Each time they cross, the sound will increase in volume because the two waves reinforce one another. Each time they diverge, the opposite will happen. In short, we will hear a sound that periodically increases and decreases volume, or *beats* . The **difference**, in Hz, between our two frequencies dictates how **often** the beating occurs. It stands to reason, therefore, that the closer together our frequencies are, the less frequently they beat. The further apart they are, the faster the beating (until, at a certain point, the beating disappears altogether and we simply perceive two different pitches - remember, this is a phenomenon that occurs **only** if the two sounds in question are very close to one another in frequency). For example, an A440 together with an A439 will beat once per second, whereas an A440 together with an A438 will beat **twice** per second.

This is a technique commonly used by guitarists and bass players everywhere. What these strange people will do (myself included - definitely!) to tune their instruments up is to play the same note - usually as a harmonic - on two different strings. They then change the tuning of one of the strings, listening to the beating, until it slows down and finally disappears. At that point, the two strings are deemed to be perfectly in tune (Anybody ever hear the story about the punk rocker who finally got his guitar in tune, so he welded the tuning heads? Never mind...).

Beating is also used to great effect by analog synthesizers. In fact, this is the main explanation for the rich, lush sounds that these instruments are known for. Most of these instruments typically employ two or more analog oscillators as their sound source, and, as we know, it is impossible to expect two voltages to ever remain stable enough long enough to avoid drifting. If you tune two analog oscillators to the "same" frequency, what you are actually doing is tuning them to **nearly** the same frequency. Even then, the differences in frequency between them will constantly be changing. Without the use of some kind of electrical synchronization circuit (which is commonly available but infrequently used), there is **no way** to get two analog oscillators perfectly in tune with one another. The end result is that the analog synthesizer is usually outputting signals that are beating in varying interesting manners, and this is what is largely responsible for their "warmth".

Acoustic instruments also beat most of the time. In the case of a piano, that's pretty obvious since each note has two or three strings, and the best piano tuner in the world cannot (and won't even **want** to) get these strings **perfectly** in tune with one another. The point is that beating is an integral part of most musical sounds in existence. Obviously, we want to be able to induce this in our DX7. And here's where a potential problem arises. Unlike our analog cousins, the DX7 has **digital** oscillators. This means that there is theoretically no potential whatever for distortions or drifting in the signal they generate. We will have to **program** these distortions, and, even then, they will be "perfect" distortions - which means that it is practically impossible for a digital synthesizer of any kind to exactly reproduce the unpredictable changes in sound that an analog synthesizer generates. In return for this restriction, however, we know that we have much finer control over what we are actually doing. There **is** a method on the DX7 for inducing beating effects - and it is a much more precise method than any found on analog machines.

We've learned that in order to make a sound beat, we need to generate two very similar frequencies. Well, one way we could do that on the DX7 would be to use the FREQUENCY FINE control. This will enable us to generate two sine waves that are slightly out of tune with one another. If, for example, operator 1 is given a ratio number of 1.00 and operator 2 a value of 1.01, then playing middle "A" on the keyboard will result in two sine waves, one of 440 Hz (440 x 1.00 = 440) and the other of 444.4 Hz (440 x 1.01 = 444.4), resulting in a beating occurring once per 4.4 seconds (444.4 - 440 = 4.4). Let's try an exercise that first allows us to confirm that no beating occurs in the initialized state, and then allows us to set up the example above and hear the result:

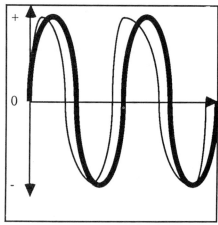

Figure 5-6

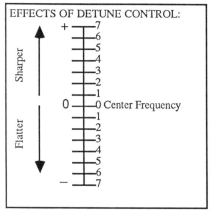

Figure 5-7

EXERCISE 15

Using the Frequency Fine control for beating effects:

1) INITIALIZE your DX7 and select algorithm #32. TURN OFF operators 2 through 6 (operator status = "100000"). Play a few notes and LISTEN, confirming that you are hearing operator 1.

2) Using edit switches 17, 18, and 19, OBSERVE that operator 1 is at its default values; MODE = FREQUENCY(RATIO), F COARSE = 1.00, and F FINE = 1.00. TURN OFF operator 1.

3) TURN ON operator 2 only ("010000"). CHANGE its output level from the default of 0 to a value of 99, using edit switch 27 and the data entry controls.

4) Using edit switches 17, 18, and 19, OBSERVE that operator 2 is at the same default values as operator 1. Play a few notes and LISTEN. There should be **no difference whatsoever** in the sound between operators 1 and 2.

5) TURN ON operator 1 ("110000") and play a few notes, LISTENing to the composite result of operators 1 and 2 together (AUDIO CUE 15A). NOTE that, apart from an increase in volume, there is no perceptible difference between the sound of **both** operators together and the sound of **either** alone. The overall volume has increased because the two operators are **exactly** in tune with one another and so their waves are reinforcing at every point: **(See Figure 5-6.)**

6) Using the OPERATOR SELECT switch, VIEW operator 2 and, with edit switch 19, CHANGE its F FINE value to 1.01.

7) Hold down Middle A on the keyboard and LISTEN (AUDIO CUE 15B). You should be hearing a composite sound of two sine waves *beating* against one another 4.4 times per second.

8) Keeping all values intact, press and hold down "A" above Middle A and LISTEN (AUDIO CUE 15C). You should now be hearing a composite sound of two sine waves beating against one another **8.8** times per second! EXPERIMENT by playing and holding down some more notes, individually, and in chords, and NOTE that, the higher the note you play, the **faster** the beating, and vice-versa. Also NOTE that each octave higher produces beats **twice** as fast, and each octave lower **half** as fast.

9) CHANGE the F FINE value for operator 2 to 1.02. Hold down a note and OBSERVE that the beating is occurring more quickly. Keeping the note held down, continue incrementing the F FINE value for operator 2 until the beating disappears and you hear two very sour notes! Reverse course and slowly decrease the F FINE value for operator 2 back to 1.00 and NOTE that the beating slows down and finally disappears altogether as we hear the composite result of two sine waves **perfectly** in tune with one another.

So far, so good. But the problem is, the FREQUENCY FINE control will allow us to get our two operators only so close to one another in pitch. If we could somehow get them closer still, we know that we would hear our beating occurring more slowly, and this will often produce a very desirable warmth to our sound. Fear not, because the *DETUNE* control lets us do just that - it is simply a **finer** fine tuning control!

What the detune control does is to break down the smallest FREQUENCY FINE increment (which we have seen changes according to the FREQUENCY COARSE value) into **fifteen** further increments! These are arranged as values of -7 to +7, with 0 as the center point: **(See Figure 5-7.)**

DETUNING an operator to a negative value will ever so slightly flatten its note whereas changing it to a positive value will ever so slightly sharpen it. This is the reason why 0 has been provided as a center point - if you don't want a particular operator to be detuned at all, you just set the DETUNE value to 0. As you might expect, the initialized default for this parameter is 0 for **all** operators. Let's try using it:

EXERCISE 16

The Detune Control:

1) INITIALIZE your DX7 and select algorithm #32. TURN OFF operators 3 through 6 (operator status = "110000").

2) Press edit switch 20 (DETUNE parameter) and use the OPERATOR SELECT switch in order to VIEW operator 1. Confirm that the default value for this is 0 (bottom line of LCD should read "OSC DETUNE = 0"). Now TURN OFF operator 1 ("010000").

3) Press edit switch 27 and CHANGE the output level of operator 2 from its default of 0 to a new value of 99, enabling us to **hear** it.

4) Press edit switch 20 and CHANGE the DETUNE value for operator 2 to "+7" (bottom line of LCD should read "OSC DETUNE = +7"). This will have the effect of making whatever frequencies operator 2 outputs slightly more sharp than normal - but not quite as much as a F FINE setting of 1.01 would do.

5) Play a few notes and LISTEN, first to operator 2 alone, and then, using the OPERATOR ON/OFF switches, to operator 1 on its own (AUDIO CUE 16A). You may not be able to tell any discernable difference between them since the change in pitch is very slight.

6) TURN ON both operators 1 and 2 ("110000") and hold down a note on the keyboard. LISTEN! (AUDIO CUE 16B) You should be hearing the composite sound of two sine waves gently and slowly beating against one another.

7) Holding down the same note, use the "no" button in the *data entry* section to slowly **decrease** the DETUNE value for operator 2 back to 0. LISTEN (AUDIO CUE 16C). NOTE that as you approach 0 the beating slows down and finally disappears altogether at the value of 0. NOTE also that this parameter changes in *real time* .

8) Keeping the same note held down, continue using the "no" button to decrease the DETUNE value for operator 2 into its negative numbers until you reach -7 (LCD reads "OSC DETUNE = -7"). LISTEN (AUDIO CUE 16D) and NOTE that the audible result is the **same** as in step 7 above. Whether we sharpen or flatten one of the frequencies doesn't matter, so long as the **difference** between the two remains constant (i.e. 441 - 440 equals 1, as 440 - 439 **also** equals 1).

9) EXPERIMENT by playing chords as well as single notes. Remember that each note is beating at a different rate! (the higher the note, the faster the beating) and so we derive strikingly beautiful effects (AUDIO CUE 16E). EXPERIMENT further by adding in various other operators at the same F COARSE and F FINE values but at different DETUNE values and NOTE that very complex and elegant movements in the sound can be obtained in this manner.

Of course, the beatings we can generate using this control will be "perfect" and unchanging effects, but with up to six different operators at our disposal, we can mask the regularity of this movement sufficiently to emulate the unpredictability of the analog synthesizer or the acoustic instrument. Beating is by far one of the most important effects we can use to "humanize" the sounds we create on the DX7. In general, it's something you do towards the end of a programming session, but it's always worth trying and usually produces a warmth to the sound which is desirable and difficult to achieve otherwise. Unlike the analog synthesizer, however, we aren't **forced** to have it present if we don't want it - just set the DETUNE control to 0 and (apart from special circumstances to be revealed later) there will be no beating coming from your DX7!

Fixed frequency mode

Earlier on, we mentioned that an alternative existed for the FRE-QUENCY(RATIO) mode. In the FREQUENCY(RATIO) mode, the pitch we hear changes as we play different notes on the keyboard because, even though the *ratio number* remains constant, the *frequency number* is continually being updated and revised (by the action of us playing the different notes!). This alternative mode is called *FIXED FREQUENCY* , and any operators put into this mode will no longer generate ratio numbers, nor will the computer do its multiplications. Instead, we will use the FREQUENCY COARSE, FREQUENCY FINE, and DETUNE controls to designate a particular **fixed** frequency at which the oscillator in question will generate its signal. This means, in plain English, that no matter what note we play on the keyboard, we will hear the same fixed pitch. There are many potential uses for this effect, but for those of you who are heavily into bagpipes, the first and most obvious is in setting up drones (sometimes called pedal tones).

Before we run an exercise showing you how to do this, let's preview the mechanics of how we set the fixed frequency we require. Edit switch 17 will allow us to put an operator into this mode in the first place, and edit switches 18, 19, and 20 together will actually determine the frequency. Edit switch 18, the FREQUENCY COARSE control will, as its name implies, set the **coarse** range, either from 1 Hz to 10 Hz; 10 Hz to 100 Hz; 100 Hz to 1000 Hz; or 1000 Hz to 10,000 Hz. The four different set FREQUENCY COARSE values available to us in fixed frequency mode are 1.000 Hz, 10.00 Hz, 100.0 Hz, and 1000 Hz. As you can see, when you cycle between these values (by pressing the "yes/no" buttons), we are simply shifting the decimal point.

Having set the coarse range, we can use the FREQUENCY FINE control to zero in on the particular frequency desired, and the DETUNE control if we wish to make further slight alterations to the pitch. NOTE that function control 1, MASTER TUNE ADJUST, will have no effect on any operators in FIXED FREQUENCY mode.

EXERCISE 17

Fixed frequency mode:

1) INITIALIZE your DX7 and select algorithm #32. TURN OFF operators 2 through 6 (operator status display = "100000").

2) Press edit switch 17 once and, using the "yes" button in the data entry section, change the MODE for operator 1 (the only operator on) to "FIXED FREQUENCY" (bottom line of LCD reads "FIXED FREQ. (Hz)").

3) Press edit switch 18 (FREQUENCY COARSE) and OBSERVE that the coarse range is currently 10 Hz - 100 Hz (bottom line of LCD reads "F COARSE = 10.00 Hz), and that the current fixed frequency is exactly 10.00 Hz.

4) Play a few notes on the keyboard and LISTEN. You should not be hearing any sound. Why is this? Because 10.00 Hz is a *subsonic* frequency, below the range of human hearing (see Chapter 1).

5) Press the "yes" button in the data entry section once to change the F COARSE value to 100.0 Hz. The range is now 100 Hz - 1000 Hz and the current fixed frequency is exactly 100 Hz, now in the *audible* range.

6) Play a few notes on the keyboard and LISTEN (AUDIO CUE 17A). NOTE that you hear the same low tone, approximately A flat below Middle A, **no matter what key you press**.

7) Press the "yes" button again and LISTEN (AUDIO CUE 17B) as you play a few notes on the keyboard. Our range is now 1000 Hz - 10,000 Hz and our fixed frequency is now exactly 1000 Hz. NOTE that we hear the same high-pitched tone regardless of which key we press on the keyboard.

8) Press the "yes" button one more time and NOTE that the range is now 1 Hz - 10 Hz, the fixed frequency is now exactly 1 Hz, and that playing keys on the keyboard yields no sound (since 1 Hz is subaudio). Press the "yes" button two more times to return us to a range of 100 Hz - 1000 Hz.

9) Press edit switch 19 (FREQUENCY FINE), and, using the controls in the data entry section, increase the F FINE value slowly. Hold down a note on the keyboard as you do so, LISTENing (AUDIO CUE 17C). NOTE that, while the pitch you hear sweeps smoothly, the LCD shows us only particular values in the range 100.0 - 977.2 Hz.* Enter a value of 436.5 Hz in the F FINE parameter.

10) Press edit switch 20 (DETUNE) and, using the data entry controls, enter a value of +7. Operator 1 is now outputting a fixed frequency of 436.5, sharpened slightly to nearly 440. LISTEN (AUDIO CUE 17D).

11) TURN OFF operator 1 and TURN ON operator 2 ("010000"). Press edit switch 27 and, using the data entry controls, enter an output level of 99, enabling us to **hear** operator 2. Play a few notes on the keyboard and LISTEN.

12) Press edit switches 17, 18, 19, and 20 in succession to confirm that operator 2 is at its default values (MODE = FREQUENCY(RATIO), F COARSE = 1.00, F FINE = 1.00, DETUNE = 0).

13) TURN ON operator 1 again ("110000") and play Middle A on the keyboard. LISTEN (AUDIO CUE 17E). There probably will be some beating, since the two operators we are hearing are close in frequency, but not exactly in with one another. Operator 2 is **close** to 440 Hz (depending upon the MASTER TUNE ADJUST setting) and operator 1 is also nearly 440 Hz (436.5, DETUNED up +7). If the beating is very rapid, go to the next step, otherwise skip ahead to step 15.

14) Place your DX7 in *function* mode by pressing the "function" key in the *mode select* section. Press function switch 1 (MAS TUNE ADJ). Hold down Middle A on the keyboard and, using the data entry slider, adjust the tuning until the beating slows down to its slowest point. Return the DX7 to edit mode by pressing the "edit" mode select switch.

15) Now try playing several different notes and a melody or two (AUDIO CUE 17F). LISTEN and NOTE that, while operator 2 *tracks* the keyboard (since it is in FREQUENCY(RATIO) mode), operator 1 is playing Middle A as a pedal tone, providing a drone.

16) Using the OPERATOR SELECT switch, VIEW operator 1. Press edit switch 19 and use the data entry slider to change the pitch of the drone. EXPERIMENT with different pitches, and also try returning to edit switch 18 to change the COARSE range. OBSERVE that this works by moving the decimal point in the LCD display (i.e. 436.5 Hz can be changed by a factor of ten up to 4365 Hz, or down to 43.65 or even 4.365 Hz!).

17) EXPERIMENT by adding in other operators and setting them to various other fixed frequencies. NOTE that you can create **chords** that drone (not just individual notes!) by using this technique.

18) EXPERIMENT by setting several operators to the same fixed frequency and then using the DETUNE control to create interesting *beating* effects **within** the drone!

* Why these particular values? Because of size restrictions in the DX7 memory, only a finite number of values can be offered to us; what Yamaha's software engineers did was to divide the entire potential F Fine range by the total number of values available, and certain frequencies happened to fall at these points. One unfortunate byproduct of this is that we cannot access an exact 440 Hz frequency for reference tuning with this parameter.

It would appear at the moment that having the option of subaudio fixed frequencies is a waste and that is certainly true when working with unmodulated carriers only. We will see in the very next chapter, however, that **everything**, however, changes very drastically when we introduce MODULATORS into the picture!

If you're ever in doubt as to whether a particular operator is in FREQUENCY(RATIO) or FIXED FREQUENCY mode, there are three easy ways to find out. First of all, you can listen to it on its own by shutting off the other operators and see whether playing different keys on the keyboard changes its pitch (of course, this will only apply to CARRIERS since you can't ever hear MODULATORS). Secondly, you can go into edit mode and press switch 17 - the LCD will clearly tell you what mode your operator is in. Thirdly, you can go into edit mode and select either switches 18 or 19 - FREQUENCY COARSE or FREQUENCY FINE. Look at the LCD. If the number is followed by a "Hz", then your operator is in FIXED FREQUENCY mode; if not, you're in FREQUENCY(RATIO).

Oscillator Key Synchronization

This is far and away the most inconsequential of all the edit parameters, but in explaining it, we will need to for the first time discuss precisely **how** the DX7 is able to play up to 16 notes at a time. The obvious answer might be that the DX7 actually has 96 (16 x 6) operators. However, this is NOT the case. The mechanics of how this **polyphony** occurs can be explained very simply.

First of all, we know that the DX7 is a computer, and that it is constantly running thousands and thousands of computations. When we want to finally hear, say, a Middle C of a flute sound, the DX7 has to come up with a mathematical equation that will deliver just that. It can do all of its computations in advance - except for one final piece of the puzzle - and that is **which note** you wish to hear. The DX7, after all, has no way of ascertaining that until you actually press a key down on the keyboard. The microprocessor in the machine - the central "brain" - receives this keyboard information a note at a time, even if you play chords! This is OK because remember that computers are capable of doing their thing at speeds so fast that these events appear simultaneous to we mere mortals. As each note value arrives at the microprocessor, it instantly completes the calculation and sends the resulting stream of numbers on their merry way to one of sixteen tone generators in the instrument. These tone generators then relay the data on to the DAC. When the next set of keyboard instructions arrive, if the first tone generator is still in use, the microprocessor simply shunts them to the next one, and so on down the line. If all sixteen tone generators are in use, the first one is reallocated for the new data (meaning that the first note we played on the keyboard is *robbed* - thus the term "voice robbing", or *last-note priority)* , and so on down the line. This entire procedure is called *voice assignment* : **(See Figure 5-8.)**

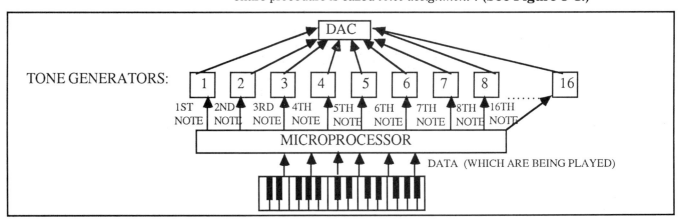

Figure 5-8

All of which brings us to the point of this discussion: What is *oscillator key sync*? When you press edit switch 17 **twice**, you will see a new message in the LCD. The bottom line will read "OSC KEY SYNC = ON" (or OFF). This parameter allows us to specify for the DX7 how we would like it to output the voice data to the DAC with each new key depression. If we set the oscillator key synchronization ON, then each new set of data (that is, each voice), will always begin with the number zero and then go positive only, causing the "wave" to always start at the **beginning** of its cycle, like this: **(See Figure 5-9.)**

Alternatively, if we set the oscillator key sync OFF, then each new tone generator will simply pick up from where it left off last time it was in use, like this: **(See Figure 5-10.)**

We turn the oscillator key sync ON or OFF by using the "yes-no" buttons (which moonlight as "on-off" buttons - look underneath them) in the data entry section.

What audible difference will we hear in having the OSC KEY SYNC on or off? This is a very subtle effect, so in most cases, none. However, you may find that having it OFF will make simulated acoustic instrument voices sound a little more natural, since each key depression will produce a wave starting at a slightly different time. Having it ON will tend to sharpen the initial attack of most sounds. But, for the most part, it will make little difference; that's why Yamaha didn't even think it merited a switch of its own and instead "buried" this parameter **beneath** the oscillator MODE switch (edit switch 17).

If you're interested in hearing the different effects of oscillator key synchronization, try initializing your DX7, select algorithm #32 and set the output level of all six operators to the maximum value of 99. Press edit switch 17 twice and note that the initialization default for this (non-operator-specific) parameter is OSC KEY SYNC = ON. Play a three-note chord on the keyboard (you'll hear this effect better with low frequencies than with high ones, so play a low three-note chord) and listen - notice that the sound is sharp and that no beating whatsoever is present since all six operators are tracking the keyboard precisely the same way, and since all three tone generators are starting their waves at the same time. Now use the "no" button to set the OSC KEY SYNC = OFF. Play the same three-note chord again and this time notice that the volume is now just a bit softer and that some gentle movements in the sound can be detected. When the sync was ON, all three tone generators output their waves perfectly in *phase* with one another (more about that in the next chapter): **(See Figure 5-11.)**

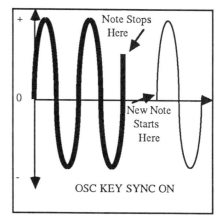

Figure 5-9

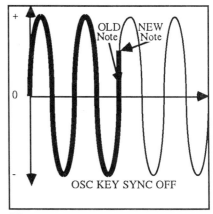

Figure 5-10

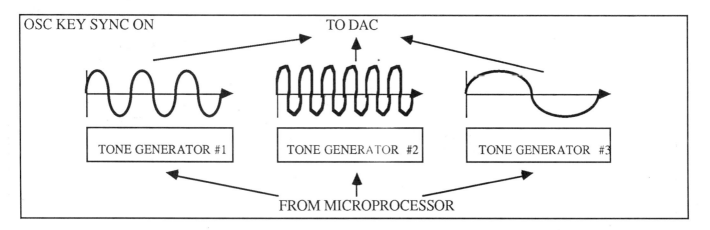

Figure 5-11

When the sync was OFF, all three tone generators started their waves at different times (actually at the point at which they last left off), so that they were slightly *out-of-phase* (again, we'll get more into this in the next chapter), accounting for the movement and slightly smoothed attack that we heard: **(See Figure 5-12.)**

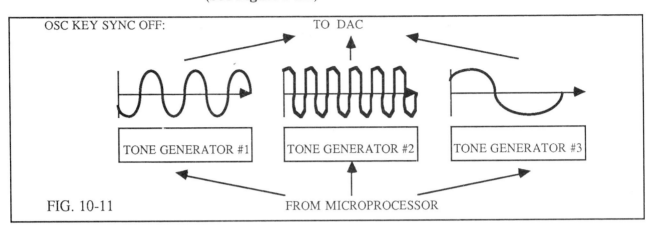

Figure 5-12

Summing up: One final word - in all the exercises in this chapter we have been careful to work **only** in algorithm #32 since this is the only algorithm with all CARRIERS. **Whenever** you work with algorithm #32 (and it is unlikely that you will use it much except for generating organ sounds) you are **not** using *digital FM* . Instead, we are using conventional digital additive synthesis techniques, and greatly simplified, this is the way that all non-FM digital synthesizers work. So even though you thought buying this book would teach you only about the DX7, we are actually touching on other areas of broader interest. Let's leave simple sine waves behind now and move on to the Wonderful World of MODULATORS and complex timbres.

SWITCHES AND CONTROLS COVERED IN CHAPTER FIVE:

SWITCH	PARAMETER	COMMENTS
Edit 17 (once)	Oscillator mode	FREQUENCY (RATIO) or FIXED FREQUENCY
Edit 17 (twice)	Oscillator Key Sync	On - Off
Edit 18	Frequency Coarse	Range 1.00 - 31.00 in FREQ(RATIO) mode; Range 1.00 Hz-1000 Hz in FIXED FREQ mode
Edit 19	Frequency Fine	Range determined by F COARSE setting
Edit 20	Detune	Range -7 to +7; 0 is center point

CHAPTER SIX:
THE MODULATOR

We have learned that the sole purpose of having modulators is to allow us to generate **complex** timbres - that is, sounds with overtones. Algorithm #32, which we examined in great detail in the previous chapter, allows to do all kinds of wonderful manipulations - but in all cases, we were working with simple **sine** waves, sounds that had **no** overtones.

When we use modulators to cause other operators to generate overtones, there are really only two things that we need to ask ourselves in order to determine what type of sound we hear, and these two questions are:

    1) What **type** of overtones are we hearing?, and
    2) How **many** of each of these overtones are we hearing?

If we can answer these questions in advance, then we can completely control and predetermine what type of sounds we will be creating. (Bear in mind, again, that until we learn more about envelope generators and a few of the other similar devices on the DX7, our sound is still not changing over time, and this **change** in a sound is obviously an important factor. But let's take things one step at a time...)

These two questions can further be described as *qualitative* and *quantitative* ones. The first question, "what **type** of overtones?" is the *qualitative* one, and can be answered in a variety of ways. For example, we may be producing **harmonic** overtones exclusively, or **disharmonic** exclusively, or (more often,) some combination of both. Then, we will have to ask the question, "**which** harmonics?", or "**which** disharmonics?", or "what combination of each?". These are all *qualitative* questions.

The second question is the *quantitative* one. Having somehow described **which** overtones we are generating, we now need to determine how **many** of each of these overtones we hear, relative to each other and to the fundamental frequency.

As we saw in Chapter One, it is the **type** and **amount** of overtones that determines a sound's characteristic *timbre* , and so asking ourselves these two questions **first** will allow us to selectively generate in our DX7 just about any kind of timbre we can envision.

For each of these questions there is an associated parameter that will serve to answer them, and these are as follows:

    1) We determine the **type** of overtones generated (the *qualitative* question) by something called *FREQUENCY RATIO* . (Note: **not** "FREQUENCY (RATIO)" - no parentheses used here).
    2) We determine the relative amplitude (**amount**) of each of these overtones generated (the *quantitative* question) by the *OUTPUT LEVEL* of the **MODULATOR** .

Let's talk about the latter one first, as it's easy to understand. If our modulator is somehow causing the carrier to generate overtones by sending it output signal: **(See Figure 6-1.)**

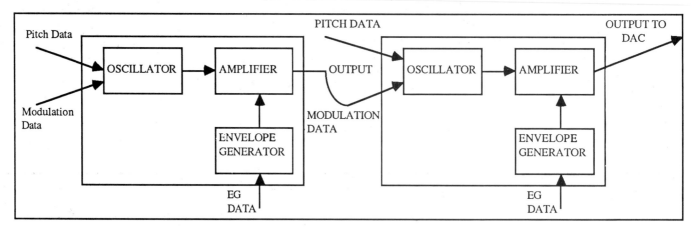

Figure 6-1

then, logically, the **more** output signal it sends, the more effect it will have - the greater the amplitude of the overtones being generated. This is precisely the way things actually work. And this brings us to another extremely important CARDINAL RULE:

CARDINAL RULE TWO: CHANGING THE *OUTPUT LEVEL* OF A *MODULATOR* WILL *ALWAYS* RESULT IN A CHANGE IN *TIMBRE* .

Specifically, a **quantitative** change in timbre: the greater the output level of the modulator, the greater the amplitude of the overtones we are generating; hence, the **brighter** the sound! The less the output level of the modulator, the lesser the amplitude of the overtones; hence, the **duller** (or **warmer**) the sound!

When I teach my DX7 class in front of a room of typically worldly and experienced musicians and DX7 owners I usually insist that they write this rule down and put asterisks all around it! I cannot stress enough how important it is to digest, understand, and thoroughly comprehend both of these CARDINAL RULES - after all, that's why they **are** CRs! (for those of you with short memories, CARDINAL RULE ONE, as put forward in the last chapter, states that whenever you change the output level of a **carrier** , you will induce a change in **volume**. This is equally as important as Cardinal Rule Two.)

Now let's go back and talk about the qualitative parameter - the mysteriously previewed *frequency ratio* . In plain English, the frequency ratio is simply the **relative speed** of the two operators involved. For example, is the modulator traveling at exactly the same speed as the carrier? Is it traveling at **twice** the carrier's speed?? Or **half** its speed?? Or 14.23 times its speed??? **(See Figure 6-2.)**

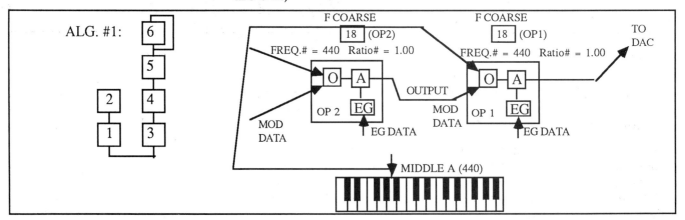

Figure 6-2

In the above example, playing a "Middle A" on the keyboard will cause the carrier to run at exactly 440 Hz, since its ratio number is set to 1.00; and the modulator will also travel 440 times per second since it has the same ratio number. Playing the "A" below "Middle A" will similarly cause both of them to run at 220 Hz. In fact, playing any note at all will cause both of them to travel at **precisely** the same frequency, since they have the **same** ratio number. The frequency ratio is usually expressed as two numbers separated by a colon, as in any algebraic ratio. The convention with digital FM instruments is that the first number of the ratio represents the **modulator** . Hence, the *frequency ratio* in the above example would be *1:1* .

On the other hand, suppose we were to double the ratio number for our modulator only: **(See Figure 6-3.)**

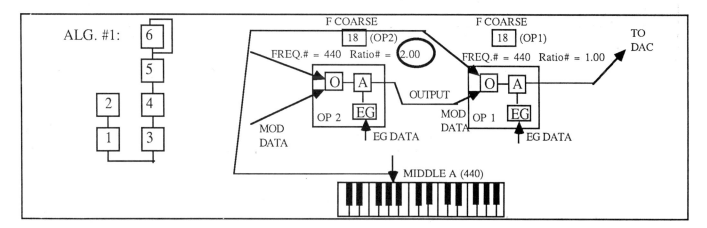

Figure 6-3

Playing "Middle A" on the keyboard would still cause operator 1, the carrier, to run at 440 Hz, since its ratio number is still 1.00. However, since operator 2, the modulator, now has a ratio number of 2.00, it will now output a signal 880 times per second! The frequency ratio in this case would be said to be *2:1*. If we reversed things so that operator 2's ratio number were restored to 1.00, and operator 1's changed to 2.00: **(See Figure 6-4.)**

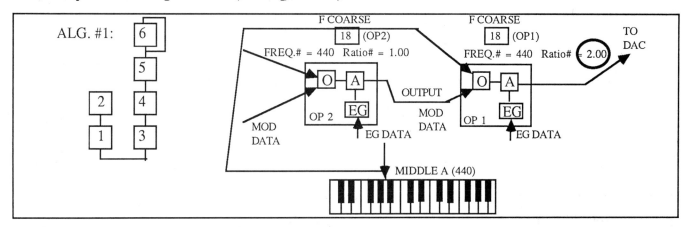

Figure 6-4

then our frequency ratio would now be *1:2* . Remember, the first number **always** represents the **modulator** , and the second, the receiving operator (in this particular example, a carrier).

Frequency ratios can of course be expressed as decimals instead of just whole numbers. For example, a frequency ratio of 4.63:1 would mean that our modulator was always traveling 4.63 times faster than the carrier. A frequency ratio of 2:7 would mean that the **carrier** was always traveling 3.5 times faster than the modulator (think about it!).

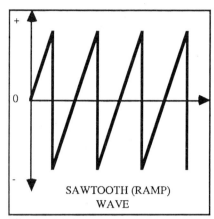

Figure 6-5A

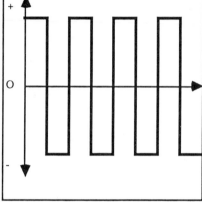

Figure 6-5B

For those of you who were never very good at math, this may be a little bit problematic, but stick with it, because this is obviously a very important factor in creating sounds on the DX7. What we are saying here is that **every time you vary the relative speeds of the modulator and the carrier, you will hear a totally different set of overtones** . The enormous value of this concept is that it allows us to construct on the DX7 virtually **any** kind of waveshape!

Later on in this chapter we will be talking more about the concept of "frequency ratio" and its importance in creating sounds but for now lets see how we can use these two controls, the *qualitative* and the *quantitative* , to make some more new sounds.

Analog synthesizers, which use subtractive synthesis systems, generate timbres by starting with one or two fixed waveshapes and then removing whatever overtones are not desired. The fixed waveshapes used in analog synthesis are important to us because analog synthesizers have, after all, been around a lot longer than the DX7; and traditional so-called "synthesized" or "electronic" sounds have generally been constructed using these particular waveshapes. The first standard analog timbre, the sine wave, is one with which we have already become very familiar. Two others that we will work with now are called the *sawtooth* , or *ramp* wave; and the *square* wave. Keeping in mind, of course, that the **timbre** of a sound determines it's wave **shape**, let's take a look at how these two waves appear on an oscilloscope: **(See Figure 6-5A and 6-5B.)**

These waves have very different **shapes** because they have very different **overtone contents** , or **timbres** . The sawtooth wave (sometimes called a ramp wave) is very rich in harmonics, and actually contains **all** the harmonic overtones, in slowly decreasing amounts. That is, it has a great deal of fundamental, followed by nearly as much second harmonic, followed by nearly as much third harmonic, etc., etc., until we can't hear any more. **(See Figure 6-6.)**

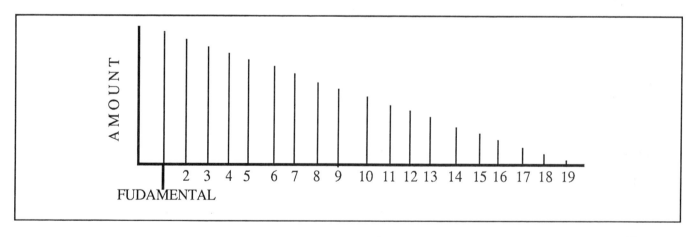

Figure 6-6

This wave, being very musical, contains little or no disharmonics. The characteristic sound of the sawtooth wave is very bright and buzzy. This makes sense since it contains **many** overtones, in large quantities (Remember - the greater the amplitude of the overtones, the brighter the sound, right?). Typically, sawtooth waves are used to generate the big, brassy sounds that analog synthesizers are so renowned for.

Not wanting to be left out, the DX7 can also generate a sawtooth wave, and quite easily, at that! There is a recipe we can follow, and it goes like this:

RECIPE: Set the frequency ratio to *1:1*. Set the output level of the modulator to maximum (99). Set in a cookie dish and bake well 45 minutes. Serves many. (Sorry 'bout that! Ignore the last two sentences, and let's get back to business...)

Seriously, this **is** the recipe for generating a sawtooth wave on the DX7 and, in just a moment, we'll run an exercise and try it. First, there must surely be those among you who are wondering, Why? Why a sawtooth wave and not a grpxkdtl wave?? (somewhere out there, I **know** someone is frantically looking up "grpxkdtl" in a dictionary. For you, sir or madam: there is no such thing.) What's so special about these particular settings (frequency ratio of 1:1 and modulator output level of 99)?? For those who truly want to know, there is a mathematical explanation, but you won't get it here! The theory of digital FM to this degree is unfortunately well beyond the scope of this book. Dr. John Chowning of Stanford University (the originator of the digital FM process) has published many scientific papers in the Computer Music Journal and in several Audio Engineering Society publications, which explain this and many other bylaws of digital FM in great detail. I would steer any of you who are interested in such detailed explanations in that direction. But just as it is unnecessary to understand the theory of combustion engines in order to drive a car, it is unnecessary to understand these complex theorems in order to use a DX7. We'll only be following a couple of these unsubstantiated recipes, so I ask your indulgence, and just say (in the magic words of the music business) - trust me! They work!!

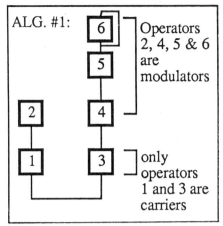

Figure 6-7

Now to run our exercise. For this exercise, and quite a few more to boot, we will be working not with algorithm #32, as in the past, but instead with the default algorithm, algorithm #1. **(See Figure 6-7.)**

Algorithm #32 is obviously unsuitable for our purposes here since it doesn't provide us with any modulators. All of the remaining 31 algorithms do but we might just as well stick with #1, as it is where the DX7 puts us when we initialize anyway. We will **not** concern ourselves with the right-hand stack of operators 3, 4, 5, and 6; but we will simply be using the *system* of operators 1 and 2: **(See Figure 6-8.)**

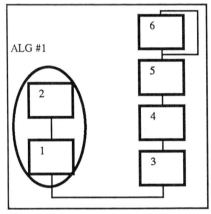

Figure 6-8

As our diagram clearly indicates (and by all means check the algorithm diagram on the machine itself to confirm that our diagram is correct!), in algorithm #1, operator 1 is a carrier, and operator 2 is being used as a modulator, **sending output into the modulation data input of operator 1** . That means that as we **increase** the output level of operator 2, operator 1 will generate greater and greater amounts of overtones. What type of overtones? In this case, all of the harmonic overtones, in a linearly decreasing fashion, since we will take care to **leave** both operators at their default ratio numbers of 1.00 (thus setting up a frequency ratio of, you guessed it!, 1:1). This will cause us to generate a particular type of waveshape: the *sawtooth* wave.

EXERCISE 18

Generating a sawtooth wave:

1) INITIALIZE your DX7 and CONFIRM that you are in the default algorithm, algorithm #1.

2) TURN OFF operators 3 through 6 ("110000").

3) CONFIRM that operator 1 is at its default **output level** of 99, and that operator 2 is at **it's** default **output level** of 0. LISTEN to the single sine wave. (AUDIO CUE 18A). Even though both operators are &on, and even though operator 2 is **modulating** operator 1, since operator 2's output level is defaulted to 0, it is currently having no effect whatever on operator 1.

4) Using the *operator select* switch, VIEW the output level parameter for operator 2 (= 0). **Slowly** begin raising the *data entry* slider, thereby increasing the value for this parameter. Make sure you keep tapping a note on the keyboard as you do this as output level does **not** change in real time (refer to Chapter Four if this doesn't sound familiar).

5) LISTEN (AUDIO CUE 18B). As you increase the output level of operator 2, the sine wave begins to change **timbre** , getting slowly but steadily **brighter** , as more and more overtones are generated. When you finally reach maximum output level (99), the sound is as bright as it is going to get (AUDIO CUE 18C). The wave you are now listening to is a *sawtooth* wave!

6) EXPERIMENT by slowly reducing the output level of operator 2 (AUDIO CUE 18D). NOTE that the sound gets warmer, as the harmonic content of the sound decreases. Also NOTE that relatively little change occurs with output levels of 0 to 50; as the numbers increase, the change becomes more drastic. The change between output levels 90 and 99, for instance, is far more noticeable than that from 80 to 89.*

7) EXPERIMENT by restoring the output level of operator 2 to 99 and then slowly reducing the output level of operator **1** (AUDIO CUE 18E). NOTE that, following the dictums of Cardinal Rule 1, **only** the volume of the sound changes, and that no timbral change whatever occurs.

For those of you with prior experience in analog synthesis, you have just heard something very similar to opening and closing an analog low-pass filter (this is a filter that selectively removes overtones, from highest to lowest). Of course, we're doing nothing of the kind, since the DX7 does not contain filters of any description, but I for one find it amazing that two totally dissimilar systems will produce exactly the same aural effect!

More importantly, we were able to **hear** just how changing the output levels of modulators and carriers differs. When we altered the output of operator 2, clearly the timbre changed, and in such a way that greater output level resulted directly in a brighter sound. When we altered the output of operator 1, clearly only the volume changed, and in such a way that lesser output level resulted directly in a softer sound. Very shortly we will be experimenting with altering the **qualitative** factor, the frequency ratio, in order to hear **different** (not just less or more) overtones, but first, let's follow another recipe, this time to build that good old analog standby, the *square* wave.

The square wave was not named by a beatnik in the early '60s, nor is it the sound generated by Lawrence Welk's bubble-blowing machine. Instead, it is an interesting timbre which consists **only** of the fundamental frequency plus the odd-numbered harmonics. For example, a square wave having a fundamental frequency of 440 Hz will also contain some 1320 Hz (the third harmonic), some 2200 Hz (the fifth harmonic), and some 3080 Hz (the seventh harmonic), etc., all in linearly decreasing amounts. Unlike the sawtooth wave, we will **not** hear any 880 Hz (the second harmonic), 1760 Hz (the fourth harmonic), or 2640 Hz (the sixth harmonic). **(See Figure 6-9.)**

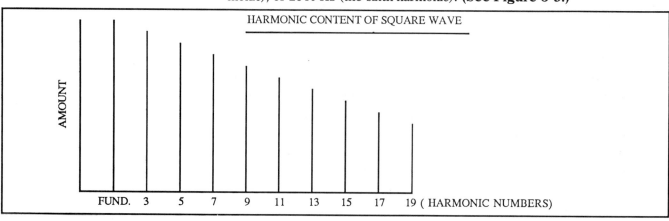

HARMONIC CONTENT OF SQUARE WAVE

AMOUNT

FUND.   3   5   7   9   11   13   15   17   19 (HARMONIC NUMBERS)

Figure 6-9

*This is because the output level is changing exponentially rather than linearly. Chapter Twelve contains a detailed explanation of these terms, but until we get to that point, just take note of this phenomenon.

This means, of course, that the square wave will sound quite different from the sawtooth wave, and indeed it does - it has a peculiar hollow sound, brought on by the fact that it is literally **missing** harmonics. Again, we will hear little or no disharmonics, since this is a very musical timbre. Square waves tend to sound very clarinetish, and are generally used in analog systems to generate woodwind or stringed sounds.

The recipe for generating a *square wave* on the DX7 is as follows:

RECIPE: Set the frequency ratio to **2:1** (modulator at exactly twice the frequency of the carrier). Set the output level of the modulator to **71** . Voila! Instant square wave souffle!!

EXERCISE 19

Generating a square wave:

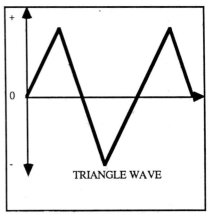

Figure 6-10

1)   INITIALIZE your DX7 and TURN OFF operators 3 through 6 ("110000"). Leave the machine in algorithm #1.

2)   Press main switch 18 (F COARSE) and use the *operator select* switch to VIEW the F COARSE value for operator **2** (F COARSE = 1.00).

3)   Using the "yes" button in the *data entry* section, CHANGE the F COARSE value for operator 2 to **2.00**. Operator 2 will now travel at precisely twice the speed of operator 1 (which is still at its default F COARSE setting of 1.00 - check to confirm) regardless of what key you play.

4)   PLAY a note on the keyboard and LISTEN (AUDIO CUE 19A). Even though we have altered the F COARSE value for operator 2, we are still only hearing a single sine wave because operator 2's output level is still at its default value of 0 (check to confirm this).

5)   Press main switch 27 and the *operator select* switch, if necessary, to VIEW the output level value for operator 2. (=0)

6)   Using the data entry slider, **slowly** increase this value to 71, tapping a note on the keyboard and LISTENing as you do so (AUDIO CUE 19B). As in the last exercise, you cannot simply hold a note down since output level does not change in real time. Once again, as you increase the output level, the sound becomes brighter. At the exact modulator output level value of 71, you are hearing a pure square wave (AUDIO CUE 19C). LISTEN to the typical "clarinet-ish" type of timbre.

7)   EXPERIMENT by increasing the value of operator 2's output level **above** 71 (AUDIO CUE 19D). Once again, the sound becomes brighter, since the amplitude of our overtones is increasing beyond the point typically found in a square wave. But NOTE that we are still only hearing **odd-numbered** overtones; the **quality** of the overtones does not change!

8)   EXPERIMENT by decreasing the value of operator **1's** output level and NOTE that once again, **only** the volume of the sound changes (AUDIO CUE 19E).

The fourth basic analog waveshape, the *triangle* wave, looks like this on an oscilloscope: **(See Figure 6-10.)**

and has very little harmonic content: essentially just a bit of the third harmonic and a pinch of the fifth. This wave generates a characteristic flute-like sound and is typically used on analog synthesizers for (you guessed it!) flute-ish sounds. We've seen that the square wave also contained the third and fifth harmonics (albeit in much larger quantities) with no in-between harmonics (specifically the second and fourth). Logically, if we can reduce the relative **amounts** of third and fifth harmonics in our square wave and somehow get rid of any harmonics above that point, we will be able to generate a triangle wave. How do we accomplish this? By returning to our *quantitative* control.

Very simply, lessening the output signal from our modulator (running at twice the speed of our carrier), will have the result of reducing the relative amounts of the third and fifth harmonic to the point where they emulate that found in the triangle wave. If we diminish these relative amounts to the point where we are only getting a very small quantity of the fifth harmonic, then all the harmonics **above** the fifth will also be reduced in quantity to the point where their contributions to the overall sound are negligible. The end result will be: A triangle wave! **(See Figure 6-11.)**

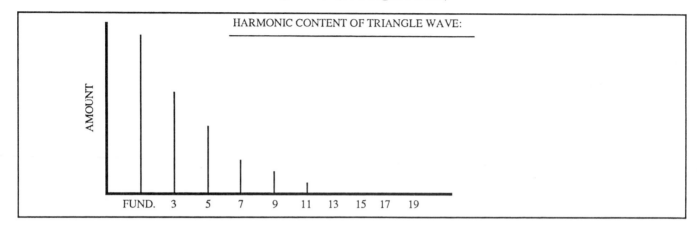

Figure 6-11

The *recipe*, then, for generating a triangle wave on the DX7 is very simple: make a square wave, and then reduce the output level of the modulator down to about 45. You will hear a very flute-ish sound, and, on an oscilloscope, you will see a very triangle-ish wave shape.

Before we leave this section, we should briefly touch upon another analog phenomenon, and that is something called *pulse width*. The square wave is in fact a particular kind of wave called a *pulse* wave. This wave, as we have seen, only exists in a simple up-down fashion, as follows: **(See Figure 6-12.)**

Remember that in these diagrams we are mapping **amplitude** (the Y-axis) versus **time** (the X-axis). The *pulse width* control on an analog synthesizer allows us to vary the **relative** amounts of time that the pulse wave spends in its "up" condition versus its "down" condition (while keeping the **total** time required for one complete cycle the same). For example, we can alter our pulse wave so that it stays "up" far longer than it drops "down": **(See Figure 6-13.)**

Or we can do precisely the reverse: **(See Figure 6-14.)**

A pulse wave that stays "up" **exactly** as long as it stays "down" is called a *square* wave: **(See Figure 6-15.)**

Therefore, all square waves are pulse waves but not all pulse waves are square waves (think about it!). In any event, when we "narrow" or "broaden" the *pulse width* by **changing** these relative times, what we are in fact doing is changing the **timbre** , and **not** the pitch or volume of the sound. The illustrations above clearly show that at no time is the height of the wave changing, and at no time are we increasing or decreasing the total number of waves generated per second.

How does the timbre change? Well, remember that our pure square wave (which can now be referred to as a 50% pulse wave; i.e. 50% "up" followed by 50% "down") contained only the **odd-numbered** harmonics. When we change the pulse width, either by narrowing or broadening it, what we are doing is reintroducing those even-numbered harmonics that previously were missing, as we **reduce** the number of odd-numbered harmonics, and of the fundamental itself. The end result is a striking timbral change, resulting in a sound that gets progressively thinner and more nasal. Surprisingly, whether you choose to narrow **or** broaden the pulse width, the aural effect is the same! That is, a 25% pulse wave (one that stays "up" 25% of the time and "down"

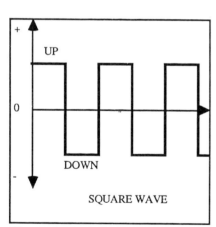

Figure 6-12

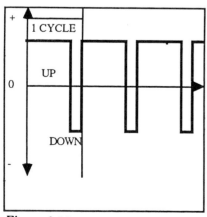

Figure 6-13

the remaining 75%) sounds exactly the same as a 75% pulse wave. A 10% pulse wave sounds the same as a 90% pulse wave, etc., etc.

This pulse width control is a powerful tool for analog synthesists, as it allows them to further specify harmonic content even after they have selected an initial waveshape (**if** they have selected a *pulse* wave - this control has no effect whatsoever on the other analog waveshapes). For example, the analog synthesist might choose a 50% pulse wave for a clarinet sound, but a 35% pulse wave instead for an oboe sound, and a 17% pulse wave for a mandolin sound.

On the DX7 we can also generate various different pulse widths, not with the degree of control found on an analog synthesizer, but enough to get by (after all, with so many more timbres available in the DX7, it's unlikely that this will worry too many people). The recipe for generating various pulse waves of different width is as follows:

RECIPE: Make a square wave (frequency ratio of 2:1 and modulator output level of 71). Now change the ratio number of the **carrier** to any **odd-number** (i.e. 2:3, 2:5, 2:7, 2:9, etc.).

As you raise the ratio number of the carrier, you will hear the sound become thinner and more nasal. In fact, whenever you set up any kind of frequency ratio where the carrier is travelling **faster** than the modulator, this effect, similar to the use of an analog *high-pass* filter (that is, a filter which increasingly removes the lowest components of a sound's harmonic spectrum), will result. Here, what we are in fact doing is altering the pulse width of our square wave, therefore changing the **timbre** of the sound. Let's try it:

EXERCISE 20

Generating different pulse waves:

    1) INITIALIZE your DX7 and leave it in algorithm #1. TURN OFF operators 3 through 6 ("110000").
    2) GENERATE a square wave (if you don't remember how, refer to Exercise 19 above).
    3) LISTEN to the clarinet-like sound made by a 50% square wave (AUDIO CUE 20A).
    4) Using the *operator select* switch, if necessary, and pressing main switch 18 (F COARSE), VIEW the ratio number value for operator **1.** (**= 1.00**)
    5) Using the "yes" button in the *data entry* section, CHANGE this value to 3.00. LISTEN (AUDIO CUE 20B).
    6) Repeat step 5 above, this time changing the value to 5.00. LISTEN (AUDIO CUE 20C).
    7) Continue repeating step 5 above, each time changing the value for operator 1 F COARSE to another **odd** number only (change to values of 7.00, 9.00, 11.00, 13.00, 15.00, 17.00, 19.00, 21.00, 23.00, 25.00, 27.00, 29.00, and 31.00). LISTEN (AUDIO CUE 20D). NOTE that as the value goes higher, the sound gets thinner and more nasal. NOTE also that at the very highest settings, *disharmonics* begin creeping in as the sound begins losing its overall discernible pitch. NOTE that at no time do we hear volume changes.
    8) EXPERIMENT. Restore the F COARSE value of operator 1 to 1.00, thereby restoring our square wave. LISTEN to confirm that. Now try changing the F COARSE value for Operator 1 to **even** numbers (2.00, 4.00, 6.00, etc.). LISTEN (AUDIO CUE 20E). NOTE that while the timbre **does** indeed change, it does not change the same way as before, and that for each of the **even** numbered ratios, the sound goes **up** an octave!

Now things are really starting to get interesting! **Why** did the sound jump up an octave? Well, let's look at exactly what we did: We began by changing the F COARSE value for operator 1 to 2.00. The F COARSE value for operator 2 had previously also been set to 2.00. Therefore, our *frequency ratio* was 2:2, **which is exactly the same as 1:1!!** Remember, the frequency ratio is a

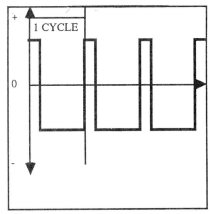

Figure 6-14

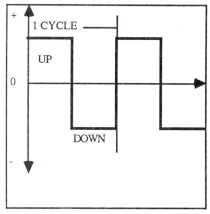

Figure 6-15

relative number, and so what we heard when we changed the ratio to 2:2 was **not** a pulse wave at all, but instead a **sawtooth** wave **an octave higher!** (Think about it, and it will make sense!)

But something else strange is starting to happen. What we did in that last exercise was change the F COARSE value for our *carrier*. Didn't we learn in Chapter Five that altering this number changes the **pitch** of the sound? We did, but I also cautioned you at the end of the chapter that carriers behave very differently once modulators are plugged into them! And here is graphic evidence that this is indeed true.

Once you plug a modulator into a carrier (by virtue of instructing the DX7 to give you an algorithm with such a configuration), you should no longer think about the modulators and carriers as separate entities. Instead, as we briefly alluded to earlier in this book, you should think of *systems*. In Exercises 18, 19, and 20, we were working with the **system** of operators 1 and 2, not just with carrier 1 and modulator 2: **(See Figure 6-16.)**

With this concept firmly in mind, it would probably be a good idea to go back and reexamine the 32 different algorithms. Note, for example, that algorithm #5 (which we will soon be working with frequently) offers us three independent **systems: (See Figure 6-17.)**

as algorithm #1, for example, only offers us two: **(See Figure 6-18.)**

and algorithm #16, only one: **(See Figure 6-19.)**

Algorithm #32, of course, offered us six systems; each system being a simple unmodulated carrier. With some other algorithms, it isn't quite so obvious. How many systems, for example, are offered us by algorithm #20? **(See Figure 6-20.)**

The correct answer is **two** . Operators 1 and 2 are **both** being modulated by operator 3, so altogether this yields one system. Similarly, operator 4 is being modulated by **both** operators 5 and 6, so they comprise another system. Let's try one more: **(See Figure 6-21.)**

The correct answer for this algorithm (#24) is **three** . Operators 3, 4, and 5 are all being modulated by operator 6 and so all together they comprise one system. Operators 1 and 2 are simply unmodulated carriers, and each can be considered an independent system.

So, when dealing with a **system** of modulator plugged into carrier, it is clear that we cannot initiate a pitch change by simply changing the pitch data input to the carrier alone. We can't accomplish a pitch change by altering the pitch data input to the modulator alone, either. So how do we accomplish a pitch change to a system? Simple. We change the pitch data input to **both** of them, **the same way** .

This makes sense when you realize that altering the pitch of one or the other alone actually upsets the *frequency ratio*: **(See Figure 6-22.)**

Changing the frequency ratio cannot and will not ever cause a pitch change, but instead a qualitative timbral change. By changing the pitch data input to **both** the modulator **and** carrier, **equally**, you maintain the current frequency ratio; hence, only a pitch change occurs: **(See Figure 6-23.)**

After all, as we have seen, a frequency ratio of 2:2 is the same as 1:1; similarly, a frequency ratio of 4:2 is the same as 2:1, and so is 8:4; 16:8; or 25.4:12.7! In each of these instances, we would be hearing a square wave at a different **pitch**. Let's try it:

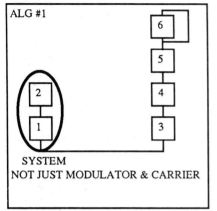

Figure 6-16

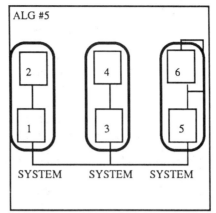

Figure 6-17

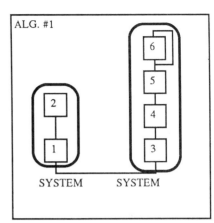

Figure 6-18

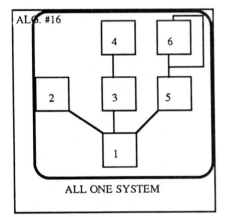

Figure 6-19

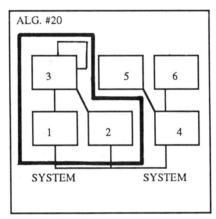

Figure 6-20

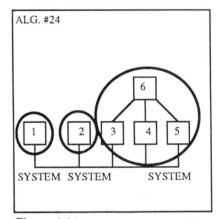

Figure 6-21

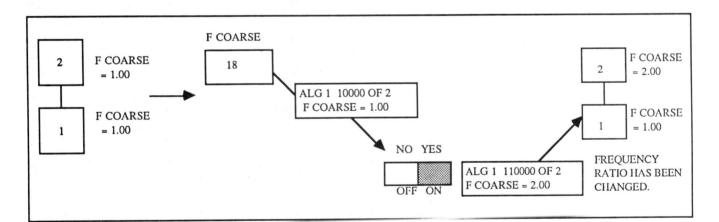

Figure 6-22

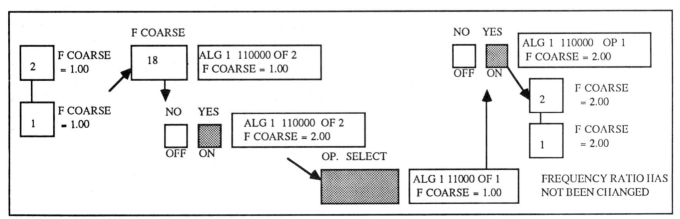

Figure 6-23

EXERCISE 21

Altering the pitch of a complex timbre:

1) INITIALIZE your DX7, leave it in algorithm #1, TURN OFF operators 3 through 6 ("110000"), and GENERATE a square wave with the system of operators 1 and 2. Hold a note down on the keyboard and LISTEN (AUDIO CUE 21A).

2) Press main switch 18 (F COARSE) and, while continuing to hold the same note down, use the appropriate operator select and data entry switches to **double** the F COARSE value for operator 1 **only** from 1.00 to 2.00 (frequency ratio is now 2:**2**) .

3) LISTEN (AUDIO CUE 21B). What you are currently hearing is a quasi-sawtooth wave (since operator 2 output level is 71 and not 99), an octave higher.

4) Continuing to hold down the same note on the keyboard, VIEW operator 2 (using the operator select switch) and **double** its F COARSE value as well, from 2.00 to 4.00 (frequency ratio is now 4:2). LISTEN (AUDIO CUE 21C). Since a frequency ratio of 4:2 is the same as a ratio of 2:1, what you are now hearing is a **square** wave, an octave higher. NOTE that we were able to keep a note held down throughout this procedure because we were changing pitch data input values, which, unlike output level values, **do** change in real time!

5) Using the appropriate operator select and data entry switches, redouble the F COARSE values for **both** operators 1 and 2 (frequency ratio of 8:4). LISTEN (AUDIO CUE 21D). What you are now hearing is the same square wave, up yet another octave. NOTE that neither the timbre nor the volume of the sound has changed in any way.

6) EXPERIMENT by setting different F COARSE and/or F FINE values for operators 1 and 2, taking care to always insure an overall ratio of 2:1 (in other words, always keeping operator 2 at **twice** the frequency of operator 1). LISTEN and NOTE that, regardless of the specific values used, the timbre remains a square wave.

All of which brings us happily to Cardinal Rule 3:

CARDINAL RULE THREE: ALTERING THE PITCH DATA INPUT VALUE FOR ONE OPERATOR IN A SYSTEM WITHOUT AFFECTING THE OTHER ONE EQUALLY, WILL ALWAYS RESULT IN A TIMBRAL CHANGE ONLY. TO OBTAIN A PITCH CHANGE IN A SYSTEM YOU MUST ALTER THE PITCH DATA INPUT VALUES FOR ALL OPERATORS EQUALLY .

This Cardinal Rule, like the two others before it, is of great importance. Again, it is my strongest advice that you eat, drink, sleep, digest, comprehend, verify, and thoroughly **understand** this rule before proceeding any further.

So far, we have limited ourselves to working with only two complex waveshapes, the sawtooth and the pulse. We've seen that setting up a frequency ratio of 1:1 with the proper modulator output level (99) yields a sawtooth wave, and that setting up a frequency ratio of 2:1 with the proper modulator output level (71) yields a square wave. But what happens if we set up a frequency ratio of 3:1? Or 4:1?? Or 27:1??? Well, obviously, changing the frequency ratio will qualitatively change the **type** of overtones we hear, so each of these manipulations will yield a new and different waveshape. What are the names of these various waveshapes? Well, they have no names! They're just - well, **new** and **different**. Beyond the obvious recipes for typical analog waveshapes lies the real strength of the DX7 - a doorway is opening up that allows us to literally generate new timbres that simply have not previously existed! Remember too that we are not limited to changing the modulator pitch data input only - as we've just seen, changing this value for the carrier will also initiate new timbres for which there are no names. Also bear in mind that setting up a frequency ratio of 4:1, for example, will yield an entirely different waveshape than a frequency ratio of 1:4. With a ratio number range of 0.50 to nearly double 31.00 (61.69, to be exact), you can see that the number of possibilities, while mathematically finite, are indeed astronomical in size!

Let's try running an exercise, firstly to examine some of these different timbres induced by **whole-number** frequency ratio changes (the next exercise will deal with **non**-whole number changes). You will notice that, as the modulator and carrier get further apart from one another in frequency, the nearest overtone to the fundamental appears at a further distance, and also that rather more disharmonics than harmonics begin to make their presence felt. This, of course, will result in an apparent change in pitch as the sound becomes more dissonant, but remember that timbre is itself a frequency-dependent phenomenon, and so what we are really hearing is a **timbral** change, albeit one that **sounds** like a pitch change.

EXERCISE 22

Generating new complex timbres using whole-number frequency ratio changes:

1) INITIALIZE your DX7, leave it in algorithm #1, TURN OFF operators 3 through 6 ("110000"), and, using the system of operators 1 and 2, GENERATE a sawtooth wave (if you don't remember how to do this, refer to Exercise 18 earlier in this chapter). Hold a note down on the keyboard and LISTEN (AUDIO CUE 22A).

2) VIEW the F COARSE parameter (edit switch 18) for operator 2, and, while continuing to hold the note down on the keyboard, use the data entry slider to **slowly** increase this value through its various numbers until you reach the maximum value of 31.00. LISTEN (AUDIO CUE 22B). NOTE that you can hear this change in **real time** since we are **not** altering output level.

3) Restore the frequency ratio to 1:1 by returning the F COARSE value for operator 2 to 1.00.

4) Using the operator select switch, VIEW the F COARSE parameter for operator **1** . Hold down a note on the keyboard, and use the data entry slider to **slowly** increase this value through its various numbers until you reach the maximum value of 31.00. LISTEN (AUDIO CUE 22C). NOTE that you are again hearing **timbral** change, but that it is qualitatively quite different from what you heard in step 2 above.

5) EXPERIMENT by altering the F COARSE value for **both** operators 1 and 2 in various ways. NOTE, for example, that setting up a frequency ratio of 14:5 yields a very different timbre from that generated by a frequency ratio of 5:14 (Try it!).

Of course, nothing in the DX7 works by itself alone. We have seen time and time again that the various parameters work in concert with one another to produce the finished result of what you hear. You've certainly noticed in the preceding exercise that running a modulator at very high frequencies induce sounds that are unpleasantly dissonant and often overbright. Well, don't forget that you can alter the *quantitative* control as well as the qualitative one at any time. So, if the sound produced by the frequency ratio of, say, 29:1 was extremely jarring to your ears, go back and reduce the output level of operator 2! All of sudden, that horrible 29:1 timbre becomes quite pleasant and musically usable! With this in mind, go back and repeat Exercise 22, and this time alter the modulator output level (that is, operator 2) from time to time as you go through the various frequency ratios.

We are certainly not limited to only working with **whole-number** frequency ratios (i.e. 19:1, 15:2, etc.). The FREQUENCY FINE parameter will, after all, permit us to set up **non-whole-number** frequency ratios. Using these types of frequency ratios will allow us to generate many more disharmonics than harmonics, resulting in non-musical, or percussive sounds. Let's run an exercise to try it!

EXERCISE 23

Generating non-musical timbres:

1) INITIALIZE your DX7, leave it in algorithm #1, TURN OFF operators 3 through 6 ("110000"), and GENERATE a sawtooth wave using the system of operators 1 and 2. LISTEN (AUDIO CUE 23A).

2) VIEW the F FINE parameter (edit switch 19) for operator 2. (= 1.00)

3) Hold a key down on the keyboard, and use the data entry slider to slowly CHANGE this value up to its maximum of 1.99, LISTENing as you do so (AUDIO CUE 23B).

4) Return the F FINE value to 1.00 and press edit switch 18 (F COARSE parameter). Use the "yes" button to change this value to 2.00.

5) Redo steps 2 and 3, this time CHANGING the F FINE value slowly up to its maximum of 2.98, LISTENing as you do so (AUDIO CUE 23C).

6) Return the F FINE value back to 2.00, and then the F COARSE value back to 1.00 (in other words, restore your sawtooth wave. LISTEN to confirm this).

7) VIEW the F FINE parameter for operator **1** .

8) Hold a key down on the keyboard, and slowly CHANGE the F FINE parameter for operator 1 up to its maximum value of 1.99, LISTENing as you do so (AUDIO CUE 23D). NOTE that there is a qualitative difference in the sound from that which you previously heard in step 3 above (i.e., a frequency ratio of, say, 1.00:1.37 produces a very different timbre from that of a ratio of 1.37:1.00. Both timbres, however, are largely **disharmonic** and therefore non-musical).

9) EXPERIMENT with other non-whole number frequency ratios by altering the F FINE and F COARSE parameters for various modulators and carriers. NOTE that any time a **non-whole number** frequency ratio is set up, a disharmonic timbre results.

As with the previous exercise, remember that we are here only manipulating the qualitative control! Using the quantitative control, that is, changing the **output** level of the modulator, will help make these jarring, disharmonious sounds a lot easier to take! Learn to balance the two controls in order to establish precisely the timbre you require.

Altering the FREQUENCY FINE parameter within a **system**, then, allows us to generate disharmonic timbres. But what effect can we expect from the DETUNE control, which, after all, is just a finer FREQUENCY FINE control? The answer is, somewhat surprisingly, very similar effects to that which we encountered when detuning lone carriers!

Try setting up a frequency ratio on your DX7 of 1.01:1.00 (for simplicity, just re-initialize, keep yourself in algorithm #1, and just use the system of operators 1 and 2. Remember to raise the output level of operator 2 from its default of 0!). Listen to the resulting timbre, and you will hear a **beating** effect very similar to that which we heard in Chapter Four. However, we are now obviously hearing only **one** wave, not two discrete sine waves. So what exactly is beating? We had learned that in order to initiate a beating effect we needed to hear **two** or more frequencies that were very close to one another. Here we are only hearing **one** sound. Or are we?

Technically, we are. But the reality is that this one sound, our complex wave, is composed of many different frequencies (the overtones), blended together. This explains why we can hear beating **within** a **single** complex sound - we are actually hearing the *overtones* beating against one another!

A frequency ratio of 1.00:1.00 generates the following set of harmonic overtones, resulting in a sawtooth waveshape: **(See Figure 6-24.)**

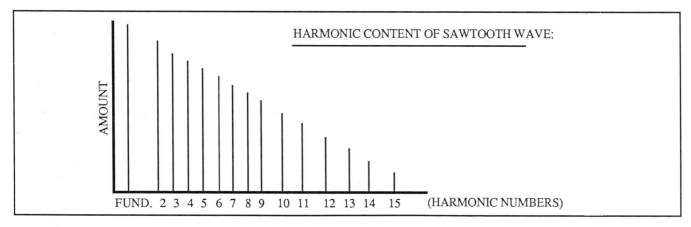

Figure 6-24

Slightly shifting the tuning of one of the two operators, resulting in a frequency ratio of 1.01:1.00, generates the same table of harmonic overtones **plus** a few disharmonic overtones which are **extremely** close in frequency to the existing harmonics: **(See Figure 6-25.)**

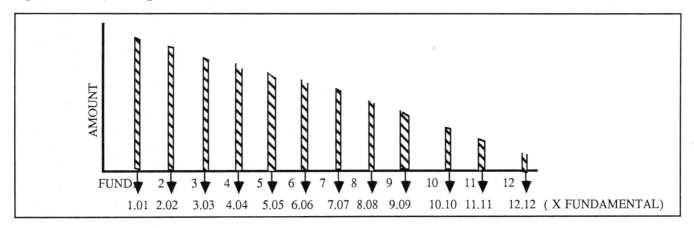

Figure 6-25

Which causes a beating effect **within** the single complex sound! Using the DETUNE parameter allows us to bring the frequency ratio even closer than 1.01:1.00, say to 1.**001 : 1.000** . This will result in the same effect, except that the disharmonics generated will be even **closer** to the harmonics than that in the previous example, hence a **slower** beating: **(See Figure 6-26.)**

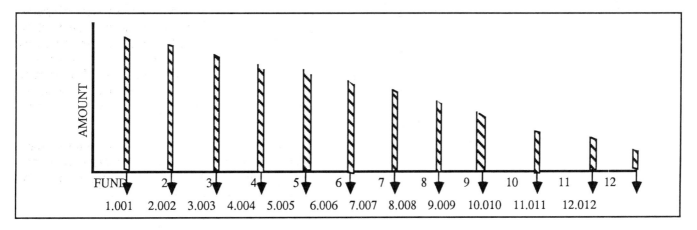

Figure 6-26

Let's try it:

EXERCISE 24

Use of the DETUNE control within a system:

1) INITIALIZE your DX7 and leave it in algorithm #1. TURN OFF operators 3 through 6 ("110000") and GENERATE a sawtooth wave (refer to Exercise 18 if you don't remember how to do this).

2) VIEW the DETUNE parameter (edit switch 20) for operator 2.

3) Using the data entry slider, CHANGE this value from its default of 0 to its maximum value of +7.

4) LISTEN (AUDIO CUE 24A). NOTE the speed of the beating. NOTE also that this sound is very harsh. To make the sound warmer,

5) VIEW the OUTPUT LEVEL parameter for operator 2. CHANGE this value to 90. LISTEN (AUDIO CUE 24B).

6) Go back to the DETUNE parameter for operator 2 . Hold down a note on the keyboard, and, using the "no" button, slowly CHANGE this value back to the center point of 0, LISTENing as you do so (AUDIO CUE 24C). NOTE that the beating effect slows down and, at the setting of 0, disappears altogether (at this setting, the frequency ratio is once again exactly 1.00:1.00, and only harmonic overtones are present).

7) Continue holding down the note and continue using the "no" button to CHANGE this value downward to its minimum setting of -7, LISTENing as you do so (AUDIO CUE 24D). NOTE that there is no perceptable difference in the effect as from when you **increased** the DETUNE value up to +7. That's because the only thing that matters here is the **relative** offset, not the absolute values. Similarly, altering the DETUNE values for operator 1 instead of operator 2 will have the same effect. EXPERIMENT and try it!

Detuning, then, provides us with one of the most powerful *animating* techniques on the DX7, and we should explain what we mean by this term.

Digital synthesizers have long had the largely undeserved stigma of being able to only produce sounds which are considered "cold" or "sterile". To a certain degree this is true because, as we discussed in Chapter One, they produce sounds which theoretically are distortion-free.*

Because acoustic instruments and acoustic sounds all have small degrees of random distortions present, the manufacturers of digital synthesizers have had to provide us with various means of digitally simulating this randomness. The various techniques and tools available for accomplishing this on the DX7 are numerous, and I like to refer to them as "animation" techniques, since they help to animate, or humanize, the sounds we generate. Inducing beating effects, whether by beating a carrier against another carrier (as we did in the last chapter), or by beating a modulator against a carrier (or vice versa) is one of the most important animation techniques available to us. My general advice is, once you've done just about everything you want to in creating a new sound, at least **try** some detuning effects. It's icing on the cake, but more often than not, it will add a dimensionality to your sound that makes it far more "real". We will discover as we examine the Yamaha presets, for example, that there are very few of them which do **not** use beating effects to some degree.

Just as we were able to beat two carriers producing simple sine waves against one another, so, too, can we beat two carriers producing complex waves

*This is not actually the case, as every DX7 owner already knows. The bits of hiss or "fizz" that you occasionally hear emanating from your instrument as you play certain sounds is known as aliasing noise, and this is essentially the result of our DAC not quite always being able to keep up with the millions of numbers per second that our microprocessor is feeding it. These "left-over" numbers are simply discarded and the aural result is a small amount of very high frequency noise. A standard low-pass filter is usually all that is necessary to reduce this to acceptable levels.

against one another. This involves shifting the **pitch** of one of two complex waves, and results in a very beautiful and pleasing effect:

EXERCISE 25

Beating effects with complex timbres:

1) INITIALIZE your DX7, leave it in algorithm #1, and TURN OFF operators 3 through 6 ("110000"). GENERATE a **square** wave using the system of operators 1 and 2 (refer to Exercise 19 if you don't remember how to do this).

2) LISTEN to confirm (AUDIO CUE 25A).

3) TURN OFF operators 1 and 2 and TURN ON operators 3 and 4 ("001100"). OBSERVE the diagram for algorithm #1 and NOTE that in this algorithm, operator 3 is a carrier being modulated by operator 4 (don't worry about what operators 5 and 6 are doing, since we've got them switched off anyway).

4) Using the system of operators 3 and 4, GENERATE another square wave and LISTEN to confirm (AUDIO CUE 25B). NOTE that there is no difference whatsoever between this square wave and the one you previously made with operators 1 and 2. Selectively TURN ON and OFF each of the two systems to confirm this.

5) Keeping all four operators ON ("111100"), VIEW the DETUNE parameter (edit switch 20) for operator 3 and CHANGE the value to + 7. Remember that in order to initiate a **pitch** change in our sound, we must also change operator 4 in the same way!! Bearing this in mind, CHANGE the DETUNE value for operator 4 **also** to + 7.

6) Play a few notes on the keyboard and LISTEN (AUDIO CUE 25C). This is an extremely beautiful effect!!

7) Let's take things a step further and add in yet another detuned square wave. NOTE that algorithm #1 will not permit us to accomplish this since neither of our remaining two operators (operators 5 and 6) are being used as carriers. Remember that you can **change algorithms at any time!** Examine the algorithm diagrams and NOTE that both algorithms #5 and #6 have configurations where operators 5 and 6 act as a modulator-carrier system, and where operators 1, 2, 3, and 4 are still configured in the same way as they currently are in algorithm #1. Either algorithm #5 or algorithm #6, then, will allow us to add in another detuned square wave without affecting what we've already generated. With this in mind,

8) Press edit switch 7 (ALGORITHM SELECT) and CHANGE to algorithm #5. TURN OFF operators 1 through 4 and TURN ON operators 5 and 6 ("000011"). Using this system, GENERATE another square wave. LISTEN to confirm (AUDIO CUE 25D). NOTE that, again, there is no difference at all in the quality of the square wave generated by these two operators from that of the other operators.

9) VIEW the DETUNE parameter for operator 5 and CHANGE this value from its default of 0 to a new value of -3. Again, in order to initiate a pitch change, we will have to change operator 6 in precisely the same manner. VIEW the DETUNE parameter for operator 6 and change it also to -3.

10) TURN ON all operators ("111111") and LISTEN (AUDIO CUE 25E). Very impressive chorusing, if I say so myself!

11) EXPERIMENT by now offsetting various carriers against their respective modulators - for example, change the DETUNE parameter of operator 1 to + 5 (AUDIO CUE 25F) or of operator 4 to -6 (AUDIO CUE 25G). NOTE that as you thereby induce beatings **within** the three square waves, the sound gets even richer and begins to take on a stronger type of movement.

12) EXPERIMENT further by repeating the above exercise with **different** complex timbres, balancing the qualitative and quantitative

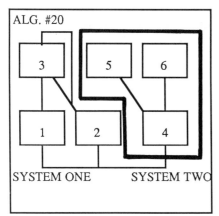

Figure 6-27

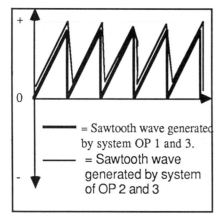

Figure 6-28

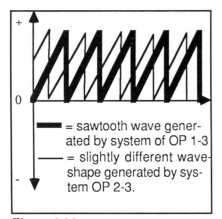

Figure 6-29

controls to achieve unusual musical timbres. Also try the same with **non-musical** timbres generated from non-whole number frequency ratios. Finally, try it yet again with *FIXED FREQUENCY* complex timbres. For example, to generate a square wave at a fixed frequency of 436.5 Hz, set your carrier to a fixed frequency value of 436.5 Hz and your modulator to a fixed frequency of 873.0 Hz (or as close as you can get), thereby maintaining a frequency ratio of 2:1! Adjust the modulator output level to 71 and you will have a square wave whose pitch doesn't change as you play different notes on the keyboard. The same detuning and beating effects can be incurred with fixed-frequency complex waves as with non-fixed timbres. Try it!

We can generate other extremely interesting and beautiful animation effects by sending a modulator's output signal to two slightly detuned carriers, or by sending two slightly detuned modulators' output signal to a single carrier. Algorithm #20 happens to conveniently provide us with both configurations in one package: **(See Figure 6-27.)**

The first system gives us two carriers (operators 1 and 2) which are both being modulated from the same source, operator 3. The second system gives us two modulators (operators 5 and 6) which are both equally affecting a single carrier (operator 4). Let's find out what we get by detuning operator 2 slightly relative to operator 1; and follow that by slightly detuning operator 6 relative to operator 5:

EXERCISE 26

Detuning with algorithm #20:

1) INITIALIZE your DX7 and, using edit switch 7, select algorithm #20.
2) TURN OFF operators 2, 4, 5, and 6. ("101000")
3) Using operators 1 and 3, GENERATE a sawtooth wave (refer to Exercise 18 if you can't remember how). LISTEN to confirm (AUDIO CUE 26A).
4) TURN OFF operator 1, and TURN ON operator 2. ("011000")
5) Using operators 2 and 3, GENERATE another *sawtooth* wave. LISTEN to confirm (AUDIO CUE 26B). NOTE that it sounds exactly the same as the one generated from operators 1 and 3.
6) Now TURN ON operator 1 again ("111000") and LISTEN (AUDIO CUE 26C). What you hearing is two sawtooth waves, perfectly in tune with one another, so they reinforce each other at every point and the sound is simply a bit louder: **(See Figure 6-28.)**

7) VIEW the DETUNE parameter for operator **2** and use the "yes" button to change this value to +7. LISTEN to the unusual beating effect (AUDIO CUE 26D). This is being caused because we have slightly altered the frequency ratio between operators 2 and 3, such that it is no longer 1.00:1.00 but is in fact closer to 1.00:1.008 . This means that not only is there beating occurring within the wave itself (as the harmonic overtones beat against their close disharmonic cousins) but that the overall wave generated by the combination of operators 2 and 3 is beating against the pure sawtooth wave generated by the combination of operators 1 and 3. The aural result is a very deep phase cancellation effect, as we hear these two waves periodically reinforcing and cancelling one another. The speed of this movement is determined by how closely detuned our "renegade" wave (operators 2 and 3) is: **(See Figure 6-29.)**

8) Continue to hold a note down and, using the "no" button, CHANGE this value slowly back down to 0 and then through the negative values all the way to -7. LISTEN as you do so (AUDIO CUE 26E) and NOTE that, as you get closer to the 0 center point, the

speed of the beating slows down. Now let's listen to the **other** system in this algorithm:

9)   TURN OFF operators 1, 2, and 3, and TURN ON operators 4 and 5. ("000110")

10)   Using operators 4 and 5, GENERATE another sawtooth wave and LISTEN to confirm (AUDIO CUE 26F).

11)   TURN OFF operator 5 and TURN ON operator 6. ("000101")

12)   Using operators 4 and **6** , GENERATE yet another sawtooth wave and LISTEN to confirm (AUDIO CUE 26G).

13)   Now TURN ON operator 5 once again ("000111") and LISTEN to the composite result (AUDIO CUE 26H). Because operator 4 (our carrier) is being modulated to the maximum degree by two separate modulators (operators 5 and 6) the sound will be unpleasantly over-bright and harsh, verging on distortion (!). We can make this much more listenable by using our front panel to

14)   VIEW the OUTPUT LEVEL parameter (edit switch 27) for operator 5 and CHANGE the value to 85. Now VIEW the same pa-rameter for operator 6 and CHANGE it also to a value of 85. LISTEN (AUDIO CUE 26I) and NOTE that our sound is much warmer (as lowering the output level of a modulator always will reduce the **num-ber** of overtones).

15)   Now VIEW the DETUNE parameter for operator **6** and CHANGE this value to + 7. LISTEN to this very unusual effect (AU-DIO CUE 26J) and NOTE that it is very different from the effect we heard previously from the other system in our algorithm. What we are doing here is setting up a different frequency ratio for operators 4 and 6 than the perfect 1:1 ratio which exists for operators 4 and 5. This new frequency ratio is in fact closer to 1.008:1.00 and will cause a wave to be generated which has internal beatings due to the dishar-monic overtones being very close in frequency to the harmonic over-tones. When this already moving wave is output alongside a pure saw-tooth wave, the movements intensify and in fact simulate a "wah-wah" type effect as we hear overtones going in and out of phase with one another: **(See Figure 6-30.)**

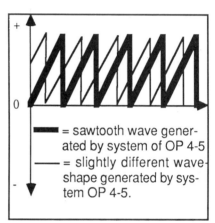

= sawtooth wave gener-ated by system of OP 4-5
= slightly different wave-shape generated by sys-tem OP 4-5.

Figure 6-30

16)   Continue to hold down a key and CHANGE the DETUNE pa-rameter slowly back to 0 and through its negative settings, down to a minimum of -7. LISTEN as you do so (AUDIO CUE 26K) and NOTE that the **speed** of the beating effect slows as you bring it nearer to the center point of 0.

17)   EXPERIMENT with timbres other than the sawtooth wave, which was picked here purely as a time-saving convenience. Also try EXPERIMENTing with altering detuning settings within algorithm #16, #17, or #18 (each of which offer **three** modulators sending output into a single carrier) and algorithm #22 or #24 (which offer three car-riers all receiving modulation data from a **single** modulator!).

We have seen that changing the DETUNE setting alters the **speed** of the ef-fect, but how would we alter the **depth** of the effect without changing the speed? The answer, again, is simple and straightforward: simply lower the output level of the "renegade" wave. If there is less actual audio signal coming from this wave, then it will beat less severely against the unaltered wave. Try it! Redo the above exercise, and lower the output level of operator 2 in the first system, and operator 6 in the second system, in order to lessen the over-all effect, with **no** change in speed.

Being able to conjure up these phase cancellation or "wah-wah" effects on our DX7 greatly expands the on-board power of the machine, but, perhaps more importantly, offers us yet another means of reducing the shortlist of available algorithms for a particular sound you have in mind. For example, if you feel strongly you will need a "wah-wah" type of effect, you will need an algorithm that provides you with at least two modulators feeding into a single carrier. If, on the other hand, you know that you will need the sound of several complex timbres beating against (and not just within) one another, than you will need two or more carriers, each with its own attached modulator (something like what is provided by algorithm #5, which is in fact used more often than any other algorithm in the Yamaha presets!). Asking yourself these types of questions, along with the "how many carriers do I need?" question mentioned previously, will help you to ultimately decide the best algorithm to use for a particular situation.

Let's suppose, for example, that we wanted to make a sound that consisted of a sawtooth wave, a square wave, and two detuned sine waves. What algorithm would we choose for this? At first glance, it may seem as if algorithms #21, #22, #23, #29, or even #30 might work: **(See Figure 6-31.)**

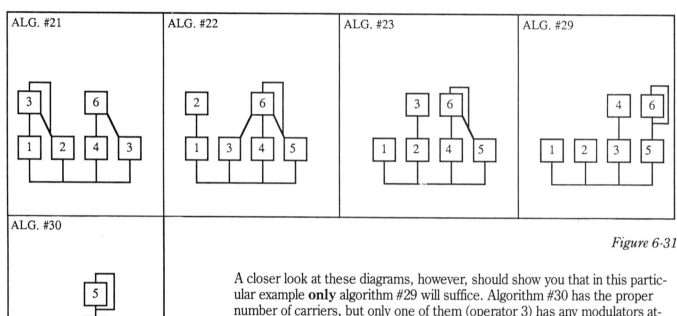

Figure 6-31

A closer look at these diagrams, however, should show you that in this particular example **only** algorithm #29 will suffice. Algorithm #30 has the proper number of carriers, but only one of them (operator 3) has any modulators attached. Algorithms #21, #22, and #23 disqualify because they all have modulators feeding more than one carrier and there is no way we can direct a modulator to send its signal one place and not another. This is a purposely simple example, and often your choice will not be so straightforward but this will give you an idea of the process involved.

Another very powerful animating technique involves the use of fixed-frequency mode with complex timbres. We have had some experience with this already in Exercise 25, where you were asked to experiment by generating fixed-frequency complex timbres and then slightly altering their tunings so as to produce beating effects. However, we should devote some time now to more closely examining the effects of fixed frequency on such complex timbres, specifically those effects generated by *offsets*, that is, placing **one** of the operators within a system into this mode while leaving the other operator in its normal frequency(ratio) mode.

First of all, what kind of effect will we initiate by placing a modulator in fixed-frequency while leaving the carrier in frequency(ratio) mode? Surprisingly, two different ones, depending upon whether the modulator is in a *sub-audio* or *audio* frequency. If the modulator is outputting a sub-audio frequency, then the effect will be exactly similar to that of feeding an analog LFO (low frequency oscillator) control voltage into an audio oscillator. For those of you unfamiliar with analog terminology, we are saying in plain English that we will hear slow, repetitive pitch change from this configuration. In the case of the DX7, since our un-modulated modulator is only capable of generating a **sine** wave, this periodic pitch change will be smooth, back and forth, in an up and down direction AND IT WILL NOT CHANGE SPEED OVER THE KEYBOARD (since our modulator, in fixed frequency mode, is **ignoring** the keyboard). In other words, if you play "middle A" on the keyboard, you will hear the pitch slowly rise above middle A and then slowly fall below middle A: **(See Figure 6-32.)**

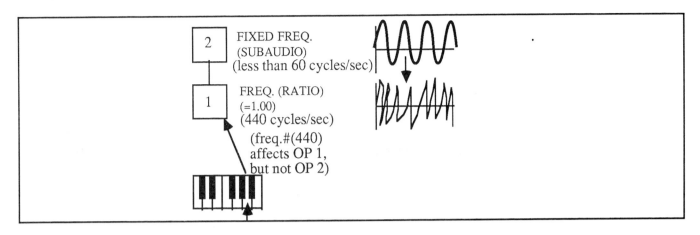

FIXED FREQ.
(SUBAUDIO)
(less than 60 cycles/sec)

FREQ. (RATIO)
(=1.00)
(440 cycles/sec)

(freq.#(440)
affects OP 1,
but not OP 2)

Figure 6-32

Let's try it:

EXERCISE 27

Repetitive pitch change with modulators in sub-audio

fixed-frequency mode:

1) INITIALIZE your DX7, leave it in algorithm #1, TURN OFF operators 3 through 6 ("110000") and, using the system of operators 1 and 2, GENERATE a sawtooth wave (refer to Exercise 18 if necessary).

2) Use the appropriate controls to VIEW the MODE of operator 2 (edit switch 17).

3) Use the "yes" button to CHANGE this from the default of "FREQUENCY(RATIO)" to a new value of "FIXED FREQUENCY".

4) VIEW the F COARSE parameter for operator 2 (edit switch 18) and CHANGE this value to 1.00 Hz.

5) Play a note on the keyboard and LISTEN (AUDIO CUE 27A). You should be hearing a single sine wave, changing pitch once per second (since operator 2 is at a frequency of 1.00 Hz). Continue holding this note down for the remainder of this Exercise.

6) VIEW the F FINE parameter for operator 2 (edit switch 19) and, using the data entry slider, slowly increase this value to its maximum of 9.772 Hz, LISTENing as you do so (AUDIO CUE 27B). NOTE that as you increase this value, the speed of the pitch change increases.

7) Return the F FINE value to 1.00 Hz and VIEW the F COARSE parameter again. Use the "yes" button to change this value to the sub-audio frequency of 10.00 Hz.

8) VIEW the F FINE value for operator 2 and once again use the data entry slider to slowly change this value up to its maximum of 97.72 Hz, LISTENing as you do so (AUDIO CUE 27C). NOTE that as the frequency of operator 2 approaches the audio range (approx. 20 Hz), the repetitive change in pitch happens so quickly that it cannot be perceived, and instead we begin to hear dissonant overtones.

Of course, if we continue in this manner, we will eventually have operator 2 well up into the audio range and different things will start to happen. As we started to hear in step 8 above, when the modulator goes into the faster audio range, disharmonic overtones are generated and the sound becomes dissonant and non-musical. Playing a series of different notes on the keyboard will produce **different timbres per note** . This is because each new note on the keyboard generates a different frequency ratio: **(See Figure 6-33.)**

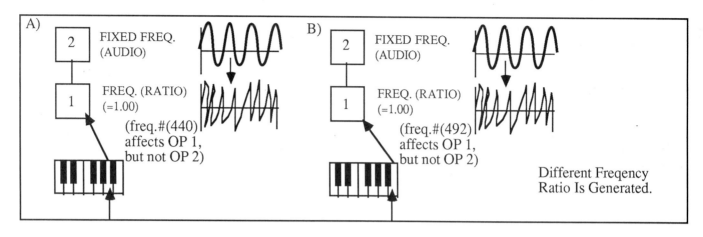

Figure 6-33

The effect generated here is very similar to that of an analog device called a *ring modulator*. A ring modulator is a component that **adds** frequencies together and also **subtracts** frequencies from one another. In analog synthesizers, they are generally used to create dissonant, ringing effects, by inputting to it two audio signals of different frequencies (normally derived from two analog oscillators). If, for example, you feed in one wave at 300 Hz, and another at 440 Hz, the ring modulator will output a signal of 740 Hz (the sum of 300 and 440) and another of 140 Hz (the difference between 440 and 300). Neither 740 Hz nor 140 Hz have any whole-number mathematical relationship to our starting frequencies of 300 Hz or 440 Hz, and so the output signal is dissonant. Furthermore, if the input signals were complex timbres and not just sine waves, the **overtones** would also sum and difference and we would hear a complex output containing many disharmonic overtones. It should be easy to see why setting up constantly different non-whole number frequency ratios on our DX7 will yield a similar dissonant effect. Try redoing Exercise 27 above, but this time put operator 2 in the **audible** F COARSE ranges of first 100 Hz and then 1000 Hz; and then try changing the F FINE parameter as before.

But what if we put our **carrier** into a fixed-frequency mode? Again, the results will be different, depending upon whether it is in an **audible** or **sub-audio** frequency. Let's try it in an audible range first. As you will see, the result is virtually the same as having our modulator in an audible fixed frequency, as we are once again setting up different frequency ratios per note. The result is the same: a dissonant, ring modulator-like effect.

EXERCISE 28

Generating dissonant effects by using a carrier in an audible fixed-frequency mode:

1) INITIALIZE your DX7, leave it in algorithm #1, TURN OFF operators 3 through 6 ("110000"), and, using the system of operators 1 and 2, GENERATE a sawtooth wave.
2) Use the appropriate switches to VIEW the MODE parameter (edit switch 17) for operator 1. Use the "yes" button to change this value for operator 1 from its default of FREQUENCY(RATIO) to FIXED FREQUENCY. 3) VIEW the F COARSE parameter for operator 1 (edit switch 18) and CHANGE this value to 100.0 Hz (which is in the **audible** range).
4) Play a scale on the keyboard and LISTEN (AUDIO CUE 28A). NOTE that each note played produces a different dissonant timbre.
5) VIEW the F FINE parameter for operator 1 and use the data entry slider to CHANGE this to a value of 436.5 Hz. Play a scale on the

keyboard and LISTEN (AUDIO CUE 28B). NOTE that, again, each note played produces a different dissonant timbre, dissimilar from that which you heard in step 4 above.

6) x EXPERIMENT by setting operator 1 to different F COARSE and F FINE values, taking care to keep it in the **audible** range (between 20 Hz and 20,000 Hz). For now, **don't** go into sub-audio values.

Finally, what will happen if we put our carrier (operator 1 in this instance) into a **sub-audio** fixed frequency? The logical answer to this question might well be that we wouldn't hear **anything** , since our carrier is actually providing the audio signal, and since a sub-audio signal is by definition outside the range of human hearing. This may be the logical answer, but it is not the correct one.

In fact, what we will hear is one of the most beautiful animation techniques available on this instrument. The explanation for this comes from the fact that our digital oscillators inside our operators are in fact **number** generators (see Chapter Three if you don't remember this). In order to generate a sine wave, these oscillators must produce numbers which are both positive and negative: **(See Figure 6-34.)**

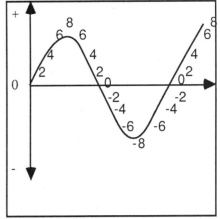

Figure 6-34

If we set our carrier to a sub-audio fixed frequency, then it is **slowly** generating the same positive and negative numbers, over and over again, at a constant slow speed. Our modulator, which we will leave in an audible range, and in FREQUENCY(RATIO) mode, is sending into our carrier a very high-speed stream of numbers, hundreds or even thousands of times per second: **(See Figure 6-35.)**

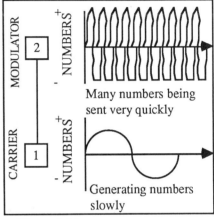

Many numbers being sent very quickly

Generating numbers slowly

Figure 6-35

The end result is that our carrier slowly **accepts** and then **rejects** this stream of numbers, resulting in a complex timbre being generated, followed by the **mirror-image of this timbre! (See Figure 6-36.)**

We literally hear a complex timbre, followed by the **inverse** of this timbre, slowly and gently, flipping back and forth. The end result is a very beautiful movement in the sound, not dissimilar to that created by a *chorusing* or *flanging* device. Let's try it!

EXERCISE 29

Animating a sound by using a carrier in sub-audio fixed frequency:

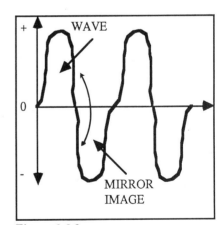

Figure 6-36

1) INITIALIZE your DX7, leave it in algorithm #1, TURN OFF operators 3 through 6 ("110000"), and, using the system of operators 1 and 2, GENERATE a sawtooth wave.

2) VIEW the MODE parameter for operator 1 (edit switch 17) and use the "yes" button to change this value from the default of FREQUENCY(RATIO) to FIXED FREQUENCY.

3) VIEW the F COARSE parameter for operator 1 and use the "no" button to change this value from 10.00 Hz to 1.00 Hz.

4) Play a note on the keyboard and LISTEN (AUDIO CUE 29A). NOTE that the sound changes timbre once per second, since the frequency of operator 1 is exactly 1.00 Hz. NOTE also that the sound, being a sawtooth wave, is quite harsh. To make the sound warmer,

5) CHANGE the OUTPUT LEVEL (edit switch 27) for operator **2** to a value of 85. Play a note on the keyboard and LISTEN (AUDIO CUE 29B) to confirm that the sound is less harsh.

6) VIEW the F FINE parameter (edit switch 19) for operator **1** and, using the *data entry* slider, slowly CHANGE this upwards to its maximum of 9.772 Hz, holding a note down on the keyboard and LISTENing as you do so (AUDIO CUE 29C). NOTE that as this value increases, the speed of the effect increases.

7) EXPERIMENT by creating different timbres and applying this effect to them.

To summarize, then, we have covered six different *animation* techniques, all of which help to add movement and "human-ness" to the sound, but all of which have qualitatively different effects:

1) DETUNE a sine wave (carrier only) relative to another sine wave.
2) DETUNE a modulator relative to its carrier (beating **within** a single sound).
3) DETUNE a complex wave (generated by a **system**) relative to another complex wave (this involved changing the frequency of **both** the modulator and carrier in the same way, in order to keep the frequency ratios intact).
4) DETUNE one carrier relative to another, both receiving modulation data from the **same** modulator (as with the first system in algorithm #20). This produces a characteristic deep phase cancellation.
5) DETUNE one modulator relative to another, both feeding modulation data into the **same** carrier (as with the second system in algorithm #20). This produces a characteristic "wah-wah" type effect.
6) Put a carrier within a system into a sub-audio FIXED FREQUENCY. This produces a characteristic chorusing or flanging effect, and is probably the most subtle of the techniques covered here.

In all instances except the last one, the depth of the effect can be lessened by decreasing the output level of one of the affected operators. In the last instance, you will probably most often use this effect on one system within an algorithm that offers you **another** system which can be set up similarly but without the sub-audio mode. This will allow the altered system to "bounce off" an un-affected system, thereby increasing the overall effect. In that case, lowering the output level of the sub-audio carrier will induce a lessening in the depth of the effect.

Modifying presets:

Congratulations to those of you who have faithfully gotten this far, initializing away and constantly creating sounds from scratch. As mentioned earlier, this is **not** a procedure you will find yourselves doing often in practice. Most of the time you will create the sounds you require by **modifying** a pre-existing sound. We now have amassed enough information to try this procedure for the first time!

When you call up a preset sound, either from the internal memory or from some outboard memory such as a cartridge, the DX7 automatically **copies** this data into your *edit buffer*. How can we view and/or change this data? Simple - we need to press only **one** button, and that button is the *edit mode* select switch.

Possibly the most remarkable thing about the DX7 is that it is absolutely incapable of keeping a secret! THERE IS NO WAY TO "PROTECT" A SOUND IN THE DX7 FROM BEING SEEN BY THE WORLD AT LARGE! And certainly no way to protect it from being changed. Companies which sell sounds for the DX7 do so at great risk, because first of all, once you have the sound, you can find out **exactly** how it was made, and, second of all, you can **copy** the data to your heart's content: to other memory storage units for your DX7 and to other DX7s. There is absolutely nothing the author of a sound can do to prevent that. Copyright laws in this country, do, however, normally prohibit you from using or reselling a copywritten sound as your own. The legal entanglements of this are complicated and well beyond the scope of this book - just bear in mind that the DX7 **always** allows you to see and learn from the programming work of others!

Let's take a look at a common preset, and experiment with making some useful changes to it. Find the "E.PIANO 1" preset, either on ROM cartridge 1A-11 or ROM 3A-8. Go into *cartridge play mode* and call up this sound. Now press the "edit" mode select switch, and let's see what we have!

No matter what parameter is currently displayed in the bottom line of your LCD, the top line will undoubtedly show you that this sound was created using algorithm #5: **(See Figure 6-37.)**

Let's take a look at what frequency ratios were used in each of the three systems available in this algorithm. Press edit switch 17 and you will note that all six operators are in FREQUENCY(RATIO) mode; to be expected, since different notes on the keyboard produce different harmonious pitches. Press edit switch 18 to see what actual ratios were used. Use the *operator select* switch to view the values for each operator, and you will see the following ratios: **(See Figure 6-38.)**

Now let's see what the OUTPUT LEVELs were for each operator. Press edit switch 27 to view this parameter, and use the operator select switch to view the value for each operator: **(See Figure 6-39.)**

Of course, there are many more factors in play here which make this sound what it is, but we will limit ourselves here to only those parameters we have already covered. Suppose, however, you have an incorrigible urge to **change** the sound a bit? No problem! The edit buffer insures that we can change away, without actually affecting the sound itself! Let's begin with the crudest change imaginable, changing the algorithm! Remember, you can change algorithm at any time, and when you do so, **no other data is changed!** So, for example, if you're curious to hear "E.PIANO 1" in algorithm #16, press edit switch 7 (ALGORITHM SELECT parameter), and use the data entry slider to change this value to 16. Play a note on the keyboard and listen - you should be hearing a really horrible noise which doesn't sound anything like "E.PIANO 1". Try going into different algorithms and note that many of them produce enormous changes to the overall sound.

Changing the algorithm is probably the grossest change you can make to the sound. Doing this is a fairly mindless exercise and will rarely be of logical help to you in modifying a sound (of course, there is nothing inherently wrong with mindless exercises, after all 8 million MTV viewers can't be wrong! Seriously, though, often just mindlessly changing algorithms will yield new and interesting sounds and I don't mean to discourage you from doing it). However, more often, changes to more subtle parameters will yield just the kind of modifications to the sound you require.

Let's try one practical example. As nice as the "E.PIANO 1" preset is, a common complaint is that it doesn't "cut" enough - that is, most people would like the sound to be somewhat harder and brighter. This preset is meant to emulate the sound of a real Fender Rhodes piano, and the Fender Rhodes is actually an acoustic instrument whose sound can be modified by certain physical adjustments to the hammers and metal tines which create the sound. In order to "harden" the sound of a Rhodes, you normally raise the hammers higher so that they strike the metal tines sooner; hence, a brighter, harder sound.

We can digitally simulate that effect in our DX7 and make the "same" change to the sound of our Fender Rhodes as a real Fender Rhodes owner can. The first step in modifying any preset, after entering edit mode to view the edit parameters, is to listen to the contribution of each individual system within the algorithm. This is accomplished by selectively switching OFF operators. The second step is to THINK about what parameter it is you want to change in order to accomplish the desired result. In this instance, we wish to **brighten** the sound, that is, to **increase** the number of overtones. We know that in order to do this, we must increase the OUTPUT LEVEL of one or more modulators within the system. The question is, how do we know **which** modulators we want to affect? The answer is usually provided by the first step. Listening to each system individually will usually indicate to you which operator or operators are the best candidates for a change. Let's try it:

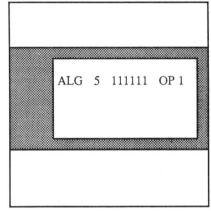

Figure 6-37

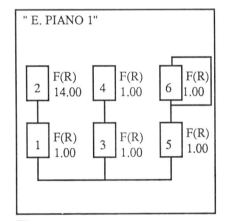

Figure 6-38

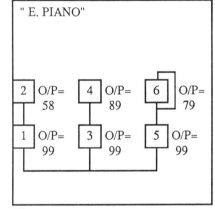

Figure 6-49

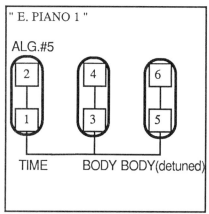

" E. PIANO 1 "

ALG.#5

TIME   BODY BODY(detuned)

Figure 6-40

EXERCISE 30

Brightening the sound of "E.PIANO 1":

1) Put your DX7 in *cartridge play mode* and call up the "E.PIANO 1" preset.

2) Press the "edit" mode select switch in order to VIEW and CHANGE the edit parameters for this sound.

3) Top line of LCD shows us that algorithm #5 was used to create this sound. This algorithm provides us with three systems; operators 1 and 2, operators 3 and 4; and operators 5 and 6. TURN OFF operators 3 through 6 ("110000") in order to hear the first system on its own. Play a note on the keyboard and LISTEN (AUDIO CUE 30A). This system provides the attack, or "tine" part of the sound.

4) TURN OFF operators 1 and 2 and TURN ON operators 3 and 4 ("001100") in order to hear the next system. Play a note on the keyboard and LISTEN (AUDIO CUE 30B). This system sounds quite different, providing the body of the sound.

5) TURN OFF operators 3 and 4 and TURN ON operators 5 and 6 ("000011") in order to hear the last system. Play a note on the keyboard and LISTEN (AUDIO CUE 30C). This system also provides the body of the sound, similar to that of the second system. **(See Figure 6-40.)**

6) TURN ON operators 3 and 4 ("001111") and play a note on the keyboard, LISTENing as you do so (AUDIO CUE 30D). NOTE that a certain amount of *beating* is present in this part of the overall sound. VIEW the DETUNE parameter for operators 3, 4, 5, and 6, and NOTE that operators 5 and 6 are heavily detuned (-7 and +7, respectively), relative to operators 3 and 4 (which are not detuned at all).

7) TURN ON operators 1 and 2 ("111111") and once again LISTEN to the overall sound. Since we now know that the first system (that of operators 1 and 2) was providing the "attack", or "tine" part of the sound, it is logically the OUTPUT LEVEL of operator **2** that we want to increase.

8) VIEW the OUTPUT LEVEL parameter of operator 2, and using the data entry slider, slowly increase this value from its present setting of 58 up to a maximum value of 99. Since we are changing OUTPUT LEVEL (which does not change in real time), you will have to tap a note on the keyboard as you LISTEN (AUDIO CUE 30E). NOTE that at the uppermost values the sound is distorted and unpleasant. CHANGE this value to 86 for a realistic "hard" Fender Rhodes sound.

9) EXPERIMENT by changing the output levels for operators 4 and/or 6 instead of operator 2. NOTE that while these changes make the sound brighter, the quality of the sound changes drastically and no longer resembles a Fender Rhodes.

10) EXPERIMENT by changing the frequency ratios within the different systems and NOTE that since this only initiates a *qualitative* change in timbre, the result is **not** a brighter sound, just a **different** sound.

The technique of modifying a preset is as much an art as a science but will usually require you to translate a subjective audio requirement into a fixed DX7 parameter change. In the example above, we wanted to "harden", or "brighten", our sound. Since there are no "harden" or "brighten" parameters on the DX7, we had to translate this desire into a command to "increase modulator output level". An examination of the contributions of individual systems within the overall sound showed us that system 1 was the system we really needed to change, and so the finger was pointed at operator 2 as the likely recipient of that change!

Okay, now that we've built a better (or at least brighter) Fender Rhodes, let's try adding in one of our animation techniques. The very last one we examined, placing a carrier in a sub-audio fixed frequency, will work very well with this sound, since we have two systems (that of operators 3 and 4, and of operators 5 and 6) which are essentially the same. Remember, this particular effect will work best when we can bounce it off of an uneffected system, in order to create maximum phase and pitch shifts.

Since it's a **carrier** we need to change, our candidates are operators 3 and 5. Which one is the better to use? That's a tough question, but I personally would opt for operator 3, since operator 5 is already contributing some beating effects to the overall sound (by reason of its detuning). Let's do it:

EXERCISE 31

Adding chorusing to "E.PIANO 1":

1)   REDO Exercise 30 through to Step 8.
2)   VIEW the MODE parameter (edit switch 17) for operator 3. Use the "yes" button to change this from FREQUENCY(RATIO) to FIXED FREQUENCY.
3)   Press edit switch 18 (F COARSE parameter) and change this value to 1.00 Hz.
4)   Press edit switch 19 (F FINE parameter and change this value to 4.365 Hz.
5)   Play a few notes on the keyboard and LISTEN (AUDIO CUE 31A). NOTE that the "E.PIANO 1" sound now has a chorusing effect.
6)   EXPERIMENT by changing the F FINE value to higher or lower speeds. NOTE that as you do so, the **speed** of the effect changes. EXPERIMENT by lowering the OUTPUT LEVEL of operator 3. NOTE that as you do so, the **depth** of the effect is lessened.

Congratulations on making your first musically useful modification to a preset! In Chapter Eight we will have an opportunity to name and store this sound, but first we must complete our discussion of the effects of modulators by discussing STACKED MODULATORS and THE FEEDBACK LOOP.

CHAPTER SEVEN: STACKED MODULATORS AND THE FEEDBACK LOOP

You've probably noticed by now that there are many algorithms that provide us with modulators modulating **other** modulators, as in algorithm #3: **(See Figure 7-1.)**

or algorithm #16: **(See Figure 7-2.)**

or algorithm #1, which actually provides us with a modulator (operator 6) modulating another modulator (operator 5) modulating yet **another** modulator (operator 4) before the signal finally reaches the carrier (operator 3)! **(See Figure 7-3.)**

These systems of more than one modulator in a row are called *stacked modulators* , or *stacks* for short. (Dr. Chowning himself refers to these as "cascades".) We can best describe the purpose and effect of these stacks by running an exercise. What we will do here is to start ourselves in algorithm #23, which looks like this: **(See Figure 7-4.)**

We'll begin by using just operators 2 and 3, which comprise a single modulator-carrier *system* , to generate a sawtooth wave. As we've learned in the previous chapter, we can change algorithms at any time, so, having made our sawtooth wave, we will next change over to algorithm #3, which looks like this: **(See Figure 7-5.)**

As you can see, in algorithm #3, operator 3 is **still** modulating operator 2, but this time operator 2 is no longer a carrier but is instead configured as another modulator, affecting operator 1 (our carrier). When you change algorithms, remember, all of your previous data is retained, and so even though operator 2 is now a modulator instead of a carrier, it is **still** a sawtooth wave, since operator 3 is still affecting it in precisely the same way: **(See Figure 7-6.)**

By sending signal from the output of operator 2 to operator 1, we are now modulating our carrier with a **sawtooth** (complex) wave, instead of just a simple sine wave. The aural results will be strikingly different. Let's do it:

EXERCISE 32

Modulating with a sawtooth wave:

1) INITIALIZE your DX7, select algorithm #23, and TURN OFF operators 1, 4, 5, and 6 ("011000").
2) Using the *system* of operators 2 and 3, GENERATE a sawtooth wave and LISTEN to confirm (AUDIO CUE 32A).
3) VIEW the OUTPUT LEVEL parameter of operator **2** and CHANGE this value to 0. Since operator 2 is a carrier in this algorithm, this will have the effect of lowering the volume to zero. NOTE that even though we can now no longer hear operator 2, it is still a sawtooth wave since operator 3 continues to have an output level of 99: **(See Figure 7-7.)**

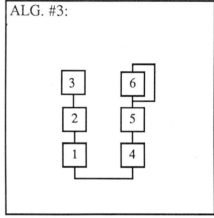

Figure 7-1

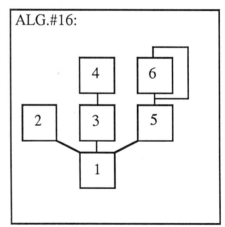

Figure 7-2

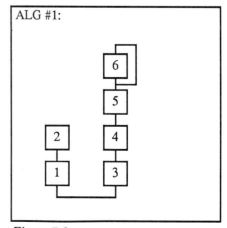

Figure 7-3

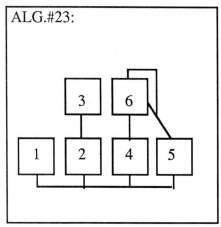

ALG.#23:

Figure 7-4

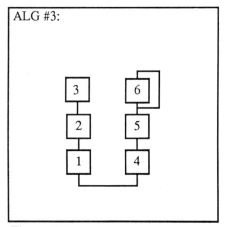

ALG #3:

Figure 7-5

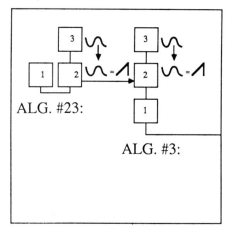

ALG. #23:

ALG. #3:

Figure 7-6

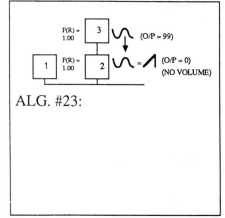

ALG. #23:

Figure 7-7

4) Press edit switch 7 (ALGORITHM SELECT parameter) and CHANGE to algorithm #3.

5) TURN ON operator 1 ("111000"). Even though operators 2 and 3 are on, we won't hear their effect since the output level of operator 2 has been reduced to 0. Examine the algorithm diagram and NOTE that there is no way that operator 3 can send any modulation data directly to operator 1: **(See Figure 7-8.)**

6) Play a note on the keyboard and LISTEN (AUDIO CUE 32B) in order to confirm that you are only hearing the sine wave generated by the currently unmodulated operator 1.

7) VIEW the OUTPUT LEVEL parameter (edit switch 27) for operator **2** , and, using the *data entry* slider, slowly increase this value up to its maximum of 99, tapping a note on the keyboard and LISTENing as you do so (AUDIO CUE 32C). NOTE that you cannot simply hold a note down, as we are altering output level, which does not change in real time.

What exactly did we hear? First of all, the overtones began appearing at a much earlier point. By the time you had increased the output level of operator 2 to a value of 20 or so, several overtones had begun to make their presence felt. Secondly, the sound got much, much brighter than anything we've heard previously, to the point where it actually overloaded and distorted when the output level was close to or at maximum. Of course, there was no reason to have to start in algorithm #23; we did that here just so you could demonstrably hear that operator 2 had in fact been changed to a sawtooth wave. When generating complex timbres with stacks of modulators, you can start directly in algorithm #3, or any other algorithm, for that matter.

The sole purpose of these stacks, then, is to allow us to use **complex** waves as modulating sources. After all, every timbre we've previously generated has been a result of feeding a sine wave output into another sine wave. What we've accomplished here is to feed a complex wave output (in this case a sawtooth wave) into our sine wave: **(See Figure 7-9.)**

The advantage of using a complex wave as our modulating source is that it enables us to generate **overbright**, twangy, biting kinds of sounds on our DX7, and, in large doses, **distorted** sounds. Crank the output level of operator 2 up to 99, play a hot guitar lick on the keyboard, and you'll hear a nastier fuzz guitar sound on your DX7 than you could ever hope to accomplish on the cheapest (and most distorted) analog synth around!

Of course, we're not limited to just using a sawtooth wave as our complex modulating source. We can use any timbre we like. Just for the sake of illustration, let's run a quick exercise to generate a **square** wave as our modulating source:

EXERCISE 33

Modulating with a square wave:

1) INITIALIZE your DX7, go straight to algorithm #3, and TURN OFF operators 4 through 6 ("111000"). Play a note on the keyboard and LISTEN to confirm that all you are hearing is the single sine wave being generated by operator 1 (AUDIO CUE 33A).

2) GENERATE a square wave in operator 2 by setting the F COARSE value of operator 3 to a value of 2.00, and the OUTPUT LEVEL of operator 3 to a value of 71: **(See Figure 7-10.)**

NOTE that even though operator 2 is now outputting a square wave, we cannot hear its effect on operator 1 since the OUTPUT LEVEL of operator 2 is still 0.

3) VIEW the OUTPUT LEVEL parameter for operator 2, and using the data entry slider, slowly increase this up to its maximum value of 99, tapping a note on the keyboard and LISTENing as you do so (AUDIO CUE 33B). NOTE that once again, the overtones appear at an

earlier stage and that the sound becomes significantly brighter than that generated by a single modulator.

4) EXPERIMENT by changing the frequency ratio between operators 2 and 3; between operators 2 and 1; between operators 3 and 1. EXPERIMENT further by changing the output level of operator 3 as well as that of operator 2. NOTE that as higher frequency ratios are set, more distortions appear as we increase the disharmonic content. NOTE also that this can be offset by **reducing** the OUTPUT LEVEL of either operator 2 or operator 3; and that each produces a qualitatively different effect.

If you plan to generate a sound on your DX7 that is harpsichord-like, clavinet-like, guitar-like, banjo-like, or any kind of twangy, sharp, biting sound, you will probably need a stack or two to accomplish this. Several algorithms, like #3 and #4, offer you two stacks, while others, like #10 or #30, offer you one stack plus several other systems. Since a stack by definition will consist of at least 3 operators, and since we only have a total of six operators at our disposal, there are no algorithms offering you **more** than two stacks. In any event, this is yet another question to ask yourself when making a decision as to the best algorithm to use for a specific situation. Since over half of the 32 available algorithms do **not** contain stacks, then deciding that you need one will effectively eliminate over half of the potential choices. Don't waste your time trying to make an accurate electric guitar sound, for example, with a single modulator-carrier system - you won't be able to generate enough overtones to do it well. Only using a complex wave as a modulating source can accomplish that, and that's precisely why *stacked modulators* are available to us.

Why would we ever need stacks of **three** modulators, as provided by algorithms #1, 2, and 18? We'll be able to better answer that question after we discuss something called *feedback* .

The feedback loop:

In every one of the 32 algorithms in the DX7, we are provided with something called a *feedback loop* . Those of you with keen sensory apparatus (or those of you who are just plain observant!) may have noticed these funny little boxes that are attached to at least one operator in every algorithm diagram, even though we have conveniently not said anything about them up until now. Algorithm #1, for example, has its feedback loop on operator 6: **(See Figure 7-11.)**

This feedback loop is an alternative means of routing an operator's output either to its **own** modulation input, or to the input of another operator stacked above it, hence the term "feedback".

Acoustic feedback is a phenomenon which occurs when a signal is re-routed, or "fed back" into itself, as when an open microphone is placed in front of an active loudspeaker: **(See Figure 7-12.)**

The output signal from the microphone goes into the loudspeaker, which reproduces it. This reproduced signal is then picked up again by the open microphone, and "fed back" into the loudspeaker; over and over again this occurs, until finally a characteristic squealing and howling is generated. Of course, in our DX7 we are not dealing with audio signals of any type, since all of our components are digital. The result of our DX7 feedback loops, then, will be simply to allow a modulator **to modulate itself** , or in a few algorithms, to allow a **carrier** to actually modulate a modulator stacked above it! (Whew! Try saying **that** three times fast...)

We do not have the power to decide where the feedback loop will be: this is determined by the algorithm we choose. Usually (but not always! - consult the algorithm diagrams!!), the feedback loop is on operator 6 and it usually is set to feed back into itself, as in algorithm #5: **(See Figure 7-13.)**

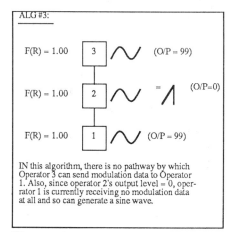

Figure 7-8

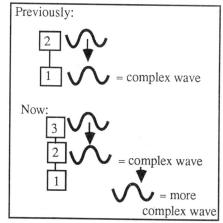

Figure 7-9

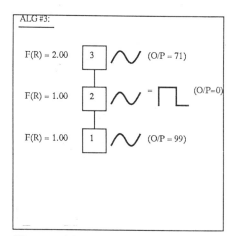

Figure 7-10

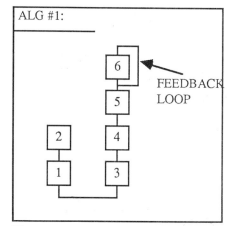

Figure 7-11

Figure 7-12

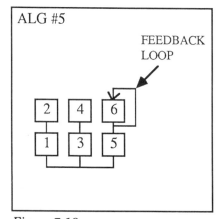

Figure 7-13

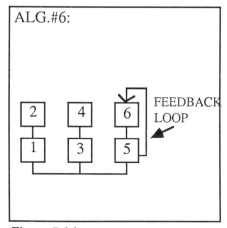

Figure 7-14

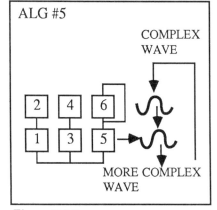

Figure 7-15

Sometimes, however, the loop specifies that operator 6 will instead be the **recipient** of modulation input fed back by a carrier below it, as occurs in algorithm #6: **(See Figure 7-14.)**

In fact, the **only** difference between algorithm #5 and algorithm #6 is in the feedback loop! Obviously, we will hear qualitatively different aural effects from each configuration.

Take a moment or two to reexamine the 32 algorithms, taking mental note of where the feedback loop is placed for each one. Observe, for example, that the only algorithm that contains a carrier feeding back into **itself** is algorithm #32, which, after all has **only** carriers. In every other algorithm the feedback loop terminates at a **modulator** .

Let's begin by examining the effect of a modulator feeding back into itself, as with algorithm #5. If operator 6 is sending its output not only to operator 5, as the algorithm indicates, but into its **own** modulation data input, then it will actually have the effect of modulating itself! (among some irreverent DX7 programmers, this is known as the auto-erotic mode) This means that operator 6 will be able to turn itself into a complex wave, without needing another modulator stacked above it, thereby "saving" you an operator: **(See Figure 7-15.)**

In the case of algorithm #6, however, operator 6 instead is the recipient of signal outputted by operator **5** , sitting below it! This means that the complex wave produced as a result of operator 6 modulating operator 5 is then **returned** , in varying amplitudes, to the modulation **input** of operator 6, causing it to output a more complex wave itself. This extra-complex wave is then outputted again into operator 5, and the whole process reoccurs again and again. **(See Figure 7-16.)**

Exercise 34, below, will let us hear the qualitative aural difference between these two feedback routings.

We can control how much signal enters the feedback loop with edit switch 8, labeled "FEEDBACK": **(See Figure 7-17.)**

The range of this switch is 0 - 7; a value of 0 indicates that **no** signal is entering this pathway, hence no feedback; a value of 7 indicates that maximum signal is in this routing and feedback is maximized. In small doses (values of 1, 2, 3, or 4), the effect of the feedback loop is very similar to that of a stacked modulator. In larger doses (values of 5, 6, or 7), so much signal will be feeding back that the sound will grossly distort and eventually break into *white noise* .

If you take all of the colors of the rainbow and mix them together, you get the color **white** ; if you take all of the audio frequencies and randomly mix them together, you get white noise. White noise is useful for generating thoroughly non-musical sounds such as handclaps, surf, wind, thunder, or engines, helicopters, and jackhammers. Using the feedback loop in its higher settings will allow us to generate white noise effects on the DX7; however, for other reasons soon to be discussed, the DX7 is not a particularly good instrument to use for these kind of effects. In any event, let's try out the feedback loop and hear its contribution to a sound. Note that the feedback loop parameter is **not** operator-specific; the upper right-hand corner of our LCD will be blank and the *operator select* switch will be inactive. This makes sense since, as we have seen, we cannot specify which operator is to have the feedback loop - it is determined for us by the algorithm we select.

EXERCISE 34
The feedback loop:

> 1) INITIALIZE your DX7 and select algorithm #5. TURN OFF operators 1 through 4 ("000011").
> 2) Using the system of operators 5 and 6, GENERATE a sawtooth wave. LISTEN to confirm (AUDIO CUE 34A).
> 3) Press edit switch 8 to VIEW the FEEDBACK parameter. NOTE that the *default* for this parameter is 0 (no feedback).

4)   Hold down a single note on the keyboard and use the "yes" button to slowly increase this value up to its maximum of 7, LISTENing as you do so (AUDIO CUE 34B). NOTE that the sound gets progressively brighter, simulating the effect of a stack, until, at the highest settings, it distorts and eventually degenerates into white noise (at a value of 7).

5)   Restore the FEEDBACK value to 0 and press edit switch 7 to VIEW the ALGORITHM SELECT parameter. CHANGE this to algorithm #6.

6)   Repeat steps 3 and 4 above, LISTENing as you do so (AUDIO CUE 34C). NOTE that, since in this algorithm operator 6 is **not** feeding back into itself but is instead the **recipient** of operator 5's output signal, **(See Figure 7-18.)**

the effect is qualitatively different. In this configuration, the feedback overtones appear earlier and distort more quickly, producing a "cleaner" type of white noise.

7)   EXPERIMENT by using timbres other than a sawtooth wave, and by trying the feedback loop in other algorithms. Try specifically using algorithm #32, as this is the only algorithm with a **carrier** feeding back into itself (NOTE that the aural results are particularly unspectacular). NOTE that regardless of the timbre selected or the algorithm used, the feedback loop **always** has the aural effect of brightening and/or distorting the overall sound. EXPERIMENT further by calling up various presets in *play mode* , examining their feedback loop settings, and CHANGING them. LISTEN to the increase in brightness as you increase the FEEDBACK value in all instances.

It should be obvious that the FEEDBACK loop can sometimes be used as a "phantom" seventh operator, since it can so closely simulate the effect of a stack. For example, suppose you've created a sound on your DX7 using all six operators in the configuration of algorithm #5, and you feel that it's lacking just that extra bit of "bite". You may already have the output levels of your modulators at or near maximum, and the sound is still not cutting through enough. Well, even if you look for another algorithm, one with a stack, you're unfortunately out of luck because there are only six operators, and you're already using them all! In this example, opening up the feedback loop already present in operator 6 may well be all you need to do in order to complete the sound to your satisfaction!

Even when, in the last Exercise, we used algorithm #6 and raised the FEEDBACK value to its maximum of 7, we didn't really come up with a very pure white noise. Noise, by definition, should be completely pitchless, and you probably noticed that quite a bit of the original carrier sine wave was still present. We can increase the purity of the noise we generate on the DX7 (that is, decrease the amount of the pitch component) by using stacks of **three** modulators, and this is the main use of such stacks.

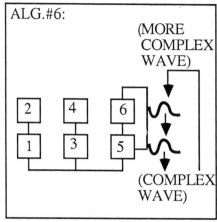

Figure 7-16

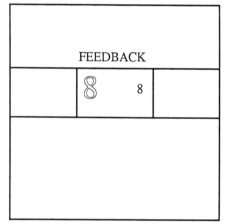

Figure 7-17

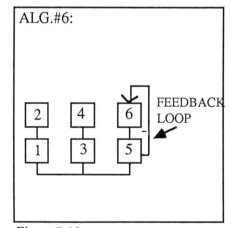

Figure 7-18

Here is a good method for creating pure unpitched white noise on the DX7, using a stack of three modulators, and using a carrier in sub-audio *fixed frequency* mode:

EXERCISE 35

Generating unpitched white noise:

1) INITIALIZE your DX7 and leave it in algorithm #1. TURN OFF operators 1 and 2 ("001111").

2) VIEW the OUTPUT LEVEL parameter (edit switch 27) for operator 3 and CHANGE it to a value of 99. LISTEN to the pure sine wave (AUDIO CUE 35A).

3) CHANGE the OUTPUT LEVEL of operator 4 to a value of 99, generating a *sawtooth* wave (remember, the frequency ratio between operators 3 and 4 is **already** 1 : 1, since these are *default values*). LISTEN to confirm (AUDIO CUE 35B).

4) CHANGE the OUTPUT LEVEL of operator 5 to a value of 99, generating a distorted sound as a result of changing operator 4 to a sawtooth wave and using that as a modulating source. LISTEN to confirm (AUDIO CUE 35C).

5) CHANGE the OUTPUT LEVEL of operator 6 to a value of 99, increasing the distortion present in the sound to a point where it is generating noise. LISTEN to confirm (AUDIO CUE 35D). NOTE that this noise is still fairly pitched, and therefore **not** yet white noise.

6) VIEW the FEEDBACK parameter (edit switch 8) and CHANGE it to its maximum value of 7. NOTE that in algorithm #1, the feedback loop is set so that operator 6 (the top modulator in the stack) is feeding back into itself. LISTEN (AUDIO CUE 35E) to confirm that the pitch component in the noise has been greatly reduced, but is still present.

7) Press edit switch 17 and VIEW the MODE parameter for operator 3 (the carrier). Use the "yes" button to CHANGE this to FIXED FREQUENCY.

8) Press edit switch 18 and VIEW the F COARSE parameter for operator 3 and note that it is currently 10.00 Hz, which is a sub-audio frequency. Leave it at this setting and LISTEN (AUDIO CUE 35F). NOTE that the pitch component has again been reduced but is still slightly present.

9) CHANGE operator 4 also to FIXED FREQUENCY mode, and VIEW its F COARSE value (which will be at the default of 10.00 Hz). LISTEN (AUDIO CUE 35G). NOTE that we have again reduced the pitch component.

10) Repeat step 9 above, for operator 5 . LISTEN (AUDIO CUE 35H) and NOTE that the pitch component is now entirely gone, and that we have succeeded in generating pure white noise.

11) EXPERIMENT by changing operator 6 (the top modulator) also to a FIXED FREQUENCY of 10.00 Hz. LISTEN (AUDIO CUE 35I) and NOTE that this produces a helicopter-like sound; interesting, but not white noise. EXPERIMENT further with other FIXED FREQUENCIES for the various operators in the stack provided by algorithm #1.

The reason why the DX7 is not generally very useful as a source for white noise-based sounds is because the action of the Envelope Generators (see Chapter Nine for a complete discussion of these little beauties!) have a tendency to restore the pitch component when they undergo complex changes. There is no doubt a mathematical explanation as to why this phenomenon occurs, but, once again, it would be beyond the scope of this book to go into it. Suffice it to say that generating typical white-noise effects, such as whip-cracks, handclaps, snare drums, thunder, wind, and surf, are best left to analog synthesizers, which are usually much more successful at generating such sounds. In any event, here's a diagram of what we constructed in Exercise 35: **(See Figure 7-19.)**

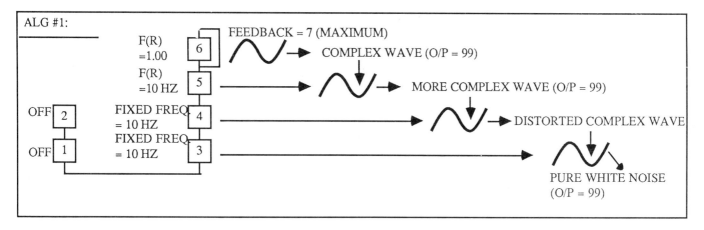

Figure 7-19

Now let's see how we can store some of the sounds we've been creating!

SWITCHES AND CONTROLS COVERED IN CHAPTER SEVEN:

SWITCH	PARAMETER	COMMENTS
Edit 8	Feedback	Range 0 to 7; Non-operator specific

CHAPTER EIGHT: STORING SOUNDS

In the overview presented in Chapter Two we spoke of the different "memories" available in the DX7 - specifically, the *internal memory* , and the *cartridge memory* . When we discuss the MIDI interface in Chapter Fourteen we will see that we can also access whatever memory and memory storage devices available in virtually any computer as well. For now, however, we'll limit ourselves to just the two above-mentioned memories available on the DX7 itself.

Let's just do a quick review of the features of each kind of memory: the internal, the RAM cartridge, and the ROM cartridge:

> 1) *Internal memory*: 32 slots, data can be read **or** written to.
> 2) *RAM cartridge memory* : also 32 slots; data can also be read or written to.
> 3) *ROM cartridge memory* : 2 sets of 32 slots, each accessed by "A/B" switch on rear of cartridge. Data can **only** be read. The information stored in these cartridges **cannot** be overwritten.

Rather than simply discuss the overall procedure, it will probably be easier (and certainly more fun) to actually store a sound we create. The sound we store can be something we've built from scratch, via the *voice initialization* procedure, or it could be a sound we've modified (or even not modified) from a preexisting one. Let's work here with a modification of a preset. Take a few minutes to go back to the end of Chapter Six and redo Exercises 30 and 31. These exercises, you may remember, modified the "E.PIANO 1" sound found on ROM 1A-11 or ROM 3A-8, adding extra brightness to the sound and then a chorusing animation effect.

Got the modified sound in your edit buffer? Good - let's carry on...

The first thing you probably noticed when simply playing back sounds on your DX7 is that every sound has a name. These names are for identification purposes only and don't actually mean anything at all - you can, for example, generate a flute sound on your DX7 and name it "TUBA", or you can generate a tuba sound and name it "FRED". Normally, of course, you'll want to give a sound a name that somehow identifies it, just for the sake of your sanity, but the point is, you have the freedom to name, or rename, any sound in any way at all. When you create a new sound via the Voice Initialization procedure, for example, the default name for that voice will always be "INIT VOICE". Obviously, you should always rename every voice you create this way, or else you may well end up with a memory full of different sounds, all named "INIT VOICE".

The edit parameter that allows us to name or rename a sound is edit switch 32, labeled "VOICE NAME". If your DX7 isn't already in edit mode, put it there by pressing the edit mode select switch, and then press switch 32. The bottom line of your LCD should read "E.PIANO 1", since that is the original name of the sound we modified. You also should be seeing a blinking black box over the "E", like this: **(See Figure 8-1.)**

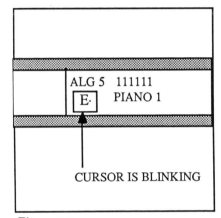

Figure 8-1

This blinking box is called a *cursor* , and those of you with any computer experience at all should be very familiar with this little guy. The cursor is simply a prompt; the computer's way of trying to get your attention and let you know what it wants you to do. In this instance, since you told the DX7 you want to name or rename this voice, it's showing you the old name and letting you know that it's ready to redo the first letter.

Nestled inside each of the 32 main switches as well as the 8 special switches on the left-hand side of the machine is a small black *character* , and these are used solely for naming sounds. Switches 1 through 9 contain the numbers 1 through 9, and switch 10 contains the number "0"; following that, switches 11 through 16 have the letters A through F, and switches 17 through 32 have the letters G through V: **(See Figure 8-2.)**

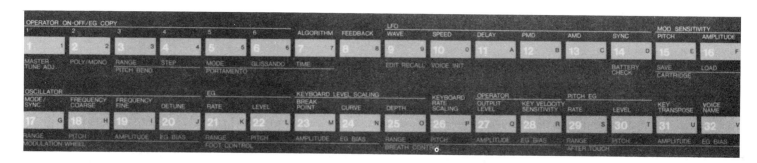

Figure 8-2

W, X, Y, and Z are inside the top row of 8 switches on the left-hand side of the machine: **(See Figure 8-3.)**

and the two memory select switches contain a hypen and a period, respectively: **(See Figure 8-4.)**

The function mode select switch doubles as a space bar, and will be used to enter blank characters, or spaces: **(See Figure 8-5.)**

and the "yes" - "no" buttons in the data entry section will move the blinking cursor to the left or right, as indicated by the arrows inside them: **(See Figure 8-6.)**

All of which leaves us with only one remaining switch on the entire front panel, and that switch is the edit mode select switch, which is labeled "CHARACTER": **(See Figure 8-7.)**

This is the switch which **activates** all of the previously remaining ones for their characters. WHEN NAMING A SOUND, YOU MUST KEEP THIS SWITCH **HELD DOWN** AT ALL TIMES. This is the only way that the DX7 will know that, for example, switch 18 is to yield the character "H" and not call up the F COARSE parameter: **(See Figure 8-8.)**

Note, again, the color-coding system. The word "CHARACTER" inside the edit mode select switch is **black**, linking this switch with the black characters inside all of the other switches.

At the moment, of course, our sound already has a name, and that name is "E.PIANO 1". Why then, do we need to rename it? Well, if we simply save it in our internal memory or on a RAM cartridge, how will we be able to distinguish it from the **original** "E.PIANO 1"? After all, we made some significant changes to the original sound. It would be a real pain to have to remember which one was which, especially if the original and the modification were stored in the same internal or cartridge memory. The solution, obviously, is to give one of them a different name. Since the original is a factory preset from a

Figure 8-3

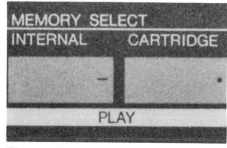

Figure 8-4

ROM cartridge, and since we can't ever overwrite data in a ROM, we will be renaming our modified sound. Let's run an exercise, and rename our new sound " - JOE -":

EXERCISE 36

Renaming a sound:

1) Your DX7 should currently have in its edit buffer the modification of "E.PIANO 1" done in Exercises 30 and 31 (Chapter Six). If not, redo these exercises.

2) You should currently be VIEWing the VOICE NAME parameter: bottom line of LCD should read "E.PIANO 1", with the cursor over the letter "E". If not, press edit switch 32 to VIEW this parameter. NOTE that the upper right-hand corner is **blank** as this is obviously not an operator-specific parameter.

3) Press and **hold down** the "edit" mode select switch, thereby activating all other switches for their characters. Keep this switch held down for the remainder of this exercise.

4) Since in the name " - JOE - " the first character is a **space** , press the "function" mode select switch once, thereby inserting a blank character over the letter "E". NOTE that the cursor automatically moves over the next character, which is a " . ".

5) We wish to replace the " . " with a hyphen, so press the "internal" *memory select* switch once to insert a " - " over the second character. NOTE that the cursor again moves on.

6) Insert a blank space into the next character by once again pressing the *spacebar* ("function" mode select switch), as in step 4 above.

7) Continue by typing in the word "JOE" by pressing the following main switches: 20, 25, and 15 (for the characters "J", "O", and "E"). Follow this with another space (function mode switch) and then another hyphen (internal memory select switch).

8) Bottom line of LCD should now read " - JOE -1. The "1" is remaining from the old name. To blank it out, press the space bar one last time. LCD should now read " - JOE - ".

9) EXPERIMENT by renaming the sound " - WOE - ", " - HOE - " or (for you Three Stooges fans) " - MOE - ". You can accomplish this easily by using the "no" button in the data entry section to move the cursor to the left, back over the letter "J", and then simply retyping the new letter. NOTE that this does **not** erase any old characters. The arrow keys located inside the "yes" and "no" buttons simply move the cursor without any erasure. To actually erase a character, you use the space bar (function mode select switch).

10) EXPERIMENT further by renaming the sound anything you like (note that the DX7 does not mind four-letter words, but your relatives might!). After EXPERIMENTing, restore the sound to its new name of " - JOE - " for identification purposes.

Okay, now we've created our sound (by modification) and we've named it. The question is, where do we want to put it? Just knowing that we want to put it in internal memory, or cartridge memory isn't enough - we need to know just which slot to put it in. This isn't just an arbitrary thing, either, since writing data into a memory slot **always** erases whatever was previously in that slot - remember, each slot can only hold **one** voice in it at a time!

We'd therefore like to be able to see what is in our internal or RAM cartridge memory **without losing our current sound**: " - JOE - "? , in order to decide what we're willing to erase in order to store " - JOE - ". At this point on most synthesizers we would be up the proverbial creek with the proverbial paddle. But not on the DX7, thanks to a wonderful little piece of memory called the *edit recall buffer* .

We know that whenever we call up or work on any sound at all in the DX7, our edit buffer presents us with a copy of that sound. The edit buffer is actually a

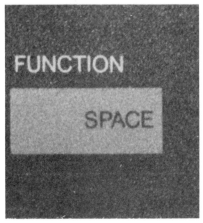

Figure 8-5

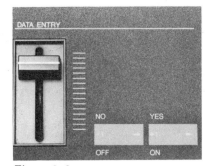

Figure 8-6

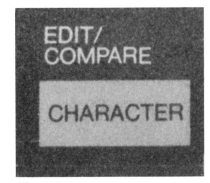

Figure 8-7

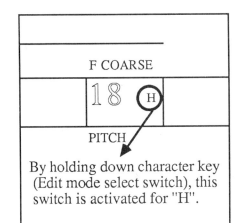

By holding down character key (Edit mode select switch), this switch is activated for "H".

Figure 8-8

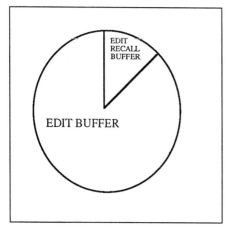

Figure 8-9

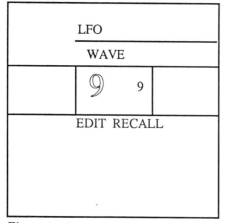

Figure 8-10

two-part memory. It contains within itself a little sub-section called the edit **recall** buffer, and this part of the edit buffer is **protected** by the back-up battery and its contents can easily be recalled from any main mode (**including** play mode!) with a simple function mode command. **(See Figure 8-9.)**

How do we get data into this special part of the edit buffer? No problem, the DX7 does it for us automatically! Take a look at your LED and you will notice a decimal point after the number. You may previously have noticed this and wondered about its significance. The decimal point appears whenever you first make **any kind of change** to a sound (**except** initializing or renaming it). That is to say, it makes its appearance the first time you enter any new data into a sound. In this particular example, we first saw the decimal point in step 8 of Exercise 30, when we first CHANGED the output level of operator 2. Note that simply turning operators ON and OFF, as we did in steps 3 through 7, is not sufficient to make the decimal point appear as these operator status switches are only temporary time saving devices (remember, operator on - off status is not remembered by DX7 when you store sound).

What exactly does this decimal point mean? Well, it's a reminder that a sound has somehow been changed, and it is confirmation from the DX7 that our current work is entered and stored in the edit recall buffer, where it will be protected and can later be recalled. THE EDIT RECALL BUFFER ALWAYS HOLDS THE MOST RECENT EDITING WORK YOU DID. As with all other memory slots, it can only hold **one** set of data at a time. That means that if you then decide to stop altering "E.PIANO 1" and instead INITIALIZE and make a sawtooth wave, all of your modification work in the edit recall buffer would be lost and instead it would contain just the sawtooth wave.

This extra bit of memory is a wonderful safety net, because it **is** protected by the back-up battery. This means that if you sit up till 5 AM constructing the most amazing DX7 sound ever heard and then you turn off the machine without remembering to store the sound, it will still be in there the next day! It also means that at any point, we can **leave** edit mode and return to play mode in order to see just what we've got in memory and decide what we're willing to erase, **without losing our modified sound!!**

Very, very few synthesizers have anything like the edit recall buffer, and that means when working with these instruments, you need to know in advance where you plan on storing a sound before you can even think about creating it! This can be very problematic unless detailed written records of the contents of the synthesizer's memory are kept - a rare occurrence!

We instruct the DX7 to recall the contents of the *edit recall buffer* into the *edit buffer* by pressing function switch 9: **(See Figure 8-10.)**

Entering this command will result in the LCD prompt "EDIT RECALL?". If we answer this question "yes" with the data entry switch, we will be asked "ARE YOU SURE?", as with the voice initialization procedure. Again, this is a drastic change that will normally cause **all** of the edit parameters to be changed (and, again, this is no tragedy since we are **always** in the edit buffer anyway).

With all of this information in hand, we can now Boldly Go Forward, etc., and **leave** edit mode in order to examine the current contents of our internal memory. Let's take a deep breath and do it:

EXERCISE 37

Using the edit recall buffer:

1) Your DX7 should currently have the modification of "E.PIANO 1" in its edit buffer, renamed " - JOE - ". If this is not the case, redo Exercise 36 above.

2) You should currently be in edit mode, viewing the VOICE NAME parameter. If this is not the case, go into edit mode and press main switch 32. Bottom line of LCD should read " - JOE - ". LED should read either "11." or "8." depending upon whether you originally ac-

cessed this sound from ROM 1 or ROM 3.

3) Turn off your DX7! Wait a couple of seconds and then switch it back on again. NOTE that the edit buffer **still** contains the same data as before. PLAY a few notes on the keyboard to confirm that the same sound is also present.

4) Press the internal memory select switch in order to **leave** edit mode and enter play mode.

5) Press the various main switches in order to hear the sounds you currently have stored in your internal memory. Be certain NOT to make any changes to any sounds by reentering edit mode - stay in play mode!

6) Insert a cartridge (RAM or ROM) into the slot and enter cartridge play mode by pressing the cartridge memory select switch.

7) Press the various main switches in order to hear the sounds you currently have stored in the cartridge memory. Once again, do NOT make any changes to any of these sounds!

8) Finally, select any sound from internal or cartridge memory that is significantly dissimilar from " - JOE - ". Play a few notes on the keyboard and LISTEN.

9) Put your DX7 in function mode by pressing the appropriate mode select switch.

10) Press function switch 9 (EDIT RECALL) and answer "yes" to both questions ("EDIT RECALL?" and "ARE YOU SURE?").

11) Play a few notes on the keyboard and LISTEN. " - JOE - " is back!! NOTE that, as in the VOICE INITIALIZATION procedure, the DX7 has automatically taken you out of function mode and returned you to edit mode.

12) Press edit switch 32 to VIEW the VOICE NAME and NOTE that it is still " - JOE - ".

You were asked to actually turn off the power switch on your DX7 in order to illustrate that the contents of the edit recall buffer are in fact protected by the back-up battery, same as the internal memory slots. The data contained in the edit recall buffer will remain there until such time as you reintroduce the decimal point by making another change to another sound, or until the back-up battery fails (normally not for a good five years). That's why you were warned **not** to make any **edit** parameter changes to any sounds you were viewing, since doing so would have automatically erased " - JOE - " from the edit recall buffer and replaced it with your new work.

In any event, you were provided - courtesy of the edit recall buffer - with an opportunity to review the sounds currently in internal memory and to decide which you consider expendable. If you didn't actually take note of which sound you're willing to erase first, go back and redo Exercise 37 and find one. Finding an "available" memory slot is a lot like doing one of those 25-cent puzzles we all grew up with - the ones where you have to move pieces around in the one empty slot in order to finally get them in order: **(See Figure 8-11.)**

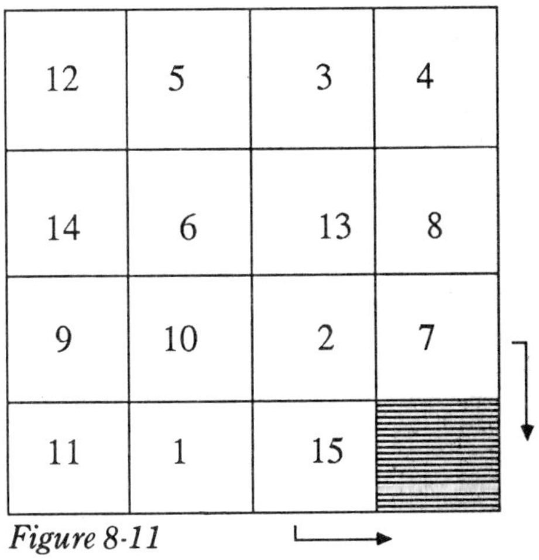

We're going to eventually be storing " - JOE - " in internal memory slot 22 (just an arbitrary number) so if you're fond of what's already in internal slot 22, go back and pick a sound somewhere else to be sacrificed. Let's suppose you decide that the sound in internal slot 3 is particularly loathsome to you. We are still going to put " - JOE - " into slot 22, not slot 3, so we're going to somehow have to **copy** the voice in slot 22 over to slot 3, so it will still exist even after we put " - JOE - " in slot 22. How do we do this?

Fortunately, just as we could move pieces of the plastic puzzle around, the data contained in each memory slot can be easily moved from place to place (the only limitation being, of course, that you cannot **enter** new data into a ROM cartridge). Since I have no way of knowing what you currently have in the internal memory of your DX7, we'll have to run an exercise to free up internal slot 22. This will require that you be prepared to erase **one** of the voices inside your DX7, and you'll have to decide which one yourself. Of course, if your DX7 internal memory currently contains the so-called "MAS-

12	5	3	4
14	6	13	8
9	10	2	7
11	1	15	

Figure 8-11

Figure 8-12

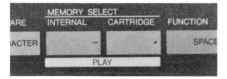

Figure 8-13

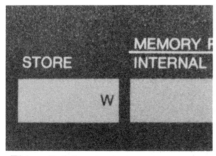

Figure 8-14

TER GROUP", that is, a duplicate of ROM 1 or ROM 3, then you have nothing to worry about. You can erase **anything** and be certain that you already have an uneraseable copy of these sounds in the ROM cartridge itself.

The *store* procedure allows us to actually **write** data to a memory slot, be it internal or RAM cartridge. This procedure is purposely a little complicated in order to prevent you from ever accidentally erasing a sound you wanted to keep. Actually, the description of this procedure is more complicated than the procedure itself, but it's set up so you have to press three different switches **in a particular order** to make it happen. There are, then, the following three stages to the store procedure:

1) Memory protect
2) Memory select
3) Store

Memory protect : Both the internal memory and the RAM cartridge memory are normally protected by circuitry in the DX7. This protection is automatically there whenever you turn on the instrument, and in fact is one of only two features on the DX7 that actually *resets* itself on power-up (the other has to do with MIDI - see Chapter Fourteen for a full explanation). The two center switches in the upper row of the eight special switches (left-hand side of the front panel) are the memory protect switches: **(See Figure 8-12.)**

If we wish to write data into the internal memory, we will need to turn the internal memory protect switch "off" by pressing the "no" button in the data entry section. Remember, the "no" button moonlights as an "off" switch, as the "yes" button doubles as an "on" switch. Press the internal memory select switch and note that it is currently "ON". Use the "no" button to turn the memory protection "OFF". If we wanted to write data in the RAM cartridge memory, we would use the cartridge memory select switch in a similar fashion.

Memory select: The second step in the procedure is to tell our dumb computer exactly **where** we wish to write our data. The DX7 does **not** necessarily assume that since you've turned the internal memory protection off that that is where you wish to send your data. You will still need to tell it the destination by pressing one of the two memory select switches (previously used as play mode select switches): **(See Figure 8-13.)**

Store: Finally, the last step, and also the last of the eight special (left-hand side of the front panel) switches that we have encountered. The pink STORE switch is used to initiate the final storage of data: **(See Figure 8-14.)**

and this switch must be **held down** with one hand while you press the appropriate main switch to tell the DX7 exactly which slot you wish the data entered into.

The prerequisite for this entire procedure is that you must have the data you wish to store **currently in the edit buffer** . This, of course, simply means that you have to have the sound actually active in the machine before you can store it anywhere (that is, if you play a note on the keyboard, you **hear** the sound you wish to store).

Finally, at the conclusion of the storage procedure, you would do well to get in the habit of turning the memory protection back ON. This is your "safety" switch - as long as it's ON, there is **no way** you can accidentally erase a sound in memory. This protection will reset when you turn the machine off but there's no point to actually powering down the DX7 after every storage. Turning the memory protection back on is optional, but it's an option you should use - in the immortal words of Roger Powell, "use it or lose it!"

We're going to take " - JOE - " and store him in internal slot 22. If your DX7 currently has the MASTER GROUP in its internal memory, then you can skip this next exercise, since you are free to erase **any** of the sounds in memory. If, on the other hand, you have a voice in internal slot 22 that you want to keep, you'll have to run this next exercise in order to "free up" internal slot 22.

As mentioned earlier, you will be asked to erase **one** of your sounds in order to do this, and presumably you now know which one is to be sacrificed. If not, go back and redo Exercise 37 again to find an expendable voice.

EXERCISE 38

Moving voice data within the internal memory:

1)   Put your DX7 in internal play mode and CALL UP the voice you have decided to erase. Make a written note of the slot number.
2)   Press main switch 22 in order to CALL UP the voice stored in internal slot 22. This has the action of making a **copy** of that voice in the edit buffer.
3)   Press the internal memory protect switch and use the "no" button to turn the protection OFF.
4)   Press the internal memory select switch. This tells the DX7 that you wish to store data in the internal memory.
5)   Press and HOLD the pink STORE switch.
6)   While continuing to HOLD the STORE button, with your other hand, press the main switch corresponding to the slot number of the sound you wish to ERASE (which you wrote down in step 1 above). WARNING: BE CAREFUL AS THIS STEP WILL IRRETRIEVABLY **ERASE** THAT SOUND. BE **SURE** YOU PRESS THE CORRECT MAIN SWITCH!!
7)   Press the internal memory protect switch once again and use the "yes" button to turn the protection back ON.
8)   Press the internal memory select machine to put your DX7 back in play mode. Press main switch 22 in order to confirm that the voice which was in slot 22 is **still there** . NOTE that copying this data over to another slot does **not** in any way alter the original data. The voice you had in slot 22 is still there, **as well as** in the other slot you moved it to.

What this exercise did, of course, was to duplicate the sound you wanted to keep into somewhere other that slot 22, effectively freeing slot 22 to receive " - JOE - " without erasing a sound you liked. We are finally ready to store " - JOE - " into a memory slot in our DX7.

EXERCISE 39

Recalling and storing a sound:

1)   Press function switch 9 in order to initiate the EDIT RECALL procedure. Answer "yes" to both questions in order to restore " - JOE - " to the edit buffer. Press edit switch 32 in order to view the name and play a few notes on the keyboard to confirm that this sound is indeed present in the edit buffer. If anything other than this comes up, you've probably done something you shouldn't have. DON'T PANIC, just go back and redo Exercises 30 and 31 once again.
2)   Press the internal *memory-protect* switch and use the "no" button to turn the protection OFF.
3)   Press the internal memory-select switch. This tells the DX7 that you are going to store data in the internal memory.
4)   Press and HOLD the pink STORE switch. While doing so, use your other hand to press main switch 22. WARNING: BE SURE TO PRESS SWITCH 22 AND NO OTHER AS THIS WILL IRRETRIEVABLY ERASE A VOICE. We know, in this instance, that erasing the voice in slot 22 is okay to do since we just copied it elsewhere in the memory (Exercise 38 above).
5)   NOTE that bottom line of LCD reads "INT 22 - JOE - ". Play a few notes on the keyboard and LISTEN: " - JOE - " should be what you are hearing.
6)   Press the internal memory protect switch once again and use the "yes" button to turn the protection back ON.

7)   Return the DX7 to play mode and CALL UP any voices, internal or cartridge, that you like. NOTE that when you call up internal voice 22, however, " - JOE - " reappears. At any point, press function switch 9 to redo an EDIT RECALL. Note that " - JOE - " is **still** in the edit recall buffer **as well as** in internal memory slot 22, and will remain there until the next time you make a change to a sound in edit mode.

Voices, of course, can also be stored onto a RAM cartridge. The procedure for storing onto a RAM is almost exactly the same, with two small differences. First of all, the RAM cartridge itself has a memory protection switch built into it. When you plan on storing data on your RAM, you must put this in its OFF position **as well as** turning the DX7 cartridge memory protect switch OFF. Remember to put this switch back ON after storing, in addition to resetting the DX7 cartridge memory protect to ON. Secondly, when data is actually leaving the machine (and entering a cartridge plugged into the slot), the LCD will briefly display the words "UNDER WRITING !". Once the data transfer is complete (and this takes just a split second), the display returns to a normal cartridge play screen (i.e. top line of LCD reads CARTRIDGE VOICE and bottom line tells you which voice). This is important because if you interrupt the flow of data (by taking your finger off the STORE button, for example) **before** the transfer is complete, only **part** of the data may be written and you may not have a complete copy of the voice. ALWAYS keep your fingers on the switches (STORE and the main switch) until the "UNDER WRITING !" display disappears. Let's try it:

EXERCISE 40

Storing data on a RAM cartridge:

1)   Insert a RAM cartridge into the slot and put your DX7 into cartridge play mode. Go through the voices currently stored on your RAM cartridge and find one that you are willing to erase. Make a written note of the slot number. (If you are using a brand-new or nearly-new RAM cartridge, you will find that several or all of the memory slots are already empty. This is indicated by a series of small black boxes in the LCD where normally the voice name would appear. Since there is no data in these slots, they obviously can be overwritten.)

2)   Press the internal play mode select switch and CALL UP internal voice 22 (yes, it's " - JOE - " again. Play a few notes on the keyboard to confirm that this voice is in fact now in the edit buffer.

3)   Remove the RAM cartridge and change its onboard memory protection switch to OFF. Reinsert the RAM cartridge.

4)   Press the cartridge memory protect switch and use the "no" button to turn this protection OFF as well.

5)   Press the cartridge memory select switch. This tells the DX7 that we wish to store data in the cartridge memory.

6)   Press and HOLD the STORE button. While continuing to hold it down, press the main switch corresponding to the cartridge memory slot of the voice you previously decided to erase (in step 1 above). WARNING: THIS WILL IRRETRIVABLY ERASE A SOUND, SO BE SURE YOU SELECT THE RIGHT SLOT NUMBER. OBSERVE the "UNDER WRITING !" prompt in the LCD and be certain to continue HOLDing the STORE button until this prompt disappears.

7)   Press the cartridge memory protect switch again and use the "yes" button to turn this protection back on.

8)   Remove the RAM cartridge and change its onboard memory protection switch back to ON. Reinsert the RAM cartridge.

9)   Put the DX7 in cartridge play mode and go through the voices cur-

rently in your RAM cartridge. NOTE that " - JOE - " is now stored in the slot that you designated.

10)   EXPERIMENT by redoing this exercise, but this time attempt to store " - JOE - " on a ROM cartridge. NOTE that when you reach step 6, the LCD will read "MEMORY PROTECTED" and you cannot continue. The ROM cartridges are **permanently** write-protected and for that reason their contents are uneraseable. 11)   EXPERIMENT further by moving data back and forth between the RAM cartridge and the internal memory. NOTE that, apart from the separate memory protection switch on the RAM and the "UNDER WRITING !" display, both memories work the same way.

At the moment, of course, " - JOE - " is living in three separate places. We've just put him into a RAM cartridge slot; he's still in internal memory slot 22; and he's also still in the edit recall buffer. **(See Figure 8-15.)**

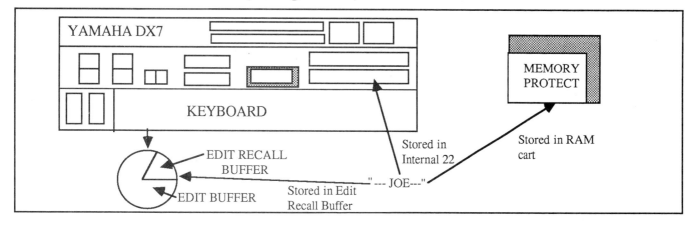

Figure 8-15

Finally, thanks to the edit buffer, we can actually move data **between cartridges!** This involves copying a voice from a cartridge into our edit buffer (done automatically by simply calling up the voice) and then writing it onto another (RAM) cartridge. If it wasn't for the edit buffer, there would be no way of accomplishing this. Let's try taking the original "E.PIANO 1" sound and storing it on our RAM. For the sake of simplicity, we'll overwrite " - JOE- " in the RAM:

EXERCISE 41

Moving voice data from cartridge to cartridge:

1)   Insert either ROM cartridge 1 or ROM cartridge 3 into the slot and set the cartridge to side "A".

2)   Put your DX7 into cartridge play mode and CALL UP either ROM 1A-11 or ROM 3A-8 ("E.PIANO 1"). This voice is now, of course, in your machine's edit buffer.

3)   Remove the ROM cartridge and insert a RAM cartridge with its onboard memory protect switch OFF.

4)   Press the cartridge memory protect switch and use the "no" button to turn the protection OFF.

5)   Press the cartridge memory select switch. This tells the DX7 that we wish to store data in the cartridge memory.

6)   Press and HOLD the STORE button. While continuing to HOLD this switch, press the main switch corresponding to the RAM slot in which you previously stored " - JOE - ". WARNING: THIS WILL IRRETRIEVABLY ERASE A SOUND, SO BE SURE YOU SELECT THE RIGHT SLOT NUMBER. If you can't remember which RAM slot held " - JOE - ", return the DX7 to cartridge play mode, and go through the various slots. When you've located it, make a written note, and go back to step 1 above.

7) Remove the RAM cartridge and turn its onboard memory protect switch back ON, then reinsert it.

8) Press the cartridge memory select switch once again and use the "yes" button to turn the protection back ON.

9) Return the DX7 to cartridge play mode and go through the various voices in your RAM cartridge. NOTE that the slot that previously had " - JOE -" in it now contains "E.PIANO 1". Play a few notes on the keyboard to confirm.

Moving data around within the DX7, then, is a fast and simple procedure once you get used to hitting the switches in precisely the right order. The contents of a memory, be it internal or cartridge, can easily be rearranged to suit your particular needs. For example, if you're doing a live performance with your DX7 and you know the first sound of the night will be ROM 2B-20, and the second sound ROM 1A-6, and the third sound Internal Voice 12, don't give yourself fits by having to continually swap cartridges and memories! Move the first sound into RAM slot 1, the second into RAM slot 2, and the third into RAM slot 3. At the performance, all you'll have to do is insert your RAM cartridge and then just increment the numbers - a much easier way of accomplishing the same thing! Your internal memory can be used the same way.

As you work through this book, or as you work on your own, you should continually **save** your work by **writing** it to memory. Your most recent edit work will, of course, continually be held in the edit recall buffer, but remember, it will only hold the single most recent work. Sometimes you will need to recall data that **wasn't** recently changed. Unless you saved that data, you're out of luck. As every session programmer knows, the saddest words in the world are, "you know, I liked it better the way you had it two minutes ago.". Those two minutes could be an eternity if you've changed several parameters and neglected to **save** as you went along.

Or at least that's the way things used to be B.D. (Before DX7 - the Stone Age of synthesis). Will wonders never cease? The DX7 actually provides us with yet another amazing piece of memory, called *compare mode*, which allows us to do real-time comparisons between a modified sound and the original!

We must enter compare mode from edit mode - that's logical since the only time we would ever actually need to make a comparison is when we are actually making some kind of change to a sound. If you press the edit mode select switch while **already** in edit mode, the DX7 will enter compare mode: the LED will begin blinking (the decimal point will disappear as well), and the original sound will temporarily be restored into the edit buffer. Furthermore, the LCD will actually display the **original data** for whatever parameter you call up! This is extremely useful, particularly if you've made many changes to a sound. Suppose, for example, you've modified twelve different edit parameters and you're satisfied with what you've done. Being naturally inquisitive, you decide to try one last change, perhaps to the output level of a particular operator, and it turns out awful! If you can't remember the original output level setting, you're in a lot of trouble, since it seems as if you've ruined the sound. Going back to play mode and calling up the original sound won't do you any good, since the twelve previous changes you made would be lost.

Here's where compare mode gallops to the rescue. Simply call up the output level parameter, press the edit switch again, and the LCD will actually **show** you what the original output level was for that operator! Returning to edit mode by pressing the edit switch again will allow you to then restore the original data by reentering that same value with the data entry section. Let's try it out:

EXERCISE 42

Compare mode:

1) Put your DX7 in cartridge play mode and select "E.PIANO 1" from either ROM cartridge 1A-11 or ROM cartridge 3A-8.

2) Put your DX7 in edit mode and press main switch 18 (F COARSE parameter).

3) VIEW operator 3 and CHANGE the F COARSE value to 5.00. OBSERVE that a decimal point appears next to the number displayed in the LED, as this is the first actual change we are making to this sound. This modified sound and all future changes we make to this sound is now in the edit recall buffer. VIEW operator 4 and CHANGE its F COARSE value to 12.00, thereby setting up a frequency ratio in this system of 12:5. Play a few notes and LISTEN (AUDIO CUE 42A). NOTE that the sound is more metallic and artificial.

4) VIEW operator 5 and CHANGE the F COARSE value to 3.00. Do the same to operator 6 (thereby setting up a frequency ratio of 3:3, raising the pitch of this system an octave and a musical fifth). Play a few notes and LISTEN (AUDIO CUE 42B). NOTE how this system pitch change has the effect of making the overall sound more nasal.

5) Press edit switch 7 (ALGORITHM SELECT parameter) and CHANGE to algorithm #11. Play a few notes and LISTEN (AUDIO CUE 42C). NOTE that the entire quality of the sound, while interesting and pleasant, has changed from the original, due to the new configuration: **(See Figure 8-16.)**

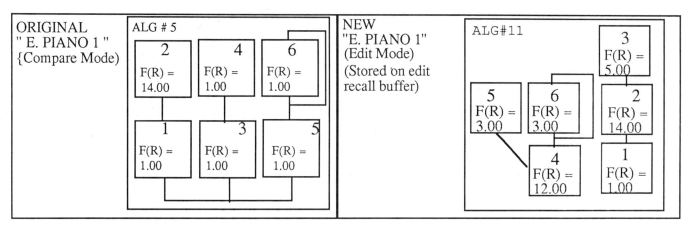

Figure 8-16

6) VIEW the OUTPUT LEVEL parameter (edit switch 27) for operator 6 and CHANGE it to a value of 99. Play a few notes and LISTEN (AUDIO CUE 42D). NOTE the unpleasant, wavering high overtone that appears. This is because of the high degree of feedback in operator 6 and because it is greatly detuned relative to operators 4 and 5.

7) Press the edit mode select switch in order to enter compare mode. NOTE that the LED begins blinking, and the decimal point disappears.

8) Play a few notes on the keyboard and LISTEN (AUDIO CUE 42E). NOTE that we are once again hearing "E.PIANO 1", a far cry from our modified sound!

9) While still in compare mode, OBSERVE the LCD, which is showing you on the bottom line that the original OUTPUT LEVEL of operator 6 **was** a value of 79 and, on the top line, that the original algorithm was #5. Press the edit mode select switch again to return the DX7 to edit mode and note that the LCD once again shows us the modified OUTPUT LEVEL value of 99 (as well as the new algorithm #11, on the top line). Use the data entry slider to CHANGE this back to its original value of 79. Play a few notes on the keyboard and LISTEN (AUDIO CUE 42F). NOTE that we have restored the sound to the point we were at in step 5 above, **not** all the way back to the original "E.PIANO 1" sound.

10) EXPERIMENT by modifying the new sound in various different ways, using compare mode to show you what the original settings

were. If you're happy with the end result, SAVE the sound to a slot in your internal or RAM memory.

The real value of compare mode, then, is that it allows you to travel down the road of modifying a sound and know that you can never stray too far. If you've made fifty changes to a sound and the fifty-first seems to ruin it, compare mode will let you restore that one parameter without having to restore the first fifty.

Notwithstanding all that, there's still a very good argument for **saving** your work periodically. The reason is simple - if you **save** your modification, then you can compare to **that** without having to compare to the original! Also note that INITIALIZING a sound in the edit buffer and then building from that point on gives you no useful basis for comparison: the DX7 will **not** compare to the initialized default settings but instead just to the original sound that was in the memory slot that you happened to be accessing before initialization. If you are creating a sound using the initialization procedure, then, you will want to save an early version of it somewhere in memory so that you're not simply comparing to something totally irrelevant. Finally, remember that you cannot **change** any data while in compare mode: changes to edit parameters can only be made while in edit mode. In other words, if the LED is blinking, the data entry section will be inactive - in order to reactivate it, you will need to return your DX7 back to edit mode by pressing the edit mode select switch again.

Now that we know how to name, store, and compare data, let's return to our discussion of the edit parameters that shape the sound in meaningful ways. Specifically, we'll move on to the devices that change our sounds dynamically over time: the ENVELOPE GENERATORS.

SWITCHES AND CONTROLS COVERED IN CHAPTER EIGHT:

SWITCH	PARAMETER	COMMENTS
Edit 32	Voice Name	CHARACTER key (edit mode select) must be held down while naming sound.
Function 9	Edit Recall	
Memory Protect (Internal)		On or Off.
Memory Protect (Cartridge)	On or Off.	
Store		Must be held down while selecting memory slot.
Compare mode select		Restores original voice and data to edit buffer.

CHAPTER NINE: THE ENVELOPE GENERATORS

In Chapter One we learned that all sound is composed of three parameters: volume, pitch, and timbre, and that typically each of these parameters will **change** during the duration of a sound. We have made great strides in unraveling the mysteries of the DX7 but up until this point every sound we have created on this instrument has been static and unchanging through its duration. We have learned how to specify the volume (carrier output level), pitch (pitch data inputs), and timbre (modulator output level and frequency ratio) of a sound, but not yet how to **vary** them over time.

The first, and most important component on the DX7 which allows us to do this is the *envelope generator*. Remember our diagram of the operator: **(See Figure 9-1.)**

Each operator has its own, totally independent envelope generator (or EG for short), and the actions of one have no bearing at all on the actions of any other. We will be issuing instructions to each EG via the *EG data input*, in order to tell it what to tell its amplifier.

The sole purpose of the EG is to effect an *aperiodic* change of some kind to the sound over time. The word "aperiodic" simply means "non-repetitive", and the way that an envelope generator in any synthesizer works is that you press a key on the keyboard; it does its thing once and **once only**; and that is that, until you press another key on the keyboard. We'll learn in the next chapter that the DX7 also has another device, the LFO, that allows you to effect a *periodic*, or repetitive change over time.

Specifically, what the EG is affecting is *output level*. This is extremely important to understand, so I'll repeat it: THE INDIVIDUAL OPERATOR ENVELOPE GENERATORS CONTROL *OUTPUT LEVEL*. The illustration above clearly shows us that the EG sends its instructions directly to the amplifier, telling it how much signal from the oscillator to pass at various times, and how to vary that level. The end result of these commands will be to change the output level over time.

Cardinal Rules One and Two tell us that if we vary the output level of a carrier, we will get a volume change, and if we vary the output level of a modulator, we will get a timbral change. Keeping these Rules in mind, it's clear that an EG living inside a **carrier** will change the **volume** over time, and that an EG living inside a **modulator** will change the **timbre** over time. Of course, it's the algorithm that decides which operators are used as carriers and which as modulators, so that the EG of, say, operator 2, would alter part of the volume of a sound if algorithm #32 were being used: **(See Figure 9-2.)**

but would affect the timbre of a sound if algorithm #5 were being used: **(See Figure 9-3.)**

Note that neither a carrier EG **nor** a modulator EG can in any way affect the pitch of a sound since neither has any bearing at all on the pitch data inputs: **(See Figure 9-4.)**

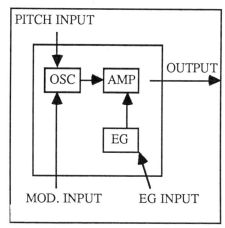

Figure 9-1

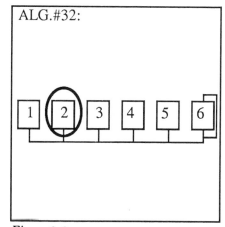

Figure 9-2

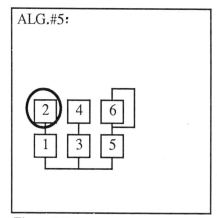

Figure 9-3

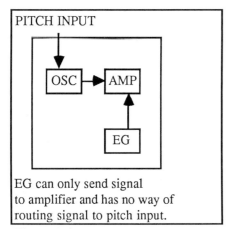

PITCH INPUT

EG can only send signal
to amplifier and has no way of
routing signal to pitch input.

Figure 9-4

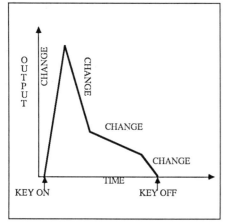

Figure 9-5

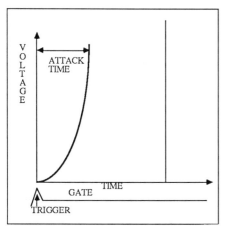

Figure 9-6

We will learn shortly that the DX7 provides us with a separate mechanism for varying the pitch over time. For now, though, let's concentrate on the individual operator EGs, which will aperiodically vary the volume or timbre of a sound over time.

In order to do its thing, the EG needs to know three important facts:

    1) When you strike a key,
    2) When you let go of the key, and
    3) How long you held the key down.

These bits of information are transmitted within the DX7 by means of what in computerese are known as *flags*. When you strike a note on the keyboard (any note at all, it doesn't matter which), the DX7 generates a specific binary number called a "KEY ON" flag. This is simply a "holler" to the six operator EGs, very much like someone waving a flag (hence the term), telling them that a key has been struck. As soon as the EGs receive this flag (a process which takes only a millionth of a second or so), they know to begin going through their paces. When you let go of a key on the keyboard, the DX7 generates another flag, called a "KEY OFF" flag. This lets the six EGs know that it's time to **stop** doing what they're doing and begin to return to their starting points.

Once again, what the EGs do is change the output level over time. We can graph these changes, as follows: **(See Figure 9-5.)**

The microprocessor in the DX7 has a small counter (or "clock") in it that is constantly ticking away, so it is able to calculate the amount of time that transpires between the KEY ON and KEY OFF flags. In this way, the EGs get the answers to the three questions posed above, namely:

    1) When you strike a key - KEY ON flag is generated.
    2) When you let go of the key - KEY OFF flag is generated.
    3) How long you hold the key down - amount of time lapsed between KEY ON and KEY OFF flags.

All of this happens quite automatically within the DX7, and very quickly, so that even if you play a lot of notes very quickly, the EGs will be able to "track" what you're doing. Remember, computers are so incredibly fast that what we as humans consider "very quickly", they consider ultra-slow-motion.

The way that the DX7 envelopes work mechanically is really very straightforward, but this seems to be the area of the instrument that most users have problems with. The first point that must be made is that using the EGs is absolutely mandatory; you can't avoid them, so you might as well master them! The amplifiers inside the operators will not pass any signal at all (which means: no sound!) if they do not receive instructions from the EGs. The second point to be made is that since the EGs take what would otherwise be static sounds and turn them into *dynamic*, "real" sounds, their contribution is essential!

Before we examine the workings of the DX7 envelope generator, (which is, happily or unhappily, one of the most complex you'll find on **any** synthesizer), we might do well to take a little time to discuss the typical analog envelope found on most analog synthesizers, which is quite a bit simpler. The analog envelope is a voltage-producing device which sends a control voltage (or CV for short), typically to a voltage-controlled amplifier (VCA) or voltage-controlled filter (VCF) in order to aperiodically vary the volume or timbre of the analog sound. Again, the envelope needs to know when you strike a note, when you let go of the key, and how long you held the note down. This information in an analog system is generated by means of electrical signals called "triggers" and "gates" (which are the analog equivalents of our KEY ON and KEY OFF flags). A "trigger" is a sharp spike in voltage which is always followed by the steady-state "gate" voltage. When a trigger occurs, the analog envelope generates first a rising voltage, followed by a falling voltage which then drops to a holding level. The amount of time it takes to rise is called the *attack* time: **(See Figure 9-6.)**

and the amount of time it takes to fall is called the *decay* time: **(See Figure 9-7.)**

and the level it drops to and holds at is called the *sustain* level: **(See Figure 9-8.)**

The envelope holds at its sustain level as long as your finger remains on the key and a "gate" voltage is present. When you let go of the key, the gate voltage disappears and the envelope then begins dropping back down to 0 volts. The amount of time it takes to return back to the 0 volt level is called the *release* time: **(See Figure 9-9.)**

These four values: attack, decay, sustain, and release, are all controllable and variable by knobs or sliders on the instrument, and altering their values has the effect of "shaping" the envelope. Thus, we can build, for example, sounds that slowly rise in volume and then rapidly fall to a lower level, or sounds that quickly increase in brightness and then slowly reduce in overtone content. The four controls in the analog envelope are so standardized that the envelopes themselves are often referred to by their initials: ADSR.

While analog envelopes have been sufficient for many years in creating interesting and useful synthesized sounds, the folks at Yamaha, with access to digital circuitry, thought that the time was right to introduce a newer, more powerful set of controls, allowing us far more flexibility in shaping sounds. We will be occasionally drawing comparisons between the DX7 EG and the standard ADSR because synthesists have become very accustomed to thinking of sounds along the lines of "attack", "decay", "sustain", and "release", but bear in mind that the DX7 offers us much more than this in the way of control.

What we are essentially going to do is to draw a road-map for our operator amplifier to follow. This map will tell the amplifier how much signal to pass at various times, and how long to take in making changes between various output levels. We are going to be able to specify four different output levels, labeled L1, L2, L3, and L4; as well as four different rates of movement **between** the four levels. These rates will be labeled R1, R2, R3, and R4. Each Level can have a value of between 0 and 99; 0 being the lowest level (corresponding to an output level of 0) and 99 being the highest level (corresponding to the **maximum set output level**, NOT NECESSARILY AN OUTPUT LEVEL OF 99. This maximum set output level is the value you entered for that particular operator with edit switch 27). Similarly, each Rate can have a value of 0 to 99, with 0 being the **slowest** possible rate of movement and 99 being the **fastest**.

When we generate a KEY ON flag by virtue of having struck a key on the keyboard, all six individual operator envelopes will begin their journey at **Level 4*** (**not** Level 1, as you might expect). Bear in mind, of course, that L4 might be different for each of the six operators as their envelopes are totally independent of one another. Let's just trace the hypothetical EG of one operator, and let's suppose that we specify a Level 4 of 0 (by far the most common Level 4 value) for this operator: **(See Figure 9-10.)**

The first thing the EG will do is to begin moving from its starting point of Level 4 to Level 1, at a rate of speed governed by Rate 1: **(See Figure 9-11.)**

As soon as the EG reaches Level 1, it immediately continues onward to Level 2, at a rate of speed determined by Rate 2: **(See Figure 9-12.)**

And it then continues onward to Level 3, at Rate 3: **(See Figure 9-13.)**

* One anomaly to be aware of here is that the operator EG won't know what you want Level 4 to be until it actually **encounters** it by reaching the end of an envelope cycle: in other words, the first time you strike a key upon calling up a new sound, the microprocessor will ASSUME that Level 4 is 0, even if you have entered in a different value. If you are working polyphonically, you will have to play 16 notes before the voice assignment system is fully aware of the Level 4 value you entered!

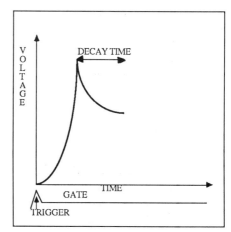

Figure 9-7

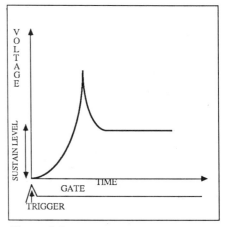

Figure 9-8

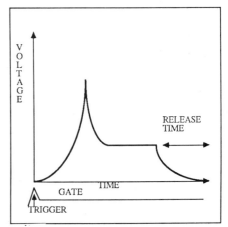

Figure 9-9

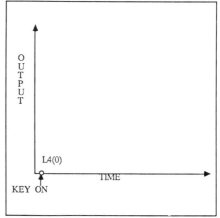

Figure 9-10

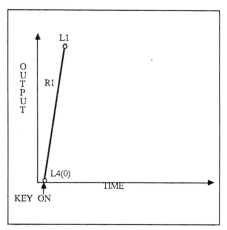

Figure 9-11

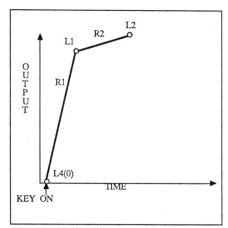

Figure 9-12

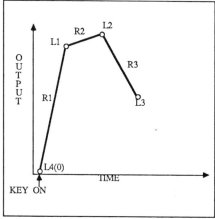

Figure 9-13

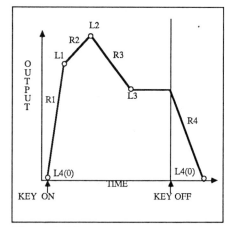

Figure 9-14

Having reached Level 3, the envelope will **hold** at this level, AS LONG AS NO KEY OFF FLAG HAS BEEN DETECTED (in other words, as long as your finger stays on the note). Once a KEY OFF is detected, however, the envelope immediately begins returning to its ending point of Level 4 (which, you may remember, was also its starting point), at a rate of speed determined by Rate 4: **(See Figure 9-14.)**

Our amplifier, then, has undergone up to four separate **changes** in output level, resulting in up to four changes in volume or timbre over the duration of the sound. This is what we mean by a dynamic sound!

Up until this point, of course, we have not heard any dynamics whatsoever in sounds we have created from scratch. How can this be, since we know that the envelopes are always somehow changing the amplifiers? The answer lies in the *default* envelope settings that occur when we initialize.

We can view and/or enter data into an operator's EG data input via edit switches 21 and 22, labeled "EG RATE" and "EG LEVEL", respectively. These two switches are *multi-level*, which means that if you press them repeatedly, you will call up different rates and levels. The switches *cycle*, that is, you will see, in the case of edit switch 21, Rate 1, Rate 2, Rate 3, and Rate 4, followed again by Rate 1 if you press the switch a fifth time. Switch 22 works the same way. When you INITIALIZE your DX7, all six operator envelopes default the same way, that is, they each have the same values for each rate and level. Let's run an exercise to see what those values are:

EXERCISE 43

The default EG values:

1) INITIALIZE your DX7, leave it in algorithm #1 and TURN OFF operators 2 through 6 ("100000").

2) Press edit switch 22 to VIEW the EG level values for operator 1 (NOTE that the upper right-hand corner of the LCD reads "OP 1" since this **is** very much an operator-specific parameter). OBSERVE that bottom line of LCD currently reads "EG LEVEL 1 = 99". This is the *default* for L1, for all operators.

3) Press edit switch 22 a second time to VIEW the default for Level 2. OBSERVE that LCD reads "EG LEVEL 2 = 99". This is the default for L2, for all operators.

4) Press edit switch 22 again to VIEW the default for Level 3. OBSERVE that LCD reads "EG LEVEL 3 = 99". This is the default for L3, for all operators.

5) Press edit switch 22 again to VIEW the default for Level 4. OBSERVE that LCD reads "EG LEVEL 4 = 0". This is the default for L4, for all operators. Press edit switch 22 once again and NOTE that it cycles back to the value for L1.

6) Press edit switch 21 to VIEW the default for R1 for operator 1. OBSERVE that LCD reads "EG RATE 1 = 99". Press edit switch 21 three more times to view the defaults for R2, R3, and R4. OBSERVE that the default for all rates, for operator 1 (and, therefore, all operators) is a value of 99. Press edit switch 21 once again and NOTE that it cycles back to the value for R1.

7) If you are naturally doubtful or from Missouri, turn on any other operator and repeat this Exercise. NOTE that the default values are the same for **all** operators.

Let's graph out what this envelope would look like, again mapping output level over time: **(See Figure 9-15.)**

As you can see, this envelope has a square shape, and so is often referred to as a "square envelope". Very simply, when we press a key, the output level of all six operators rises to maximum (Once again, **not** necessarily 99, but whatever output level you set with edit switch 27. An L1 of 99 simply means "maximum **set** output level". The EG **cannot** under any circumstances increase the value entered with edit switch 27). They then travel instantly (since R2 and R3 are at 99) to the same maximum output level (L3) and hold there until you let go of the key, at which time they instantly (R4) travel back to minimum output level (L4). This is the reason why, although we have been unknowingly using the six operator envelopes, they haven't been doing anything useful, just giving instant on and instant off, for all operators.

One point must be made about rates: they are **rates**, not absolute times. That is, they vary according to the distance they have traverse. Suppose, for example, you were struck with a sudden urge to visit Tibet, right now. There are probably millions of different rates of speeds that you could travel at, since Tibet is so far away (for those of you Tibetans currently reading this, substitute Brooklyn for Tibet). You could fly, you could swim, you could even walk (but only if you wore real good shoes). On the other hand, suppose you were struck with a sudden urge to visit the door of the room you're sitting in right now. Since it's a much shorter distance to that door than it is to Tibet, there are many fewer rates of speed at which you could travel. Finally, let's suppose you were struck with a sudden urge to go nowhere at all. In that case, it doesn't matter what rate you travel at, since you're not going anywhere anyway.

In the square envelope example above, R1 and R4 could be many different values since in the case of R1 we were traveling from an L4 of 0 to an L1 of 99; and in the case of R4 we were traveling from an L3 of 99 to an L4 of 0; in other words, we had the maximum allowable distance to traverse. **(See Figure 9-16.)**

On the other hand, we can see that in this particular envelope both R2 and R3 are meaningless, since in both cases we were going from a level of 99 to a level of 99; in other words, we were going nowhere: **(See Figure 9-17.)**

The speed of the rates, then, are **relative** to the distances they have to travel, and that distance is determined by the relative level settings. However, Yamaha has thrown in a couple of very unusual "rules" for the EGs to follow, rules which unfortunately can in certain circumstances negate this statement. The first of these anomalies is that, when traveling from a lower EG level to a higher EG level, the rate will be faster than the same rate going from higher to lower. In other words, an R2 of 50 will be **faster** if L1 is 0 and L2 is 99 than if L1 were 99 and L2 were 0. This has been done deliberately because naturally occurring "attack" times of sounds are typically faster than "decay" or "release" times. By making this "smart programming" modification to the envelope logic, we can accurately reflect this in our DX7 sounds. The second quirk in our EGs is that they have been programmed by Yamaha to have their rates respond slightly differently when traveling **between** two inaudible level values (that is, level values of about 20 or less: unless you've got your amplifier set ridiculously loud, you can't ever hear levels this low) - even if the level values are precisely the same!

Normally, you would expect a slow (40 or less) rate value to always yield a slow increase or decrease in output level: **(See Figure 9-18.)**

However, when a rate is traveling from an inaudible level of 20 or less to another inaudible level of 20 or less - even if both of those levels are the same - it won't respond in that manner. Instead, that rate will act as a *delay line*, and will simply **delay** the onset of the next movement. The lower this rate value, the longer the delay, so that, for example, setting an EG with an L1 of 0 and an L2 of 3, with an R2 value of 25, will cause the following to occur: **(See Figure 9-19.)**

The actual initial attack time is here determined by **R3**, not R1. The logic behind this is that the EG assumes that if you instruct it to slowly go from an inaudible level (20 or less) to another inaudible level, what you really want from it is a **delay**, since those movements couldn't be heard anyway. This anomaly will allow you to produce sounds which have "delayed attacks", but will work

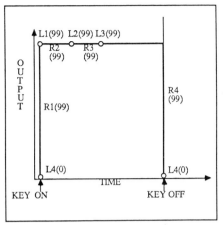

Figure 9-15

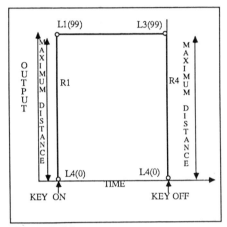

Figure 9-16

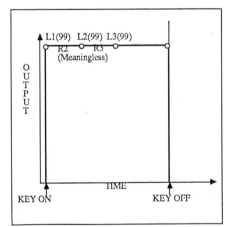

Figure 9-17

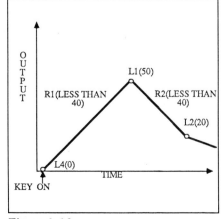

Figure 9-18

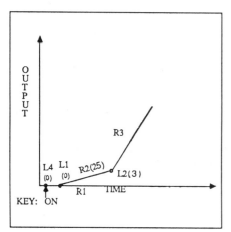

Figure 9-19

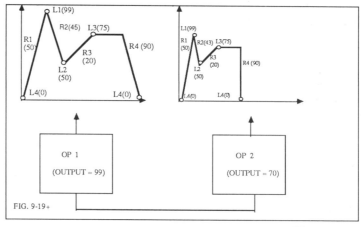

Figure 9-20

only when you set up the EG with two **adjacent** level values of 20 or less. One byproduct of utilizing this is that, when using very slow delay rates (25 or less), the DX7 voice assignment system seems to have trouble following what is happening. If you therefore play a simultaneous chord, the notes will come back in a randomly arpeggiated form, and if you arpeggiate the notes in a particular order, they may well reattack in a different order. This is probably a software "bug", but one which we can occasionally use to great advantage. We'll soon run an Exercise to try out these strange effects (Exercise 48, coming up soon).

Finally, the DX7 software will always automatically scale the EG values as a function of the nominal output level of the operator (as determined by edit switch 27). In other words, if you set up two different operators with different output levels, but precisely the same EG settings, the operator with the **lesser** output will cycle through its EG movements somewhat faster than the operator with the greater output level. This is because all the EG Levels in the operator with the lesser output have been equivalently lowered, therefore reducing the relative distances the Rates in that envelope have to traverse. We'll talk more about this phenomenon, and potential applications, in Chapter Fifteen: **(See Figure 9-20.)**

In any event, no one expects you to memorize all of these complicated movements, and so Yamaha has put a model EG diagram on the front panel of the machine itself: **(See Figure 9-21.)**

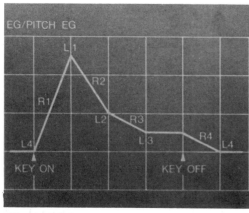

Figure 9-21

This is purely for reference purposes and should not be construed as the only shape available! If, however, we were to actually construct this envelope (and we will, in a moment), we could predict how it would affect the sound we hear, as follows: If this envelope happened to be living inside a carrier, we would hear the volume rapidly (R1) rise to maximum (L1), and then just as rapidly (R2) fall to a point about halfway (L2). It would then somewhat more slowly (R3) drop to near-minimal volume (L3) and continue to hold there as long as our finger remained on the key. Once we let go, the sound would slowly (R4, in this case about the same speed as R3) fade away to no volume (L4). **(See Figure 9-22.)**

If, on the other hand, this envelope were inside a modulator, we would hear a sound whose brightness rapidly (R1) increased to maximum (L1), and then just as rapidly (R2) fell to about halfway (L2 - meaning the overtone content would quantitatively drop to about half what it was). The sound would then somewhat more slowly (R3) decrease in brightness to a near-sine wave (L3) as long as our finger remained on the key. Once we let go, the sound would just as slowly (R4) return to a pure sine wave (L4). **(See Figure 9-23.)**

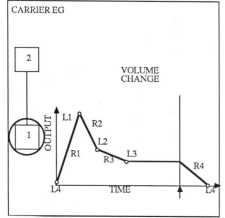

Figure 9-22

Let's run an exercise now to try and actually construct the model envelope drawn on the front panel. We'll do it first for a carrier in a single modulator-carrier system, and then for the modulator:

EXERCISE 44
Generating the model EG:

1) INITIALIZE your DX7 and leave it in algorithm #1. TURN OFF operators 3 through 6 ("110000").

2) Using the system of operators 1 and 2, GENERATE a sawtooth wave by setting the OUTPUT LEVEL value for operator 2 to 99. NOTE that the OUTPUT LEVEL for both operators is now at 99. Play a few notes on the keyboard and LISTEN to confirm (AUDIO CUE 44A).

3) Use the *operator select* switch to VIEW operator 1 (the carrier) and press edit switch 22 (EG LEVEL parameter) four times in order to VIEW the EG L4 value. NOTE that it is at its default of 0 and leave it that way. Press the switch again to VIEW the L1 value, currently at its default of 99. Leave it at that value, and press the switch once again to VIEW the L2 value. CHANGE this value to 75. Press the switch once again to VIEW the L3 value and CHANGE this value to 35.

4) Press edit switch 21 (EG RATE parameter) once to VIEW the value for R1. NOTE that it is currently at its default of 99 and CHANGE it to a new value of 60. Press the switch again to VIEW the value for R2 and CHANGE it to 50. Press the switch again to VIEW the value for R3 and CHANGE it to 30. Press it one last time to VIEW the value for R4 and CHANGE it to a new value of 22. Our newly constructed envelope for operator 1 now looks like this: **(See Figure 9-24.)**

5) Play a note on the keyboard and LISTEN (AUDIO CUE 44B). NOTE that the volume quickly increases and just as quickly decreases to a lower level. This movement is followed by a slower movement (R3) down to an even lower, barely audible level. NOTE that when you let go of the key, the sound slowly dies away (R4) but **that a drastic timbral change occurs**. The final sound you hear is a simple sine wave. That's because the default envelope still in operator 2 has been unaffected by the changes we made to the EG of operator 1. Since R4 for operator 2 is still 99, it drops instantly (an R4 of 99) to an output level of 0 (a L4 of 0) once we let go of the key. If operator 2 sends no output to operator 1, we hear a sine wave only: **(See Figure 9-25.)**

6) As you play various notes, look at the model EG diagram on the front panel. You should be able to hear the volume changes that you are seeing. NOTE that only the volume, not the timbre, and not the pitch, is affected since we are changing only the output level of our carrier. EXPERIMENT by changing the OUTPUT LEVEL parameter for operator 1 to a lesser value. NOTE that while our carrier undergoes virtually the same changes, its overall volume is reduced. (As we mentioned earlier, these changes will now all be a bit faster since the EG Levels have all been automatically rescaled to reflect this output level reduction).

7) Re-INITIALIZE your DX7 and repeat steps 1 through 6 above, this time making the EG changes to your modulator, operator 2. Play a few notes on the keyboard and LISTEN (AUDIO CUE 44C). NOTE that this time the changes you hear are only timbral changes and that the volume and pitch remain constant. NOTE also that the R4 portion of operator 2's EG appears to be non-functioning. Why should this be? Again, changing the values for operator 2's EG in no way affects operator 1. Since R4 for operator 1 is currently at its default value of 99, that means that as soon as you let go of the key, the volume instantly drops to 0 - in other words, you won't hear anything after you take your finger off the key. **(See Figure 9-26.)**

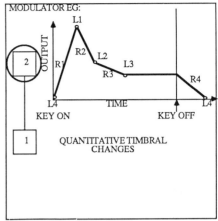

Figure 9-23

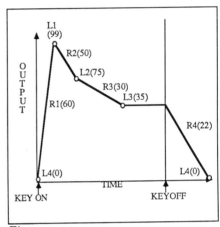

Figure 9-24

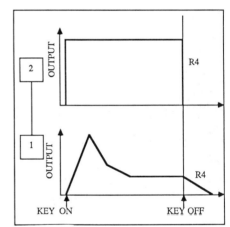

Figure 9-25

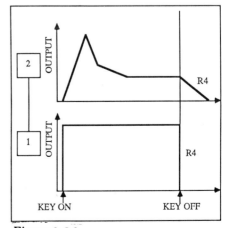

Figure 9-26

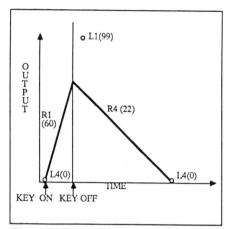

Figure 9-27

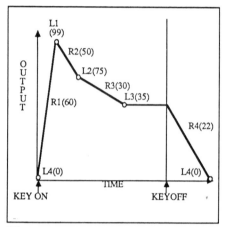

Figure 9-28

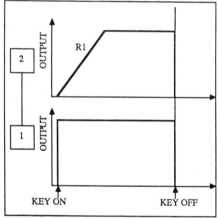

Figure 9-29

8) EXPERIMENT by changing the OUTPUT LEVEL for operator 2 to a lesser value. NOTE that while the EG still undergoes virtually the same changes (just a bit more quickly), the sound never gets as bright as it did before. EXPERIMENT further by changing the *frequency ratio* within the system of operators 1 and 2. NOTE that while the EG still undergoes the same changes, the type of timbre that is generated is qualitatively different.

What happens if you take your finger off the key before the EG has a chance to reach its holding point of L3? The answer is simple - the envelope will **immediately** begin traveling from wherever it happens to be, back to L4, at R4. This means that you can set up sounds which will actually do different things depending upon whether you play notes staccato or legato (sharply or slowly). Try redoing Exercise 44 above, changing the EG values for operator 1 only, and this time try playing some notes on the keyboard quickly instead of holding the key down. If you play it so quickly that, for example, the EG only gets halfway up to L1 before KEY OFF, then this is what would happen: **(See Figure 9-27.)**

and the sound would never actually reach maximum volume. Try it! The DX7 envelopes have been "trained" by Yamaha's software engineers to always automatically return to L4, at R4, **whenever** a KEY OFF flag is detected. This automatic return to the starting point is not unusual, and in fact is found even on analog ADSRs.

Let's take another look at the envelope we just created, because you may be wondering about a few of the values we selected: **(See Figure 9-28.)**

If we are trying to get the speed of the first drop in output level (R2) to be the same speed as the initial rise in output level (R1), why did we pick such different values for R1 and R2? The reason is, again, that these are relative rates and not absolute speeds. R1 has to travel a far greater distance (0 to 99) than R2 (99 to 75); therefore, matching their absolute speeds means entering different relative rates. Similarly, since the angle of R3 and R4 appears to be the same on the model diagram, and since R3 and R4 have to travel different distances (R3 is going from 75 to 35 and R4 from 35 to 0), their values have to be different also.

Another point is that the model diagram appears to show L2 at a little less than half the volume of L1. Why then did we pick an L2 value of 75 instead of, say 45? The answer is that, as we discovered when we first learned about the output level control, all of the controls on the DX7 are **exponential**, and not linear. Therefore, the greatest change is always at the top of the control, and an L2 of 75 will in fact be a little less than half the volume of an L1 of 99. Similarly, we had to set L3 at a value of 35 since the model diagram illustrates a volume only slightly above no volume. Levels much below 35 are virtually inaudible unless you've got your amp up really high, which you wouldn't want to do since it would make the L1 of 99 pretty nearly blow your speakers up! The point is, the DX7 being a digital instrument, we have an enormous amount of *dynamic range* (the difference between the loudest and softest sound) available to us, even though in normal circumstances you won't make use of such a wide range.

Let's continue our examination of the EGs with a step-by-step experimentation with the different levels and rates. We'll start with R1, since that's the first thing that occurs in every instance.

EXERCISE 45

Changing rate 1:

1) INITIALIZE your DX7, leave it in algorithm #1, TURN OFF operators 3 through 6 ("110000"), and, using the system of operators 1 and 2, GENERATE a sawtooth wave.

2) Use the operator select switch to VIEW the EG RATE parameter (edit switch 21) for operator 1. NOTE that all four rates are currently

at their default values of 99. CHANGE the R1 value for operator 1 to a new value of 50 and LISTEN (AUDIO CUE 45A). NOTE that the volume of the sawtooth wave fades in slowly now. CHANGE the R1 value to 25 and LISTEN (AUDIO CUE 45B). NOTE that the volume fades in even more slowly. HOLD DOWN a key on the keyboard, and as the sound reaches its maximum volume, play a new note (while continuing to HOLD DOWN the old one). NOTE that each note fades in independently, as the DX7 treats each new voice as an independent equation (this is due to the DX7's voice assignment system- see Chapter Five for a further explanation). NOTE also that if you release your finger from the key before it reaches maximum volume, the volume instantly returns to 0 since R4 is still at its default of 99.

3) EXPERIMENT with different R1 values for operator 1 and NOTE that smaller values lead to longer fade-in times and that higher values just have the effect of "softening" the attack of the sound.

4) Restore the R1 value for operator 1 back to its default of 99 and use the operator select switch to VIEW this value for operator 2.

5) CHANGE the R1 value for operator 2 to 50, play a few notes and LISTEN (AUDIO CUE 45C). NOTE that, while the volume remains constant, the sound now begins as a pure sine wave and quickly changes into a sawtooth wave as the OUTPUT LEVEL of operator 2 is somewhat rapidly increased by its EG to maximum: **(See Figure 9-29.)**

6) CHANGE the R1 value for operator 2 to 25, play a few notes and LISTEN (AUDIO CUE 45D). NOTE that the sine-wave-to-sawtooth-wave transformation occurs more slowly. EXPERIMENT by altering the R1 value for operators 1 and/or 2 in various ways and LISTEN to the volume and/or timbral changes that result.

Rate 1, then, would at first glance appear to be the same as the "attack" component of the analog ADSR. This is true most of the time, but the additional flexibility of the DX7 envelope over the analog ADSR means that in special circumstances, R1 will **not** be equivalent to "attack". We'll discuss these special circumstances shortly but for now let's continue with an examination of Rate 4.

Rate 4 is the only thing that will occur **after** you let go of a key (following the KEY OFF flag) and so it always emulates the "release" portion of the analog ADSR. Let's run an exercise to experiment with setting different R4 values:

EXERCISE 46

Changing rate 4:

1) INITIALIZE your DX7, leave it in algorithm #1, TURN OFF operators 3 through 6 ("110000"), and, using the system of operators 1 and 2, GENERATE a sawtooth wave.

2) VIEW operator 1 (the carrier in this system), and press edit switch 21 (EG RATE parameter) four times in order to VIEW R4 for operator 1.

3) CHANGE this R4 from its default of 99 to a new value of 30. Play a note on the keyboard, release it and LISTEN (AUDIO CUE 46A). NOTE that while the sound lingers and slowly dies away after you release the key, the sound you hear after KEY OFF is a simple sine wave, not the sawtooth wave we previously generated. The reason for this is that altering R4 for operator 1 in no way affects R4 for operator 2, which is still at its default of 99: **(See Figure 9-30.)**

4) Now let's try the opposite: Restore R4 for operator 1 to its default value of 99. VIEW operator 2 and CHANGE its R4 value to 30. Play a note, release the key and LISTEN (AUDIO CUE 46B). NOTE that you hear nothing at all after releasing the key. Again, this is because altering R4 for operator 2 in no way affects R4 for operator 1. Since operator 1 in this system is acting as the carrier, the total volume

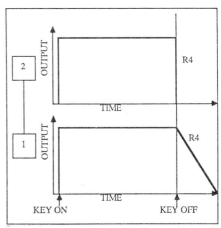

Figure 9-30

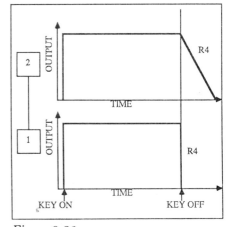

Figure 9-31

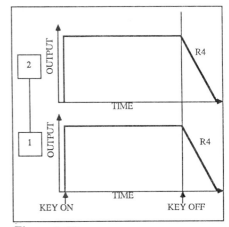

Figure 9-32

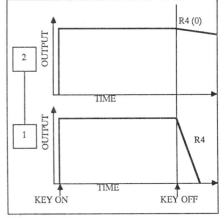

Figure 9-33

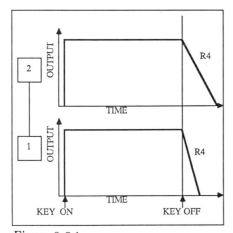

Figure 9-34

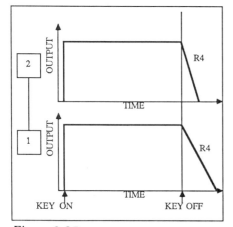

Figure 9-35

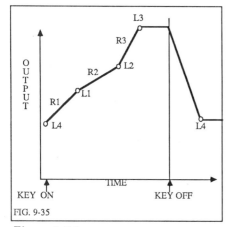

Figure 9-36

shuts down upon KEY OFF. Operator 2 is continuing to fade away after KEY OFF, but you just can't hear it! **(See Figure 9-31.)**

5) Let's try setting R4 for the carrier the same as R4 for the modulator. Leave R4 for operator 2 at its current setting of 30, and CHANGE R4 for operator 1 to the same value of 30. Play a note, release it and LISTEN (AUDIO CUE 46C). NOTE that, as the volume fades away, so too do the overtones, at the same rate of speed. What you are hearing is a sawtooth wave slowly dropping in volume and changing back into a sine wave at the same time. By the time the sound becomes inaudible, the overtones are practically all gone: **(See Figure 9-32.)**

6) What if we simply wanted to hear our sawtooth wave fade away in volume with no timbral change at all? One method would be to set the modulator's R4 to a minimal value (0). This would ensure that as the carrier dies away, the modulator changes minimally. Try it: CHANGE R4 for operator 2 to 0, play a note, release it, and LISTEN (AUDIO CUE 46D): **(See Figure 9-33.)**

7) Another way of accomplishing virtually the same effect would be by setting R4 for the carrier to a significantly higher value than that for R4 of the modulator. This will ensure that the sound will fade away quickly enough that the change in timbre is simply not heard. Try it: Restore R4 for operator 1 to 50, and CHANGE R4 for operator 2 back to 30. Play a note on the keyboard, release it, and LISTEN (AUDIO CUE 46E): **(See Figure 9-34.)**

8) On the other hand, we may want the timbral change to occur more rapidly than the fade in volume. We can accomplish this by setting R4 for the modulator to a higher value than that of the carrier. Try it: CHANGE R4 for operator 2 to 50, and restore R4 for operator 1 back to 30. Play a note on the keyboard and LISTEN (AUDIO CUE 46F): **(See Figure 9-35.)**

9) EXPERIMENT with different R4 values for operator 1 and operator 2. EXPERIMENT further with creating different timbres using the same system of operators 1 and 2. NOTE how different R4 values and offsets between the operators affect the overall sound in different ways.

10) EXPERIMENT by using algorithm #5 to create a sound with three different timbres blended together. Offset the R4 values for the different systems and NOTE how this varies the overall sound. Don't forget that you can adjust the balance between the different timbres by altering the OUTPUT LEVEL for the individual carriers.

While R1 and R4 can both be equivalent to ADSR values, Level 4 is truly unique in that it allows the DX7 user to actually begin and end envelopes at points other that 0 - after all, there is nothing to prevent you from entering a value greater than 0 for L4 (bearing in mind, as mentioned earlier, that the **first time** you call up a voice, the DX7 **assumes** that L4 is 0). If you use an L4 of greater than 0 in a carrier, you will generate a continuous sound, as the volume will never completely die away: **(See Figure 9-36.)**

Of course, having an L4 of greater than 0 can't automatically start the envelope since it still requires a KEY ON flag from the keyboard.

The relative values of L3 and L4 can also be quite important in the carrier. Having an L4 greater than 0 but equal to L3 will result in a sound whose volume is unchanging from its sustain level, even after you let go of the key; in other words, you can dramatically remove your fingers from the keys and no change in the volume will occur! This can fall into the category of Amuse Your Friends At Parties, or it can have a similar effect to that of a "drone" or "hold" switch typically found on the analog synthesizer: **(See Figure 9-37.)**

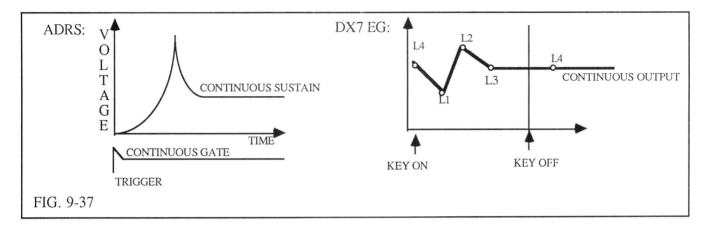

FIG. 9-37

Figure 9-37

In the modulator, having an L4 greater than 0 but equal to L3 will result in a sound which undergoes **no timbral change whatever** after you release the key. This is actually the best method of accomplishing what we tried to do in steps 6 and 7 of the Exercise above.

Synthesizers are often used in recording studios for gating effects - a continuous white noise sound, for example, might be set up and a device called a *noise gate* would control the output signal and perhaps only allow it to pass when triggered by a snare drum. This is a typical application, but by no means the only one. On the analog synthesizer, a commonly found "drone" switch allows the sound to be continuously heard without you having to literally keep your finger on the key continuously, or by (more commonly) holding the key down with a piece of tape. DX7s are usually found in recording studios with remnants of pieces of tape stuck to their keys as there is no obvious DX7 switch labeled "drone". L4, as we have seen, can accomplish precisely the same effect.

On the other hand, L4 in our carrier, while still being greater than 0, can be either greater or less than the value for L3. An L4 value greater than L3 will result in a sound that actually gets louder after you let go of the key: **(See Figure 9-38.)**

In our modulator, this would result in a sound that gets brighter after you let go of the key. Of course, the speed with which either change occurs will be determined by R4. Similarly, an L4 in our carrier which is less than L3, but still greater than 0, will result in a sound which is continuous but at a lower volume level: **(See Figure 9-39.)**

Again, the speed with which the volume will drop is determined by R4. Remember that the aural effect caused by altering L4 for a **modulator** will always largely depend on the L4 value for the carrier, since the carrier controls the overall volume. Let's run an Exercise to try some of these changes:

EXERCISE 47

Changing level 4 :

    1) INITIALIZE your DX7, leave it in algorithm #1, TURN OFF operators 3 through 6 ("110000"), and, using the system of operators 1 and 2, GENERATE a sawtooth wave.
    2) Press edit switch 22 (EG LEVEL parameter) and VIEW operator 1. CHANGE the value for L4 from its default of 0 to a new value of 99. NOTE that L3 (as well as L1 and L2) are also at 99 (their defaults).
    3) Play a note on the keyboard, release the key and LISTEN (AUDIO CUE 47A). NOTE that you hear a continuous **sine wave** when you let go of the key. This is because altering L4 for operator 1 in no way alters L4 for operator 2, which is still at its default of 0.

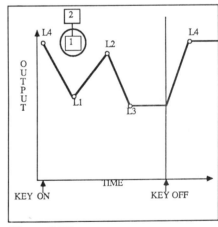

Figure 9-38

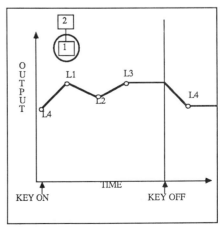

Figure 9-39

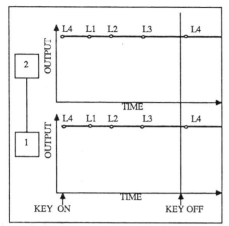

Figure 9-40

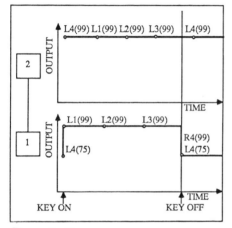

Figure 9-41

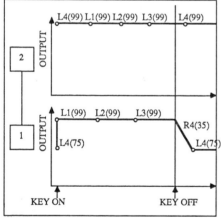

Figure 9-42

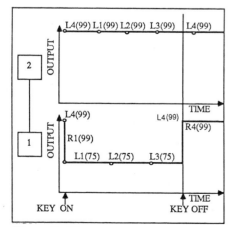

Figure 9-43

4) Restore the L4 value for operator 1 back to its default of 0. NOTE that this does not result in any change to the sound, which should still be droning away! This is because the Levels in the EG are **output levels**, and output level never changes in real time! In order to enter this new value of 0 into the audio signal, we will have to retrigger the keyboard 16 times. This is because of the voice assignment system used by the DX7 (refer to Chapter Five for a full explanation of this). If, for example, the last note you played happened to be voice #4 (and you will have no way of knowing which voice it actually was), the computer will have to recycle through voices 5, 6, 7, 8, 9, 10, 11, 12, 13, 14, 15, 16, 1, 2, and 3 before it finally comes back to voice #4 and has the opportunity to insert the new L4 value into it. Try it: tap the keyboard 16 discrete times and NOTE that the 16th time, the note you are hearing finally drops out! (AUDIO CUE 47B) Of course, you could accomplish the same thing more quickly by playing a fast arpeggio or simply doing a Jerry Lee Lewis-type slide on the keyboard. Alternatively, you can stop the sound by returning to any other mode on the machine (*play mode*, *function mode*, or, best of all, *compare mode*).

5) Now that we finally got the DX7 to shut up, let's try getting a continuous sawtooth wave. CHANGE the L4 value for both operator 1 and operator 2 to 99. Play a note, release the key, and LISTEN (AUDIO CUE 47C). This EG graph illustrates why we are now hearing a continuous sawtooth wave: **(See Figure 9-40.)**

6) Restore L4 for operator 1 only to a new value of 0 and remember to retrigger the keyboard 16 times in order to actually stop the sound. Now CHANGE L4 for operator 1 only to a new value of 75. Play a note on the keyboard, release it, and LISTEN (AUDIO CUE 47D). You should be hearing a continuous sawtooth wave, but at a lower level: **(See Figure 9-41.)**

NOTE that the volume dropped instantly to this lower level immediately upon KEY OFF. This is because R4 is still at its default of 99. CHANGE R4 for operator 1 to a new value of 35 and LISTEN (AUDIO CUE 47E). NOTE that the volume slowly dies down to its lower, continuous level: **(See Figure 9-42.)**

EXPERIMENT with different L4 and R4 values for operator 1.

7) Let's now construct a sawtooth wave that actually gets louder when we release the key. Restore the L4 and R4 values for operator 1 back to their default settings and retrigger the keyboard 16 times in order to stop the continuous sound. Leave L4 for operator 2 at its current value of 99. CHANGE L1, L2, and L3 for operator 1 to values of 75 for each, and CHANGE L4 for operator 1 to a new value of 99. Play a note on the keyboard, release it, and LISTEN (AUDIO CUE 47F). The envelopes now look like this: **(See Figure 9-43.)**

NOTE that the volume **instantly** increases upon KEY OFF. That is because R4 of operator 1 is currently at its default of 99. CHANGE operator 1's R4 to a new value of 35 and LISTEN (AUDIO CUE 47G). NOTE that the sound now **slowly** increases in volume: **(See Figure 9-44.)**

EXPERIMENT with different L4 and R4 values for operator 1.

8) Restore all EG values for both operators 1 and 2 to their default settings (refer to Exercise 43, above, or Appendix B for these values). CHANGE L4 for both operators 1 and 2 to a new value of 99, but CHANGE L1, L2, and L3 for operator 2 only to 30. Play a note on the keyboard, hold it down a moment, release it, and LISTEN (AUDIO CUE 47H). NOTE that after KEY OFF, the sound instantly gets brighter, because our envelopes look like this: **(See Figure 9-45.)**

Of course, changing R4 to a lesser value will cause the sound to slowly get brighter after KEY OFF. Try it: CHANGE R4 for operator 2 to a new value of 35. Play a note on the keyboard, hold it down a moment, release it, and LISTEN (AUDIO CUE 47I). The envelope now looks like this: **(See Figure 9-46.)**

EXPERIMENT further with different R4, and different Level values for operator 2.

Obviously, there is a degree of interaction between the EG of our carrier and that of our modulator even though the two are quite independent of one another. Since the carrier EG is actually controlling the amount of total sound we hear, it will tend to sometimes appear to be more in control. Steps 2 and 3 above illustrate that best. But we can also use that interaction to great advantage in setting up complex movements in DX7 sounds which couldn't possibly exist on any other synthesizer.

Consider ROM 1A-19 (or ROM 3A-2, if you have an American DX7), the "HARPSICHORD 1" preset. In perfect mimicry of an acoustic harpsichord, when you play a note, you actually hear the "hammer" spring back! Call up the sound, try it, and take note of the additional "after-sound" you hear after releasing the key. Any time you hear anything happen after releasing a key, you know that R4 and L4 in the EGs are at play. Put your DX7 into edit mode so we can examine this sound and see exactly how this effect is conjured up. The first thing you will notice is that "HARPSICHORD 1" was constructed with algorithm #5, an old favorite: **(See Figure 9-47.)**

Operators 1, 3, and 5 are our carriers in this configuration, and they all have precisely the same EG values, as follows: **(See Figure 9-48.)**

You may view these values by simply calling up any of the carriers and viewing the EG rate and level values. Turn off their modulators (operators 2, 4, and 6) and just listen to the carriers alone. The sound you hear is nothing at all like a harpsichord, since we are only hearing sine waves, and a harpsichord sound obviously has many overtones.

Turn off the three carriers and turn on the three modulators (operators 2, 4, and 6). If you play a note on the keyboard, you won't hear anything, but that doesn't prevent us from looking at the data contained within these operators. Somewhat surprisingly, each of the three modulators also has precisely the same EG values, as follows: **(See Figure 9-49.)**

Again, you can confirm these by simply viewing the EG rate and level parameters and cycling through them. Let's overlay the carrier EG with the modulator EG, as follows: **(See Figure 9-50.)**

Turn off everything except one system - operators 3 and 4, for example. Play a note, release it, and listen as you look at this diagram. Can you "see" what you're "hearing"?* You should be able to: the carrier dies away at a moderate rate of speed (an R4 value of 47) to an L4 of 0 - in other words, the sound disappears. On the other hand, the modulator **instantly** (an R4 of 99) rises in output level to nearly maximum (an L4 of 98) **even as the sound is dying away**! That's why the **brightness** of the sound increases greatly after KEY OFF.

The reason that algorithm #5 was selected for this sound is because even though each system has the same EG values for its modulator and its carrier, each system is generating a qualitatively different set of overtones by virtue of the different frequency ratios for each: **(See Figure 9-51.)**

Also note that a small amount of feedback (a value of 1) has been added to operator 6. Try increasing this value and listen to the added harshness and distortion this adds to the overall sound. Note that, even at the maximum feedback value of 7, the sound doesn't break into white noise. This is because the

* You'll be able to hear these EG changes more clearly for low notes than for high ones. The reason for this? Another edit parameter called *keyboard rate scaling*, which will be discussed in detail shortly.

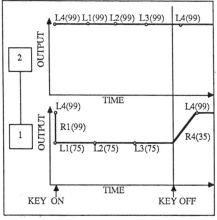

Figure 9-44

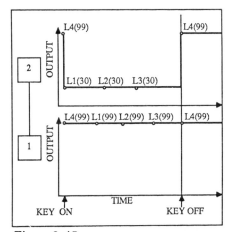

Figure 9-45

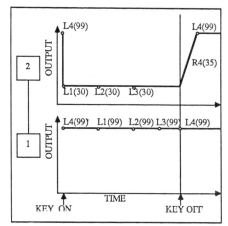

Figure 9-46

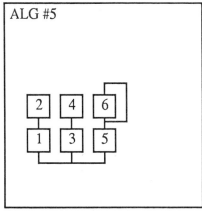

Figure 9-47

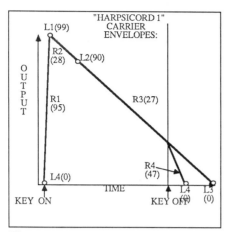

Figure 9-48

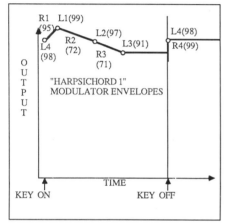

Figure 9-49

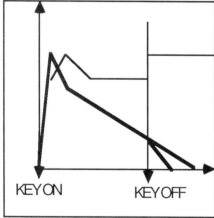

Figure 9-50

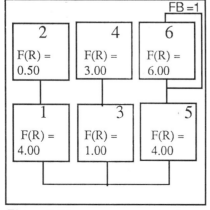

Figure 9-51

feedback loop in this algorithm is altering operator 6 only, and the output level of operator 6 has been set at the moderate value of 87, giving it relatively little effect on the carrier, operator 5.

Level 4, then, is a powerful tool that allows us to change the sound in various different ways after we let go of the key we are playing, and this is one of many DX7 envelope effects that normally cannot be duplicated on other synthesizers.

Let's quickly summarize the comparisons we have discovered between the DX7 envelope and the standard analog ADSR:

1) DX7 Rate 1 = Analog attack time (usually),
2) DX7 Rate 4 = Analog release time, and
3) DX7 Level 3 = Analog sustain level.

The only one of the analog parameters for which we have no DX7 EG equivalent is the **decay** time. Instead, we can initiate a complicated series of movements by using R2, L2, and R3. It is in this section that we can generate very complex movements within a sound **while still holding down a key on the keyboard**, but before the envelope ever reaches and holds at its **sustain** level (L3). This will allow us to create aural effects quite unlike those typically produced by analog synthesizers.

For example, there's nothing that says that L2 cannot have a value of 0. If we leave the other EG levels at their default values and just make this one change, we'll have an envelope that looks like this: **(See Figure 9-52.)**

If this EG happened to be living inside a carrier, we would actually hear a sound with **two** separate attacks! On the other hand, if we set L1 and L2 both to 0 (or, for that matter, any value less than 20) but leave all the other EG values at their defaults, we have learned that R2 will **not** operate in the usual manner but will in fact allow us to set up a **delayed** attack: **(See Figure 9-53.)**

Let's run an Exercise to try out both of these unusual effects:

Exercise 48

Creating a delayed attack and a double attack:

1) INITIALIZE your DX7, leave it in algorithm #1, TURN OFF operators 3 through 6 ("110000"), and, using the system of operators 1 and 2, GENERATE a sawtooth wave.
2) Press edit switch 22 (EG LEVEL parameter) and VIEW L1 for operator 1. Use the *data entry* slider to CHANGE this to a new value of 0. Press this switch a second time in order to VIEW the L2 value for operator 1, and CHANGE this also to a value of 0.
3) Press edit switch 21 (EG RATE parameter) and VIEW R2 for operator 1. CHANGE it to a new value of 40. Play a note on the keyboard and LISTEN. NOTE that the initial attack is now **delayed**, but that the sound attacks **instantly** when it does come in. This is because R3 is currently at its default value of 99: **(See Figure 9-54.)**

Changing R3 to a lesser value will cause the same delayed attack (the amount of delay being determined by R2), but a **slow** delayed attack. Press edit switch 21 and CHANGE R3 for operator 1 to a new value of 30. Play a note on the keyboard and LISTEN (AUDIO CUE 48A). NOTE that the attack is delayed, but is now a slow fade-in. Restore R3 for operator 1 back to its default value of 99. **(See Figure 9-54.)**

4) CHANGE the R2 value for operator 1 to 20. Play a key and LISTEN. NOTE that our sound is now delayed for a longer period of time, but that the initial attack is still instantaneous. Arpeggiate several notes, hold them down and LISTEN (AUDIO CUE 48B). NOTE that they re-arpeggiate in the same order, but that all their appearances are delayed. Now CHANGE the R2 value for operator 1 to

15. Arpeggiate several notes, hold them down, and LISTEN (be patient, as this will take 20 seconds or so to attack!) (AUDIO CUE 48C). NOTE that the original timing of your arpeggiation is somewhat altered, as the voice assignment operation of the DX7 becomes somewhat "confused" (because the Rate value was less than 25). Finally, play a chord, hold it down and LISTEN (AUDIO CUE 48D). NOTE that some of the notes reappear at slightly different times, again due to this "confusion".

5) Press edit switch 22 (EG LEVEL parameter) and restore both L1 and L2 for operator 1 back to their default values of 99. Press edit switch 21 (EG RATE parameter) and restore R2 for operator 1 back to its default value of 99. You should now be back to your default square envelope.

6) CHANGE L2 for operator 1 to a new value of 0. This causes an "M"-shaped envelope, like this: **(See Figure 9-55.)**

to be generated. We may now expect to hear a sound with **two** separate attacks. .IN 10

7) Play a note and LISTEN (AUDIO CUE 48E). NOTE that we do **not** hear what we predicted - the sound is exactly the same as it was before we changed the L2 value. Why is this? Because the **rates** are still all at their default values of 99. Even though our sound is changing levels twice, from 0 to 99 back to 0, back to 99 again, it is making these changes so rapidly that we, as mere humans, cannot possibly hear it: **(See Figure 9-56.)**

In order to hear these changes, we will have to slow down either R2 or R3, or both. R2 is the rate of speed our envelope takes to get from its first peak of 99 (L1) to its first drop to 0 (L2). Slowing this rate down, then, will have the audible effect of allowing us to hear a sawtooth wave with a rapid initial attack (R1 = 99) which then slowly fades away before again rapidly **re-attacking: (See Figure 9-57.)**

8) Press edit switch 21 (EG RATE parameter) and VIEW the R2 value for operator 1. CHANGE this to a new value of 45. Play a note on the keyboard and LISTEN (AUDIO CUE 48F). NOTE that we now hear the double attack, as predicted.

9) Arpeggiate several notes on the keyboard and continue to hold the keys down and LISTEN (AUDIO CUE 48G). NOTE that the note reattack in the same order. The voice assignment system treats each note and each EG independently. EXPERIMENT with greater or lesser R2 values for operator 1 and NOTE how they change the overall sound. If you have time to kill, try entering the minimum value of "0" and NOTE that our sound now takes over **five full minutes** to die away completely and reattack! Because we are traveling from one extreme level (99) to the other (0), this is the longest rate of change available on the DX7 - far longer than EG values available on most other synthesizers! Restore the R2 value for operator 1 back to 45. **(See Figure 9-58.)**

10) R3 is the amount of time it takes for the sound to reattack. Because R3 is currently at its default of 99, the sound is now reattacking instantly. Let's try lowering this value: Press edit switch 21 once again in order to VIEW R3 for operator 1. CHANGE this to a new value of 45, play a note on the keyboard and LISTEN (AUDIO CUE 48H). NOTE that the sound now takes virtually as long to reattack as it did to die away in the first place.* CHANGE this value further to 30, arpeggiate a few notes on the keyboard, hold the keys down and LIS-

---

* The reason it won't take **exactly** as long is because, remember, "attack" rates in the DX7 EG are preset to always be slightly **faster** than equivalent "decay" rates.

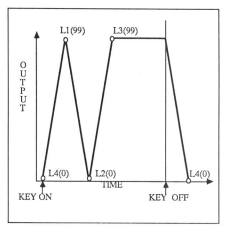

Figure 9-52

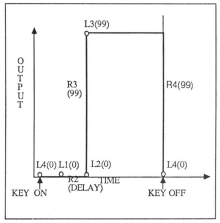

Figure 9-53

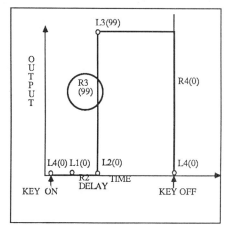

Figure 9-54

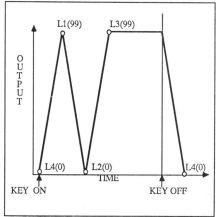

Figure 9-55

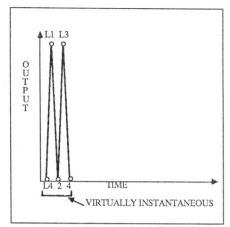

Figure 9-56

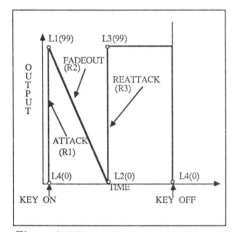

Figure 9-57

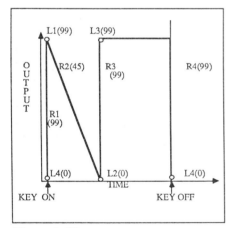

Figure 9-58

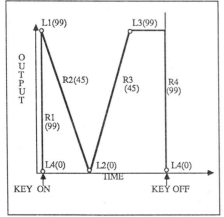

Figure 9-59

TEN (AUDIO CUE 48I). NOTE that we can create some interesting "fade-in" affects with low R3 values. Restore R3 for operator 1 back to 45. **(See Figure 9-59.)**

11) R1, in this instance, is acting as the initial attack time. Because R1 for operator 1 is currently at its default of 99, the sound initially attacks instantaneously. Press edit switch 21 two more times to VIEW R1 for operator 1 and CHANGE its value to 45. Play a note on the keyboard and LISTEN (AUDIO CUE 48J). NOTE that the sawtooth wave now takes just as long in its first attack as it does in its second: **(See Figure 9-60.)**

EXPERIMENT by entering new values for R1, R2, and R3 and NOTE the changes that are made to the overall sound.

12) Restore R1, R2, and R3 to values of 45, and leave your DX7 set up this way for the next Exercise, which follows shortly.

Because all of the changes we made in the preceding exercise were to our carrier, we heard, of course, only volume changes. If, on the other hand, the same changes were made to our modulator, we would hear a similar kind of timbral change, which in this particular instance could be described as a double "wah-wah" effect: **(See Figure 9-61.)**

As the output level for the modulator increases from L4 (0) to L1 (99), the sound gets brighter. As it then decreases from L1 (99) to L2 (0), the sound gets duller. It then returns back to L3 (99) for a brighter effect again, hence the double "wah".

We can do this, or we can take things a step further by having **both** the modulator and carrier envelopes **the same**. This, of course, would result in a sound that gets louder and brighter, all at the same time, followed by a similar decrease in both volume and overtones, followed by yet another increase.

There are two ways to get both operator's EGs set up with the same data: the hard way and the easy way. The hard way is to do it manually. In other words, you'd VIEW R1 for operator 1, make a mental (or written) note of the value, then VIEW R1 for operator 2 and enter that value. You'd then have to go back and do the same for R2, for R3, for R4, and for all the levels. In the best instance, this is a time-consuming and conceivably problematic way of doing things. In the worst instance, of course, it can be the proverbial pain in the proverbial you-know-what, especially if you're in a studio costing hundreds of dollars per hour with an unfriendly producer glaring at you.

But there **will** be many instances when you will want to have more than one operator set up with a similar envelope. For that reason, Yamaha has provided us with the easy way, better known as the *EG copy* function.

This is one of the few controls on the DX7 which is unlabeled. It is important to realize that you can only access this control from edit mode. We give the DX7 the EG copy command by pressing and HOLDING DOWN the pink store button, while in edit mode. Let's try it. Your DX7 should still be set from the last step of Exercise 48, and you should currently be viewing operator 1 (the carrier). Press and HOLD DOWN the pink store button. Your LCD should look like this: **(See Figure 9-62.)**

The "?" is a prompt from the microprocessor, and it is simply asking you where you want to copy this EG data to. You can instruct it to copy this data to any of the remaining operators by now pressing any of the first six *operator ON-OFF* switches, edit switches 1 through 6. NOTE that these switches are also labeled "EG COPY". It is important to realize that this control copies EG data **only**. No other information about the operator (such as output level or pitch data) is copied.

The reason why, in this particular instance, our LCD said "from OP1 to OP?" was because we had been VIEWING operator 1. If we had, for example, been viewing operator 5 instead, it would have said "from OP5 to OP?". You therefore must always first VIEW the operator whose envelope you wish to copy. Copying the EG data in no way affects the original (source) operator; it still will retain its same values. Let's run a short Exercise to try it:

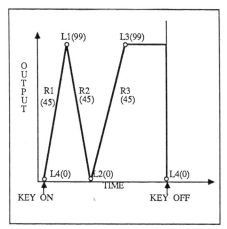

Figure 9-60

EXERCISE 49

EG copy:

1) Your DX7 should currently be set up as per the last instruction in step 8 of Exercise 48. If it is not, re-INITIALIZE your DX7, leave it in algorithm #1, TURN OFF operators 3 through 6, GENERATE a saw-tooth wave using the system of operators 1 and 2, and enter the following values into the EG of operator 1 **only**: R1 = 45; R2 = 45; R3 = 45; and L2 = 0. Leave all other EG values at their default settings and **don't** change any EG defaults for operator 2. Make sure you are currently VIEWing operator 1.

2) Press and HOLD DOWN the pink *store* switch. NOTE that the LCD reads: **(See Figure 9-63.)**

3) While still HOLDING DOWN the store switch, with your other hand, press edit switch 2 . NOTE that LCD now reads: **(See Figure 9-64.)**

4) Release both switches. The EG data from operator 1 has now been copied exactly into the EG of operator 2. Play a note and LISTEN (AUDIO CUE 49A). Use the operator select switch to VIEW operator 2. Press edit switch 21 in order to VIEW the R1, R2, and R3 values for operator 2, and NOTE that they are now the same as those for operator 1 (they should all be = 45). Press edit switch 22 twice in order to VIEW the L2 value for operator 2, and NOTE that it has now also changed to 0.

5) Leave your DX7 set up this way for the next Exercise.

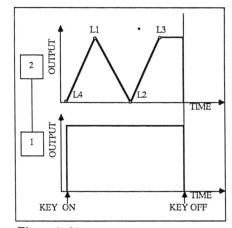

Figure 9-61

Of course, we have used the store button before. In the last Chapter, we saw how the store button initiates the storage of voice data into any memory slot. However, remember that we alway **preceded** pressing the store button in that instance with one of the *memory select* switches. Here we are not: instead, we press the store button directly from edit mode. This is how the DX7 "knows" that we wish to use this switch as an EG COPY switch, and not a STORE switch. The EG COPY function is of enormous value because often, when creating sounds using multi-system algorithms, you will want to set up systems with similar envelopes to one another. Note that I said "similar", and **not** "the same". This is because the randomness in naturally occurring sounds dictates that they will never undergo precisely the same volume and timbral changes at precisely the same time. For that reason, it will probably always be a good idea to **offset** any similar envelopes to one another so you avoid having any two operators with precisely the same EG settings. Doing so would introduce an artificial quality to the sound and would reinforce the fact that we are here digitally **simulating** sounds. While this may be occasionally desirable, most of the time it will be preferable to disguise the DX7's digital precision.

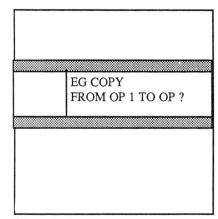

Figure 9-62

We still have quite a bit more to explore with envelopes, but let's digress just a bit while we have this characteristic "double-attack" sound set up in our machine, and examine a related edit parameter called *EG rate* scaling.

The purpose of this control is to allow us to shape - or "scale" - the timing of our envelopes according to which note we actually play on the keyboard. It is therefore a geographic control, but one which does **not** affect output level in any way. Instead, it affects the **speed** - or "rate" - of movement of the operator EGs. Hence the term "EG rate scaling".

If you play the lowest note of an acoustic piano and hold it down, the note will linger on for a good minute or two before it finally dies away. On the other hand, if you play and hold down the **highest** note, it will rapidly disappear.

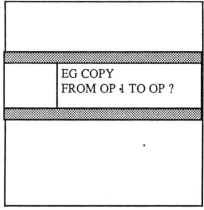

Figure 9-63

This is because of physical considerations within the piano - most significantly, the length of the strings. Because the low note has a much longer string, it can vibrate back and forth for a greater period of time before it loses energy and dies away. The high note, with its shorter string, cannot sustain its vibrations as long: **(See Figure 9-65.)**

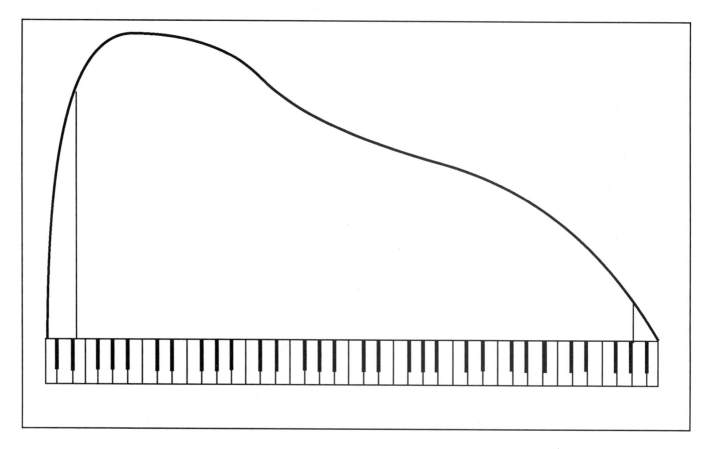

Figure 9-65

We, of course, don't have strings or moving parts of any kind in our DX7, but we can digitally simulate this effect with the EG rate scaling control. Specifically, what this control will do is to **increase** the four EG rates for each operator, as you play higher notes on the keyboard. This will naturally cause the envelopes to cycle through much faster than those being triggered from the action of lower notes being played. The result, of course, is very similar to that which naturally occurs in most acoustic instruments, particularly stringed ones, where, as we have seen, lower notes sustain much longer than higher notes.

The edit switch that we use to access this control is main switch 26, and interestingly, this is an **operator-specific** parameter! This will allow the DX7 user to set up sounds which scale in different ways for different operators within the overall sound, allowing you to construct unusual (but acoustically unrealistic) effects, as well as the accurate acoustic simulation we just described.

The range of this switch is 0 to 7, allowing us to choose from among eight different rate scaling amounts. A value of 0, naturally, will call for **no** rate scaling effects, and a value of 7 will call for the maximum effect. The default value for this parameter, as you may have guessed, is 0 for all six operators, indicating that when you initialize, no Keyboard Rate Scaling will be occurring.

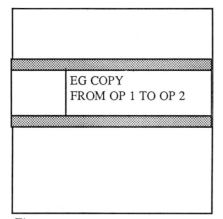

EG COPY
FROM OP 1 TO OP 2

Figure 9-64

EXERCISE 50

Keyboard rate scaling:

1) Your DX7 should still be set up as at the conclusion of Exercise 49. If it is, skip ahead to the next step. If not, re-INITIALIZE it, leave it in algorithm #1, TURN OFF operators 3 through 6 ("110000"), GENERATE a sawtooth wave with the system of operators 1 and 2, and enter the following values into the EG of operator 1: R1 = 45; R2 = 45; R3 = 45; and L2 = 0. Leave all other EG values at their defaults. Use the EG copy control (the STORE button) to **copy** this EG data into operator 2.

2) Press edit switch 26 to VIEW the *keyboard rate scaling* parameter. Use the *operator select* switch to VIEW the value for operator 1. OBSERVE that the current value is at its default of 0. Use the data entry slider to CHANGE this to the maximum value of 7. VIEW operator 2 and CHANGE its keyboard rate scaling value also to 7.

3) Play C1 (the lowest note on the keyboard) and LISTEN (AUDIO CUE 50A). NOTE that the amount of time the sound takes to attack and reattack is virtually the same as before (it will actually be a little faster since C1, while the lowest physical note on the keyboard is not actually the lowest note the DX7 recognizes. This feature enables you to use the DX7 with larger external keyboards. For more information on this, see Chapter Twelve (Keyboard Level Scaling).

4) Play C2 and LISTEN (AUDIO CUE 50B). NOTE that the amount of time the sound takes to both attack and reattack is slightly lessened. Continue by playing and LISTENING to C3 (AUDIO CUE 50C), C4 (AUDIO CUE 50D), C5 (AUDIO CUE 50E), and C6 (highest note on the keyboard - AUDIO CUE 50F). NOTE that each time, the envelopes need shorter and shorter time periods to cycle through to L3, and that for the highest notes of the keyboard this becomes so short as to be virtually instantaneous. **(See Figure 9-66.)**

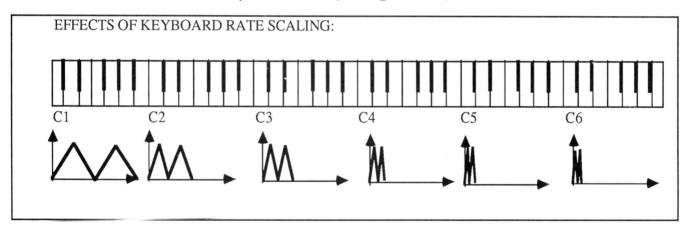

EFFECTS OF KEYBOARD RATE SCALING:

C1   C2   C3   C4   C5   C6

Figure 9-66

5) EXPERIMENT by setting the keyboard rate scaling value for both operators 1 and 2 to a new value of 4. Repeat steps 3 and 4 above and NOTE that the same effect occurs, but less drastically, as we have set the sensitivity of these operators to a lower level. EXPERIMENT further by OFFSETTING the keyboard rate scaling control to **different** values for operators 1 and 2 and NOTE the unusual effects that can be generated by doing this.

Most of the time, if you use the keyboard rate scaling control when creating simulated acoustic instrument sounds on your DX7, you will probably want to set all operators to the same roughly the same scaling value. Major offsetting of scaling values between operators will accomplish unusual but acoustically odd effects - something you may also want to accomplish from time to time!

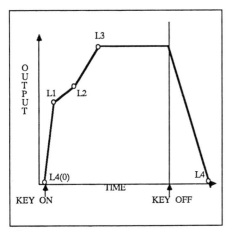

Figure 9-67

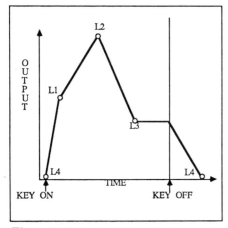

Figure 9-68

This effect is very easy to hear with the "double-attack" sound, but you should try using it to greater or lesser degrees with various preset sounds in order to become fluent in its operation.

Let's continue our discussion of the EGs now with Level 3. L3 is, of course, the **sustain** level, the level that all our envelopes **hold** at while a KEY ON situation exists. Consequently, it is of great importance because its value indicates at what output level we will remain while our finger stays on the keyboard. Because L2 always immediately precedes L3, the **relative** values for these two levels becomes important. If you are, for example, looking to create a sound that becomes either brighter or louder as you hold the key down, then you will want L3 to be **greater** than L2: **(See Figure 9-67.)**

If, on the other hand, you are looking to build a sound that diminishes in volume or in overtone content as you hold the key down, then you will want L3 set at a **lesser** value than L2: **(See Figure 9-68.)**

Some acoustic instruments, like the violin or tuba, are known as "sustaining" instruments, since they are theoretically capable of sustaining their sound indefinitely as long as they are played (of course, a violinist's arms will fall off eventually, and the tuba player's lungs will collapse before very long, but we are talking **theoretically** here). If you are trying to imitate a "sustaining" instrument on the DX7, then you will obviously want to designate carrier L3 values greater than 0.

Other acoustic instruments, like the piano or snare drum, are "nonsustaining"; in other words, you can keep your finger on the key of a piano as long as you like, but the sound of the piano will die away sooner or later, regardless. If you are using your DX7 to imitate these types of instruments, then you will want to set your carrier L3 values to 0, thus yielding this typical reduction in volume over time. Of course, with careful use of R3, we can have this degeneration of volume occur just as slowly or as quickly as we like.

Let's go back to "E.PIANO 1" - a preset which is meant to simulate the sound of a Fender Rhodes piano, which is an **acoustic** instrument. By calling this sound up and putting our DX7 into edit mode, we can see just how the carrier envelopes are set up:

EXERCISE 51

Examining Level 3 and Rate 3 for E. PIANO 1 :

1) Put your DX7 into *cartridge play mode* and CALL UP the "E.PIANO 1" sound from either ROM cartridge 1A-11 or 3A-8.
2) Use the mode select switch to put your DX7 in edit mode. TURN OFF the modulators (operators 2, 4, and 6). ("101010")
3) Use the operator select switch to VIEW operator 1 and press edit switch 22 (EG LEVEL parameter) four times in order to VIEW L4 for operator 1. VIEW L4 also for operators 3 and 5, and NOTE that this value is 0 for each of the three operators we have examined.
4) Press edit switch 22 three more times to VIEW the value for L3 for each of the three carriers. NOTE that this value is **also** 0 for each of them.
5) Use the appropriate switches in order to VIEW the L1 and L2 values for operators 1, 3, and 5. The EG level values for the three carriers are as follows:

Operator	L1	L2	L3	L4
1	99	75	0	0
3	99	95	0	0
5	99	95	0	0

6) TURN ON operators 2, 4, and 6 ("111111"). NOTE that so far we have merely OBSERVED the sound and have made no CHANGES to it, and that is why there should currently be no decimal point in the LED. Play a chord and HOLD DOWN the keys and LISTEN (AUDIO CUE 51A). NOTE that the sound eventually fades away to no volume, but that it takes a long time to do so, as does a real Fender Rhodes.

7) Using the data entry slider, CHANGE the L3 values for operators 1, 3, and 5 to a new value of 60. Play a chord, HOLD DOWN the keys, and LISTEN (AUDIO CUE 51B). NOTE that the sound slowly fades away, but **not** to no volume. Instead, the sound sustains at a lower level and will continue to do so as long as your fingers remain on the keys, no matter how long you do so. This is obviously **not** the way a real Fender Rhodes responds.

8) Restore the L3 values for each of the three carriers back to its original value of 0 (if you're from that immortalized state of Missouri, use compare mode to prove to yourself that these were in fact the original values).
NOTE that at the very highest range, some odd distortions occur as disharmonic sidebands become more prominent.

9) Press edit switch 21 (EG RATE parameter) three times in order to view R3. NOTE the R3 values for the carriers (operators 1, 3, and 5). They are as follows:

Operator	L2	R3	L3
1	75	25	0
3	95	20	0
5	95	20	0

Rate 3 is the amount of time it takes each of these carriers to die away to their sustain level of 0. L2 for operator 1 has been set at a slightly higher value (25) than that of operators 3 and 5 (both set at 20), but the end result is that they all die away at fairly equal, but all slow, rates of speed.

10) Use the data entry slider to CHANGE the R3 values for the carriers to the following new values: 45, 40, and 40. Play a chord on the keyboard, HOLD DOWN the keys, and LISTEN (AUDIO CUE 51C). NOTE that the sound now takes a much shorter time to fade away altogether.

11) EXPERIMENT with different R3 and L3 values for each of the carriers and NOTE how these changes affect the overall sound.

The sustain pedal:

When you buy an American DX7, you normally receive two footpedals: one is a push-pull type (whose operation will be covered in the next Chapter) and the other is a piano-like *sustain pedal*. If you own a Japanese DX7, you may not have received these pedals with the instrument, but you can buy them separately at any Yamaha dealer. We will concern ourselves here with one of the functions of the sustain pedal because it is tied in with the operation of the EGs.

The sustain pedal can be plugged into one of two different jacks on the back of your DX7 - either the "sustain" input or the "portamento" input. The actions of the "portamento" input will be covered in Chapter Thirteen (Function Controls). If, however, you plug it into the "sustain" input, then stepping on the pedal will supply a KEY ON flag to the EGs, the same one generated by the action of you holding a key down on the keyboard.

Of course, depressing the pedal alone (either by stepping on it or playing it Neil Young songs) is not enough to initiate the actions of the EGs. The operators still need to receive some pitch input data in order to know what notes to

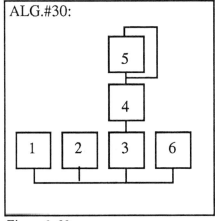
Figure 9-69

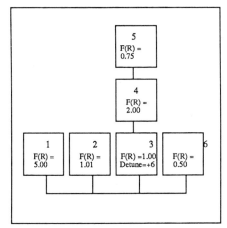
Figure 9-70

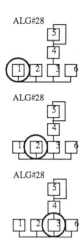

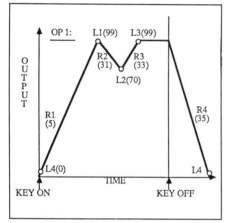

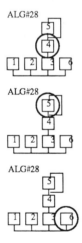

Figure 9-71A

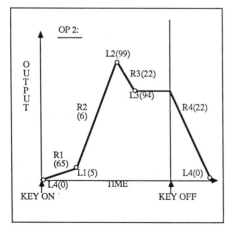

Figure 9-71B

play - therefore, you'll still always have to actually play a key in order to start the envelopes.* However, the use of the sustain pedal ensures that you won't have to HOLD DOWN the key in order to get the envelopes to cycle through to L3, the sustain level. This is what makes this pedal a true **sustain** pedal, and not a release pedal as is often found on analog synthesizers. As long as you keep your foot on the pedal, all the DX7 EGs will cycle through until they reach L3 and will continue to hold there until you release the pedal, at which time they all return to L4 at R4, same as if you took your finger off the key. So, stepping ON the pedal generates a KEY ON flag and stepping OFF the pedal generates a KEY OFF flag.

Try repeating Exercise 51 above, but this time, every time you encounter the instruction "HOLD DOWN a key", simply touch a key and simultaneously step on the sustain pedal instead. NOTE that the result is precisely the same. The sustain pedal is also commonly used when you have created a sound that takes a very long time to develop because of very slow Rates in the EGs. As we've seen, we can take up to 5 whole minutes in order to get from Level to Level (at their extreme settings), and so we can literally build sounds on the DX7 that take up to 20 minutes to develop in their entirety! We won't go that far, but let's run a quick Exercise to create a long-developing sound and use the sustain pedal to save ourselves wrist cramps as we play it!

EXERCISE 52

Generating a long swelled sound:

1) INITIALIZE your DX7 and select algorithm #30, which looks like this: **(See Figure 9-69.)**

This algorithm has four systems; one stack and three simple carriers.

2) Using the appropriate operator select and data entry controls, set up the following frequency ratio for the stack:

0.75 : 2.00 : 1.00

and the following frequencies for the single carriers: operator 1 = 5.00; operator 2 = 1.01; operator 6 = 0.50. Also set the detuning control for operator 3 only to +6. The final pitch inputs to our six operators should be as follows: **(See Figure 9-70.)**

3) Set the OUTPUT LEVELS of the six operators as follows: op 1 = 99; op 2 = 96; op 3 = 97; op 4 = 71; op 5 = 81; op 6 = 99.

4) Use the appropriate controls to enter the following EG data into the six operators:

Op	L4	R1	L1	R2	L2	R3	L3	R4	L4
1	0	5	99	31	70	33	99	35	0
2	0	65	5	6	99	22	94	22	0
3	0	36	99	79	82	99	99	23	0
4	99	11	85	9	85	99	85	10	99
5	0	7	99	99	99	99	99	27	0
6	0	13	99	20	67	84	99	23	0

A graph of these envelopes would look like this: **(See Figure 9-71.)(A through F.)**

5) Leave all other edit parameters at their default values. Play a note on the keyboard and HOLD it DOWN - this sound takes over a minute to fully develop. LISTEN (AUDIO CUE 52A). Now play a chord, HOLD it DOWN, and LISTEN. NOTE that the notes **re-attack** an

---

* This is true even for operators in fixed-frequency mode - you'll **always** have to depress a key on the keyboard in order to start the EGs.

octave lower some thirty seconds in. This is the envelope of operator 6 (a sine wave tuned an octave lower; i.e., F COARSE = 0.50) quickly (R3 = 84) rising back up to maximum level after slowly reaching about half-volume (L2 = 67).

6) We know that instead of HOLDING DOWN a note physically, we can generate the same KEY ON flag by keeping the sustain pedal depressed. Press down the sustain pedal and keep it held down **without** playing a note. NOTE that no sound is heard. While keeping it depressed, play a series of arpeggiated notes and LISTEN (AUDIO CUE 52B) as each note develops independently. Because of the long R4 values for each operator, you can let go of the sustain pedal and the notes will hang on for several seconds (also NOTE that the slightly **different** R4 values for each operator ensure that they all drop out at slightly different times, making for a very pleasant effect). Even as the previous notes are hanging on, you can re-depress the sustain pedal and add new notes to the total sound. Try it!

7) NAME and STORE this sound in a free memory slot (RAM cartridge or internal - the choice is yours). Then EXPERIMENT by listening to each system independently and, referring to Figures 9-71 (A through F), visually following each envelope as it goes through its travels. NOTE that every operator except operator 5 (whose output to operator 3 is governed by the movements of operator 4) undergoes several OUTPUT LEVEL changes over its duration. Also note that the two operators contributing beating effects (operators 2 and 3) each fade in rather slowly by virtue of their EG settings. NOTE that beating in this sound does **not** occur right away, but consequently fades in as well! This is a particularly subtle way to "fade in" beating effects and is often more pleasing than simply introducing them right away. As you EXPERIMENT with this sound, remember to STORE your changes (or OVERWRITE the original) if you want to keep them. Use the compare mode to return to these settings whenever you make a change you **don't** like.

This particular sound was created by me for use in an ambient composition written for a holography exhibition, and so I've named it "HOLOGRAM". You may, of course, name it anything you like, and for the sake of concerned copyright lawyers everywhere, I declare this software to be public domain freeware. That means that you're more than welcome to use it in any applications you like.

A couple of interesting things occur in this sound that some of you astute envelope-watchers may have realized. Step 5 above points out how the octave-lower re-attack occurs, so you know about that already. Another interesting observation would be that L4 for the middle modulator in the stack (operator 4) is set to 99. The other Levels for this operator are all at 85 and R4 is quite slow so obviously what happens here is that the brightness of the sound actually **increases** after KEY OFF. Also, if you play this sound with extensive use of the sustain pedal (and it really lends itself to this) you may find that after you have 16 notes held down and you add a 17th, the voice assignment system suddenly "realizes" that L4 for operator 4 is **not** 0, and you will begin hearing a sharper timbre for these new notes! Of course, operator 5 (the top modulator in the stack) has a more-or-less default square envelope, with a long R1 and R4, but its contribution to operator 3, as mentioned earlier, is defined by the movements of operator 4: **(See Figure 9-72.)**

Because operator 5 is set to a non-whole number frequency (0.75) relative to operator 3 (set at 1.00), it will have the effect of inducing disharmonic overtones as it fades in. This is why, about 45 seconds into the sound, you hear some low disharmonics enter for the first time. If you allow the envelopes to progress to this point and then let go of the key (KEY OFF) you'll actually hear the sound become even **more** disharmonic afterwards! The frequency ratio between operators 4 and 3, coupled with operator 4's OUTPUT LEVEL of 71, tells us that initially a square wave is generated, and that is the case **un-**

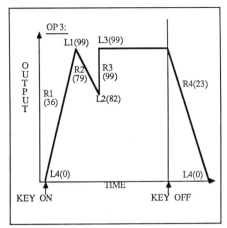

Figure 9-71C

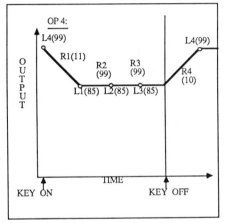

Figure 9-71D

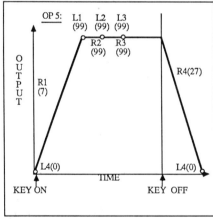

Figure 9-71E

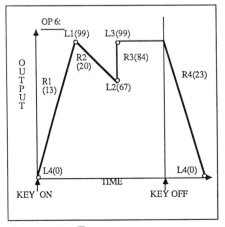

Figure 9-71F

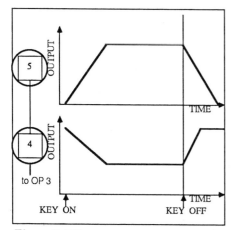

Figure 9-72

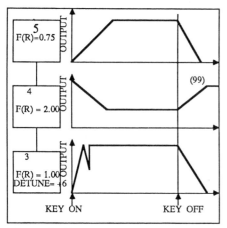

Figure 9-73

til operator 5 begins fading in and contributing its disharmonics. When we let go of the key, operator 4 (which is being continually changed as operator 5 fades in) increases its output level as it rises to an L4 of 99: **(See Figure 9-73.)**

Another factor that makes this sound so interesting is the several **different** complex movements that each operator's EG is making. This means that you can let go of the key at different points and individual notes will have developed to different degrees, making for many different timbres combining and resonating at once.

We can conclude our discussion of the operator EGs by running an Exercise to construct a simulated acoustic sound. We'll work with a relatively simple one here (more complex examples are given in Chapter Fifteen) and try to make the sound of a woodblock.

There are many ways of describing the sound of a woodblock: our job here is to find those descriptions which are the most directly translatable into DX7 commands. A woodblock, of course, is a clean, hollow, wooden sound which is percussive and therefore basically pitchless (you can pick out some kind of pitch, but you couldn't, for example, tune a woodblock to an A440). It is also a sound of brief duration which does not sustain at all, but, depending upon external acoustics, may hang on a little bit afterward.

Now let's translate these plain English descriptions of the sound into "DX7-ese": Because a woodblock is not a particularly complex sound, we won't need more than one system to generate it. Because it isn't a particularly bright or distorted sound, we won't need more than one modulator or the feedback loop. This means that we can create our woodblock with any algorithm except #32 (which doesn't provide **any** modulators). The fact that we know this sound to be "hollow" points us in the initial direction of a timbre like a square wave (which is actually missing harmonics) and the fact that it is percussive tells us that we will need to generate disharmonics by using a non-whole number frequency ratio. A wooden timbre, unlike a metallic timbre, is one which undergoes a great deal of timbral change over its duration (specifically, a sharp **decrease** in the amount of overtones generated), and the fact that the sound is of brief duration tells us a good deal about how to construct the carrier envelope. So we've really got enough to go on. For the sake of simplicity, we'll just use the system of operators 1 and 2 in algorithm #1 (the default algorithm) since we've determined that we don't need a stack or feedback to accurately construct this sound. Here goes nothing!

EXERCISE 55

Generating a woodblock sound:

1) INITIALIZE your DX7, leave it in algorithm #1, TURN OFF operators 3 through 6 ("110000"), and, using the system of operators 1 and 2, GENERATE a **square** wave. Play a note on the keyboard and LISTEN (AUDIO CUE 53A).

2) In order to generate some disharmonics within this square wave, we need to set up a non-whole number frequency ratio. Press edit switch 19 (F FINE parameter) and VIEW operator 2. CHANGE this value to 2.84 (just an arbitrary value I selected for demonstration), play a note and LISTEN (AUDIO CUE 53B).

3) We now have created a dissonant clarinet-ish sound. The reason we are still far from the woodblock is because both operators in the system still have their default square envelope settings. Let's begin with the carrier envelope. CHANGE the values for operator 1's EG Levels as follows:

L4	L1	L2	L3	L4
0	99	99	0	0

which generates an envelope which looks like this: **(See Figure 9-74.)**

The reasons for picking these Levels 1, 3, and 4 should be fairly obvious: Level 1 is set at maximum output because there's no reason to have any less than maximum output. In fact, whenever constructing **any sound at all** on the DX7, you should always ensure that at least one carrier has at least one of its EG Levels set at 99. If not, you are going to output more noise and less signal than would be desirable (for more on this *signal-to-noise ratio*, refer back to Chapter One). Level 3 is set at 0 because a woodblock is a non-sustaining instrument, and Level 4 is similarly set to 0 because we don't want a continuous sound. The only question, in fact, is where you want to put Level 2. If you think it through, there are only three options available to you:

    (a) L2 can be the same as L1; or
    (b) L2 can be the same as L3; or
    (c) L2 can be somewhere in-between L1 and L3.

The only reason for picking option (c) above would be if you wanted to have two **different** volume changes within the overall sound, like this: **(See Figure 9-75.)**

or like this: **(See Figure 9-76.)**

A woodblock is not that complex a sound that it actually undergoes two separate changes in volume, so we can eliminate option (c) in this particular example. Well, then, should L2 be the same as L1, or should it be the same as L3? The answer is, it doesn't make the slightest bit of difference. If L2 is set the same as L1 (as we did above), then it is R3 that acts as the "decay" time: **(See Figure 9-77.)**

On the other hand, if we set L2 the same as L3, then it is **R2** that acts as the "decay" time: **(See Figure 9-78.)**

The Levels, then, for this particular sound actually suggest themselves when you stop and analyze what it is you need to accomplish. My advice is that you always begin setting up an EG by determining and entering the Levels first. In this way, you are delineating the points on the "road-map". Next, we will specify to the DX7 how **quickly** or **slowly** we wish to travel from point to point by specifying the EG Rates.

4) Press edit switch 21 (EG RATE parameter) and enter the following EG Rates for operator 1:

L4	R1	L1	R2	L2	R3	L3	R4	L4
0	99	99	99	99	72	0	52	0

which generates an envelope which looks like this: **(See Figure 9-79.)**

The reason we picked these particular rates should also be fairly obvious. Rate 1 has been set at its maximum value of 99 since a woodblock attacks instantaneously. Rate 2 is, of course, completely meaningless since L1 and L2 are the same - this value could be anything at all, and I simply left it at its default of 99. Rate 3, the "decay" time in this example, has been set at a value that sounds close to the way a real woodblock decays, and Rate 4 has been set at a value close to the way a woodblock sound might typically ring after the fact.

5) Play a note on the keyboard and LISTEN (AUDIO CUE 53C). Our sound is closer, but it's much more like a metallic cowbell than a wooden woodblock. The reason for this, as stated earlier, is that wooden timbres typically undergo a great deal of timbral change.

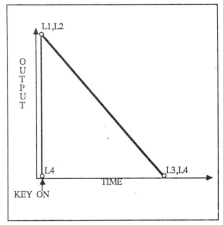

Figure 9-74

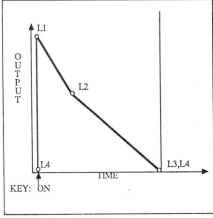

Figure 9-75

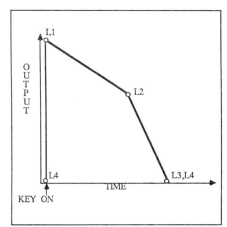

Figure 9-76

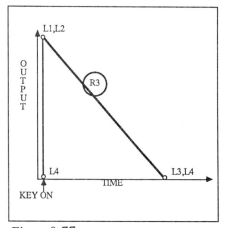

Figure 9-77

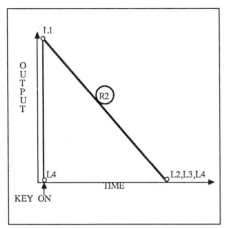

Figure 9-78

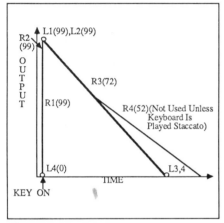

Figure 9-79

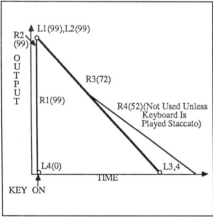

Figure 9-80

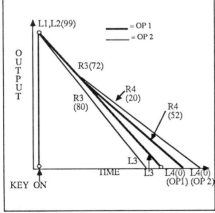

Figure 9-81

Since our modulator still has the default square envelope, our sound is currently undergoing no timbral change even though the EG of operator 1 is ensuring a significant volume change. Since we have learned that a characteristic of wooden sounds is that they undergo a rapid decrease in overtone amount, we can use the same EG we have already constructed for operator 1: **(See Figure 9-80.)**

to do the job for operator 2. Use the EG copy function to copy the EG data for operator 1 into operator 2. Play a note on the keyboard and LISTEN (AUDIO CUE 53D). We're definitely getting closer!

6)   The reason we're not quite there yet is twofold: First of all, we haven't yet **offset** the envelopes, and we know that in reality there's no way the volume and the timbre of a woodblock would change precisely the same way. Second of all, when we created the timbre in the first place, we really were only guessing. Now that we've got the envelopes closer, we'll have a much better idea of the frequency ratio and modulator output levels we'll need to accurately simulate this sound. First, let's do the offsets:

7)   CHANGE R3 and R4 for operator **2** to new values of 80 and 20, respectively, generating offset envelopes that look like this: **(See Figure 9-81.)**

The overtone content, then, dies away more rapidly than the volume, unless you strike a key staccato, in which case the overtones change little as the volume fades away: **(See Figure 9-82.)**

Play a note and LISTEN (AUDIO CUE 53E). Nearly there! Now we're ready to do the final tweaking to our timbre:

8)   CHANGE the OUTPUT LEVEL of operator 2 (our quantitative control) to a new value of 78. Use the F COARSE and F FINE parameters to change the pitch of operator 2 (thereby changing our qualitative timbral control - the frequency ratio) to 3.69 (you'll have to change the F COARSE value to 3.00 in order to enter in an F FINE value of 3.69. Pretty sneaky, huh?). Play a note on the keyboard and LISTEN (AUDIO CUE 53F). Instant woodblock!

9)   NAME and STORE this sound somewhere in your DX7's memory. Then EXPERIMENT by changing different values and see how you can improve on the sound created here. NOTE that the sound never sounds perfect over the full five octave range, and that it is usually unrealistic to expect this with almost any sound. EXPERIMENT further by finding one good pitch at which this sound is particularly realistic and then setting that pitch over the whole keyboard by using FIXED FREQUENCY mode. Remember that you must keep your frequency ratio intact!

In none of the Exercises in this chapter were we able to affect the pitch of the sound in any way. A quick look at our diagram of the operator makes this clear: **(See Figure 9-83.)**

as there is no way that an operator EG can possibly affect the pitch data input. There will, however, be times when you will want to aperiodically change the pitch of a sound, and so the DX7 provides us with a completely separate, seventh envelope generator called the pitch EG.

The pitch EG is an independent device which resides outside of the six operators and sends data to **ALL SIX** of them simultaneously. This is an important point, worth repeating:

THE PITCH EG ALWAYS SENDS PITCH DATA TO ALL SIX OPERATORS SIMULTANEOUSLY.

There is a good reason why Yamaha set things up this way. If we are generating a sound with, say, a system of operators 1 and 2, as follows: **(See Figure 9-84.)**

, and we could use an EG to alter the **pitch** of operator 2 without in any way affecting operator 1, would we accomplish a pitch change? Cardinal Rule Three (Chapter Six) says we would not. Instead, of course, we would be altering the frequency ratio, which would result in a **timbral** change.

Since the whole purpose of a pitch EG is to allow us to alter the pitch of a sound aperiodically, the wonderful software engineers at Yamaha simply made the pitch EG *non-operator-specific*. Of course, if they **had** made it operator-specific, we would be able to generate even more exciting sounds on the DX7 (hint, hint, you guys) but I suppose we must learn to accept what is provided us.

All kidding aside, the pitch EG is a powerful tool and it is in fact rare to find a separate EG on **any** synthesizer which is dedicated to pitch change. It is perhaps worth mentioning that any operators in fixed frequency mode (see Chapter Six for details) will **ignore** any Pitch EG data sent to them and will therefore remain at the fixed frequency you designate.

The pitch EG operates exactly the same way as the individual operator EGs in that it has four Levels and four Rates. It also initiates its activity from the same KEY ON flag, and reacts the same way to KEY OFF (immediately returning from whatever point it's at, back to L4, at R4). In fact, the only real difference lies in its default values: all four Levels default at a value of 50. The four Rates, like their individual operator cousins, default at the maximum value of 99: **(See Figure 9-85.)**

Because the pitch EG defaults this way, there is no pitch change occurring when you INITIALIZE (since all four Levels are the same value). The reason that a value of 50 was selected for the default is to allow you to use the pitch EG to either sharpen or flatten the pitch; if 0 had been selected, you could only sharpen the pitch: **(See Figure 9-86.)**

and if 99 had been chosen, you could only flatten it: **(See Figure 9-87.)**

Because the four Levels are the same, the values for the four Rates are completely irrelevant and could in fact be anything. Levels, then, which are greater than 50 will cause the pitch to rise and Levels less than 50 will cause the pitch to fall. Levels much greater than 50 or much less than 50 will cause gross pitch changes (to a maximum range of four octaves sharper or flatter), and Levels around the default of 50 will allow us subtle wavers in pitch. In all instances, of course, the Rates determine the speed of the pitch change.

We access the Pitch EG controls from edit switches 29 and 30, labeled "PITCH EG RATE" and "PITCH EG LEVEL" respectively: **(See Figure 9-88.)**

Let's run an Exercise to try out some of our options:

EXERCISE 54

The Pitch EG:

1) INITIALIZE your DX7, leave it in algorithm #1, TURN OFF operators 3 through 6 ("110000"), and use the system of operators 1 and 2 to generate a sawtooth wave.

2) Press edit switch 30 (PITCH EG LEVEL parameter) once to VIEW L1. NOTE that upper right-hand corner of the LCD is **blank** as this is a **non**-operator-specific parameter.

3) Press edit switch 30 four more times to OBSERVE the PITCH EG LEVEL default values (all Levels = 50). Press edit switch 29 (PITCH EG RATE parameter) four times to OBSERVE the PITCH EG RATE default values (all Rates = 99).

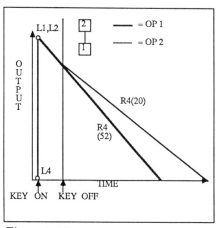

Figure 9-82

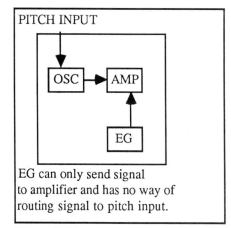

Figure 9-83

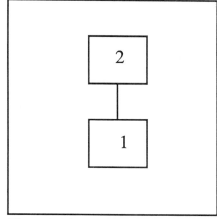

Figure 9-84

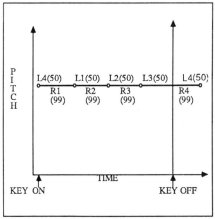

Figure 9-85

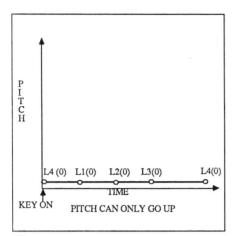

Figure 9-86

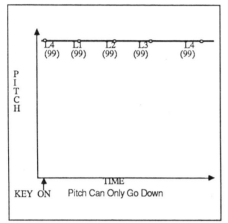

Figure 9-87

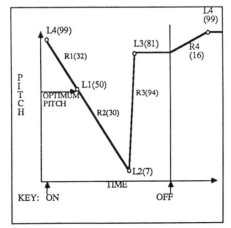

Figure 9-88

4) CHANGE the PITCH EG L1 to a new value of 75. Play a note on the keyboard and LISTEN (AUDIO CUE 54A). NOTE that the pitch quickly rises (R1 = 99) and falls (R2 = 99) just a bit more slowly, as the PITCH EG, like the operator EGs, has attack times which are scaled to be slightly quicker than equivalent decay times.

5) CHANGE the values for the PITCH EG R1 and R2 both to 35. Play a note on the keyboard and LISTEN (AUDIO CUE 54B). NOTE that the pitch now slowly rises and falls a bit more slowly.

6) CHANGE the value of the PITCH EG L1 to 25. Play a note on the keyboard and LISTEN (AUDIO CUE 54C). NOTE that the pitch now **falls** instead of rising. NOTE also that the fall ("decay") time is again somewhat slower than the rise ("attack") time, even though the R1 and R2 values are still equal to one another.

7) CHANGE L1 of the PITCH EG to its minimum of 0 without changing the Rates. Play a note and LISTEN (AUDIO CUE 54D). NOTE that the pitch drops down and then returns a full four octaves and that this change occurs more slowly than in step 6. This is because even though the Rate settings are the same, they have a greater distance to travel.

8) CHANGE L1 of the PITCH EG to its maximum of 99. Play a note and LISTEN (AUDIO CUE 54E). NOTE that the pitch now rises a full four octaves before returning to its starting pitch (L2).

9) CHANGE L1 of the PITCH EG to a new value of 52. Play a note and LISTEN (AUDIO CUE 54F). NOTE that we now hear a very subtle wavering in pitch as we are accomplishing an aperiodic pitch change of less than a quarter tone.

10) CHANGE L1 of the PITCH EG to a new value of 48, play a note and LISTEN (AUDIO CUE 54G). NOTE that we hear a slightly different wavering in pitch as we are now rising up to our pitch from a slightly flatter note. These kinds of subtle pitch changes bring to mind the kind of gentle pitch bends that are characteristic of much Eastern music.

11) EXPERIMENT by making various CHANGES to different PITCH EG Levels and Rates, and NOTE the way this affects the overall sound. NOTE also that whatever sound you affect with the PITCH EG, **only** a pitch change occurs because it always affects **all** operators equally.

While there are relatively few presets that utilize the gross settings of the Pitch EG, there are quite a few that utilize the subtler effects possible. The Pitch EG, like beating effects, generally falls under the category of Icing On The Cake: it will usually be something you try at the end of creating a sound, and it usually won't be an integral part of the sound.

Having said all that, let's examine one preset which does utilize, as an integral component, the Pitch EG for gross pitch change. This is, of course, the "TAKE OFF" preset, found on ROM 1A-32 or ROM 3A-32:

EXERCISE 55

Examining the "TAKE OFF" Pitch EG:

1) Put your DX7 into cartridge play mode and call up either ROM 1A-32 or ROM 3A-32 ("TAKE OFF").

2) Press the edit mode select switch in order to VIEW the edit parameters for this sound.

3) Press edit switch 30 (PITCH EG LEVEL parameter) and OB-SERVE the Pitch EG Level settings. Press edit switch 29 and NOTE the Pitch EG Rate settings. The PITCH EG values are set as follows:

L4	R1	L1	R2	L2	R3	L3	R4	L4
99	32	50	30	7	94	81	16	99

Figure 9-89

which generates an envelope something like this: **(See Figure 9-89.)**

4) Play a note on the keyboard and LISTEN (AUDIO CUE 55A). As you LISTEN, follow the diagram above so you can hear the following pitch changes: First, a slow (R1) fall in pitch from a high note (L4) to optimum pitch (L1). This is immediately followed by a slightly slower (R2) continued drop in pitch to a very low note (L2). As soon as this low note is reached, the pitch very rapidly (R3) springs back up to a higher point (L3) and holds there as long as your finger remains on the key or your foot remains on the sustain pedal. Once you release the key or pedal (KEY OFF), the pitch very slowly (R4) rises back up to its starting point (L4). Striking effects can be obtained by **arpeggiating** notes on the keyboard. By keeping your foot on the sustain pedal, you won't have to actually keep your fingers on the keys while the sound develops. Releasing the footpedal will cause the characteristic "after" rise in pitch. Try it! (AUDIO CUE 55B).

5) EXPERIMENT by changing the various Pitch EG Levels and Rates and NOTE how they change the overall sound. One particularly nice sound can be generated by simply de-activating the Pitch EG in "TAKE OFF" altogether. To do this, simply set all four Pitch EG Levels to their defaults of 50. At this point, there will be no pitch change whatever, and, of course, the Rates become irrelevant. Play a note on the keyboard and LISTEN (AUDIO CUE 55C). If you like the sound, RENAME it "V.PRICE" and use it the next time you are scoring a horror movie!

NOTE that, unlike operator EGs, the DX7 is able to "recognize" a starting L4 point in the Pitch EG right away - it doesn't automatically assume a starting L4 of 0 since we are here dealing with pitch change and not output level change.

Bear in mind also that the actions of the Pitch EG are somewhat tied in with the actions of the individual operator EGs. If, for example, your carrier EGs have L4s of 0 and very fast R4s, then you won't be able to hear Pitch EG changes from L3 to L4: **(See Figure 9-90.)**

On the other hand, if your carrier EGs have very slow attack rates, then you won't be able to hear quick initial pitch EG changes: **(See Figure 9-91.)**

If you want to set up a sound that drops in pitch after you let go of the note, you can be sure that it will always **begin** by **rising** in pitch, since L4 is both the starting and ending point: **(See Figure 9-92.)**

And, of course, the reverse holds true as well. If the pitch is to rise after KEY OFF, then it must fall on KEY ON: **(See Figure 9-93.)**

Also note that the EG copy function **cannot** be used with the Pitch EG. This can only be used to copy data to and from individual operator EGs.

Hopefully, the Exercises and examples in this chapter have demonstrated how incredibly important the use of envelopes are in synthesizing sounds. The use of the DX7 EGs is absolutely mandatory in the creation of ALL sounds with this instrument. Their very complexity allows us new freedom in audio synthesis. For these reasons, an entire volume could be written on them. The good news is that this book won't be it. It's time we move on now to the cousin of the EG, the device that allows us to make **periodic** changes to our sounds, the *LFO*.

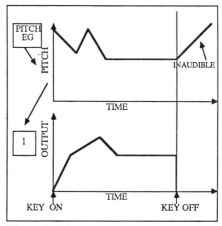

Figure 9-90

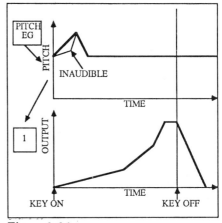

Figure 9-91

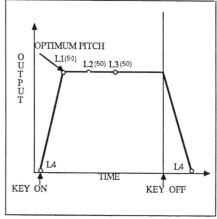

Figure 9-92

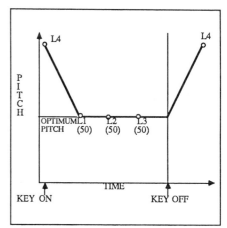

Figure 9-93

SWITCHES AND CONTROLS COVERED IN CHAPTER NINE:

SWITCH	PARAMETER	COMMENTS
Edit 21	EG Rate	Operator-specific; Multi-level; Four Rates, ranges 0 - 99.
Edit 22	EG Level	Operator-specific; Multi-level; Four Levels, ranges 0 - 99.
Edit 26	Keyboard Rate Scaling	Operator-specific sensitivity control Range 0 - 7.
Edit 29	Pitch EG Rate	Non-operator specific; Multi-level; Four Rates, ranges 0 - 99.
Edit 30	Pitch EG Level	Non-operator specific; Multi-level; Four Levels, ranges 0 - 99.

CHAPTER TEN: THE LFO

Sounds always change over time; we have seen in the last chapter how applying an envelope to a sound causes it to become dynamic and "real". However, envelope generators by their very definition are only capable of causing an **aperiodic** change to a sound; in other words, the change caused by an EG can never be repeated without actually repeating the sound itself.

Often, however, within the duration of a **single** sound, repetitive changes will be observed. For example, a *vibrato* is a repetitive pitch change; as a *tremolo* is a repetitive volume change. Therefore, we will require some kind of device in our synthesizer that is capable of effecting a periodic change to a sound over time; and that device, on all synthesizers, is called a *low frequency oscillator*, or **LFO** for short.

The digital oscillators inside our six operators were capable of generating numbers at very high speeds, and so the analog voltages produced by our DAC as a result of their signals underwent high-speed changes, in the audible (20 Hz to 20 kHz) range. In other words, they were capable of producing digital signals which became audible sounds. The LFO is a different kind of digital oscillator that lives entirely outside of the six operators. There is only one LFO on a DX7, not six, and that lone LFO is only capable of generating signal at **low** speeds (in the 0.10 Hz to 60 Hz range). That means that the signals it generates are mostly **subsonic**. The fact that the LFO only produces inaudible signals is largely irrelevant, since there is no way of routing its signal to the DAC anyway - in other words, we can never actually hear the LFO - like the EG's, we will only be able to hear its effect on our operators. The LFO on our DX7, then, is an independent digital component, completely separate from our six operators, which will send data to some or all of those operators, causing them to *periodically* (repeatedly) change their **pitch** and/or **output level**. Of course, Cardinal Rule One tells us that if the output level of a **carrier** is periodically changed, the result will be a periodic volume change. Cardinal Rule Two tells us that if the output level of a **modulator** is periodically changed, the result will be a periodic quantitative **timbral** change.

We can send this LFO signal to either of two different destinations. It can terminate at the pitch data input of our operators: **(See Figure 10-1.)**

or it can terminate at the **amplifiers** of our six operators: **(See Figure 10-2.)**

If we decide to use our LFO as in the first example, (LFO data to the pitch data inputs) then we are said to be accomplishing *pitch modulation*. Pitch modulation is always **non-operator-specific**; that is, this data will always be sent to all six operators simultaneously. This is exactly the same logic that was used with our aperiodic pitch controller, the *pitch EG*. If you remember, the pitch EG also only ever affected all six operators at once. Again, if we apply any kind of pitch change to certain operators and not all of them, Cardinal Rule Three tells us that we will not get a pitch change, but a qualitative timbral change instead.

On the other hand, if we decide to follow the second example and route the LFO data to the operator amplifiers, then we are said to be accomplishing *am-*

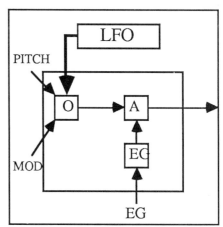

Figure 10-1

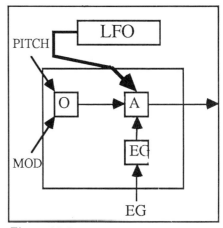

Figure 10-2

LFO						MOD SENSITIVITY	
WAVE	SPEED	DELAY	PMD	AMD	SYNC	PITCH	AMP
9 ⁹	10 ⁰	11 ᴬ	12 ᴮ	13 ᶜ	14 ᴰ	15 ᴱ	16 ꜰ
EDIT/ RECALL	VOICE INIT				BATTERY CHECK	SAVE CARTRIDGE	LOAD

Figure 10-3

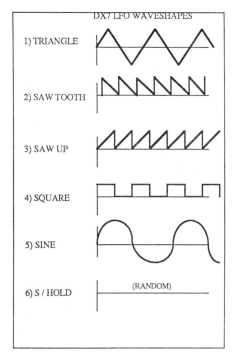

Figure 10-4

plitude modulation. Amplitude modulation is operator-specific; that is, we can specify which operators will respond to the LFO data and which will not. This means that, depending upon whether we have carriers or modulators responding to the LFO commands, we will hear either a periodic volume change or a periodic quantitative timbral change.

There are no less than eight edit switches which relate to the use of the LFO, and they are switches 9 through 16, as follows: **(See Figure 10-3.)**

We will also be using most of the lower row of *function* switches in order to route the LFO signal via the DX7's *real-time controllers*, the *modulation wheel*, the *foot controller*, the *breath controller*, and the *keyboard after-touch*. Let's begin, however, with a brief description of the eight LFO *edit switches*:

EDIT SWITCH #	NAME
9	Waveshape
10	Speed
11	Delay
12	PMD (Pitch Modulation Depth)
13	AMD (Amplitude Modulation Depth)
14	Sync
15	Pitch modulation sensitivity
16	Amplitude modulation sensitivity

Edit switch 9: LFO waveshape

When we used the EGs to change our sounds, we were able to "shape" them in various different manners by specifying different Levels and Rates. Our LFO signal cannot be "shaped" in this manner; instead, we are provided with six fixed LFO waveshapes and we are asked to select one of them. The shape of the wave will of course have a great impact on the type of periodic movement we will ultimately hear when we apply this signal. The six different waveshapes we have to choose from are as follows: **(See Figure 10-4.)**

The triangle, square, and sine waves should already be familiar to you. So, too, should be the sawtooth, although here we are offered the choice of a negative-going sawtooth wave (sawtooth down) or a positive-going sawtooth wave (sawtooth up). The S/HOLD (sample/hold) waveshape is a new one, but that's OK since it isn't really any kind of wave at all. Instead, when you select the S/HOLD shape, the DX7 generates a stream of **random** data. This will allow us to generate random periodic changes to our sounds, and will, in specific usages, yield quite interesting effects. Remember that as we only have one LFO, we can only select one LFO waveshape for any given sound.

Press edit switch 9 to access this parameter. The voice initialization default is a *triangle* wave. You can use the "yes-no" buttons or the data entry slider to VIEW the six different waveshape options available. OBSERVE that the upper-right hand corner of the LCD is blank, as this parameter is most definitely non-operator specific: we're not dealing with the operators at all here, but a separate component **outside** of the operators! **(See Figure 10-5.)**

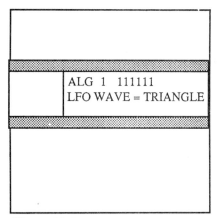

Figure 10-5

Edit switch 10: LFO speed

This one's real easy - and pretty much self-explanatory. The range of this control is 0 - 99, with 0 being the slowest possible speed (about 0.10 Hz - or one wave generated every ten seconds) and 99 being the fastest (about 60 Hz). The voice initialization default for this parameter is a speed of 35. Press edit switch 10 to VIEW this and use the data entry slider to CHANGE it. OBSERVE again that the upper right-hand corner of the LCD is blank. **(See Figure 10-6.)**

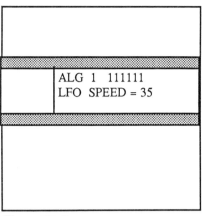

Figure 10-6

Edit switch 11: LFO delay

This is a digital delay line built into the DX7 which will serve to delay the onset of the LFO signal by a certain amount. The range of this switch is, again, 0 to 99, with 0 indicating minimum (no) delay; and 99 indicating maximum (about 3 seconds) delay. This will be useful in setting up sounds which will not undergo any periodic change upon their initial attack - for example, you could set up a sound which undergoes no change if played staccato but develops a pronounced tremolo when played legato! One unfortunate thing about this control: while the delay to the onset of the LFO signal can be quite long, once the LFO signal actually begins arriving, the "fade-in" time is actually very short and so fairly unrealistic. Another one for the Yamaha suggestion box...

Press edit switch 11 to access this control and use the data entry slider to step it through its possible values. The voice initialization default for this parameter is 0 (no delay). NOTE that the upper right-hand corner of the LCD is still blank, as this parameter again has no reference to individual operators. **(See Figure 10-7.)**

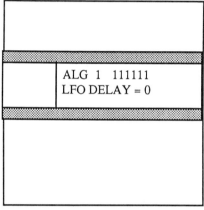

Figure 10-7

Edit switch 12: PMD

PMD stands for "Pitch Modulation Depth" and this control is used for the **direct** routing of LFO signal to the pitch inputs of all six operators simultaneously. The range of this control is also 0 - 99; with 0 indicating minimum (no) signal being routed and 99 indicating maximum (all) signal being routed. We will be running an Exercise shortly to try this out. For now, just press edit switch 12 to VIEW this parameter and use the data entry slider to CHANGE it through its range of 0 to 99. The voice initialization default for this is a value of 0 (no PMD). Again, the upper right-hand corner of the LCD is blank. **(See Figure 10-8.)**

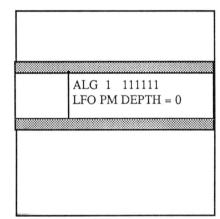

Figure 10-8

Edit switch 13: AMD

AMD stands for "Amplitude Modulation Depth" and this control is used for the **direct** routing of LFO signal to the amplifiers of all six operators simultaneously. As with the PMD control, the range is again 0 (minimum, or no routing) to 99 (maximum, or all routing). Press edit switch 13 to VIEW this parameter and use the data entry slider to CHANGE it through its range of 0 to 99. Like the PMD control, the voice initialization default is also 0 (no AMD). Again, the upper right-hand corner of the LCD will be blank. **(See Figure 10-9.)**

Edit switch 14: Sync

This parameter is the LFO keyboard synchronization control. In plain English, it will allow us, if we desire, to trigger the LFO from the KEY ON flag generated by the action of depressing a key on the keyboard. We'll run an Exercise later to demonstrate its use, but for now just NOTE that we access this control by pressing edit switch 14, and that it is either ON or OFF (according to which "on-off", that is, "yes-no" data entry button we press). Upon initialization, this parameter will default as being ON. Once again, the upper right-hand corner of the LCD is blank as we are again dealing with an LFO variable. **(See Figure 10-10.)**

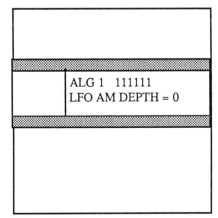

Figure 10-9

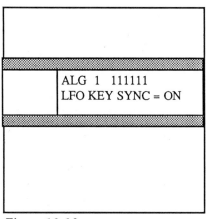

Figure 10-10

ALG 1 111111
LFO KEY SYNC = ON

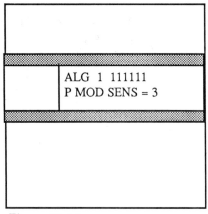

Figure 10-11

ALG 1 111111
P MOD SENS = 3

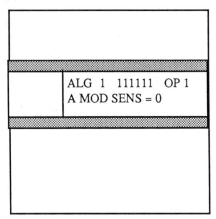

Figure 10-12

ALG 1 111111   OP 1
A MOD SENS = 0

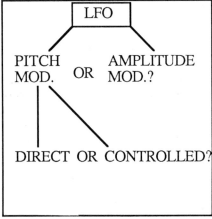

Figure 10-13

LFO

PITCH   AMPLITUDE
MOD.   OR   MOD.?

DIRECT OR CONTROLLED?

Edit switch 15: Pitch modulation sensitivity

This is the parameter that determines **how sensitive** our six operators will be to pitch modulation. The range of this switch is 0 to 7, with 0 indicating minimum (no) sensitivity; and 7 indicating maximum sensitivity. Press edit switch 15 to VIEW this parameter and OBSERVE that the upper right-hand corner of the LCD is still blank. Even though this control has to do with the six operators, remember that pitch modulation in the DX7, whether by the Pitch EG or by the LFO, is always non-operator-specific. The voice initialization default for this parameter is somewhat surprisingly a value of 3 (**not** 0). **(See Figure 10-11.)**

Edit switch 16: Amplitude modulation sensitivity

This control allows us to determine which operators will be sensitive to amplitude modulation, and also how sensitive they will be. The range of this switch is a mere 0 to 3, with 0 indicating minimum (no) sensitivity; and 3 indicating maximum sensitivity. Press edit switch 16 to access this parameter and OBSERVE that, for the first time in this chapter, we finally have an "OP" number appearing in the upper right-hand corner of the LCD! As promised, amplitude modulation is operator-specific, and so, by setting different degrees of sensitivity for different operators, we can decide which operators will respond to these LFO commands, and how much response there will be. Whenever you initialize, a default value of 0 will be assigned to all six operators for this parameter (no sensitivity for any of them). **(See Figure 10-12.)**

Let's begin by exploring the actions of the LFO being used for pitch modulation. This will, of course, give us a periodic change to the pitch of the sound we are generating. Having decided that we want to use the LFO for this purpose, the DX7, in true computer fashion, now brings us to another fork in the road: **(See Figure 10-13.)**

We have the option of either **directly** routing the LFO signal to the pitch inputs of our six operators, in which case we will need to use edit switch 12 (PMD parameter) to accomplish *direct modulation*, or, we can route the LFO signal **indirectly**, via any one of our four real-time controllers (the modulation wheel, the foot pedal, the breath controller, or the keyboard after-touch) in which case we will accomplish *controlled modulation*. Let's begin by running an Exercise to set up a **direct** pitch modulation:

EXERCISE 56

Direct Pitch Modulation:

1) INITIALIZE your DX7, leave it in algorithm #1, TURN OFF operators 3 through 6 ("110000"), and use the system of operators 1 and 2 to generate a sawtooth wave.
2) Press edit switch 9 and OBSERVE the default value of a TRIANGLE wave. Press edit switch 10 and OBSERVE the default speed of 35. Press edit switch 11 and OBSERVE the default delay value of 0 (no delay). Press edit switch 12 and OBSERVE the PMD default of 0, and press edit switch 15 and OBSERVE that there currently is a sensitivity for pitch modulation (since this parameter defaults to a value of 3).
3) Play a note on the keyboard and LISTEN (AUDIO CUE 56A). NOTE that there is currently no periodic change occurring to the pitch of the sawtooth wave. This is because no LFO modulation is being routed as yet to the pitch inputs of operators 1 and 2 (since PMD= 0) even though both are already sensitive to such a modulation (since Pitch Modulation Sensitivity = 3).
4) Press edit switch 12 (PMD parameter) and use the data entry slider to CHANGE this value to its maximum value of 99. Play a note on the keyboard and LISTEN (AUDIO CUE 56B). NOTE that you are now hearing a rapid periodic pitch change in the sound.
5) Press edit switch 10 (LFO SPEED parameter) and CHANGE this

value to a slower speed value of 8. Play a note and LISTEN (AUDIO CUE 56C). NOTE that the speed of the pitch change has now slowed appreciably and that you can now clearly hear the pitch gradually rising and falling, equivalent to the current TRIANGLE LFO waveshape: **(See Figure 10-14.)**

6)   Press edit switch 9 and press the "yes" button once to hear the effect of a SAW DOWN LFO wave (AUDIO CUE 56D). NOTE that the pitch now instantly rises and slowly drops, as equivalent to the wave shape: **(See Figure 10-15.)**

7)   Press the "yes" button once again to hear the effect of a SAW UP LFO wave (AUDIO CUE 56E). NOTE that the pitch now changes in the opposite manner, slowly rising and quickly dropping, as equivalent to the wave shape: **(See Figure 10-16.)**

8)   Press the "yes" button once again to hear the effect of a SQUARE LFO wave (AUDIO CUE 56F). NOTE that the pitch now instantly rises, followed by an instant fall, as equivalent to the wave shape: **(See Figure 10-17.)**

NOTE that this produces a *trill* effect to the sound. Press edit switch 12 (PMD parameter) and use the data entry slider to slowly change this value to its minimum of 0, HOLDing DOWN a key and LISTENing as you do so (AUDIO CUE 56G). NOTE that changing the PMD value has the effect of changing the two notes you hear; so that varying the depth of the pitch modulation effectively changes the higher and lower points of the modulating SQUARE wave: **(See Figure 10-18.)**

9)   Restore the PMD value to 99. Press edit switch 9 and then press the "yes" button once again to hear the effect of a SINE LFO wave (AUDIO CUE 56H). NOTE that the pitch now gently rises and falls, in a manner equivalent to the wave shape: **(See Figure 10-19.)**

and similar to the effect of the TRIANGLE wave, but more gently, as the SINE wave is a more rounded shape.

10)   Press the "yes" button one last time to hear the effect of a S/HOLD LFO wave (AUDIO CUE 56I). NOTE that you now hear a random pitch change as the DX7 is now periodically *sampling* from a stream of random numbers, and *holding* the number just long enough to send the data to the pitch inputs of the six operators.

11)   Restore the LFO shape to that of a TRIANGLE wave. Press edit switch 10 (LFO SPEED parameter) and, using the data entry slider, slowly CHANGE this value up to its maximum of 99, HOLDing DOWN a key and LISTENing as you do so (AUDIO CUE 56J). NOTE how this change in speed does not in any way alter the **type** of pitch change you hear, nor the **amount** of pitch change. NOTE also that this change is recognized by the DX7 in *real time*. Now use the data entry slider to slowly CHANGE this value back to its minimum of 0, HOLDing DOWN a key and LISTENing as you do so (AUDIO CUE 56K). NOTE that the speed of the pitch change now decreases, and that at the absolute minimum speed of 0, it occurs only about **once** every **ten seconds** (indicating an LFO frequency of approximately 0.10 Hz) - and that you can hear the "digitizing" (or quantization) of the LFO wave at the very low speed.

12)   Restore the LFO speed back to a value of 8 and press edit switch 12 (PMD parameter). Use the data entry slider to slowly CHANGE this value back to the minimum of 0, HOLDing DOWN a key and LISTENing as you do so (AUDIO CUE 56L). NOTE that this has the effect of lessening the **depth** of the change but in no way alters the shape of the change nor the speed.

13)   Restore the PMD value back to 99 and press edit switch 15 (P MOD SENS. parameter). Use the "yes" button to slowly CHANGE this value to its maximum of 7, HOLDing DOWN a key and LISTEN-

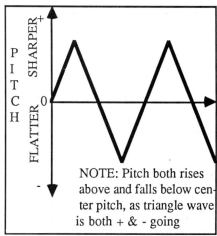

NOTE: Pitch both rises above and falls below center pitch, as triangle wave is both + & - going

Figure 10-14

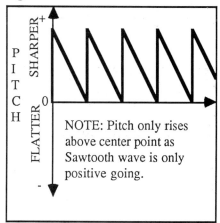

NOTE: Pitch only rises above center point as Sawtooth wave is only positive going.

Figure 10-15

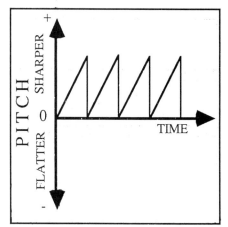

Figure 10-16

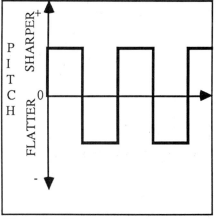

Figure 10-17

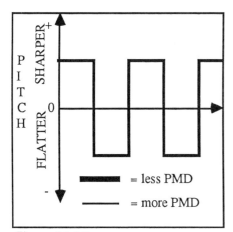

Figure 10-18

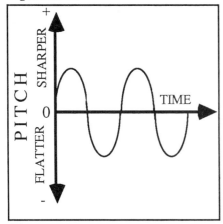

Figure 10-19

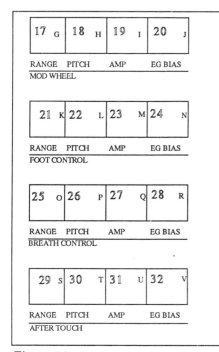

Figure 10-20

ing as you do so (AUDIO CUE 56M). NOTE that this has a similar effect to increasing the PMD value, but more so. Now use the "no" button to CHANGE this slowly back to its minimum value of 0, HOLDing DOWN a key and LISTENing as you do so (AUDIO CUE 56N). NOTE that this has the same audible effect as decreasing the PMD value, and that at a value of 0 there is no pitch change whatsoever.

14)   Restore the P MOD SENS. parameter back to a value of 3 and press edit switch 11 (LFO DELAY parameter). Use the data entry slider to CHANGE this to a value of 50. Play a note on the keyboard and LISTEN (AUDIO CUE 56O). NOTE that the effect of the LFO on the pitch is now delayed by about a second, but that the ultimate pitch change is precisely the same as before. CHANGE the LFO DELAY value to its maximum of 99, play a note and LISTEN (AUDIO CUE 56P). NOTE that the onset of the LFO is now delayed by some 3 seconds.

15)   EXPERIMENT by setting various different LFO waveshapes with various speeds and delay times. Also EXPERIMENT with different PMD and P MOD SENS. values until you feel confident in understanding how each of these different controls affect the final modulation effect.

What have we learned from this Exercise? Clearly, the LFO shape determines the qualitative **type** of pitch modulation; the LFO **speed** determines the speed of the pitch modulation; and a combination of the PMD and Pitch Modulation Sensitivity determine the quantitative depth of the pitch modulation (that is, how far the pitch strays from its original setting). Why are we given two controls for the modulation **depth**, and what is the difference between them?

The PMD control is used **only** when you wish to set up a **direct modulation**. If you wish instead to route the LFO signal via one of the four real-time controllers, then you would want the PMD value to be 0. PMD, then, simply determines how much **direct** LFO pitch modulation is accomplished. The Pitch Modulation Sensitivity control, on the other hand, determines how sensitive our six operators are to any kind of pitch modulation, be it direct or controlled (or, in certain instances, both).

We route the LFO signal through one or more of our four real-time controllers by using the bottom row of function switches (switches 17 through 32). These sixteen switches are actually four sets of four switches each, as follows: **(See Figure 10-20.)**

The potential actions of each of the four real-time controllers is exactly the same, but each controller is, of course, physically quite different. The first of these, the MOD WHEEL, is located directly to the left of your keyboard, and is labeled as such. This wheel has a smooth action and normally should be at its bottom-most (labeled "MIN") position. This ensures that it is not currently routing any signal. The second, the FOOT CONTROLLER, is a push-pull type foot pedal (NOT the piano-like sustain pedal that we discussed in Chapter Nine) that is normally supplied with American DX7s but is only available as an option with Japanese DX7s. If you are using one, make sure it is plugged into the "MODULATION" input jack on the back of your machine: **(See Figure 10-21.)**

Figure 10-21

and that it is kept at the fully-back position when not in use. This ensures that it is not currently active (you can also use this same pedal as a simple volume pedal for the DX7, if you plug it into the "VOLUME" input jack instead). The third controller is the BREATH CONTROLLER and this is optional on both American and Japanese machines. It is a small device normally held between the lips which is capable of reacting to wind pressure; you blow into it. As you blow harder or softer, it will route greater or lesser amounts of modulation signal. This must be plugged into the "BREATH CONT" mini-jack input on the front of your instrument, next to the pre-amplified PHONES jack (used for headphones): **(See Figure 10-22.)**

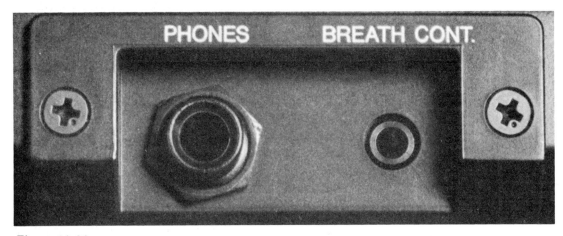

Figure 10-22

The fourth controller is the KEYBOARD AFTER-TOUCH and this requires just a bit of explanation. This controller, like the MOD WHEEL, is available on all DX7s, be they American, Japanese, or European, and is a pressure sensor located beneath every key on the keyboard. The harder you press down on a key, the more this sensor "complains" and the more modulation signal is allowed to pass. This is a **monophonic** control (unlike the *Keyboard Velocity Sensitivity*, which will be covered in Chapter Eleven), which means that whichever key in a group of keys is pressed the hardest will determine the overall amount of signal routed. In other words, you cannot have varying degrees of signal routed for specific notes in a chord, just by pressing some notes harder and other notes softer.

The first function switch in each group of four is the RANGE switch, and this simply determines **how much** LFO signal is to be routed via that particular controller, from 0 (no signal routed) to 99 (all signal routed), with all of the various smaller increments in-between. The next three switches are the **destination** switches, where we designate to the DX7 precisely where we wish the signal to terminate. These three are all "on-off" switches and can be changed using the "on-off" ("yes-no") buttons in the data entry section. The first of these, labeled PITCH is used to send the LFO signal to the pitch data inputs of the operators, if ON. The second, labeled AMP, routes the LFO signal to the amplifiers of the six operators; and the third, labeled EG BIAS, is used for a special kind of non-LFO modulation that we will be covering in Chapter Eleven.

With this in mind, let's run an Exercise to set up a controlled pitch modulation:

EXERCISE 57

Controlled pitch modulation:

    1) INITIALIZE your DX7, leave it in algorithm #1, TURN OFF operators 3 through 6 ("110000"), and, using the system of operators 1 and 2, GENERATE a sawtooth wave.
    2) Press edit switch 15 (P MOD SENS. parameter) and OBSERVE that it is currently at its default value of 3. This means that all six operators are slightly sensitive to LFO data, even though no data is

currently being sent them. If we can find a way of routing that data, they will react to some degree. We access this alternate routing by using the lower row of function switches.

3) Use the function mode-select switch to put your DX7 into function mode. Because function controls do not reset themselves, we will need to first ensure that none of the real-time controllers on your DX7 is currently active. Therefore, press function switch 17 (MOD WHEEL RANGE control) and use the data entry slider to enter a value of 0 (no data being routed). Do the same with function switches 21 (FOOT PEDAL RANGE), 25 (BREATH CONTROLLER RANGE), and 29 (AFTER TOUCH RANGE), making sure they **all** have values of 0. We also must be certain that all potential destinations are currently OFF. Press function switch 18 (WHEEL PITCH) and use the "off" data entry button to turn this destination OFF if it is not already so. Do the same with function switches 19 (WHEEL AMP), 20 (WHEEL EG BIAS), 22 (FOOT PITCH), 23 (FOOT AMP), 24 (FOOT EG BIAS), 26 (BREATH PITCH), 27 (BREATH AMP), 28 (BREATH EG BIAS), 30 (AFTER PITCH), 31 (AFTER AMP), and 32 (AFTER EG BIAS), setting all of these controls to OFF.*

4) Now we are ready to set our routing. Begin by pressing function switch 17 (WHEEL RANGE) and use the data entry slider to enter a value of 99. This means that all of the LFO signal (which currently consists of a default TRIANGLE wave traveling at a default speed of 35) is being routed through the modulation wheel.

5) Press function switch 18 (WHEEL PITCH) and turn this destination ON, using the data entry "on" ("yes") button. We have now instructed our DX7 to send that LFO signal to the pitch data inputs of our six operators.

6) Begin with the modulation wheel all the way at MIN (towards you). Play a note on the keyboard, HOLD it DOWN, and slowly move the wheel up towards MAX as you LISTEN (AUDIO CUE 57A): **(See Figure 10-23.)**

Figure 10-23

* This is a procedure you should follow whenever first programming or playing any DX7 - remember that function controls **never** reset themselves. The only way you can be certain of knowing that your controllers are not active is by checking and resetting each of these switches. For that reason, it's probably a good idea to go through this procedure every time you sit down at **any** DX7, even your own. With a little practice, it will only take you a few seconds, and you'll have the security of knowing that, whatever strange phenomenon may be occurring within your sounds, the controllers won't be to blame! You don't want to put yourself in a position of not knowing precisely what is occurring in your DX7 at all times.

NOTE: that as you raise the wheel up towards its MAX setting (furthest from you), the **depth** of the pitch modulation increases, just as it did when increasing the PMD setting in the last Exercise. This is because, just as in the last Exercise, we are routing LFO signal to the pitch inputs of our operators, but this time that signal is traveling through the Modulation Wheel instead of directly getting there. Therefore, with the Modulation Wheel at its MIN setting, it is as if we are routing no LFO signal in the first place. You can think of the real-time controller as acting like a valve, which can be fully closed (MIN), fully open (MAX), or anywhere in between. The maximum allowable signal which is routed at any one time by our controller is determined by the RANGE control.

7) The actions of each of the four real-time controllers is absolutely identical - THERE IS NOTHING ONE CONTROLLER CAN DO THAT ANY OTHER CONTROLLER CAN'T DO THE SAME WAY. With this in mind, restore the WHEEL RANGE value back to 0 and turn the WHEEL PITCH destination back to "OFF". Now press function switch 29 (AFTER RANGE) and CHANGE this to a new value of 99. Press function switch 30 (AFTER PITCH) and CHANGE it to "ON". Play a note very lightly on the keyboard and LISTEN (AUDIO CUE 57B). Depending on the current calibration of your instrument, you may hear no pitch modulation at all, or you may hear a small amount of "bleed-through" modulation*. Now press down on the same key, exert a steadily increasing pressure, and LISTEN (AUDIO CUE 57C). NOTE that the depth of the pitch modulation increases in the same way as previously raising the MOD WHEEL did.

8) Play the highest note on the keyboard (C6) as lightly as you can. Continue HOLDing this note DOWN, and play the lowest note on the keyboard (C1) with as much pressure as you can (if your last name is Schwarzenegger, or even if it isn't - don't go crazy! These keys can and do break off if abused! You have been warned!!). LISTEN (AUDIO CUE 57D). NOTE that the high note begins undergoing the same pitch change as the low one. This is because AFTER-TOUCH is a **monophonic** control. EXPERIMENT and NOTE that you can control the modulation depth for a group of notes by simply exerting increasing and decreasing pressure on a single note within that group.

9) The effects of the real-time controllers are **cumulative** - if you decide to use more than one controller for a signal routing (something which admittedly is not commonly done), then the effects of one controller will add on, or accumulate, onto the effects of any other. CHANGE the AFTER RANGE value to 50. Press function switch 17 and CHANGE the WHEEL RANGE to 75. Press function switch 18 and turn the WHEEL PITCH destination ON. We now have both the AFTER-TOUCH and the MOD WHEEL routing LFO signal to our operators' pitch inputs. Play a note on the keyboard with maximum finger pressure and LISTEN (AUDIO CUE 57E). Now slowly raise the MOD WHEEL and LISTEN (AUDIO CUE 57F). NOTE that the depth of the modulated sound increases still further as MOD WHEEL routes yet more LFO signal. These cumulative signals can in **no event** increase beyond the maximum of 99. Even though in this instance, the action of the two controllers appears to be greater than 99 (50 + 75 = 125, not 99), the DX7 "tops out" at its maximum. This is roughly equivalent to the action of an EG Level, which in no event can increase an operator's output level beyond its nominal setting (edit switch 27).

* If this is happening, don't panic! It probably just means that your DX7 needs recalibrating - an inexpensive and painless maintenance procedure your Authorized Service Center can do for you.

10)   Restore the AFTER RANGE to 0; restore the AFTER PITCH to OFF; restore the WHEEL RANGE to 99; and leave the WHEEL PITCH destination switch ON. Use the edit mode-select switch to return your DX7 to edit mode.

11)   Press edit switch 15 (P MOD SENS. parameter) and use the data entry slider to CHANGE this to a new value of 0. Place the MOD WHEEL at its MAX (furthest from you) position, play a note and LISTEN (AUDIO CUE 57G). NOTE that we now hear no pitch modulation at all. This is because even though we are routing LFO signal via our MOD WHEEL to the pitch inputs of our operators, they have all been made **insensitive** to the LFO's commands: **(See Figure10-24.)**

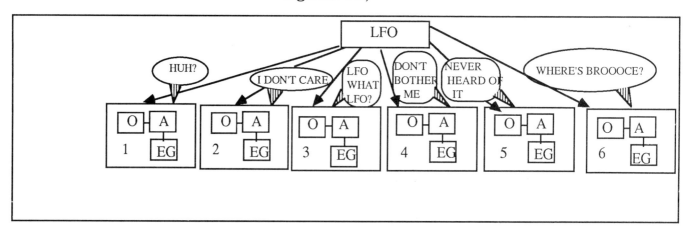

Figure 10-24

12)   Use the "yes" button to slowly CHANGE the P MOD SENS. value up to its maximum of 7, HOLDing DOWN a note and LISTENing as you do so (AUDIO CUE 57H). NOTE that as the P MOD sensitivity increases, so too does the **depth** of the pitch modulation.

13)   Familiarize yourself with different controlled pitch modulation routings. Press edit switch 9 and EXPERIMENT with different wave shapes. Press edit switch 10 and EXPERIMENT with different LFO speeds. Use different P MOD sensitivities and different controller RANGE values to determine the maximum allowable pitch modulation depth in every instance. If you have a FOOT CONTROLLER and/or a BREATH CONTROLLER, EXPERIMENT with using them as signal routers and NOTE that they affect the sound in precisely the same way as the WHEEL and AFTER-TOUCH do. Be careful to use the appropriate mode-select switch as you flip your DX7 back and forth from edit (LFO wave, speed, and P MOD sens controls) to function (RANGE and PITCH destination controls) mode. Get a good feel for the way the RANGE and SENSITIVITY controls interact.

NOTE that when using controlled modulation, the LFO DELAY (edit switch 11) has no effect whatever. The whole idea behind controlled modulation is that you yourself will, in real time, determine when, and to what degree, the LFO signal affects the sound. For that reason, the LFO DELAY parameter is only ever active for direct modulations.

Pitch modulation, then, can be used for a wide variety of effects: vibrato (with a SINE or TRIANGLE LFO wave), trill (with a SQUARE LFO wave), or even random arpeggiation (with a S/HOLD LFO wave). Very fast LFO speeds will yield periodic changes which are so fast they can barely be perceived as individual changes and will instead sound like a growl. The PMD, RANGE, and P MOD SENS. controls allow us to set up everything from a barely noticeable, subtle wavering, to a severe swooping in pitch. And, of course, the use of the real-time controllers allows us expressiveness - something that some keyboard purists have long claimed synthesizers lack.

Let's turn now to the use of the LFO for amplitude modulation. As with pitch modulation, we again have the option of either direct or controlled routings, and they are set up pretty much the same way. Edit switch 13, AMD, is used for the direct routing of LFO signal to the operator amplifiers. The real-time controllers can also send the same signal to the operator amplifiers with the use of the AMP destination function switch. In either circumstance, a certain degree of A MOD SENSitivity must be set, but here, unlike P MOD SENS., we have individual operator controls - we can specify which operators will react and which will not. Whereas the P MOD SENS. control had a range of 0 - 7, the A MOD SENS. control only has a range of 0 - 3. This limits our options quite a bit, as 0 represents no sensitivity, and 3 represents maximum sensitivity, leaving us only two different settings (1 and 2) in-between. More range in this control would have been nice, but one can only assume that memory limitations prevented it in the original DX7 design. Perhaps a future update will offer us a little more control here.

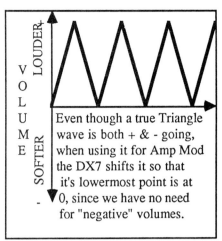

Even though a true Triangle wave is both + & - going, when using it for Amp Mod the DX7 shifts it so that it's lowermost point is at 0, since we have no need for "negative" volumes.

Figure 10-25

As mentioned previously, because amplitude modulation is operator-specific, we can use it to either periodically change the **volume** of a sound (if applied to a carrier) and/or the **timbre** of a sound (if applied to a modulator). This also gives us the freedom to apply amplitude modulation to specific **systems** within an overall sound. Let's begin with an Exercise to try out some of the effects of amplitude modulation on a **carrier**:

EXERCISE 58

Direct LFO amplitude modulation applied to a carrier:

1)   INITIALIZE your DX7, leave it in algorithm #1, TURN OFF operators 3 through 6 ("110000"), and use the system of operators 1 and 2 to GENERATE a sawtooth wave.
2)   Press edit switch 13 (AMD parameter) and OBSERVE that it is currently at its default value of 0. Press edit switch 16 (A MOD SENS. parameter) and use the operator select switch to OBSERVE that there is currently no sensitivity for amplitude modulation for either of our two operators (A MOD SENS. = 0 for all operators).
3)   Play a note on the keyboard and LISTEN (AUDIO CUE 58A). NOTE that there is currently no periodic change occurring to either the volume or timbre of the sawtooth wave. This is because no LFO modulation is being routed as yet to the amplifiers of either operators 1 or 2 (since AMD = 0) and that in any event neither are sensitive to such a modulation (since A MOD SENS. = 0).
4)   Press edit switch 16 and use the data entry slider to CHANGE the A MOD SENS. value for operator 1 **only** to its maximum value of 3. Make sure that operator 2 remains at its default value of 0. Press edit switch 13 and use the data entry slider to CHANGE the AMD to its maximum value of 99. Play a note on the keyboard and LISTEN (AUDIO CUE 58B). NOTE that you are now hearing a rapid change to the volume of the sound.
5)   Press edit switch 10 and use the data entry slider to CHANGE the LFO SPEED value to 8. Play a note and LISTEN (AUDIO CUE 58C). NOTE that the speed of the volume change has now slowed appreciably and that you can now clearly hear the volume gradually rising and falling, equivalent to the current TRIANGLE LFO waveshape:

This has precisely the same effect as slowly moving the VOLUME slider up and back. At a higher LFO SPEED value of 40 or so this will cause a typical **tremolo** effect. Tremolo is a steady back-and-forth change in the volume of a sound. Try it! (AUDIO CUE 58D).

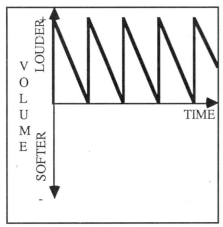

Figure 10-26

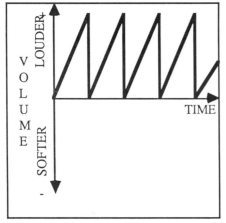

Figure 10-27

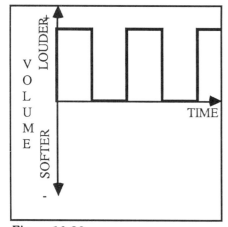

Figure 10-28

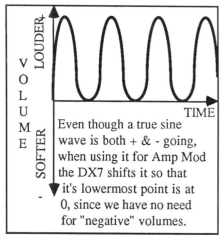

Even though a true sine wave is both + & - going, when using it for Amp Mod the DX7 shifts it so that it's lowermost point is at 0, since we have no need for "negative" volumes.

Figure 10-29

6) Restore the LFO SPEED (edit switch 10) back to a value of 8. Press edit switch 9 (LFO WAVE parameter) and press the "yes" button once to hear the effect of a SAW DOWN LFO wave (AUDIO CUE 58E). NOTE that the volume now instantly rises and slowly drops, as equivalent to the wave shape: **(See Figure 10-26.)**

7) Press the "yes" button once again to hear the effect of a SAW UP LFO wave (AUDIO CUE 58F). NOTE that the volume now changes in the opposite manner, (See Figure 10-27) slowly rising and quickly dropping, as equivalent to the wave shape: **(See Figure 10-27)**

8) Press the "yes" button once again to hear the effect of a SQUARE LFO wave (AUDIO CUE 58G). NOTE that the volume now instantly rises, followed by an instant fall, as equivalent to the wave shape: **(See Figure 10-28.)**

NOTE: that this produces an ON-OFF effect, useful in having sounds that repeat themselves periodically (yes, we were able to do this with the EG, but we were limited then to **one** repeat, maximum. See Exercise 48 in Chapter Nine if you don't remember how we did this).

9) Press the "yes" button once again to hear the effect of a SINE LFO wave (AUDIO CUE 58H). NOTE that the volume now gently rises and falls, in a manner equivalent to the wave shape: **(See Figure 10-29.)**

and similar to the effect of the TRIANGLE wave, but more gently, as the SINE wave is a more rounded shape. The SINE wave is in fact probably a better choice for most standard tremolo effects.

10) Press the "yes" button one last time to hear the effect of a S/HOLD LFO wave (AUDIO CUE 58I). NOTE that you now hear a random volume change as the DX7 is now periodically sampling from a stream of random numbers, and holding the number just long enough to send the data to the amplifiers of the six operators.

11) Restore the LFO shape to that of a TRIANGLE wave. Press edit switch 10 (LFO SPEED parameter) and, using the data entry slider, slowly CHANGE this value up to its maximum of 99, HOLDing DOWN a key and LISTENing as you do so (AUDIO CUE 58J). NOTE how this change in speed does not in any way alter the **type** of change you hear, nor the **amount** of change. NOTE also that this change in LFO SPEED is recognized by the DX7 in *real time*. Now use the data entry slider to slowly CHANGE this value back to its minimum of 0, HOLDing DOWN a key and LISTENing as you do so (AUDIO CUE 58K). NOTE that the speed of the volume change now decreases, and that at the absolute minimum speed of 0, it occurs only about once every **ten seconds** (indicating an LFO frequency of approximately 0.10 Hz).

12) Restore the LFO speed back to a value of 8 and press edit switch 13 (AMD parameter). Use the data entry slider to slowly CHANGE this value back to the minimum of 0, HOLDing DOWN a key and LISTENing as you do so (AUDIO CUE 58L). NOTE that this has the effect of lessening the depth of the volume change but in no way alters the shape of the change nor the speed.

13) Restore the AMD value back to 99 and press edit switch 16 (A MOD SENS. parameter). Use the "no" button to slowly CHANGE this value for operator 1 to its minimum of 0, HOLDing DOWN a key and LISTENing as you do so (AUDIO CUE 58M). NOTE that this has the same effect as lessening the AMD did, but because of its coarser range, it is much less subtle, and therefore less useful as a modulation depth control.

14) Restore the A MOD SENS. parameter for operator 1 back to a value of 3 and press edit switch 11 (LFO DELAY parameter). Use the data entry slider to CHANGE this to a value of 50. Play a note on the keyboard and LISTEN (AUDIO CUE 58N). NOTE that the effect of

the LFO on the volume is now delayed by about a second, but that the ultimate volume change is precisely the same as before. CHANGE the LFO DELAY value to its maximum of 99, play a note and LISTEN (AUDIO CUE 58O). NOTE that the onset of the LFO is now delayed by some 3 seconds.

15) EXPERIMENT by setting various different LFO waveshapes with various speeds and delay times. Also EXPERIMENT with different AMD and A MOD SENS. values for operator 1 and NOTE how changing these different controls affects the final sound. Try creating a second, different timbre within algorithm #1 by using the system of operators 3 and 4. Then apply an LFO amplitude modulation to operator 3 only. NOTE that we now have only one of the two timbres in our total sound (the operator 3-4 system) periodically changing in volume, while the other timbre (the operator 1-2 system) remains unchanged: **(See Figure 10-30.)**

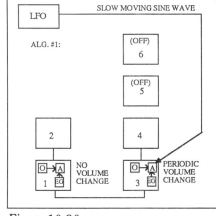

Figure 10-30

Of course, we can also accomplish the same exact modulation effects with our real-time controllers:

EXERCISE 59

Controlled LFO amplitude modulation applied to a carrier:

1) INITIALIZE your DX7, leave it in algorithm #1, TURN OFF operators 3 through 6 ("110000"), and, using the system of operators 1 and 2, GENERATE a sawtooth wave.

2) Press edit switch 16 (A MOD SENS. parameter) and CHANGE it to a new value of 3 for operator 1 only. Make sure operator 2 remains at its current default value of 0. This means that our carrier (operator 1) is now sensitive to amplitude modulation, even though no data is currently being sent to it. If we therefore route that data via one of our real-time controllers, operator 1 will react as much as possible. possible.

3) Use the function mode-select switch to put your DX7 into function mode. Using the procedure outlined in step 3 of Exercise 57 above, make sure none of your real-time controllers are currently active.

4) Press function switch 17 (WHEEL RANGE) and use the data entry slider to enter a value of 99. This means that all of the LFO signal (which currently consists of a default TRIANGLE wave traveling at a default speed of 35) is now being routed through the modulation wheel.

5) Press function switch 19 (WHEEL AMP) and use the "on" ("yes") data entry button to turn this ON. We have now instructed our DX7 to send the LFO signal to the **amplifiers** of our six operators and not to their pitch data inputs: **(See Figure 10-31.)**

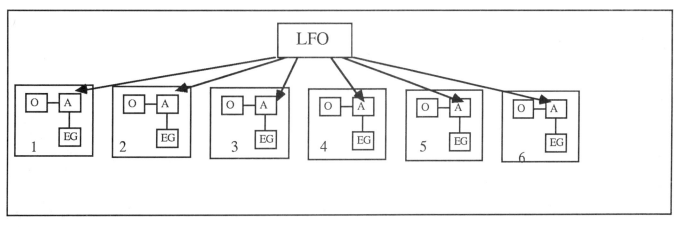

Figure 10-31

6)   Begin with the modulation wheel all the way at MIN (towards you). Play a note on the keyboard, HOLD it DOWN, and slowly move the wheel up towards MAX as you LISTEN (AUDIO CUE 59A). NOTE that as you raise the wheel up towards its MAX setting (furthest from you), the **depth** of the amplitude modulation increases, just as it did when increasing the AMD setting in the last Exercise. This is because, just as in the last Exercise, we are still routing LFO signal to the amplifiers of our operators, but this time that signal is traveling via the Modulation Wheel instead of directly getting there. Because currently only operator 1 is **sensitive** to amplitude modulation, we are currently only hearing a periodic **volume** change.

7)   Restore the WHEEL RANGE value back to 0 and turn the WHEEL AMP destination switch back to "OFF". Now press function switch 29 (AFTER RANGE) and CHANGE this to a new value of 99. Press function switch 31 (AFTER AMP) and CHANGE it to "ON". Play a note very lightly on the keyboard and LISTEN (AUDIO CUE 59B). Depending on the current calibration of your instrument, you may hear no amplitude modulation at all, or you may hear a small amount of "bleed-through" modulation. Now press down on the same key, exert a steadily increasing pressure, and LISTEN (AUDIO CUE 59C). NOTE that this causes the depth of the volume change to increase in the same way as previously raising the MOD WHEEL did.

8)   Play the highest note on the keyboard (C6) as lightly as you can. Continue HOLDing this note DOWN, and play the lowest note on the keyboard (C1) with as much pressure as you can and LISTEN (AUDIO CUE 59D). NOTE that the high note begins undergoing the same volume change as the low one. This is because AFTER-TOUCH is a **monophonic** control. EXPERIMENT and NOTE that you can control the modulation depth for a group of notes by simply exerting increasing and decreasing pressure on a single note within that group.

9)   As with pitch modulation routings, the effects of the real-time controllers are **cumulative**. CHANGE the AFTER RANGE value to 50. Press function switch 17 and CHANGE the WHEEL RANGE to 75. Press function switch 19 and turn the WHEEL AMP destination ON. We now have **both** the AFTER-TOUCH and the MOD WHEEL routing LFO signal to our operators' amplifiers. Play a note on the keyboard with maximum finger pressure and LISTEN (AUDIO CUE 59E). Now slowly raise the MOD WHEEL and LISTEN (AUDIO CUE 59F). NOTE that the depth of the modulated sound increases still further as MOD WHEEL routes yet more LFO signal. NOTE that these cumulative signals will in no event increase beyond the maximum of 99.

0)   Restore the AFTER RANGE to 0; restore the AFTER AMP to OFF; restore the WHEEL RANGE to 99; and leave the WHEEL AMP destination switch ON. Use the edit mode-select switch to return your DX7 to edit mode.

11)   Press edit switch 16 (A MOD SENS. parameter) and use the data entry slider to CHANGE this for operator 1 only to a new value of 0. Place the MOD WHEEL at its MAX (furthest from you) position, play a note and LISTEN (AUDIO CUE 59G). NOTE that we now hear no amplitude modulation at all.

12)   Use the "yes" button to slowly CHANGE the A MOD SENS. value for operator 1 up to its maximum of 3, HOLDing DOWN a note and LISTENing as you do so (AUDIO CUE 59H). NOTE that as the A MOD sensitivity increases, so too does the depth of the amplitude modulation.

13)   Familiarize yourself with different controlled amplitude modulation routings to carriers. Press edit switch 9 and EXPERIMENT with different wave shapes. Press edit switch 10 and EXPERIMENT with different LFO speeds. Use different A MOD sensitivities for operator 1 and different controller RANGE values to determine the maximum

The LFO / 157

allowable amplitude modulation depth in every instance. If you have a FOOT CONTROLLER and/or a BREATH CONTROLLER, EX-PERIMENT with using them as signal routers and NOTE that they affect the sound in precisely the same way as the WHEEL and AFTER-TOUCH do. Be careful to use the appropriate mode-select switch as you flip your DX7 back and forth from edit mode to function mode. Get a good feel for the way the RANGE and SENSITIVITY controls interact. Try creating, as before, a second timbre within algorithm #1 with the system of operators 3 and 4, and apply controlled amplitude modulation to operator 3 only. NOTE that once again, one timbre within the sound undergoes a periodic volume change while the other remains steady.

It is the operator-specificity of amplitude modulation in the DX7 that makes it such a powerful tool. With that in mind, let's try once again setting up a **direct** amplitude modulation, but this time we'll be affecting our modulator, resulting in periodic quantitative **timbral** changes:

EXERCISE 60

Direct LFO amplitude modulation applied to a modulator:

1) INITIALIZE your DX7, leave it in algorithm #1, TURN OFF operators 3 through 6 ("110000"), and use the system of operators 1 and 2 to GENERATE a sawtooth wave.

2) Press edit switch 13 (AMD parameter) and OBSERVE that it is currently at its default value of 0. Press edit switch 16 (A MOD SENS. parameter) and use the operator select switch to OBSERVE that there is currently no sensitivity for amplitude modulation for either of our two operators (A MOD SENS. = 0 for all operators).

3) Play a note on the keyboard and LISTEN (AUDIO CUE 60A). NOTE that there is currently no periodic change occurring to either the amplitude or timbre of the sawtooth wave. This is because no LFO modulation is being routed as yet to the amplifiers of either operators 1 or 2 (since AMD = 0) and that in any event neither are sensitive to such a modulation (since A MOD SENS. = 0).

4) Press edit switch 16 and use the data entry slider to CHANGE the A MOD SENS. value for operator 2 only to its maximum value of 3. Make sure that operator 1 remains at its default value of 0. Press edit switch 13 and use the data entry slider to CHANGE the AMD to its maximum value of 99. Play a note on the keyboard and LISTEN (AUDIO CUE 60B). NOTE that you are now hearing a rapid change to the **timbre** of the sound.

5) Press edit switch 10 and use the data entry slider to CHANGE the LFO SPEED value to 8. Play a note and LISTEN (AUDIO CUE 60C). NOTE that the speed of the timbral change has now slowed appreciably and that you can now clearly hear the overtones coming in and out, as the LFO's TRIANGLE wave gradually increases and then decreases the OUTPUT LEVEL of operator 2 (because it is controlling operator 2's amplifier). **(See Figure 10-32.)**

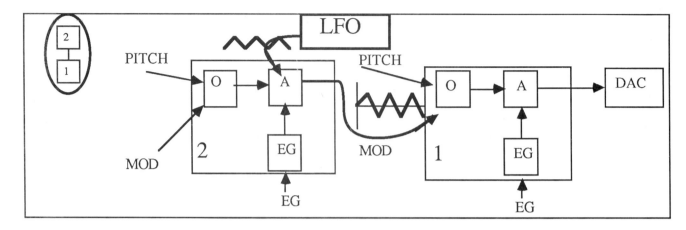

Figure 10-32

At a higher LFO SPEED value of 40 or so this will cause a typical wah-wah effect. Try it! (AUDIO CUE 60D).

6)   Restore the LFO SPEED (edit switch 10) back to a value of 8. Press edit switch 9 (LFO WAVE parameter) and press the "yes" button once to hear the effect of a SAW DOWN LFO wave (AUDIO CUE 60E). NOTE that the overtone content now instantly rises and slowly drops, as equivalent to the wave shape: **(See Figure 10-33.)**

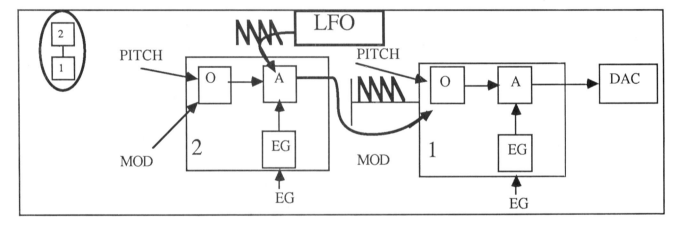

Figure 10-33

7)   Press the "yes" button once again to hear the effect of a SAW UP LFO wave (AUDIO CUE 60F). NOTE that the timbre now changes in the opposite manner, with the overtone content slowly increasing and quickly decreasing, as equivalent to the wave shape: **(See Figure 10-34.)**

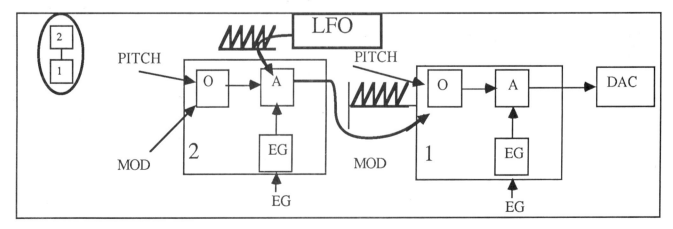

Figure 10-34

8) Press the "yes" button once again to hear the effect of a SQUARE LFO wave (AUDIO CUE 60G). NOTE that we now hear **two** different timbres, a sawtooth wave when the LFO SQUARE WAVE is positive: **(See Figure 10-35.)**

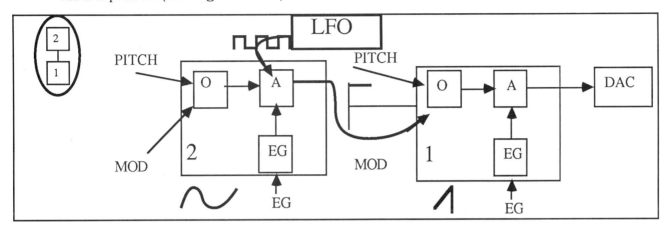

Figure 10-35

and a sine wave when the LFO SQUARE WAVE is negative: **(See Figure 10-36.)**

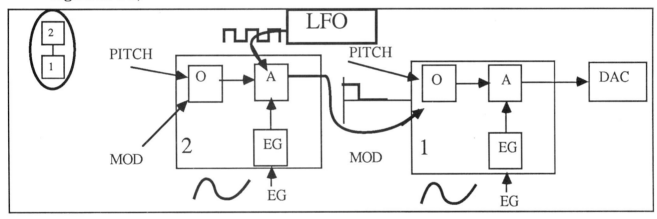

Figure 10-36

9) Press the "yes" button once again to hear the effect of a SINE LFO wave (AUDIO CUE 60H). NOTE that the overtone content now gently rises and falls, producing a gentle repeating "wah-wah", in a manner equivalent to the wave shape: **(See Figure 10-37.)**

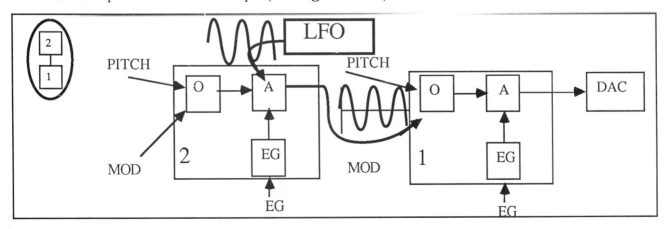

Figure 10-37

and similar to the effect of the TRIANGLE wave, but more gently, as the SINE wave is a more rounded shape.

10) Press the "yes" button one last time to hear the effect of a S/HOLD LFO wave (AUDIO CUE 60I). This is probably the most interesting and typical use of the S/HOLD waveshape, as you now hear a random **timbral** change. Increase the LFO SPEED control (edit switch 10) to about 40 or so to hear a pleasing, rhythmic random change in timbre (AUDIO CUE 60J).

11) Restore the LFO shape to that of a TRIANGLE wave. Press edit switch 10 (LFO SPEED parameter) and, using the data entry slider, slowly CHANGE this value up to its maximum of 99, HOLDing DOWN a key and LISTENing as you do so (AUDIO CUE 60K). At the highest LFO speeds you will start to hear some dissonant overtones (called *sidebands*) creeping in. This is because our LFO is now in an audible (greater than 20 Hz) range. NOTE, however, that these changes in speed do not in any way alter the **type** of change you hear, nor the **amount** of change. NOTE also that changes in LFO SPEED are recognized by the DX7 in real time. Now use the data entry slider to slowly CHANGE this value back to its minimum of 0, HOLDing DOWN a key and LISTENing as you do so (AUDIO CUE 60L). NOTE that the speed of the timbral change now decreases, and that at the absolute minimum speed of 0, it occurs only about **once** every **ten seconds**.

12) Restore the LFO speed back to a value of 8 and press edit switch 13 (AMD parameter). Use the data entry slider to slowly CHANGE this value back to the minimum of 0, HOLDing DOWN a key and LISTENing as you do so (AUDIO CUE 60M). NOTE that this has the effect of lessening the **depth** of the timbral change (we hear **more** overtones coming in and out) but in no way alters the shape of the change nor the speed.

13) Restore the AMD value back to 99 and press edit switch 16 (A MOD SENS. parameter). Use the "no" button to slowly CHANGE this value for operator 2 to its minimum of 0, HOLDing DOWN a key and LISTENing as you do so (AUDIO CUE 60N). NOTE that this has the same effect as lessening the AMD did, but because of its coarser range, it is much less subtle, and so generally less useful as a modulation depth control.

14) Restore the A MOD SENS. parameter for operator 2 back to a value of 3 and press edit switch 11 (LFO DELAY parameter). Use the data entry slider to CHANGE this to a value of 50. Play a note on the keyboard and LISTEN (AUDIO CUE 60O). NOTE that the effect of the LFO on the overtone content is now delayed by about a second, but that the ultimate timbral change is precisely the same as before. CHANGE the LFO DELAY value to its maximum of 99, play a note and LISTEN (AUDIO CUE 60P). NOTE that the onset of the LFO is now delayed by some 3 seconds.

15) EXPERIMENT by setting various different LFO waveshapes with various speeds and delay times. Also EXPERIMENT with different AMD and A MOD SENS. values for operator 2 and NOTE how changing these different controls affects the final sound.

16) Because amplitude modulation is operator-specific, we can apply it to both our modulator and carrier, in the same or different degrees, if we so desire. EXPERIMENT by redoing this entire Exercise with both operators 1 and 2 set to maximum A MOD SENSitivity. NOTE how both the volume and the timbre are affected by the LFO in the same manner. Then EXPERIMENT by redoing this EXERCISE with operator 1 set to a sensitivity of 3 and operator 2 at a sensitivity of 1. NOTE how the same LFO manipulations now affect mostly the volume, but with slight amounts of timbral change as well. Finally, EXPERIMENT by reversing the sensitivities (operator 1 = a value of 1 and operator 2 = a value of 3). NOTE that we now generate the op-

posite effect: a great deal of timbral change and only a small amount of volume change.

Again, whatever kinds of modulation effects we can set up directly, we can also route via our real-time controllers:

EXERCISE 61

Controlled LFO amplitude modulation applied to a modulator:

1)   INITIALIZE your DX7, leave it in algorithm #1, TURN OFF operators 3 through 6 ("110000"), and, using the system of operators 1 and 2, GENERATE a sawtooth wave.

2)   Press edit switch 16 (A MOD SENS. parameter) and CHANGE it to a new value of 3 for operator 2 **only**. Make sure operator 1 remains at its current default value of 0. This means that our modulator (operator 2) is now sensitive to amplitude modulation, even though no data is currently being sent to it. If we therefore route that data via one of our real-time controllers, operator 2 will react as much as possible, giving us a quantitative change in the timbre of the sound.

3)   Use the function mode-select switch to put your DX7 into function mode. Using the procedure outlined in step 3 of Exercise 57 above, make sure none of your real-time controllers are currently active.

4)   Press function switch 17 (WHEEL RANGE) and use the data entry slider to enter a value of 99. This means that all of the LFO signal (which currently consists of a default TRIANGLE wave traveling at a default speed of 35) is now being routed through the modulation wheel.

5)   Press function switch 19 (WHEEL AMP) and use the "on" ("yes") data entry button to turn this ON. We have now instructed our DX7 to send the LFO signal to the amplifiers of our six operators. However, only operator 2 in this instance will react.

6)   Begin with the modulation wheel all the way at MIN (towards you). Play a note on the keyboard, HOLD it DOWN, and slowly move the wheel up towards MAX as you LISTEN (AUDIO CUE 61A). NOTE that as you raise the wheel up towards its MAX setting (furthest from you), the depth of the amplitude modulation increases, just as it did when increasing the AMD setting in the last Exercise. This is because, just as in the last Exercise, we are routing LFO signal to the amplifiers of our operators, but this time that signal is traveling via the Modulation Wheel instead of directly getting there. Because currently only operator 2 is **sensitive** to amplitude modulation, we are currently only hearing a periodic timbral change.

7)   Restore the WHEEL RANGE value back to 0 and turn the WHEEL AMP destination switch back to "OFF". Now press function switch 29 (AFTER RANGE) and CHANGE this to a new value of 99. Press function switch 31 (AFTER AMP) and CHANGE it to "ON". Play a note very lightly on the keyboard and LISTEN (AUDIO CUE 61B). Depending on the current calibration of your instrument, you may hear no amplitude modulation at all, or you may hear a small amount of "bleed-through" modulation. Now press down on the same key, exert a steadily increasing pressure, and LISTEN (AUDIO CUE 61C). NOTE that the depth of the timbral change increases in the same way as previously raising the MOD WHEEL did.

8)   Play the highest note on the keyboard (C6) as lightly as you can. Continue HOLDing this note DOWN, and play the lowest note on the keyboard (C1) with as much pressure as you can and LISTEN (AUDIO CUE 61D). NOTE that the high note begins undergoing the same periodic timbral change as the low one. This is because AFTER-TOUCH is a monophonic control. EXPERIMENT and NOTE that you can control the modulation depth for a group of notes by sim-

ply exerting increasing and decreasing pressure on a single note within that group.

9)   As with pitch modulation routings, the effects of the real-time controllers are cumulative. CHANGE the AFTER RANGE value to 50. Press function switch 17 and CHANGE the WHEEL RANGE to 75. Press function switch 19 and turn the WHEEL AMP destination ON. We now have both the AFTER-TOUCH and the MOD WHEEL routing LFO signal to our operators' amplifiers. Play a note on the keyboard with maximum finger pressure and LISTEN (AUDIO CUE 61E). Now slowly raise the MOD WHEEL and LISTEN (AUDIO CUE 61F). NOTE that the depth of the modulated sound increases still further as MOD WHEEL routes yet more LFO signal. NOTE that these cumulative signals will in no event increase beyond the maximum of 99.

10)   Restore the AFTER RANGE to 0; restore the AFTER AMP to OFF; restore the WHEEL RANGE to 99; and leave the WHEEL AMP destination switch ON. Use the edit mode-select switch to return your DX7 to edit mode.

11)   Press edit switch 16 (A MOD SENS. parameter) and use the data entry slider to CHANGE this for operator 2 only to a new value of 0. Place the MOD WHEEL at its MAX (furthest from you) position, play a note and LISTEN (AUDIO CUE 61G). NOTE that we now hear no amplitude modulation at all.

12)   Use the "yes" button to slowly CHANGE the A MOD SENS. value for operator 2 up to its maximum of 3, HOLDing DOWN a note and LISTENing as you do so (AUDIO CUE 61H). NOTE that as the A MOD sensitivity increases, so too does the depth of the amplitude modulation.

13)   Familiarize yourself with different controlled amplitude modulation routings to **modulators**. Press edit switch 9 and EXPERIMENT with different wave shapes. Press edit switch 10 and EXPERIMENT with different LFO speeds. Use different A MOD sensitivities for operator 2 and different controller RANGE values to determine the maximum allowable amplitude modulation depth in every instance. If you have a FOOT CONTROLLER and/or a BREATH CONTROLLER, EXPERIMENT with using them as signal routers and NOTE that they affect the sound in precisely the same way as the WHEEL and AFTER-TOUCH do. Be careful to use the appropriate mode-select switch as you flip your DX7 back and forth from edit mode to function mode.

Setting up LFO effects is one area in the DX7 where having non-voice-specific function controls can be a real problem. It should be clear that in order to create a sound in which you wish the option of either controlled pitch or controlled amplitude modulation, you must take the precaution of setting a predetermined amount of either P MOD SENSITIVITY or A MOD SENSITIVITY in edit mode when actually programming the sound. Furthermore, you'll have to remember to assign the appropriate RANGE amount to the controller you wish to use and remember to turn the correct destination switch ON in order to actually get that modulation!

This can lead to confusion. For example, suppose you generated a flute sound with the LFO set at a SINE wave, and with a certain amount of P MOD SENSitivity pre-programmed. Let's suppose the very next internal memory slot contained a tuba sound with the LFO set at a SQUARE wave and no P MOD SENSitiviy, but with the carriers sensitive for a slight amount of amplitude modulation. Let's go further and assume that the next internal memory slot contained a Squeaking Breadbox sound with no modulation sensitivity of any kind. You're at a gig, the first sound of the night is the flute sound, and you want to use the keyboard AFTER-TOUCH to fade in and out the vibrato effect you pre-set, so you set the AFTER RANGE to, say, 50, and you turn the AFTER PITCH ON. No problem, you play a few notes, you press down a bit harder, and the vibrato comes in and out, just as you'd planned. Next song, next sound: the tuba. If you don't make any function control changes, then pressing down on the key harder won't do anything! Why? Because the tuba sound has no P MOD SENSitivity, only A MOD SENSitivity, and the AFTER-TOUCH is currently only routing LFO signal to the PITCH inputs of your operators. So, in the middle of the song, you frantically turn the AFTER PITCH OFF and you turn the AFTER AMP ON. Whew! Next song, next sound, and you find, of course, that your Squeaking Breadbox sound won't modulate at all, no matter how hard you press down on the key, step on the FOOT CONTROLLER, move the MOD WHEEL, or toot into the BREATH CONTROLLER. You may get a sudden burst of inspiration in the middle of your lead bagpipist's solo and want to add a tremolo to your Squeaking Breadbox, but it won't work! Why? Because you neglected to pre-program any modulation sensitivity. Of course, you can always put your DX7 back into edit mode and frantically do it, but, believe me, the last thing you want to do in a live situation is put your DX7 into edit mode...

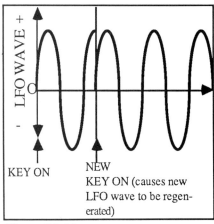

Figure 10-38

Another very common problem is encountered by the new DX7 owner who excitedly gets his machine out of the box (usually with only a cursory glance at the manual), sees a button marked "PITCH" next to that old analog standby, the MOD WHEEL, figures out how to turn it ON, and then expects that the MOD WHEEL will deliver a screaming Jan Hammer-type vibrato to any and all sound he calls up. Chances are that a few sounds will react with a vibrato when the wheel is raised, but chances are some other sounds will react very weirdly, with bubbling noises, repeated trills, or even random nonsense. Other sounds won't react at all to the MOD WHEEL. This often precipitates a "My DX7's Broken!" phone call to the store, to Yamaha, or worse yet, to me. What's happening, of course, is that various sounds have been programmed with different types of sensitivity, different LFO wave shapes, different LFO speeds. You can play trial-and-error games with sounds, just trying different controllers sending different amounts of modulation signal to different destinations, and just see what happens, but it makes far more sense to simply take a minute, put the DX7 in edit mode, and HAVE A LOOK. The data contained in edit switches 9 through 16 will tell you everything you need to know about modulation routings and sensitivities within that sound.

It would probably be a good idea to devote an evening to going through all the preset sounds you have for your DX7 (ROM presets and things you may have bought or gotten from friends in your RAM cartridge or internal memory) and examine each of them to see precisely what kind of modulation effects they have been set up for. You'll probably be very surprised at the number of expressive sounds you have already: many of them are probably already set to deliver vibratos, tremolos, trills, bubbles, random effects, or just plain weirdness - if only you'd use your controllers to route modulation signal to the correct destination! Get to know what you already have in your DX7 and new avenues of creativity will probably open themselves up to you!

Okay, we're ready now to check out the final LFO control, the LFO KEY SYNC parameter, accessed by edit switch 14. As mentioned earlier, this switch allows you to trigger the LFO from the KEY ON flag, thereby **synchronizing** it to the rhythms you play on the keyboard. When the LFO KEY SYNC is OFF, the LFO ignores you, me, and the world at large, and simply spits out its slow-moving waves, oblivious to the beauty and wonder of Nature or, for that matter, anything else. When the LFO KEY SYNC is ON, however, the LFO will be "listening" for KEY ON flags. Whenever it perceives one, it will immediately stop spitting out its wave and will instantly return to the beginning of its wave cycle: in other words, the act of you playing a note will actually cause it to *re-trigger*. **(See Figure 10-38.)**

This parameter, unlike (and not to be confused with) the OSC KEY SYNC parameter (see Chapter Five) can be very useful. If you are using the LFO for rhythmic effects (as with a SQUARE or SAW DOWN waveshape, for example), then having the LFO KEY SYNC ON will allow you to control the

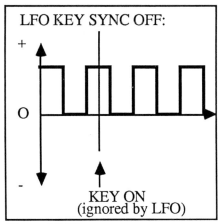

Figure 10-39

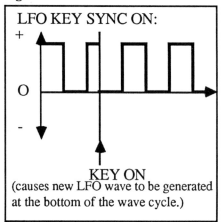

Figure 10-40

rhythms with your own keyboard technique. On the other hand, having it OFF will force you to play to the **LFO's** sense of rhythm (which, unless your name is Charlie Watts, is probably better than yours!). Let's run an Exercise now to try it out. For the sake of a little variety, we'll work with a square wave as our audio source. We'll begin by setting up a very obvious volume change with a SQUARE LFO wave, and we'll see how turning the LFO KEY SYNC ON and OFF affects the sound:

EXERCISE 62

LFO Key Sync:

1)   INITIALIZE your DX7, leave it in algorithm #1, TURN OFF operators 3 through 6 ("110000"), and use the system of operators 1 and 2 to GENERATE a **square wave**.

2)   Press edit switch 14 (LFO KEY SYNC parameter), OBSERVE that it is currently at its default value of ON, and use the "no" button to turn it OFF.

3)   Press edit switch 9 (LFO WAVE parameter) and use the data entry slider to CHANGE this to a SQUARE wave.

4)   Press edit switch 13 (AMD parameter) and CHANGE this from its default of 0 to its maximum value of 99, thereby setting up a direct amplitude modulation.

5)   Press edit switch 16 (A MOD SENS. parameter) and VIEW operator 1. CHANGE the sensitivity for operator 1 only from its current default of 0 to the maximum value of 3.

6)   Play a note on the keyboard and LISTEN (AUDIO CUE 62A). NOTE that we are hearing a periodic on-off volume change, as only our carrier (operator 1) is reacting to the SQUARE LFO wave.

7)   Play a rhythmic tune on the keyboard (AUDIO CUE 62B). NOTE that, regardless of any syncopations or poorly timed notes you may strike, the LFO continues inducing this on-off pattern at the same speed and without ever changing. **(See Figure 10-39.)**

8)   Now press edit switch 14 and turn the LFO KEY SYNC ON. Play the same rhythmic tune (AUDIO CUE 62C) and NOTE that any syncopations or out-of-time notes you play have the effect of causing the LFO to **restart** its SQUARE WAVE, always at the bottom of its cycle: **(See Figure 10-40.)**

9)   EXPERIMENT with different LFO waves and speeds and different AMD or PMD, A MOD SENS. and P MOD SENS. settings. For each new setting, turn the LFO KEY SYNC first OFF, then ON. NOTE that regardless of the LFO shape, speed, or type of modulation, the LFO KEY SYNC always has the effect of re-triggering the LFO wave at the beginning of its cycle.

LFO modulation effects are like any other edit parameters - they can be modified at will, simply by putting your DX7 into edit mode, and entering in new data. This allows us, of course, to modify any LFO settings in any preset, and this is yet another "customizing" job that you should do to the sounds you use in order to optimize them for your particular needs.

Since we have already devoted a good deal of time to examining and modifying the "E.PIANO 1" preset, let's take a look at what the LFO is doing for this sound and how we can modify it:

EXERCISE 63

Modifying the LFO in E.PIANO 1:

1)   Put your DX7 into play mode and call up "E.PIANO 1" either from ROM 1A-11 or ROM 3A-8.

2) Use the edit mode select switch to put your machine in edit mode and press edit switch 12 (PMD). OBSERVE that this value is 0, telling us that there is no direct pitch modulation in this sound.

3) Press edit switch 13 (AMD) and OBSERVE that this value is also 0, telling us that there is no direct amplitude modulation in this sound either.

4) Press edit switch 15 (P MOD SENS.) and OBSERVE that this currently has a value of 3 (for all operators, of course).

5) Press edit switch 16 (A MOD SENS.) and, using the operator select switch, observe that this value for each of the six operators is set at 0.

6) The information gleaned from steps 2, 3, 4, and 5 above tell us what the LFO is intended to be doing for this sound: there is no amplitude modulation intended since both the AMD and the A MOD SENS. settings are all 0. But obviously, even though there is no direct pitch modulation, the LFO is intended for this use, since a certain degree (3) of P MOD SENS. has been pre-programmed. With this in mind, let's VIEW the SHAPE and SPEED of the LFO (the DELAY is inactive, since there is no direct modulation). Press edit switch 9 and OBSERVE that the LFO WAVE is a SINE wave, and press edit switch 10 and OBSERVE that the LFO SPEED has been given a value of 34.

7) Because there is a certain amount of P MOD SENSitivity, we can route our LFO SINE WAVE, traveling at a speed of 34, to the pitch inputs of our operators via any of our real-time controllers, and be confident that the intended pitch modulation will in fact occur. Use the function mode select switch to put your DX7 in function mode, and use the technique outlined in Exercise 57 above to make sure that all your controllers are currently deactivated. Now press function switch 17 (WHEEL RANGE). Use the data entry slider to set this at a value of 55 (chosen instead of 99 for a more subtle effect).

8) Press function switch 18 (WHEEL PITCH) and use the "yes" button to turn this ON.

9) Play a note on the keyboard, move the MOD WHEEL up towards its MAXimum setting, and LISTEN (AUDIO CUE 63A). NOTE that the use of the MOD WHEEL, or any other controller, for that matter, induces the pre-programmed *vibrato* effect.

10) Let's change this to a *tremolo* effect instead. Press function switch 18 and turn the WHEEL PITCH destination OFF. Turn the WHEEL AMP destination ON and CHANGE the WHEEL RANGE to the maximum setting of 99.

11) Use the edit mode select switch to return your DX7 to edit mode. Press switch 16 (A MOD SENS.), and, using the operator select switch, CHANGE this value for operators 1, 3, and 5 (the carriers for algorithm #5 - don't forget that the upper left-hand corner of the LCD is telling you this) to their maximum of 3. Leave the A MOD SENSitivity for operators 2, 4, and 6 at their current value of 0.

12) Play a note on the keyboard, move the MOD WHEEL up towards its MAXimum setting, and LISTEN (AUDIO CUE 63B). With this one small change, we have changed the vibrato effect to a tremolo effect.

13) But what of the vibrato? Since the P MOD SENS. control still has a value of 3, surely we can use the LFO for that as well! The most common use of the real-time controllers is to set up different ones to route modulation signal to different destinations. Press function switch 29 (AFTER RANGE) and set a value of 55. Then press function switch 30 (AFTER PITCH) and turn it ON. Now the MOD WHEEL will control the tremolo depth and the keyboard AFTER-TOUCH will control the vibrato depth! Try it!! (AUDIO CUE 63C).

14) EXPERIMENT with other presets. Begin by examining their PMD and AMD values to find out if an LFO modulation is an intrinsic part of the sound. If not, examine their P MOD SENS. and A MOD SENS. settings to see if there is an intended controller modulation. If

so, set up one (or more) of your controllers to deliver the LFO signal to the appropriate destination. Then CHANGE various parameters, including the LFO WAVE shape, the LFO SPEED, and the RANGE and SENSitivity controls in order to modify these sounds in interesting ways.

In summary, the LFO is a powerful tool that allows us to make a periodic change to the volume, pitch, or timbre of any sound we create or call up on our DX7. Depending upon the LFO shape, its speed, and its destination, we can set up a wide variety of different effects - but these effects will always repeat throughout the duration of the sound. The LFO signal can be routed directly, so that its effect becomes an intrinsic part of the sound itself, or it can be routed through any of our real-time controllers, allowing the user expressiveness. All in all, it's amazing what a slow-moving digital oscillator can do!

SWITCHES AND CONTROLS COVERED IN CHAPTER TEN:

SWITCH	PARAMETER	COMMENTS
Edit 9	LFO Wave	Select from one of six preset shapes.
Edit 10	LFO Speed	Range 0 - 99 0 = slowest speed; 99 = fastest speed.
Edit 11	LFO Delay	Range 0 - 99 0 = minimum delay; 99 = maximum delay.
Edit 12	PMD	Direct pitch modulation depth.
Edit 13	AMD	Direct amplitude modulation depth.
Edit 14	LFO key sync	"On" or "Off"; LFO triggered from keyboard if ON.
Edit 15	Pitch modulation sensitivity	Non-operator-specific; Range 0 - 7.
Edit 16	Amplitude modulation sensitivity	Operator-specific Range 0 - 3.
Function 17	Mod wheel range	Range 0 - 99.
Function 18	Mod wheel pitch destination	"On" or "Off".
Function 19	Mod wheel amp destination	"On" or "Off".
Function 21	Foot controller range	Range 0 - 99.
Function 22	Foot controller pitch destination	"On" or "Off".
Function 23	Foot controller amp destination	"On" or "Off".

Function 25	Breath controller range	Range 0 - 99.
Function 26	Breath controller pitch destination	"On" or "Off".
Function 27	Breath controller amp destination	"On" or "Off".
Function 29	After-touch range	Range 0 - 99.
Function 30	After-touch pitch destination	"On" or "Off".
Function 31	After-touch amp destination	"On" or "Off".

CHAPTER ELEVEN: EG BIAS MODULATION AND KEYBOARD VELOCITY SENSITIVITY

EG BIAS MODULATION

The DX7 has provision for four *real-time controllers*: the *modulation wheel*, the *foot controller*, the *breath controller*, and the *keyboard after-touch*. Each of these can perform identical functions, and in the last chapter we learned about two of those functions: routing LFO signal to the pitch inputs of our operators (*pitch modulation*) and routing LFO signal to the amplifiers of our six operators (*amplitude modulation*). There is a third type of controlled modulation, however, called *EG bias modulation*. This type of modulation has nothing whatsoever to do with the LFO, even though its associated operator-specific sensitivity control "shares" one of the LFO edit switches.

In order to explain EG bias modulation, let's first return to our diagram of an operator:**(See Figure 11-1.)**

The oscillator initiates our audible signal and then passes this signal on to the amplifier, which will shape its amplitude **according to the instructions received by the EG**. The EG, of course, receives its instructions from us, via the EG data input. Finally, after the amplifier processes it according to the EG commands, the signal exits the operator as an **output**. The purpose of EG bias modulation is to control, in real time, the following signal flow: **(See Figure 11-2.)**

This becomes particularly useful when you realize that **the amount of output is always proportional to the amount of EG control signal received by the amplifier**. Taking this a step further, we can see that if an operator's amplifier receives no signal from its EG, then it won't pass any signal at all - hence no output. **(See Figure 11-3.)**

EG bias modulation, then, allows us to DIRECTLY CONTROL, IN REAL TIME, THE OUTPUT OF PARTICULAR OPERATORS. Cardinal Rules One and Two tell us that this will allow us direct, real-time control of either **volume** or **timbre** *, or both, depending upon whether we are affecting carriers or modulators. The only question remaining now is, how do we determine which of our operators will be sensitive to this type of modulation?

The answer, unfortunately, is not an obvious one. I'd love to be able to tell you that there is a switch on your DX7 labeled "EG Bias Sensitivity" but a quick look at your front panel will tell you that this switch simply doesn't exist. For reasons that we can only guess at, Yamaha does not provide us with such a dedicated switch - instead, the operator-specific EG Bias Sensitivity is determined by the operator-specific Amplitude Modulation Sensitivity control - edit switch 16. In other words, whichever operators are made sensitive for amplitude modulation will also automatically be sensitive for this EG bias modulation.

How do we determine how much effect our real-time controller has on the EG-to-amplifier signal flow? The **depth** of our modulation is determined by

---

* Direct, real-time control of pitch is possible on the DX7 by the use of the *pitch-bend wheel*. See Chapter 13 for a detailed description of this device.

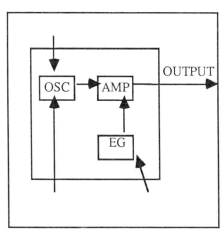

Figure 11-1

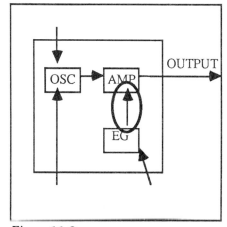

Figure 11-2

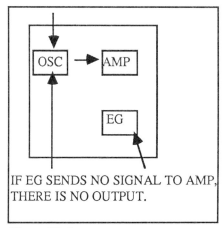

IF EG SENDS NO SIGNAL TO AMP, THERE IS NO OUTPUT.

Figure 11-3

the controller range switch; that is, function switches 17, 21, 25, and 29. As before, we have complete freedom to decide which real-time controller we wish to use for this modulation effect. So, the "patch" for setting up an EG bias modulation on your DX7 is as follows:

1) Decide which operators you wish to have sensitive for EG bias modulation, and make them sensitive by pressing edit switch 16 and assigning values greater than 0 for those particular operators (in most cases, you will probably want to assign the maximum value of 3 and then use the associated controller range control for fine-tuning the depth).

2) Decide which controller you wish to use for EG bias modulation, and use the appropriate range control to determine **how much** effect that controller will have on the signal flow. If, for example, you wish the Mod Wheel to have maximum effect, you would set the Mod Wheel's RANGE switch (function switch 17) to a value of 99.

3) Tell the DX7's microprocessor that you wish to use that particular controller for EG bias modulation by turning the EG BIAS **destination** switch (function switch 20, 24, 28, or 32) ON. If you'd like the Mod Wheel, for example, to be routing EG bias modulation signal only, then be sure and turn its other two destinations (WHEEL PITCH and WHEEL AMP - function switches 18 and 19) OFF.

Bear in mind that even when using EG bias modulation to control the EG-to-amp signal flow, the EG is still cycling normally in response to KEY ON and KEY OFF flags. In other words, even if you are completely attenuating the EG bias so that the operator amplifier is totally shut down, the EG is still going through whatever movements you programmed in, regardless. It doesn't know, nor does it care, that the amplifier is not receiving its instructions. Therefore, if you try applying EG bias modulation to a carrier with a short, percussive envelope, for example, its envelope may already be at 0 level by the time you get around to routing the signal via a real-time controller. This is something to be aware of when using this control.

Let's run an exercise now to try out EG bias modulation, as applied to a carrier in a single-system sound:

EXERCISE 64

EG bias modulation applied to a carrier:

1) INITIALIZE your DX7, leave it in algorithm #1, TURN OFF operators 3 through 6 ("110000"), and, using the system of operators 1 and 2, GENERATE a sawtooth wave.

2) Press edit switch 16 (A MOD SENS. parameter) and use the operator select switch to VIEW operator 1. CHANGE this value from its default of 0 to a new value of 3 for operator 1 only. Remember that by doing so, we are not only making operator 1 sensitive to amplitude modulation, but we are also making it sensitive to EG bias modulation.

3) Press the function mode select switch to put your DX7 into function mode. Using the procedure outlined in Exercise 57 (Chapter 10), make sure none of your real-time controllers is currently activated.

4) Press function switch 17 (WHEEL RANGE parameter) and enter a value of 99. Press function switch 20 (WHEEL EG BIAS destination switch) and set it to ON. We have now "instructed" our DX7 that we wish to use the MOD WHEEL to completely control the EG-to-AMP signal flow for operator 1. Because in algorithm #1, operator 1 is a carrier, we can expect to hear a volume change. Specifically, we can expect the MOD WHEEL to completely control the volume of our sound, since operator 1 is the only carrier we are currently using.

5) Put the MOD WHEEL at its MIN position, play a note on the keyboard and LISTEN. Depending on the current calibration of your machine, you may be hearing no sound at all, or you may be hearing a

slight amount of "bleed-through" (see Exercise 57, Chapter 10, for an explanation of this phenomenon). Now slowly raise the MOD WHEEL up to its MAX position, HOLDing DOWN a note and LISTENing as you do so (AUDIO CUE 64A). NOTE that the MOD WHEEL is currently acting as a volume control.

6)   Because the RANGE of the MOD WHEEL is currently at a value of 99, we currently have complete control of the volume of the sound - from the maximum set output level of 99 down to the minimum of 0 (or, depending on the amount of bleed-through, near 0). Inputting a lesser RANGE value will give us less complete control over the *dynamic range*. Press function switch 17 (WHEEL RANGE parameter) and enter a new value of 65. Put the MOD WHEEL back to its MIN position, play a note and LISTEN (AUDIO CUE 64B). NOTE that, instead of hearing little or no volume, we are now hearing about half-volume. This is because the output level of operator 1 is now currently at about 65% of 99. Slowly raise the MOD WHEEL back up to its MAX position, HOLDing DOWN a note and LISTENing as you do so (AUDIO CUE 64C). NOTE that the volume still returns to its previous maximum set output level of 99. As with our other output level controls (i.e. the EGs or the LFO), IN NO EVENT CAN THE EG BIAS MODULATION INCREASE AN OPERATOR'S OUTPUT LEVEL BEYOND ITS MAXIMUM SET LEVEL (as determined by edit switch 27).

7)   As with LFO modulations, whatever effect we can accomplish with one real-time controller, we can do with any other. CHANGE the MOD WHEEL RANGE control (function switch 17) back to 0, and turn the WHEEL EG BIAS destination control (function switch 20) OFF. Press function switch 29 (AFTER RANGE) and set it to a value of 99, and press function switch 32 (AFTER EG BIAS destination) and turn it ON. Now press a note lightly on the keyboard and LISTEN. Again, you should be hearing little or no sound. Slowly increase your key pressure up to maximum (don't go crazy!) and NOTE that the volume swells proportionally. In this usage, your actual finger pressure is acting as a volume control!

8)   If you have the FOOT CONTROLLER or BREATH CONTROLLER, EXPERIMENT by using them for EG bias modulation with the same sensitivity setting (for operator 1 only). NOTE that each has precisely the same effect. Wind players particularly will appreciate this usage of the breath controller to directly control the volume of our sound via wind pressure - the harder you blow, the louder it gets!

What if, however, we apply this EG bias modulation to our **modulator** instead? This will allow us to set up a real-time timbral control, of course, since altering the output level of a modulator always initiates a quantitative timbral change! Let's run an exercise to try it:

EXERCISE 65

EG bias modulation applied to a modulator:

1)   INITIALIZE your DX7, leave it in algorithm #1, TURN OFF operators 3 through 6 ("110000"), and, using the system of operators 1 and 2, GENERATE a sawtooth wave.

2)   Press edit switch 16 (A MOD SENS. parameter) and use the operator select switch to VIEW operator 2. CHANGE this value from its default of 0 to a new value of 3 for operator 2 only. Remember that by doing so, we are not only making operator 2 sensitive to amplitude modulation, we are also making it sensitive to EG bias modulation.

3)   Press the function mode select switch to put your DX7 into function mode. Again, using the procedure outlined in Exercise 57 (Chapter 10), make sure none of your real-time controllers is currently activated.

4) Press function switch 17 (WHEEL RANGE parameter) and enter a value of 99. Press function switch 20 (WHEEL EG BIAS destination switch) and set it to ON. We have now "instructed" our DX7 that we wish to use the MOD WHEEL to **completely** control the EG-to-AMP signal flow for operator 2. Because in algorithm #1, operator 2 is a modulator, we can expect to hear a **timbral** change. Specifically, we can expect the MOD WHEEL to completely control the **overtone content** of our sound, since operator 2 is the only modulator we are currently using.

5) Put the MOD WHEEL at its MIN position, play a note on the keyboard and LISTEN (AUDIO CUE 65A). NOTE that you are currently hearing only a sine wave, even though operator 2 is ON, and has an OUTPUT LEVEL of 99! This is because the MOD WHEEL is completely controlling its EG-to-AMP signal flow, and hence its output level! Because the MOD WHEEL is currently at its MIN position, there is currently no output signal leaving operator 2 at all: **(See Figure 11-4.)**

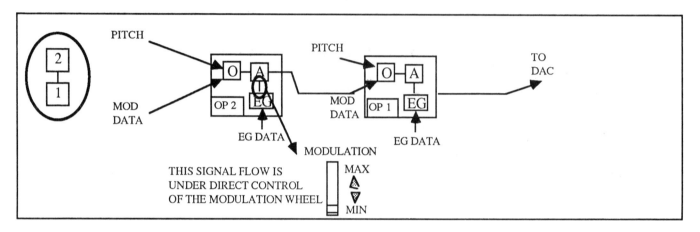

Figure 11-4

6) Now slowly raise the MOD WHEEL up to its MAX position, HOLDing DOWN a note and LISTENing as you do so (AUDIO CUE 65B). NOTE that the MOD WHEEL is currently acting as a **timbral** control, and that raising it towards its MAX position has the effect of increasing the relative amplitude of the overtones you hear - therefore, it is a quantitative timbral control. NOTE also that only at its MAX position do we actually hear the sawtooth wave we originally generated.

7) Because the RANGE of the MOD WHEEL is currently at a value of 99, we currently have **complete** control of the overtone content of the sound - from the maximum set output level of 99 (which gives us a sawtooth wave) down to the minimum of 0 (which gives us a pure sine wave, since there is no modulation data input to our carrier). Inputting a lesser RANGE value will give us less complete control over the overtone content. Press function switch 17 (WHEEL RANGE parameter) and enter a new value of 65. Put the MOD WHEEL back to its MIN position, play a note and LISTEN (AUDIO CUE 65C). NOTE that, instead of hearing a pure sine wave, we are now hearing a gentle timbre with few overtones. This is because the output level of operator 2 is now currently at approximately 65% of 99. Slowly raise the MOD WHEEL back up to its MAX position, HOLDing DOWN a note and LISTENing as you do so (AUDIO CUE 65D). NOTE that the timbre still returns to its previous maximum set output level of 99, still giving us a sawtooth wave at the MAX setting. Again, IN NO EVENT CAN THE EG BIAS MODULATION INCREASE AN OPERATOR'S OUTPUT LEVEL BEYOND ITS MAXIMUM SET LEVEL (as determined by edit switch 27).

8) As with LFO modulations, whatever effect we can accomplish with one real-time controller, we can do with any other. CHANGE the MOD WHEEL RANGE control (function switch 17) back to 0, and turn the WHEEL EG BIAS destination control (function switch 20) OFF. Press function switch 29 (AFTER RANGE) and set it to a value of 99, and press function switch 32 (AFTER EG BIAS destination) and turn it ON. Now press a note lightly on the keyboard and LISTEN. Again, you should be hearing a pure sine wave. Slowly increase your key pressure up to maximum and NOTE that the overtone content increases proportionally. In this usage, your actual finger pressure is acting as a quantitative timbral control!

9) If you have the FOOT CONTROLLER or BREATH CONTROLLER, EXPERIMENT by using them for EG bias modulation with the same sensitivity setting (operator 2 only). NOTE that each has precisely the same effect. Wind players will also appreciate this usage of the breath controller to directly control the brightness of our sound via wind pressure - the harder you blow, the brighter it gets!

10) Because EG bias modulation is operator-specific, we can use it to affect volume and timbre, in differing degrees, if we so desire. Put your DX7 back into edit mode, press edit switch 16 (A MOD SENS. parameter) and enter a value of 3 for both operator 1 and operator 2. Now return to function mode, and use one of your real-time controllers to route this EG bias modulation signal. As you change the real-time controller from its MIN to MAX position (either by raising the MOD WHEEL, stepping on the FOOT CONTROLLER, blowing harder into the BREATH CONTROLLER, or pressing down harder on the keyboard (AFTER-TOUCH), HOLD a note DOWN and LISTEN (AUDIO CUE 65E). NOTE that your controller is now acting as a volume and quantitative timbral control!

11) EXPERIMENT further by using different A MOD SENS. (EG BIAS SENS.) values for operators 1 and 2. NOTE that this allows you to CHANGE the volume of a sound a great deal, while only causing a slight timbral change, or vice-versa. EXPERIMENT also by using EG bias modulation with single timbres other than a simple sawtooth wave.

So far, so good. However, the limitations of having two different modulation sensitivities sharing the same switch (edit switch 16) should be apparent. For one thing, you won't be able to have some operators undergoing amplitude modulation, and different ones undergoing EG bias modulation. However, we can have **different** controllers routing each of the two different signals, and this can allow for some elegant and complex expressiveness as we play this instrument. The exercise below demonstrates how we can set this up:

EXERCISE 66

Dual modulations:

1) INITIALIZE your DX7, leave it in algorithm #1, TURN OFF operators 3 through 6 ("110000"), and, using the system of operators 1 and 2, GENERATE a square wave.

2) Press edit switch 16 (A MOD SENS. parameter) and VIEW operator 1. CHANGE this from its default of 0 to the maximum value of 3 for operator 1 only. Operator 1 is now sensitive for both amplitude modulation and EG bias modulation.

3) Put your DX7 into function mode. Using the procedure outlined in Exercise 57 (Chapter 10), make sure none of your real-time controllers is currently active.

4) Press function switch 17 (WHEEL RANGE) and enter a value of 99. Press function switch 19 (WHEEL AMP) and turn it ON. Press function switch 29 (AFTER RANGE) and enter a value of 99. Press function switch 32 (AFTER EG BIAS) and turn it ON.

5) Put the MOD WHEEL at its MIN position, play a note lightly on the keyboard and LISTEN. NOTE that you are currently hearing little or no sound. Press down the key with steadily increasing pressure and LISTEN. NOTE that the volume slowly increases proportionally to your finger pressure. This is occurring because the AFTER TOUCH is currently controlling the EG-to-AMP signal for operator 1 to the maximum degree.

6) The MOD WHEEL, on the other hand, is not controlling this signal flow but is instead routing LFO signal (currently a default TRIANGLE wave at the default speed of 35) to the amplifiers of all six operators. At this moment, however, only operator 1 is sensitive to this signal and so we will hear a periodic volume change, a *tremolo* effect, when we raise the MOD WHEEL. Hold a note down with half-pressure, slowly raise the MOD WHEEL towards its MAX position, then slowly increase your finger pressure, and LISTEN (AUDIO CUE 66A). NOTE that the MOD WHEEL determines the depth of the tremolo, while the AFTER-TOUCH determines the strength of the overall volume!

7) If you have the BREATH CONTROLLER or FOOT CONTROLLER, EXPERIMENT by using either of them instead of the MOD WHEEL or AFTER TOUCH to route either EG bias or amplitude modulation. EXPERIMENT further by setting up some **pitch** modulation sensitivity with edit switch 15, and using a real-time controller to route LFO signal to the PITCH inputs of your operators as well. In this manner, you can actually set up **triple** modulation effects! The limitations are, firstly, that we only have the one LFO, so we can only use one waveshape and speed at a time; and secondly, that we cannot have some operators respond to amplitude modulation and different ones respond to EG bias modulation. We can, however, use any of our controllers to route any or all of these modulation signals.

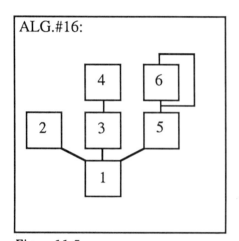

ALG.#16:

Figure 11-5

Up until now, we have only applied EG bias modulation to simple timbres; that is, sounds created with a single modulator-carrier system. The importance of this particular modulation becomes more apparent when we work with either multi-system sounds, or multi-modulator systems. For example, some of you may still be wondering about the potential use of a single-carrier algorithm like algorithm #16: **(See Figure 11-5.)**

By using EG bias modulation, we can, for example, create a sound with algorithm #16 where the upper modulators (operators 4 and 6) don't ever contribute to the sound at all unless a real-time controller routes their signal: **(See Figure 11-6.)**

or where, perhaps an entire *stack* (like operators 5 and 6) makes no contribution unless routed via a controller: **(See Figure 11-7.)**

Try setting up these two possibilities on your DX7, and it should become apparent that this tool, plus the actions of the EGs (which allow operators to "fade in" and "fade out") make the potential applications for single-carrier algorithms such as these more obvious.

An even more interesting application for EG bias modulation, however, is selective use with one or more carriers in a **multi-carrier** algorithm (which, of course, is everything **except** algorithms #16, 17, and 18). One preset sound which is a particularly good candidate for this type of treatment is "PIPES 1", found on ROM 1A-18, or 3A-10. Let's run an exercise to examine this sound and then modify it with EG bias modulation:

EXERCISE 67

Adding EG bias modulation to "PIPES 1":

1) Put your DX7 into *cartridge play* mode, and select either ROM 1A-18 or ROM 3A-10 - "PIPES 1". Play a key on the keyboard to confirm that this preset is now in your edit buffer (AUDIO CUE 67A). NOTE that this sound apparently consists of two distinct pitches, tuned several octaves apart.

2) Use the edit mode select switch to put your DX7 into edit mode. OBSERVE that algorithm #19 was used to create this sound: **(See Figure 11-8.)**

This algorithm contains two systems: the stack of operators 1, 2, and 3; and the dual-carrier, single-modulator system of operators 4, 5, and 6.

3) TURN OFF operators 4, 5, and 6 ("111000") in order to hear the first system alone. Play a key and LISTEN (AUDIO CUE 67B). NOTE that this system is providing the lower of the two perceived pitches. Now TURN ON operators 4, 5, and 6, and TURN OFF operators 1, 2, and 3 ("000111") in order to hear the contribution of the second system. Play a key and LISTEN (AUDIO CUE 67C). NOTE that this system is providing the higher of the two perceived pitches. TURN ON operators 1, 2, and 3 ("111111") and press edit switch 18 (F COARSE parameter) in order to VIEW the following frequency ratios: **(See Figure 11-9.)**

confirming our perceptions of the pitch contributions of each system to the overall sound.

4) We'll begin our modification of this sound by using the MOD WHEEL to control the volume of the lower of the two pitches - effectively making it capable of bringing in and out half of our total sound. Press edit switch 13 (AMD) and OBSERVE that since the value is currently 0, amplitude modulation is not an intrinsic part of this sound. This is an important thing to note since the EG bias sensitivity is determined by the amplitude modulation sensitivity control (edit switch 16) and we don't want to alter the actual character of the sound. Now press edit switch 16 (A MOD SENS. parameter) and NOTE that the value for this is currently 0 for all operators. Since we have decided to put the lower pitch on the MOD WHEEL and we have determined in step 3 above that it is the system of operators 1, 2, and 3 that is creating this part of the sound, it should be apparent that it is operator 1 only - our carrier - that we wish to make sensitive for EG bias modulation: **(See Figure 11-10.)**

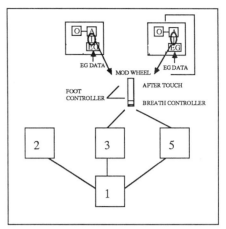

Figure 11-6

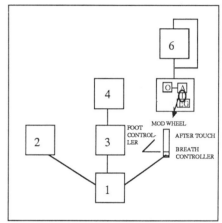

Figure 11-7

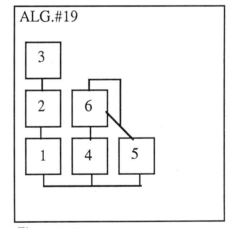

Figure 11-8

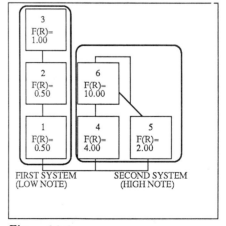

Figure 11-9

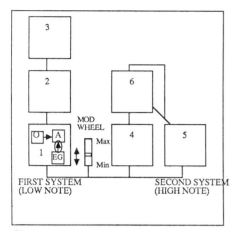

Figure 11-10

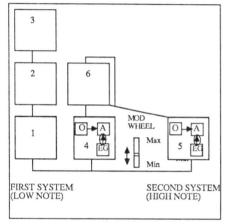

Figure 11-11

5) CHANGE the A MOD SENS. value for operator 1 only to its maximum value of 3. Press the function mode select switch to put your DX7 into function mode. Using the procedure outlined in Exercise 57, be sure that none of your real-time controllers is currently activated. Press function switch 17 (WHEEL RANGE) and enter a value of 99. Press function switch 20 (WHEEL EG BIAS) and turn this destination ON.

6) Put the MOD WHEEL at its MIN setting, play a key and LISTEN (AUDIO CUE 67D). NOTE that you are now only hearing the higher pitch, even though all six operators are currently ON. That's because the MOD WHEEL is currently controlling the EG-to-AMP signal flow in operator 1, effectively controlling the overall volume of this entire **system**. Because the other carriers - operators 4 and 5 - are not currently sensitive for EG bias modulation, they are unaffected by the actions of the MOD WHEEL and send their outputs to the DAC regardless.

7) Slowly raise the MOD WHEEL to its MAX position, while HOLDing DOWN a key and LISTENing (AUDIO CUE 67E). NOTE that the MOD WHEEL is now completely controlling the **volume** of the lower pitch in this sound.

8) Deactivate the MOD WHEEL by turning the EG bias destination switch OFF and setting the WHEEL RANGE back to 0. Play a key and NOTE that we are once again hearing the entire unaffected sound. Return your DX7 to edit mode and CHANGE the A MOD SENS. value for operator 1 back to 0. Now we'll try the opposite modification - controlling the volume of the **higher** of the two pitches, this time with the AFTER-TOUCH control:

9) Because we have determined that it is the system of operators 4, 5, and 6 that are contributing the higher of the two pitches, it is operators 4 and 5 (the carriers) that we wish to make sensitive for EG bias modulation: **(See Figure 11-11.)**

Press edit switch 16 and CHANGE the A MOD SENS. value for operators 4 and 5 to the maximum of 3. Put your DX7 into function mode, and set the AFTER RANGE (function switch 29) to a value of 99. Turn the AFTER EG BIAS destination (function switch 32) ON. Play a key gently on the keyboard and LISTEN (AUDIO CUE 67F). NOTE that we now only hear the **lower** of the two pitches, since the output from carriers 4 and 5 (which are providing the higher pitch) is being directly controlled by your finger pressure.

10) Slowly increase your pressure on the key until it reaches maximum force, HOLDing DOWN a key and LISTENing as you do so (AUDIO CUE 67G). NOTE that as you increase your keyboard pressure, the volume of the higher note increases proportionally as well.

11) EXPERIMENT by finding other presets whose total sound is composed of two or more significantly different systems, and apply EG bias modulation to each system in turn. Use different real-time controllers with different degrees of depth (RANGE switches) in order to become totally familiar with this powerful technique.

The reason we didn't apply the EG bias modulation to any of the **modulators** in the above exercise was, of course, because we were not looking to make any kind of **timbral** change to our sound. Don't forget, however, that EG bias modulation can and often will be applied to modulators as well as carriers. Bear in mind also that, just as with pitch or amplitude modulation, if you plan on using EG bias modulation in a sound, you will have to set it up in advance in edit mode by using the A MOD SENS. parameter (edit switch 16). There are, for example, several Yamaha presets: ROM 2A-5 and 3A-17 ("SAX BC"); ROM 2A-19 ("HRMNCA2 BC"); and ROM 3A-24 ("VOICES BC"), that have all been pre-programmed for EG bias modulation. The "BC" in the name is meant as a suggestion that you use the breath controller to route this modulation, but, of course, you can in fact use any of the four real-time controllers. These are all sounds which have been given expressive controls - they will all get realistically louder and/or brighter when you use the routing controller to increase the EG bias signal flow. The point is that you yourself can add this expressiveness to any sound you create.

One further point needs to be made before we leave this subject. The real-time controller parameters are all function mode controls. Therefore, if you leave one of your real-time controllers ON for the EG bias modulation destination, it will stay ON for any sound you call up into your edit buffer in future. This can be problematic if you call a sound up where one or more of its operators has a certain amount of A MOD SENSitivity, particularly if that controller is resting in its MIN position. In this instance, what you will be doing is actually **shutting down** a part of the total sound, and you may not even realize it!

Call up the "TRAIN" preset (ROM 1A-31 or ROM 3A-30). Play several notes on the keyboard and NOTE that the upper half of the keyboard provides a bell-like sound, while the lower half provides a whistle (the answer to this particular mystery will be found in the very next Chapter, via a control called KEYBOARD LEVEL SCALING), while a constant choo-choo locomotive sound is heard no matter what note you play. The constant choo-choo is a result of - you guessed it (I hope!) - an L4 the same as L3 in the choo-choo carrier's EG. But the sound itself is a result of a periodic amplitude change, so not only is the LFO at work (since that's the only device that can issue a periodic change - if you don't believe me, try lowering the LFO SPEED and listen to the train slow down and pull into the station!) but we also know that that particular operator is **sensitive** for amplitude modulation. Call up a different preset for a moment. Now put your DX7 into function mode, and turn ON the MOD WHEEL's EG BIAS destination (function switch 20) and set the WHEEL RANGE (function switch 17) to 99. Put the MOD WHEEL at its MIN position, and go back to the "TRAIN" preset. The bell's still there, the whistle's still there, but where has our choo-choo gone? (sounds like a great album title, don't you think?)

Obviously, whichever carrier was responsible for making that part of the sound* now has its EG-to-AMP signal in the "hands" of the MOD WHEEL. If you raise the WHEEL up to its MAX position, you'll - lo and behold - hear the choo-choo return. This may be an unusually silly example, but the point is this: DON'T LEAVE YOUR CONTROLLERS ON FOR THE EG BIAS DESTINATION. EVER. UNLESS YOU ENJOY GRIEF. Because what will invariably happen someday is you'll call up a sound and it won't come back the way you remembered it to be. After a call to the store, a call to Yamaha, a call to me (please, no!), and perhaps even an embarrassing trip to the Authorized Service Center, you will realize that your DX7 is not "broken": you've just forgotten to turn a controller OFF for the EG BIAS destination.

* If you're a good student and/or naturally inquisitive, you can of course put your DX7 into edit mode and find out which carrier it is. A quick glance at the algorithm being used - #5 - should tell you that it must be operator 5. Why? Because the choo-choo is a *white noise* sound, and operator 6 - operator 5's modulator - is the only operator in this algorithm with the feedback loop!

Figure 11-12

These problems would disappear if the function controls were voice-linked and not global. But as of this writing, on the DX7 (as opposed to later Yamaha digital FM synthesizers) they are not. Until Yamaha comes through with the T.P.U. (Theoretical Promised Update) - BE AWARE!!

KEYBOARD VELOCITY SENSITIVITY

As mentioned in the last chapter, after-touch is only one of two keyboard sensitivities on the DX7, the other being *velocity sensitivity*. Here the term "velocity" refers to speed, but not **horizontal** speed. In other words, the keyboard velocity sensitivity has nothing to do with how quickly you play your Keith Emerson licks (God, am I showing my age!) but instead is responsive to **vertical** speed: how quickly each key travels from its resting position down to the fully depressed position: **(See Figure 11-12.)**

Underneath each key of the DX7 keyboard is a timing mechanism, actually a computer clock which "counts" how many clock pulses it took that particular key to drop all the way down. If the key drops very slowly, it will count many of these pulses and our microprocessor will inversely generate a very **small** number. If it drops rapidly, far fewer pulses are counted, and an inversely **large** number will be generated: **(See Figure 11-13.)**

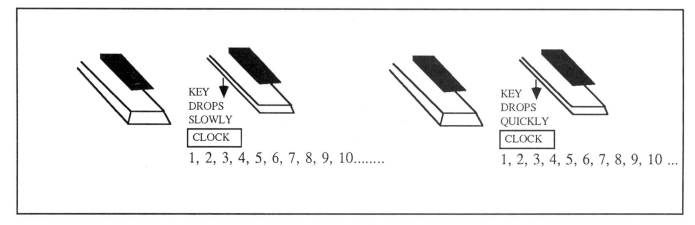

Figure 11-13

This timing mechanism, remember, is independent for each key, making keyboard velocity sensitivity a *polyphonic* control. If you play a chord, for example, but depress each of the individual notes at slightly different speeds, each of the associated keys will generate a different velocity number.

The obvious question now is, what on earth is done with that number? The answer is simple - it is applied to each of our six operators' OUTPUT LEVEL. This is very important, so I'll repeat it:

KEYBOARD VELOCITY SENSITIVITY IS AN OUTPUT LEVEL CONTROL.

Applied to all six operators, did he say? Does this make it a non-operator-specific control? Not at all, because, as with amplitude modulation, we can set each operator individually to a different sensitivity to this control. This will, of course, allow us to control the volume and/or the timbre of any sound or portion of a sound. The keyboard velocity sensitivity switch is edit switch 28: **(See Figure 11-14.)**

and the range of this operator-specific switch is 0 to 7. 0 represents no sensitivity, and any operator given a velocity sensitivity of 0 will simply ignore the velocity number being sent it by the key timing mechanism. A value of 7 represents maximum velocity sensitivity, and an operator assigned a value of 7 will have the full range of its maximum set output level (as determined by edit switch 27) controlled by the speed of the key depressions. The in-between sensitivity values (1 through 6) simply allow different shadings of

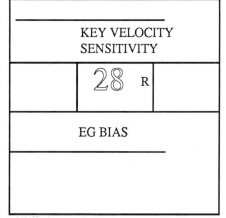

Figure 11-14

sensitivity to this control. As with the EG, LFO, and EG bias modulation controls, KEYBOARD VELOCITY SENSITIVITY CANNOT EVER INCREASE AN OPERATOR'S OUTPUT LEVEL BEYOND THE VALUE SET WITH EDIT SWITCH 27. Upon initialization, the default for this parameter is 0 (no sensitivity) for all six operators.

Often, people think of this velocity sensitivity as something which measures how hard you strike the key, and in the interests of extending the life of your keyboard, you should avoid this erroneous assumption. Logically, the harder you strike a key, the faster the key will drop, but this control is not measuring how hard the key is struck at all. With a little practice, you should be able to refine your keyboard technique so that you can depress specific notes quickly without slamming your hand down on the aching keyboard! The two keyboard sensitivities - after-touch and velocity - have been as much a curse as a blessing to certain DX7 owners who have ended up spending many unhappy hours in the lobby of their Authorized Service Center waiting for broken keys to be replaced. While the keyboard is generally robust, it can succumb to over-enthusiasm! Learn to use these keyboard sensitivities without going nuts, and you'll spare yourself unnecessary headaches...

Okay, with that Stern Admonishment out of the way (cla-a-a-ss!), let's run an exercise to try it out:

EXERCISE 68

Keyboard velocity sensitivity:

1) INITIALIZE your DX7, leave it in algorithm #1, TURN OFF operators 3 through 6 ("110000") and, using the system of operators 1 and 2, GENERATE a sawtooth wave. Play a key on the keyboard and LISTEN (AUDIO CUE 68A). NOTE the current volume of the sound.

2) VIEW operator 1 and press edit switch 28 (VELOCITY SENSITIVITY parameter). OBSERVE that it is currently at its default of 0. CHANGE this to the maximum value of 7 for operator 1 only.

3) Play a key on the keyboard, but depress the key **as slowly as possible**. LISTEN (AUDIO CUE 68B). NOTE that, because operator 1 in this system is a carrier, we hear little or no volume (again, if you are hearing a little bleed-through, not to worry. See Exercise 57, Chapter 10, for more details.). Now play the same note, with a quicker attack; attempt to get the key depressed as quickly as possible without mashing it down neanderthal-style. LISTEN (AUDIO CUE 68C). NOTE that we now hear the sawtooth wave at its original, full volume.

4) Try playing the key at varying speeds and NOTE the many different volumes available to us with the maximum sensitivity value of 7 (AUDIO CUE 68D). This is because the maximum sensitivity setting gives us control over the full dynamic range, from an operator 1 output level of 0 (note struck at slowest speed) to the current maximum set output level of 99 (note struck at fastest speed).

5) Remember that VELOCITY SENSITIVITY is a polyphonic effect. Try striking the lowest key of the keyboard as slowly as possible and simultaneously striking the highest key as quickly as possible (if you're fairly uncoordinated, or your name is Jerry Ford, you might want to have a friend help you do this). You should now be hearing the high note only. Try repeating this in reverse, striking the highest key as slowly as possible and the lowest as quickly as possible. The reverse now occurs and you should now be hearing the low note only.

6) CHANGE the VELOCITY SENSITIVITY for operator 1 only to a new value of 4. Again, play a key on the keyboard as slowly as possible and LISTEN (AUDIO CUE 68E). NOTE that, this time, we do hear some volume, but at a greatly reduced level. That's because VELOCITY SENSITIVITY, like KEYBOARD RATE SCALING (see Chapter Nine), is a **negative** sensitivity control: **(See Figure 11-15.)**

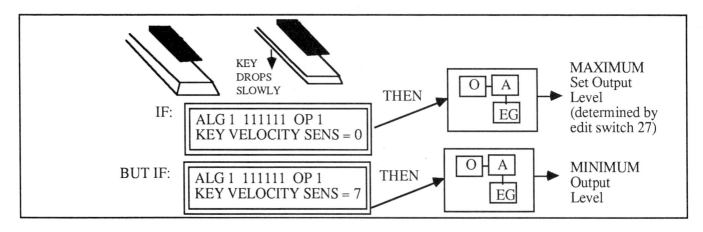

Figure 11-15

7) Now play the same key as quickly as possible and LISTEN (AUDIO CUE 68F). NOTE that, as before, we hear the note at its original, full volume.

8) Once again, play the key at varying speeds and LISTEN (AUDIO CUE 68G). NOTE that, while we still hear many different volumes, we don't have the full dynamic range at our disposal because the VELOCITY SENSITIVITY is only at about half. This means that we are hearing between half-volume and full volume only. In all instances, however, this is a volume control, which will always result in higher volumes with faster key depressions. There is no way to invert this effect on the DX7 (in other words, you can't ever get softer volumes by pressing the key harder, or vice versa).

9) Restore operator 1's VELOCITY SENSITIVITY value back to 0 and VIEW operator 2. CHANGE this value from its current default of 0 to the maximum value of 7. Play a key on the keyboard as slowly as possible and LISTEN (AUDIO CUE 68H). NOTE that we are now hearing a simple sine wave only. This is because the OUTPUT LEVEL of operator 2 (the modulator in this system) is under the full control of the velocity timing mechanism. Because you depressed the key as slowly as possible, the timing mechanism generated a velocity number of 0, and this number was applied to operator 2's OUTPUT LEVEL: **(See Figure 11-16.)**

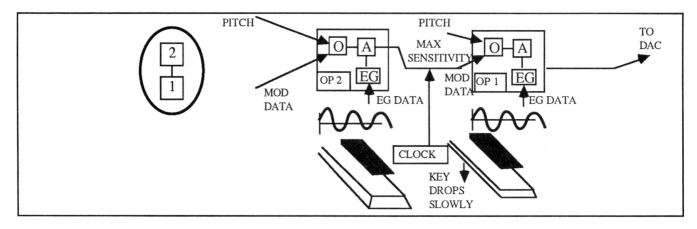

Figure 11-16

We are hearing the sine wave at full volume because operator 1 (the carrier) is currently insensitive (having a value of 0) to this control.

10) Play the same key as quickly as possible and LISTEN (AUDIO CUE 68I). NOTE that we now hear the sawtooth wave, as before!

Now play the key at several different speeds and NOTE the varying timbres that result because the keyboard VELOCITY SENSITIVITY is controlling the OUTPUT LEVEL of our modulator (which Cardinal Rule Two tells us is the *quantitative* timbral control). (AUDIO CUE 68J).

11) Again, the polyphonic aspect of this control can be demonstrated by repeating step 5 above. NOTE that in the first instance, you now hear the lowest note as a sine wave and the highest as a sawtooth; and in the second instance, the reverse occurs.

12) CHANGE the VELOCITY SENSITIVITY for operator 2 only to a new value of 4, play a key on the keyboard as slowly as possible, and LISTEN (AUDIO CUE 68K). NOTE that, instead of hearing a pure sine wave, we are now hearing an "in-between" timbre; a sine wave with a few overtones, but not enough of them to be called a sawtooth wave. This is because we have lowered the sensitivity of operator 2 to the key timing mechanism, giving us less dynamic range in our control: **(See Figure 11-17.)**

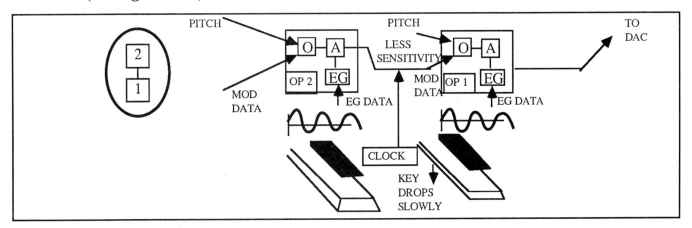

Figure 11-17

13) Now play the same key on the keyboard as quickly as possible and NOTE that we once again hear the sawtooth wave as before (AUDIO CUE 68L). Play the key with varying speeds and NOTE that, while the timbre still undergoes many different changes, NOTE that we do not have the full range of sine wave-to-sawtooth wave (AUDIO CUE 68M). In every instance, however, this control is acting as a **brightness** control, with brighter sounds always resulting from faster key depressions. As before, there is no way to invert this control (which would give us brighter sounds as we struck the key slower).

14) Because VELOCITY SENSITIVITY is operator-specific, we can affect the volume and timbre of a sound, and to differing degrees if we so desire. Leave operator 2's VELOCITY SENSITIVITY at its current value of 4 but CHANGE this value for operator 1 to the maximum of 7. Play a key at varying speeds and LISTEN (AUDIO CUE 68N). NOTE that this results in a great amount of volume change and a relatively smaller amount of timbral change as you strike the key faster and faster. Now try reversing the sensitivities, giving operator 1 a sensitivity value of 4, and operator 2 the maximum value of 7. Again, play a key at varying speeds and LISTEN (AUDIO CUE 68O). NOTE that we now hear a great amount of timbral change, but only a small amount of volume change.

15) EXPERIMENT by creating different single timbres and applying this VELOCITY SENSITIVITY control in different degrees to the carrier and/or to the modulator, NOTING how each change affects the overall sound.

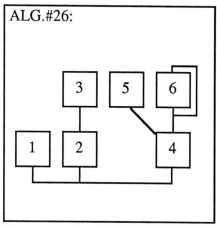

ALG.#26:

Figure 11-18

As with EG bias modulation, the real power of this control lies in the fact that it is operator-specific. This will allow us to apply it, for example, to specific systems within an overall sound. Let's try creating a complex sound, composed of two notes a fifth apart, with the root note as a square wave, and the fifth as a louder, brighter timbre, and then use the VELOCITY SENSITIVITY to selectively "fade in" one note or the other:

EXERCISE 69

Velocity sensitivity applied to a multi-system voice:

1) INITIALIZE your DX7, and CHANGE it from the default of algorithm #1 to algorithm #26: **(See Figure 11-18.)**

2) TURN OFF operators 1 and 4 through 6 ("011000"), and, using the system of operators 2 and 3, GENERATE a square wave.
3) TURN OFF operators 2 and 3, and TURN ON operators 4 and 5 ("000110"). Using the system of operators 4 and 5, GENERATE a square wave as well.
4) TURN OFF operator 5 and TURN ON operator 6 ("000101"). Using the system of operators 4 and 6, GENERATE yet another square wave. TURN ON operator 5 ("000111") and LISTEN (AUDIO CUE 69A). NOTE that the sound is now considerably brighter than a square wave, since both operators 5 and 6 are now providing modulation data input to our carrier (operator 4).
5) NOTE that in this algorithm, operator 6 has the *feedback loop*. Press edit switch 8 (FEEDBACK parameter) and change this to the maximum value of 7. Play a note on the keyboard and LISTEN (AUDIO CUE 69B). NOTE that the sound is now brighter still.
6) CHANGE the pitch of this entire system (that of operators 4, 5, and 6) so it is a musical fifth higher (if you can't remember how to do this, refer to Chapter Six).*
7) TURN ON operators 2 and 3 ("011111") and use the operator select switch to VIEW operator 2. Press edit switch 27 (OUTPUT LEVEL parameter) and CHANGE this value for operator 2 only to a new value of 92. Play a key and LISTEN (AUDIO CUE 69C). NOTE that you are now hearing two different timbres, a fifth apart, with the higher note being both louder and brighter than the root note.
8) Press edit switch 28 (VELOCITY SENSITIVITY parameter) and VIEW operator 6. CHANGE this to a new value of 3 for operator 6 only. Play a key at several different speeds and NOTE that a slight change in timbre now occurs at higher key velocities (AUDIO CUE 69D).
9) VIEW operator 4 and CHANGE its VELOCITY SENSITIVITY to the maximum value of 7. Play a key at the slowest possible speed and LISTEN (AUDIO CUE 69E). NOTE that we now hear only the root note produced by the system of operators 2 and 3. Now play the same key at the quickest speed possible and LISTEN (AUDIO CUE 69F). NOTE that we now hear both notes together, as in step 7 above. Play the key at several different speeds and NOTE that you can "cross-fade" the higher note in and out as you play at higher or lower speeds

---

* For those of you with poor memories, or those of you who have skipped ahead to this point without ever reading Chapter Six, or those of you who are just plain too lazy to turn the pages back, here's how you do it: Cardinal Rule Three tells us we must affect the carrier and modulator the same way. Since 3 times the fundamental is an octave and a fifth higher, then 1.5 times the fundamental will be a simple fifth higher. Therefore, you'll need to set up a frequency ratio between operators 5 and 4 of 3.00 : 1.50, and the same ratio between operators 6 and 4.

(AUDIO CUE 69G). Among other things, this will allow you to play boring root-to-fifth bass lines by playing just a single key! (AUDIO CUE 69H).

10) You can make this sound far more interesting by working with the operator EGs. EXPERIMENT by changing them to sharp, percussive shapes, for example. EXPERIMENT further by bringing operator 1 (in this algorithm, an unmodulated carrier) into play: tune it to a different pitch, or perhaps route some LFO signal to it; or control its output with one of the real-time controllers using EG BIAS. With a little work, you can turn this basic patch into a good, usable sound. Try it!

The potential of this VELOCITY SENSITIVITY should start becoming apparent to you as you begin experimenting with it for different sounds. For example, try redoing Exercise 67 (from earlier this chapter), but this time, instead of bringing the high or low note in the "PIPES 1" sound in and out with EG BIAS, do it with VELOCITY SENSITIVITY instead. This means that the high or low note will enter when you strike the key more sharply, as opposed to pressing down harder on the key.

In summary, VELOCITY SENSITIVITY is an *expressiveness* control, allowing us to make a sound louder or brighter when we strike a key with greater speed. By applying this control to specific systems within an overall sound, we can set up novel effects as in the Exercise above. Let's conclude with a look at an old friend, "E.PIANO 1", and see how the VELOCITY SENSITIVITY control is utilized in this preset:

EXERCISE 70

Velocity sensitivity in "E.PIANO 1":

1) Put your DX7 in cartridge play mode and call up ROM 1A-11 or ROM 3A-3, the "E.PIANO 1" preset.

2) Use the edit mode select switch to put your DX7 into edit mode and press edit switch 28 (VELOCITY SENSITIVITY parameter). Use the operator select switch to VIEW each of the six operators in turn, and OBSERVE the following values: **(See Figure 11-19.)**

3) Therefore, we might well expect our "E.PIANO 1" sound to get slightly louder but significantly brighter as we strike keys faster. Is this what occurs? Play a note at varying speeds and LISTEN (AUDIO CUE 70A). NOTE that this indeed is what happens, as predicted. A real Fender Rhodes, being an acoustic instrument, will respond in just this manner - as the key is depressed faster, the hammer hits the tine faster, and the sound gets a good deal brighter, but due to the physical construction of a Rhodes, only slightly louder.

4) But what if we wanted to create a Fender Rhodes sound that didn't change its sound **at all**, no matter how we struck the key? That would be tough (if not impossible) to do on the real McCoy, but is no problem on the DX7! Simply CHANGE the VELOCITY SENSITIVITY value for all operators to 0. Try it! Play a key as slowly as possible and LISTEN (AUDIO CUE 70B). NOTE that the sound is EXACTLY THE SAME as it previously was, when you struck the key FASTEST! This is because the VELOCITY SENSITIVITY control is a **negative** control: **(See Figure 11-20.)**

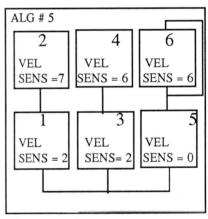

Figure 11-19

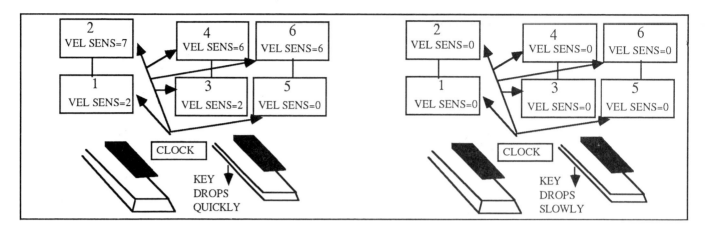

Figure 11-20

Put your DX7 momentarily into *compare* mode (by pressing the edit mode select switch again) in order to confirm this. If you wished to actually keep and use this modified sound, you'd probably want to lower the output levels of your modulators equally, so as to restore it back to the sound of a moderately struck Rhodes. Try lowering the output levels of each of your modulators (operators 2, 4, and 6) by a value of 25 (so that operator 2 = an output level of 33; operator 4 = 64; and operator 6 = 54). You'll also have to lower the output level of carriers 1 and 3 slightly since they also originally had a small degree of velocity sensitivity. Try reducing both of them by a value of 5 (so that their output levels are both equal to 94 instead of the original 99). Now put the DX7 once again into compare mode and back in order to hear that we have accomplished this!

5) EXPERIMENT by setting different degrees of VELOCITY SENSITIVITY for different operators within the "E.PIANO 1" sound, and NOTE the effects on the overall sound.

You will find that many of the ROM presets, like those that emulate acoustic instruments, have a certain amount of VELOCITY SENSITIVITY. If you don't care for this effect on a particular sound, or you feel there's too much or too little, CHANGE IT! That's what edit mode is for! Conversely, there are quite a few presets with no VELOCITY SENSITIVITY. Often you can unlock new doors of expressive sounds by **adding** this control to specific operators within the sound. Go through your presets and try changing this control for each of them - you'll probably find many ways of improving the sounds you've already got. Bear in mind that whenever you **decrease** the velocity sensitivity for a particular operator, its OUTPUT LEVEL will appear to increase, since it's now back at its nominal setting. Often you will have to compensate for this by lowering this value accordingly, as we did in the Exercise above with our modified "E.PIANO 1" sound.

Once you feel conversant with EG BIAS and VELOCITY SENSITIVITY, turn the page and let's move on to our **geographic** output level control, *keyboard level scaling.*

SWITCHES AND CONTROLS COVERED IN CHAPTER ELEVEN:

SWITCH	PARAMETER	COMMENTS
Edit 16	EG Bias sensitivity	Also A MOD SENS. control. Operator-specific; Range 0 - 3.
Function 20	Mod. wheel EG bias destination	"On" or "Off".
Function 24	Foot controller EG bias destination	"On" or "Off".
Function 28	Breath controller EG bias destination	"On" or "Off".
Function 32	After-touch EG bias destination	"On" or "Off".
Edit 28	Keyboard Velocity Sensitivity	Operator-specific; Range 0 - 7.

CHAPTER TWELVE: KEYBOARD LEVEL SCALING

The DX7 provides us with many tools which allow the control of operator *output level*. We've already explored several of these: the EGs (which change output level aperiodically over time), the LFO (which, when used for *amplitude modulation*, changes output level periodically over time), EG bias modulation (which allows real-time control of output level), and keyboard velocity sensitivity (which allows timed keyboard control over output level). In addition to these, a *geographic* output level control is also provided, and this is known as *keyboard level scaling*.

In this instance, of course, the term "geographic" does not refer to whether you are playing your DX7 in Tibet or in Brooklyn, but instead refers to **which notes you are playing on the keyboard**. By the use of this control, then, we will be able to decrease or **increase** the output level of any particular operator by simply playing different notes on the keyboard!

And, yes, you did read correctly: I did say "increase". This is in fact the **only** output level control on the DX7 which will actually allow you to increase an operator's output level **beyond its maximum set level** (as determined by edit switch 27). However, in no event will you be able to ever increase it above a maximum value of 99.

The three edit switches associated with this control are as follows:

SWITCH	PARAMETER
Edit 23	Break Point
Edit 24	Curve
Edit 25	Depth

All of these switches are operator-specific; once again, this will allow us control of either the **volume** or **timbre** of a sound.

The mechanics of keyboard level scaling are actually fairly straightforward. We will begin by specifying for each operator a note on the keyboard which is called the *break point*. We will then be able to either increase or decrease that operator's output level as we play notes above the break point, or below it: **(See Figure 12-1.)**

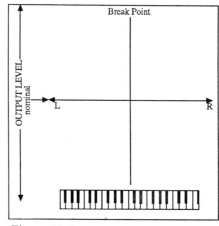

Figure 12-1

The break point can be any note on the keyboard, or, surprisingly, a note that doesn't even exist on our DX7 keyboard! We have seen that all the notes on the DX7 keyboard are numbered, since that is the only way our microprocessor can understand things. The lowest actual note is numbered C1 and the highest is called C6: **(See Figure 12-2.)**

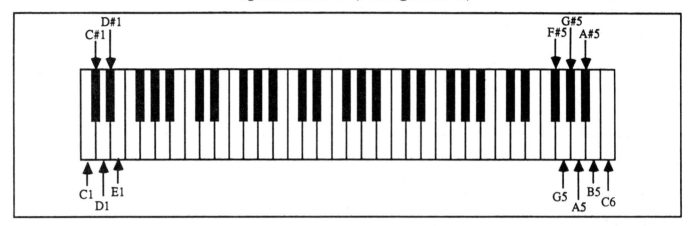

Figure 12-2

But the DX7 keyboard is only a five-octave keyboard. Through the use of the MIDI interface (see Chapter Fourteen for a complete introduction to MIDI), we can control our DX7 from an external keyboard - even one with a full 88 keys (or more!). How could we do this if our DX7 microprocessor only recognized 60 keys? We couldn't. And that's why it's been "trained" by Yamaha to recognize an additional 3 1/2 octaves worth of notes. Our ever gullible computer "believes" that there's an extra octave and a half **below** C1, and these notes are numbered A-1 to B0: **(See Figure 12-3.)**

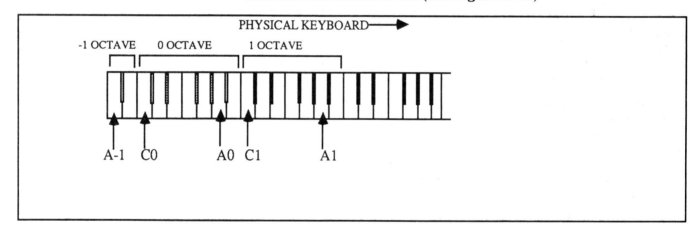

Figure 12-3

And it also believes that there are an extra two full octaves **above** C6, from C#6 to C8: **(See Figure 12-4.)**

It also doesn't seem to realize (or care) that these keys aren't ever depressed — I told you before: computers are very fast but very stupid.

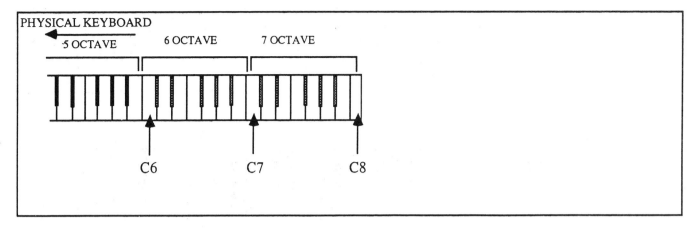

Figure 12-4

We set the break point with edit switch 23 (BREAK POINT parameter). Initialize your DX7 and press this switch in order to view the default. Note that this is A-1 (the lowest possible note) for all six operators. Use the data entry slider to step through all of the different possible break points, from A-1 all the way up to C-8. We will see shortly why we might want to set break points that are off the scale of the physical DX7 keyboard. Remember again that each operator can have its own individual break point. One little known anomaly of the DX7 is that the actual keyboard level scaling effect always begins three semitones below that actual break point you use. To avoid confusion, we'll ignore this fact in our text from here on in, but we just thought you might like to know this.

If we were to graph out the output level change initiated by keyboard level scaling, it would look like this: **(See Figure 12-5.)**

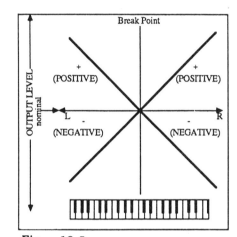

Figure 12-5

If we choose to **increase** an operator's output level above or below the break point, then we are said to be applying a **positive** curve; and if we choose to **decrease** the output level, we are said to be applying a **negative** curve. We can choose two different curves, to the left of our break point, and to the right: **(See Figure 12-6.)**

Both positive and negative curves can have one of two different shapes. The type of curve we are currently displaying in this diagram is called a linear curve. When you use a linear curve, the change will be either additive (if a positive linear curve) or subtractive (if a negative linear curve). In plain English, a positive linear curve to the right of our break point will result in a greater operator output level as we work our way up the keyboard: **(See Figure 12-7.)**

whereas a negative linear curve to the right of our breakpoint would result in a lesser output level as we work our way up the keyboard: **(See Figure 12-8.)**

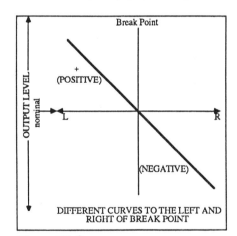

Figure 12-6

The second kind of curve available to us is called an *exponential* curve. With this type of curve, our computer performs multiplication (for a positive exponential curve) or division (for a negative exponential curve) operations. When you multiply two positive numbers together over and over again, the results soon become astronomical:

1) 2 x 2 = 4
2) 4 x 2 = 8
3) 8 x 2 = 16
4) 16 x 2 = 32
5) 32 x 2 = 64
6) 64 x 2 = 128
7) 128 x 2 = 356
8) 356 x 2 = 712
9) 712 x 2 = 1424
10) 1424 x 2 = 2848

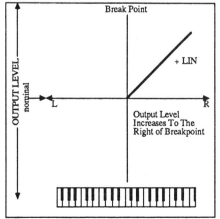

Figure 12-7

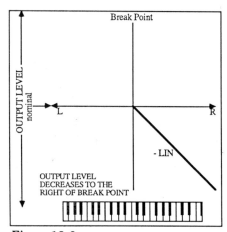

Figure 12-8

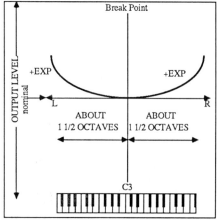

Figure 12-9

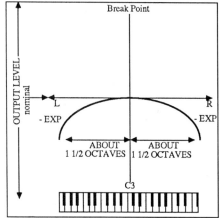

Figure 12-10

as opposed to a simple additive (linear) operation:

1) 2 + 2 = 4
2) 4 + 2 = 6
3) 6 + 2 = 8
4) 8 + 2 = 10
5) 10 + 2 = 12
6) 12 + 2 = 14
7) 14 + 2 = 16
8) 16 + 2 = 18
9) 18 + 2 = 20
10) 20 + 2 = 22

Therefore, the positive exponential curve will result in a much more drastic eventual increase in output level. Of course, we can't increase the output level above 99, so getting to these astronomical numbers won't help us much. Instead, the computer "squeezes" the curve down by dividing the result of this operation by some fixed value, and the end result is a curve which undergoes very little change at all for some period (about 1 1/2 octaves on the keyboard) and then begins a very rapid increase, an increase that accelerates for each new note played: **(See Figure 12-9.)**

Similarly, a series of division operations:

1) 100 / 2 = 50
2) 50 / 2 = 25
3) 25 / 2 = 12.5
4) 12.5 / 2 = 6.25
5) 6.25 / 2 = 3.125

yields a much more severe decrease in result than a series of subtraction operations:

1) 100 - 2 = 98
2) 98 - 2 = 96
3) 96 - 2 = 94
4) 94 - 2 = 92
5) 92 - 2 = 90

So that, once again, our "squeezed" negative exponential curve yields very little change for the same 1 1/2 octaves, and then a sharper decrease in output level for each new note played: **(See Figure 12-10.)**

Let's summarize. The four different curves available to us are as follows:

1) *Negative linear* (-LIN) - each note will have slightly less output level than the preceding one.
2) *Negative exponential* (-EXP) - very little change at all for about 1 1/2 octaves, then a more drastic decrease in output level for each note played.
3) *Positive exponential* (+EXP) - very little change at all for about 1 1/2 octaves, then a more drastic increase in output level for each note played.
4) *Positive linear* (+LIN) - each note will have slightly greater output level than the preceding one.

Since Yamaha doesn't expect you to memorize the effects of these curves (any more than they expect you to memorize the effects of the various EG levels and rates), there is a convenient diagram of these curves located on the front panel of the DX7 itself, on the far right-hand corner. Use it as a quick reference guide when working with keyboard level scalings.

Press edit switch 24 and you will see the default curve: "R KEY SCALE = -LIN" in the LCD display. Use the "yes" button in the data entry section to scroll through your four different curve choices. Press edit switch 24 a second time to view the L KEY SCALE curve, and note that it has the same default -LIN curve. Whenever you initialize, both the right and left curves for all six operators will default to a negative linear curve. Be aware that edit switch 24 is a bit tricky as you will need to press it a second time in order to view the other curve. Keep your eye on the first character of the LCD and be aware of which curve you are currently viewing and/or changing.

The last control is our DEPTH control - edit switch 25. Having selected a break point and a curve to the right and left of that point, you must now specify to the DX7 how much effect you wish that curve to have on the operator's output - the depth of our scaling. The range of this control is 0 to 99, with 0 indicating no depth at all. In other words, no matter what curve you select, if you give it a depth value of 0, it will be as if there is no curve. On the other hand, a depth value of 99 will indicate that the curve has maximum effect. On our graph, we can represent the various depths as the steepness of the angle of the curve, as follows: **(See Figure 12-11.)**

As you might expect, the initialization default for this parameter is 0 for all curves, for all operators. In other words, when you initialize, there is no keyboard level scaling occurring. Let's run an Exercise now to hear the effect of this control on a carrier in a single-system voice:

EXERCISE 71

Keyboard level scaling applied to a carrier:

1) INITIALIZE your DX7, leave it in algorithm #1, TURN OFF operators 3 through 6 ("110000"), and, using the system of operators 1 and 2, GENERATE a sawtooth wave.

2) Use the operator select switch to VIEW operator 1 (the carrier in this system) and press edit switch 23 (BREAK POINT parameter). OBSERVE that it is currently at its default value of A-1. CHANGE this for operator 1 only to a new value of C3 (Middle C on the DX7 keyboard), by using the data entry slider.

3) Press edit switch 24 (CURVE parameter) and OBSERVE that both the right curve and the left curve are currently at their defaults of -LIN (press the switch repeatedly to cycle between the R KEY SCALE value and the L KEY SCALE value).

4) Press edit switch 25 (DEPTH parameter) and OBSERVE that both the right curve and the left depths are currently at their defaults of 0, indicating no current keyboard level scaling (press the switch repeatedly to cycle between the R SCALE DEPTH value and the L SCALE DEPTH value). VIEW the R SCALE DEPTH value and CHANGE it to the maximum value of 99.

5) Play a chromatic scale (all notes) on your keyboard, starting at Middle C (C3) and going up to the highest note (C6), LISTENing as you do so (AUDIO CUE 71A). NOTE that because we have applied a -LIN curve to the **right** of C3, with maximum DEPTH (99), the volume of our sawtooth wave decreases rather rapidly, disappearing altogether by the uppermost note (C6): **(See Figure 12-12.)**

6) Play a chromatic scale from C3 **down** to C1 and LISTEN (AUDIO CUE 71B). NOTE that we hear no volume change whatsoever as we go to the **left** of C3 because the L SCALE DEPTH value is currently 0: **(See Figure 12-13.)**

7) CHANGE the R SCALE DEPTH value (edit switch 25 - and be sure you're VIEWing the **right** and not the left scale depth) for operator 1 only to a new value of 55. Play a chromatic scale on your keyboard, from C3 to C6, LISTENing as you do so (AUDIO CUE 71C). NOTE that the volume again decreases, but not as rapidly, and that even at the uppermost note (C6), we still have a significant amount of volume: **(See Figure 12-14.)**

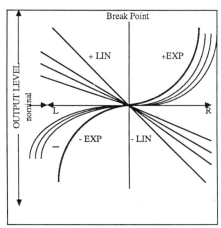

Figure 12-11

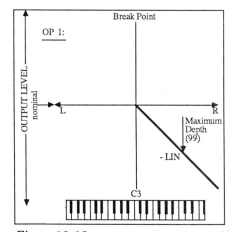

Figure 12-12

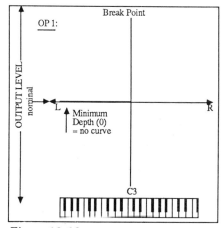

Figure 12-13

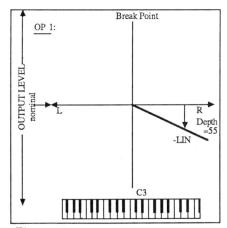

Figure 12-14

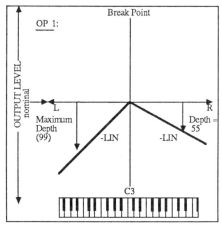

Figure 12-15

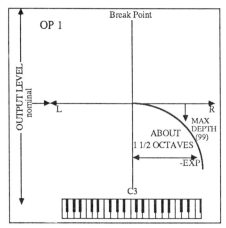

Figure 12-16

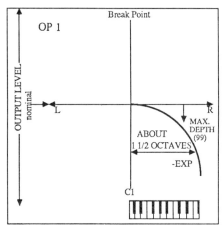

Figure 12-17

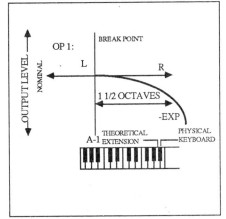

Figure 12-18

8)   CHANGE the L SCALE DEPTH value for operator 1 only to a the maximum value of 99. Play a chromatic scale on your keyboard, starting this time at the lowermost key (C1) all the way to the top key (C6), LISTENing as you do so (AUDIO CUE 71D). NOTE that the volume starts low, gets louder with its maximum at C3 (our break point for operator 1), and then gets softer again; effectively, this makes Middle C the loudest note on the keyboard: **(See Figure 12-15.)**

9)   Restore the R SCALE DEPTH value and the L SCALE DEPTH value for operator 1 back to their defaults of 0. This effectively removes the entire keyboard level scaling effect from our sound. Press edit switch 24 (CURVE parameter) and VIEW the **right** KEY SCALE value, which is currently still at its default of -LIN. Press the "yes" button once to CHANGE this for operator 1 only to a new value of -EXP, giving us a negative exponential curve.

10)   Press edit switch 25 (DEPTH parameter) and VIEW the R SCALE DEPTH value. CHANGE this value for operator 1 only to its maximum of 99. Play a chromatic scale on your keyboard, from C3 to C6, and LISTEN (AUDIO CUE 71E). NOTE that there is no apparent change in volume. Why should this be? Remember that the exponential curves induce virtually no change for a period of approximately 1 1/2 octaves: **(See Figure 12-16.)**

You may have been able to detect a slight volume decrease from A5 to C6, but this would have been slight. However, if we shift the **break point** for operator 1 so that this curve begins at a lower key, we should be able to hear the full effect of this curve, so:

11)   Press edit switch 23 (BREAK POINT parameter) and change this to a new value of C1 (the lowest physical note on the DX7 keyboard) for operator 1 only. Now play a chromatic scale up the length of the keyboard, starting at C1 all the way on up to C6, and LISTEN (AUDIO CUE 71F). NOTE that we hear virtually no volume change at all from C1 to A2, a gradual decrease in volume from A#2 to about A4, and then a drastic decrease in volume from A#4 on up to C6: **(See Figure 12-17.)**

NOTE that even then, the volume does not disappear completely even at C6. In general, then, the exponential curve will yield a more subtle effect than the linear curve.

12)   If we set our break point, however, at the very lowest note possible - right off the scale of the physical DX7 keyboard - then it will undergo its 11/2 octave no-change period before we ever hear a note, and we'll be able to hear its effect right away: **(See Figure 12-18.)**

This is the reason why the DX7 allows us to set break points right off the scale of our physical keyboard. Press edit switch 23 and CHANGE the break point for operator 1 only to a new value of A-1. Play a chromatic scale on the keyboard from C1 to C6 and LISTEN (AUDIO CUE 71G). NOTE that we are now able to hear a discernable decrease in volume from the very first note played, and that this change accelerates as we go higher up the keyboard. The volume is now completely gone by about D5.

13)   We can reverse this effect completely by making the following changes for operator 1 only: Set the BREAK POINT to C8. Set the L KEY SCALE to -EXP. Set the L SCALE DEPTH to 99. Play a chromatic scale from the **uppermost** note (C6) **down** to the lowest note (C1) and LISTEN (AUDIO CUE 71H). The effect we have created is precisely as follows: **(See Figure 12-19.)**

14) Now let's see how **positive** curves work. Restore the BREAK POINT for operator 1 only to C3. Restore both the L SCALE depth and the R SCALE depth to 0, which will have the effect of making the curves inactive. Now CHANGE the R KEY SCALE (edit switch 24) to a + LIN curve by moving the data entry slider to its uppermost position (or by pressing the "yes" button) and CHANGE the R SCALE depth (edit switch 25) back to the maximum value of 99. Play a chromatic scale on the keyboard from C3 to C6 and LISTEN (AUDIO CUE 71I). NOTE that there is currently no volume change. Why should this be? - especially since we've established that keyboard level scaling, unlike any of our previous output level controls, can be used to increase an operator's output level beyond its set value? The answer lies in the fact that we can never increase that output level beyond the maximum value of 99. And that's exactly where operator 1 is already: **(See Figure 12-20.)**

We have simply left ourselves no headroom. Press edit switch 27 (OUTPUT LEVEL parameter) and CHANGE this for operator 1 only to a new value of 50. Now play the chromatic scale again, from C3 to C6 , and LISTEN (AUDIO CUE 71J). NOTE that we now hear the volume **increase** as we play higher notes on the keyboard.

15) Press edit switch 25 and CHANGE the **right** SCALE DEPTH for operator 1 only to a new value of 75. Play a chromatic scale from C3 to C6 and LISTEN (AUDIO CUE 71K). NOTE that we hear the same volume increase, but less drastically so.

16) Play a chromatic scale from C3 **down** to C1 and LISTEN (AUDIO CUE 71L). NOTE that there is no volume change in this part of the keyboard, and that all the notes are at the lower output level. This is because there is currently no **left** SCALE DEPTH: **(See Figure 12-21.)**

17) Press edit switch 24 and CHANGE the **left** KEY SCALE curve for operator 1 only to + LIN. Now press edit switch 25 and CHANGE the **left** SCALE DEPTH for operator 1 only to the maximum value of 99. Restore the **right** SCALE DEPTH back to the maximum value of 99. Play a chromatic scale on the keyboard from C1 all the way up to C6 and LISTEN (AUDIO CUE 71M). NOTE that Middle C (C3) is now the softest note on the keyboard: **(See Figure 12-22.)**

18) Press edit switch 23 and CHANGE the BREAK POINT for operator 1 only to the lowest possible value of A-1. Press edit switch 24 and CHANGE the right KEY SCALE curve to + EXP. Play a chromatic scale up the entire keyboard, from C1 to C6 and LISTEN (AUDIO CUE 71N). NOTE that the volume now steadily increases from C1 to C5, with the greatest increase occurring in the range C3 to C5. Above C5, NOTE that there is no discernible volume increase, because the output level has already reached its absolute maximum of 99 by C5. **(See Figure 12-23.)**

19) Let's reverse that effect by doing the following: Press edit switch 23 and CHANGE the BREAK POINT for operator 1 only to a new value of C8. Press edit switch 24 and CHANGE the left KEY SCALE curve to + EXP. Press edit switch 25 and ensure that the left SCALE DEPTH value is still 99. Play a chromatic scale from C6 down to C1 and LISTEN (AUDIO CUE 71O). NOTE that the volume now steadily increases as you go down the keyboard from C6 to F2, with the greatest increase occurring in the range F4 to F2. Below F2, NOTE that there is no discernible volume increase, because the output level of operator 1 is already at its maximum of 99 by that point: **(See Figure 12-24.)**

20) Of course, we can combine positive and negative curves for the same operator, if we so desire. Press edit switch 23 and CHANGE the BREAK POINT for operator 1 only to C2. Press edit switch 27

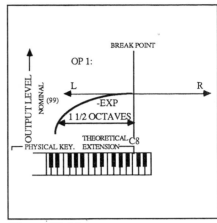

Figure 12-19

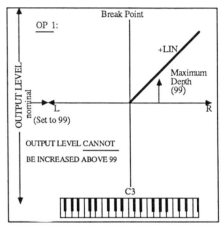

Figure 12-20

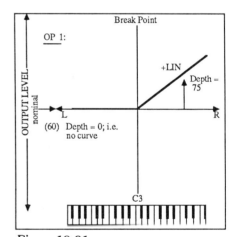

Figure 12-21

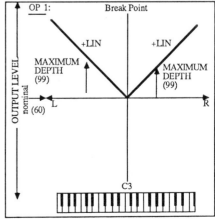

Figure 12-22

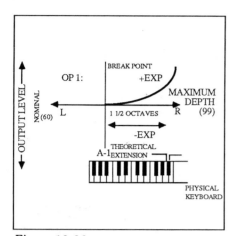

Figure 12-23

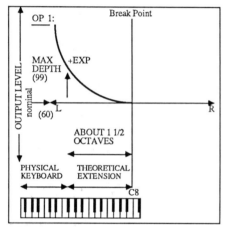

Figure 12-24

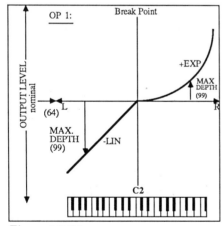

Figure 12-25

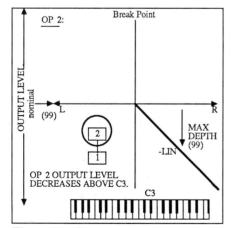

Figure 12-26

and change operator 1's OUTPUT LEVEL to a new value of 64. Press edit switch 24 and set the left KEY SCALE curve to -LIN. Press the same switch again and CHANGE the right KEY SCALE curve to + EXP. Press edit switch 25 twice and ensure that the SCALE DEPTH value for both curves is still at the maximum of 99. Play a chromatic scale up the keyboard from C1 to C6 and LISTEN (AUDIO CUE 71P). NOTE that the volume rises from near-inaudible to a low level by the time you reach C2, and then remains at that low level until about A3, at which point it begins increasing, gently at first, and then more dramatically at the upper end of the keyboard: **(See Figure 12-25.)**

21)   EXPERIMENT by changing the SCALE DEPTH values for either or both of the curves and NOTE how this affects the overall sound. EXPERIMENT further with different timbres, using different BREAK POINTS, CURVES, and DEPTHS, until you feel comfortable with the way keyboard level scaling affects carriers.

We can apply keyboard level scaling effects to our **modulator** as well. This will allow us to quantitatively change the **overtone content** of our sound, according to what note we play on the keyboard:

EXERCISE 72

Keyboard level scaling applied to a modulator:

1)   INITIALIZE your DX7, leave it in algorithm #1, TURN OFF operators 3 through 6 ("110000"), and, using the system of operators 1 and 2, GENERATE a sawtooth wave.
2)   Use the operator select switch to VIEW operator 2 (the modulator in this system) and press edit switch 23 (BREAK POINT parameter). OBSERVE that it is currently at its default value of A-1.

CHANGE this for operator 2 only to a new value of C3 (Middle C on the DX7 keyboard).
3)   Press edit switch 24 (CURVE parameter) and OBSERVE that both the right curve and the left curve are currently at their defaults of -LIN.
4)   Press edit switch 25 (DEPTH parameter) and OBSERVE that both the right and the left SCALE DEPTHs are currently at their defaults of 0, indicating no current keyboard level scaling. VIEW the R SCALE DEPTH value and CHANGE it for operator 2 only to the maximum value of 99.
5)   Play a chromatic scale on your keyboard, starting at Middle C (C3) and going up to the highest note (C6), LISTENing as you do so (AUDIO CUE 72A). NOTE that because we have applied a -LIN curve to the right of C3, with maximum DEPTH (99), the overtone content decreases rather rapidly, changing our sawtooth wave completely back to a pure sine wave by the uppermost note (C6): **(See Figure 12-26.)**

6)   Play a chromatic scale from C3 down to C1 and LISTEN (AUDIO CUE 72B). NOTE that we hear no timbral change whatsoever as we go to the left of C3 because the L SCALE DEPTH value is currently 0: **(See Figure 12-27.)**

7)   CHANGE the R SCALE DEPTH value (edit switch 25 - and be sure you're VIEWing the **right** and not the left scale depth) for operator 2 only to a new value of 55. Play a chromatic scale on your keyboard, from C3 to C6, LISTENing as you do so (AUDIO CUE 72C). NOTE that the overtone content again diminishes, but not as rapidly, and that even at the uppermost note (C6), we still hear some overtones; we never quite revert all the way back to the sine wave: **(See Figure 12-28.)**

8) CHANGE the L SCALE DEPTH value for operator 2 only to a the maximum value of 99. Play a chromatic scale on your keyboard, starting this time at the lowermost key (C1) all the way up to the top key (C6), LISTENing as you do so (AUDIO CUE 72D). NOTE that C1 is virtually a sine wave and that the overtone content steadily increases until C3 (our break point); it then begins diminishing again, until C6. Because of the combination of these two curves, C3 is now the brightest note on the keyboard: **(See Figure 12-29.)**

9) Restore the R SCALE DEPTH value and the L SCALE DEPTH value for operator 2 only back to their defaults of 0. This effectively removes the entire keyboard level scaling effect from our sound. Press edit switch 24 (CURVE parameter) and VIEW the right KEY SCALE value, which is currently still at its default of -LIN. Press the "yes" button once to CHANGE this for operator 2 only to a new value of -EXP, giving us a negative exponential curve.

10) Press edit switch 25 (DEPTH parameter) and VIEW the R SCALE DEPTH value. CHANGE this value for operator 2 only to its maximum of 99. Play a chromatic scale on your keyboard, from C3 to C6, and LISTEN (AUDIO CUE 72E). NOTE that there is no apparent timbral change. Again, the exponential curve induces virtually no change for a period of approximately 1 1/2 octaves: **(See Figure 12-30.)**

You may have been able to detect a slight overtone content decrease from A5 to C6, but this would have been slight. However, if we shift the break point for operator 2 so that this curve begins at a lower key, we should be able to hear the full effect of this curve, so:

11) Press edit switch 23 (BREAK POINT parameter) and change this to a new value of C1 (the lowest physical note on the DX7 keyboard) for operator 2 only. Now play a chromatic scale up the length of the keyboard, starting at C1 all the way on up to C6, and LISTEN (AUDIO CUE 72F). NOTE that we hear virtually no timbral change at all from C1 to A2, a gradual decrease in overtone content from A#2 to about A4, and then a drastic decrease in overtones from A#4 on up to C6: **(See Figure 12-31.)**

NOTE that even then, the overtones do not disappear completely even at C6.

12) If we set our break point, however, at the very lowest note possible - right off the scale of the physical DX7 keyboard - then it will undergo its 1 1/2 octave no-change period before we ever hear a note, and we'll be able to hear its effect right away: **(See Figure 12-32.)**

Press edit switch 23 and CHANGE the break point for operator 2 only to a new value of A-1. Play a chromatic scale on the keyboard from C1 to C6 and LISTEN (AUDIO CUE 72G). NOTE that we are now able to hear a discernable decrease in overtone content from the very first note played, and that this change accelerates as we go higher up the keyboard. By the time we reach D5, we are back to a pure sine wave.

13) We can reverse this effect completely by making the following changes for operator 2 only: Set the BREAK POINT to C8. Set the L KEY SCALE to -EXP. Set the L SCALE DEPTH to 99. Play a chromatic scale from the uppermost note (C6) down to the lowest note (C1) and LISTEN (AUDIO CUE 72H). The effect we have created is as follows: **(See Figure 12-33.)**

14) Now let's try a **positive** curve for our modulator. Restore the BREAK POINT for operator 2 only to C3. Restore both the L SCALE depth and the R SCALE depth to 0, which will have the effect of making the curves inactive. Now CHANGE the R KEY SCALE to a + LIN curve and the R SCALE depth to 99. Play a chromatic scale on

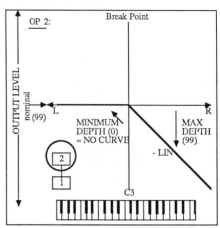

Figure 12-27

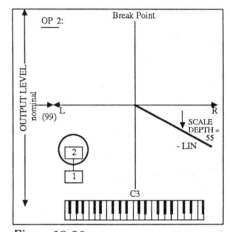

Figure 12-28

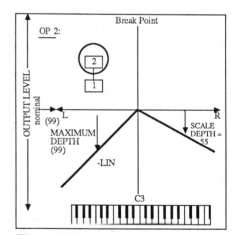

Figure 12-29

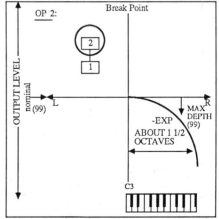

Figure 12-30

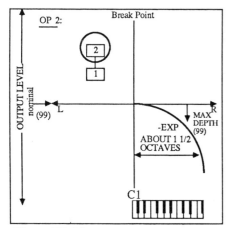

Figure 12-31

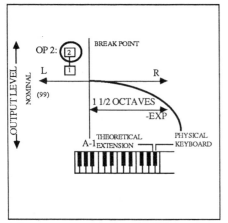

Figure 12-32

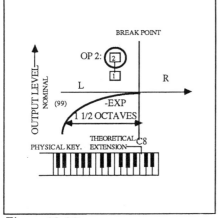

Figure 12-33

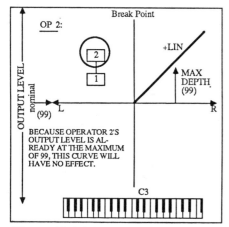

Figure 12-34

the keyboard from C3 to C6 and LISTEN (AUDIO CUE 72I). NOTE that there is currently no timbral change whatever. Again, even though keyboard level scaling can be used to increase an operator's output level beyond it's set value, we can still never increase that output level beyond the maximum value of 99. And that's exactly where operator 2 is already: **(See Figure 12-34.)**

Once again, we have left ourselves no headroom. Press edit switch 27 (OUTPUT LEVEL parameter) and CHANGE this for operator 2 only to a new value of 50. Now play the chromatic scale again, from C3 to C6 , and LISTEN (AUDIO CUE 72J). NOTE that we now hear the overtone content increase as we play higher notes on the keyboard, so that C3 is little more than a sine wave, but C6 is a full-blown sawtooth wave.

15)   Press edit switch 25 and CHANGE the right SCALE DEPTH for operator 2 only to a new value of 75. Play a chromatic scale from C3 to C6 and LISTEN (AUDIO CUE 72K). NOTE that we hear the same quantitative overtone increase, but less drastically so.

16)   Play a chromatic scale from C3 down to C1 and LISTEN (AUDIO CUE 72L). NOTE that there is no timbral change in this part of the keyboard, and that all the notes are quasi-sine waves. This is because there is currently no left SCALE DEPTH: **(See Figure 12-35.)**

17)   Press edit switch 24 and CHANGE the left KEY SCALE curve for operator 2 only to +LIN. Now press edit switch 25 and CHANGE the left SCALE DEPTH for operator 2 only to the maximum value of 99. Restore the right SCALE DEPTH back to the maximum value of 99. Play a chromatic scale on the keyboard from C1 all the way up to C6 and LISTEN (AUDIO CUE 72M). NOTE that Middle C (C3) is now the **least bright** note on the keyboard: **(See Figure 12-36.)**

18)   Press edit switch 23 and CHANGE the BREAK POINT for operator 2 only to the lowest possible value of A-1. Press edit switch 24 and CHANGE the right KEY SCALE curve to +EXP. Play a chromatic scale up the entire keyboard, from C1 to C6 and LISTEN (AUDIO CUE 72N). NOTE that the overtone content now steadily increases from C1 to C5, with the greatest increase occurring in the range C3 to C5. Above C5, NOTE that there is no discernible overtone content increase, because the output level has already reached its absolute maximum of 99 by C5: **(See Figure 12-37.)**

19)   Let's reverse that effect by doing the following: Press edit switch 23 and CHANGE the BREAK POINT for operator 2 only to a new value of C8. Press edit switch 24 and CHANGE the left KEY SCALE curve to +EXP. Press edit switch 25 and ensure that the left SCALE DEPTH value is still 99. Play a chromatic scale from C6 down to C1 and LISTEN (AUDIO CUE 72O). NOTE that the overtone content now steadily increases as you go down the keyboard from C6 to F2, with the greatest increase occurring in the range F4 to F2. Below F2, NOTE that there is no discernible timbral change, because the output level of operator 2 is already at its maximum of 99 by that point: **(See Figure 12-38.)**

20)   Of course, we can also **combine** positive and negative curves for the same operator (by having one type of curve to the left of our break point and a different type to the right). Press edit switch 23 and CHANGE the BREAK POINT for operator 2 only to C2. Press edit switch 27 and change operator 2's OUTPUT LEVEL to a new value of 64. Press edit switch 24 and set the left KEY SCALE curve to -LIN. Press the same switch again and ensure that the right KEY SCALE curve is still +EXP. Press edit switch 25 twice and ensure that the SCALE DEPTH value for both curves is still at the maximum of 99. Play a chromatic scale up the keyboard from C1 to C6 and LISTEN (AUDIO CUE 72P). NOTE that the timbre changes from a sine wave

to a gentle, triangle-like wave by the time you reach C2, and then remains that way until about A3, at which point it begins increasing in overtone content, gently at first, and then more dramatically at the upper end of the keyboard: **(See Figure 12-39.)**

21) EXPERIMENT by changing the SCALE DEPTH values for either or both curves and NOTE how this affects the overall sound. EXPERIMENT further with different timbres, using different BREAK POINTS, CURVES, and DEPTHS, until you feel comfortable with the way keyboard level scaling affects modulators.

Because keyboard level scaling is **operator-specific**, and because each operator in our sound can have independent break points, curves, and depths, it is an enormously powerful tool for creating both "real" and "unreal" sounds. No acoustic instrument, for example, responds precisely the same way for each note you play on it: played with equal force, a low note on a piano is much louder than a high note; similarly, a high note on a trumpet is much brighter than a low note. We can simulate these and many more naturally occurring acoustic phenomena with keyboard level scaling, but we can also use it to create some very unusual effects. Take a look at a sound I programmed some time ago, a sound I refer to as my "Escher" sound, called "PLAYASCALE":

EXERCISE 73

Examining "PLAYASCALE": using keyboard level scaling for pitch change:

1) INITIALIZE your DX7 and put it into algorithm #32 (bet you never thought we'd go back to this old chestnut!).

2) TURN OFF operator 6 ("111110") - for this sound, we will only be using operators 1 through 5. Even though our microprocessor will not be able to remember that operator 6 was off when you store this sound, its output level is currently defaulted at 0, so we won't hear it anyway.

3) Press edit switch 27 and set the OUTPUT LEVELs of operators 1 through 5 all to the maximum value of 99.

4) Press edit switch 18 (F COARSE parameter) and enter in the following values:

Operator #	F COARSE
1	16.00
2	8.00
3	4.00
4	2.00
5	1.00

5) Press edit switch 23 (BREAK POINT parameter) and enter in the following values:

Operator #	BREAK POINT
1	G# 1
2	G# 2
3	G 3
4	G 4
5	C 6

6) Press edit switch 25 (DEPTH parameter) and enter in the following values:

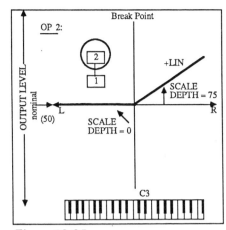

Figure 12-35

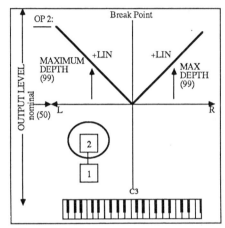

Figure 12-36

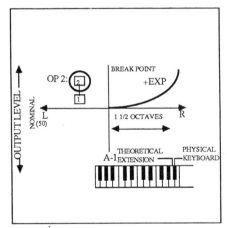

Figure 12-37

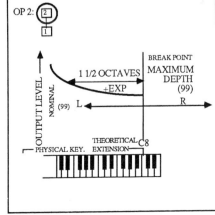

Figure 12-38

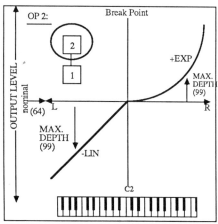

Figure 12-39

Operator # L SCALE DEPTH R SCALE DEPTH

Operator #	L SCALE DEPTH	R SCALE DEPTH
1	0	99
2	99	99
3	99	99
4	99	99
5	99	0

7) NOTE that all CURVES (edit switch 24) should be left at their default -LIN value. This process gives us a keyboard level scaling like this: **(See Figure 12-40.)**

8) Now do just what the name of the sound tells you to do - PLAYASCALE - from the bottom of the keyboard to the top, and LISTEN (AUDIO CUE 73A)! NOTE the unusual effect: C1 sounds like the same note as C2, C3, C4, C5, or C6! In fact, each octave on the keyboard sounds pretty much the same as the octave below it or above it! This creates an interesting aural illusion, similar, I think, to the kind of visual illusions created by the great artist, M. C. Escher.

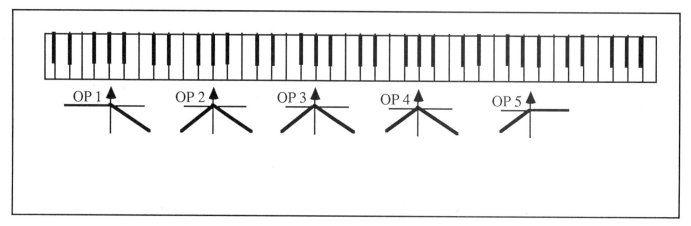

Figure 12-40

If you listen very closely to "PLAYASCALE", you can, in fact hear some slight differences in overtone content from octave to octave. But how can we have overtones when we're working with algorithm 32? Simple: the keyboard level scaling causes the differently pitched operators to overlap in various different ways over various parts of the keyboard. At no time are we ever hearing purely one of the carrier sine waves to the exclusion of the others, due to this overlap. The end result is that we usually are hearing two or three differently pitched sine waves - an additive synthesis process. The illusion is not only that the pitches appear to be the same from octave to octave but that the sound we hear appears to contain overtones as well!

As with other original sounds presented in this book, I declare this patch to be in the public domain; and that means you're welcome to store it and use it at will.

Here's another potential use of keyboard level scaling: instead of scaling different carriers over different parts of the keyboard, let's use a single-carrier algorithm, like #16, and scale different modulators over different parts of the keyboard, creating different timbres for each note we play:

EXERCISE 74

Keyboard level scaling used for timbral change:

1) INITIALIZE your DX7 and select algorithm #16: **(See Figure 12-41.)**

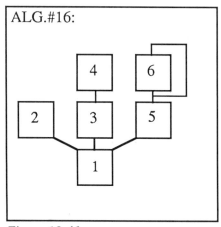

Figure 12-41

2) Press edit switch 27 and enter the following OUTPUT LEVELs for the six operators:

Operator #	OUTPUT LEVEL
1	9
2	99
3	71
4	99
5	55
6	99

3) Press edit switch 17 and/or 18 (F COARSE and F FINE parameters) to enter the following frequencies for the six operators:

Operator #	F COARSE
1	1.00
2	1.00
3	2.00
4	11.20
5	14.00
6	15.00

4) Press edit switches 21 and 22 (EG RATE and EG LEVEL parameters) to enter the following EG data for the six operators:

Op #	L4	R1	L1	R2	L2	R3	L3	R4	L4
1	0	99	99	99	99	99	99	52	0
2	0	99	99	99	99	99	99	9	0
3	0	99	99	99	99	99	99	25	0
4	0	99	99	43	0	99	0	12	0
5	0	99	99	58	0	99	0	48	0
6	0	99	99	99	99	99	99	82	0

5) Press edit switch 8 (FEEDBACK parameter) and enter the maximum value of 7. NOTE that in this algorithm the feedback loop is on operator 6.

6) Press edit switch 23 (BREAK POINT parameter) and enter in the following values for the six operators:

Operator #	BREAK POINT
1	A -1
2	C 1
3	B 1
4	F# 3
5	B 4
6	D 5

7) Press edit switch 24 (CURVE parameter) and CHANGE the right KEY SCALE for operator 3 only to -EXP. Leave all other operators at their default curve of -LIN.

8) Press edit switch 25 (DEPTH parameter) and enter in the following values:

Operator #	L SCALE DEPTH	R SCALE DEPTH
1	0	0
2	99	99
3	99	99
4	99	99
5	99	99
6	99	99

9) Play a chromatic scale from C1 to C6 and LISTEN (AUDIO CUE 74A). NOTE that our sound undergoes six distinct timbral changes as the five different modulators fade in and out over the keyboard and finally disappear altogether from E5 to C6, as according to their keyboard scaling, as follows: **(See Figure 12-42.)**

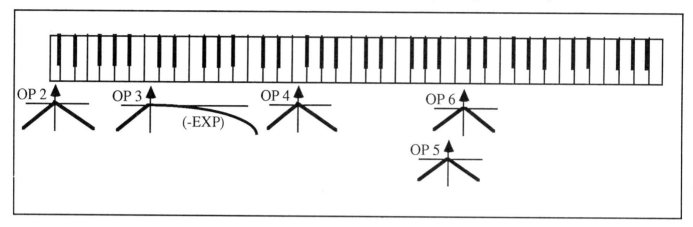

Figure 12-42

C1 is essentially just a sawtooth wave, containing a "square" envelope with a moderate release time. Because R4 for operator 2 is so slow (a value of 9), there is very little timbral change as the sound dies away. As we get to the area E1 - C2, we hear this sawtooth timbre change to a hollower square wave timbre, with a very similar type of envelope. The square wave is, of course, being generated by the action of operator 3, and because its right curve is a negative **exponential** curve, it will be present across a larger area of the keyboard than any of the other modulators. As we get towards the area C#2 - D4, we hear the steadily increasing presence of the upper modulator in this stack, operator 4. This operator has been set to a non-whole number frequency value and is at its maximum output level; furthermore, its envelope is quite percussive. The disharmonics it generates are most present at its break point of F#3 and they begin to tail off after this point. From D#4 to F#4 we begin to hear operator 5 fade in, with the

characteristic 14:1 frequency ratio and slightly percussive envelope yielding a faint reminder of the first system in "E.PIANO 1". From G4 to E5 we hear the snare-drum like sound being contributed by the feedback modulator, operator 6. Finally, above E5, the actions of all the modulators die away and disappear, and at the upper end of the keyboard we are left with just the single sine wave being generated by operator 1.

10) EXPERIMENT with altering the various scaling parameters for this sound - try, for example, reversing the entire process so that the single sine wave appears only at the **bottom** end of the keyboard. EXPERIMENT further by altering the various frequency ratios and operator output levels and NOTE how these changes affect the entire sound.

It should be apparent that keyboard level scaling, then, can be used for a variety of unique effects. However, what most people use it for most of the time is to accomplish something called *keyboard splits*.

A "keyboard split" allows you to play two separate sounds simultaneously on one keyboard. Usually, the way this works is that you assign a *split point* on the keyboard, and you will hear one sound to the left of that point, and the other sound to the right. The only way this can be accomplished on most synthesizers is by incorporating two independent sets of voice-generating circuitry into one instrument. Each of these can be thought of as a complete synthesizer unto itself - so what we essentially have is two synthesizers in one box. Typically, these will be designated the "right" and "left", or "upper" and "lower" synthesizers.

With our DX7, we can't do things that way, because we only have one set of voice-generating circuitry.* But we have learned that any one sound we create on this instrument is composed of the sum of **six** independent operators. And we have learned that we can scale the outputs of each of these operators over different points on the keyboard. Therefore, the "keyboard splits" we can accomplish using keyboard level scaling are bogus ones - since what we are doing is splitting up one voice into two or more parts, as opposed to actually having two or more independent voices.

But it works, nonetheless! Obviously, in order to accomplish this, we need a sound with more than one carrier. That eliminates algorithms 16, 17, and 18. But, what the heck, that still leaves us with 29 of our 32 algorithms that will work!

Before we run an exercise to try this out, you should realize the limitations of this quasi-split. The main restriction is that we cannot accomplish what are called *hard splits*. A "hard" split is where you have one sound on this key **completely** and a totally different sound on the next key completely: **(See Figure 12-43.)**

We can't do that on our DX7 because in every instance we have to work with curves. A linear curve with maximum depth will roll off pretty severely, but it won't be severe enough to imitate a hard split: **(See Figure 12-44.)**

The exponential curve, of course, can become more severe in its effect than the linear curve, but because of the extended (approximately 1 1/2 octave) area in which it is inactive, it will generally be of less value in trying to accomplish keyboard splits. Let's try working with one of the dual sounds provided by Yamaha, and see how we can "split" it over our keyboard. We'll work with "ORCH-CHIME", found on ROM 1A-25 or ROM 4B-5 (where, for some unknown reason, it has been renamed "STR-CHIME").

Several Yamaha presets are set up the way this one is, that is, with two distinct sounds combined together within a single algorithm, including ROM 2B-17 ("HARP-FLUTE"), 2B-18 ("BELL-FLUTE"), or 2B-22 ("B DRUM-SNARE"). (NOTE: Some of the American presets in ROM 4B have already been pre-split.) Using keyboard level scaling, we can take any of these and "split" them over different sections of the keyboard, just as the "TRAIN" sound (ROM 1A-31 or ROM 3A-30) we examined in the last chapter contains a bell at the top of the keyboard, and a whistle at the bottom (with the choo-

choo throughout). The use of curves, as opposed to hard splits (unavailable on the DX7 but available on some of the later model Yamaha digital FM machines - see Chapter Fifteen) means that we will have a "gray area" on the keyboard where both sounds will be present but crossfading with one another. However, with careful manipulation of our break points and curves, we can minimize this area to about half an octave - the DX7 "DMZ", if you like: **(See Figure 12-45.)**

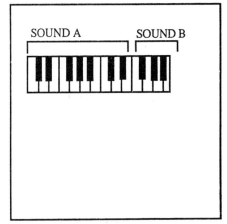

Figure 12-43

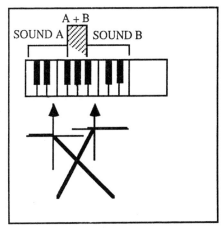

Figure 12-44

---

* see Chapter Sixteen for a description of three Yamaha digital FM synthesizers that each have two sets of voice-generating circuitry - the DX5, DX21, and DX1.

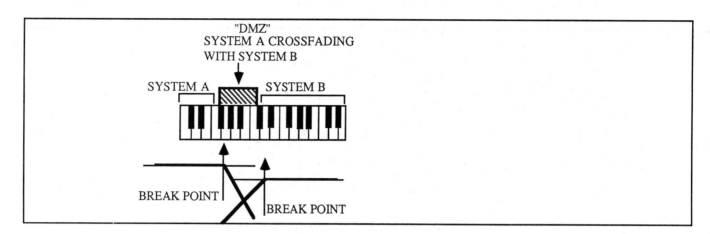

Figure 12-45

Before we actually run this exercise, let's plan out exactly what we're going to do. Put your DX7 into cartridge play mode and call up "ORCH-CHIME" from ROM 1A-25 or ROM 4B-5 (in which case it will be called "STR-CHIME"). Now go to edit mode and take a look at the algorithm used for this sound, our old friend (from "E.PIANO 1"), algorithm #5: **(See Figure 12-46.)**

A quick listen to each one of the three systems should quickly confirm that it is the **second** system, operators 3 and 4, that are creating the CHIME part of the sound. System one (operators 1 and 2) and system three (operators 5 and 6) are together creating the ORCH - really just a string sound. Let's say that we want to split our keyboard so that the CHIMES are in the upper half - let's say from F3 on up - and the ORCH is in the lower half. Since we are looking for a pure **volume** control here - we are not looking to change the timbre of either of our two sounds - we will be applying keyboard level scaling to our CARRIERS - operators 1, 3, and 5, only. For operator 3 (the carrier in the CHIME sound), we wish a keyboard scaling as follows: **(See Figure 12-47.)**

and for operators 1 and 5 (the carriers in our ORCH sound), we wish to generate this kind of curve: **(See Figure 12-48.)**

Note that in NEITHER INSTANCE do we require a **positive** curve - we are NOT looking to increase the volume in any way - only to **decrease** it above (in the case of operators 1 and 5) and below (in the case of operator 3) a certain point (in this case, F3).

Okay, now that we know what we need to do, let's do it!

EXERCISE 75

Keyboard splits: "ORCH-CHIME":

1) Put your DX7 into cartridge play mode and call up the "ORCH-CHIME" sound from either ROM 1A-25 or ROM 4B-5 ("STR-CHIME"). Play a note to confirm that this is now in your edit buffer (AUDIO CUE 75A).

2) Use the mode select switch to go to edit mode. OBSERVE that algorithm #5 was used to create this sound.

3) TURN OFF operators 3 through 6 ("110000") in order to hear system one only. Play a key and LISTEN (AUDIO CUE 75B). NOTE that this system is contributing the string ("ORCH") section to the overall sound.

4) TURN OFF operators 1 and 2, and TURN ON operators 3 and 4 ("001100") in order to hear system two only. Play a key and LISTEN (AUDIO CUE 75C). NOTE that this system is contributing a chime sound to the total sound we hear.

ALG #5

```
[2]  [4]  [6]
[1]  [3]  [5]
```

Figure 12-46

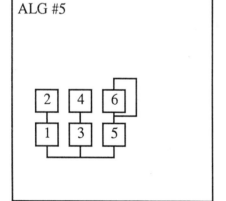

Figure 12-47

5) TURN OFF operators 3 and 4, and TURN ON operators 5 and 6 ("000011") in order to hear system three only. Play a key and LISTEN (AUDIO CUE 75D). NOTE that this system is also contributing a string sound. TURN ON operators 1 and 2 ("110011") in order to hear the complete ORCH part of "ORCH-CHIME". NOTE that system three (operators 5 and 6) is pitched an octave higher than system one (operators 1 and 2). Press edit switch 18 (F COARSE parameter) and use the operator select switch to VIEW each of these four operators. OBSERVE that the frequency ratio in system one is 0.50 : 0.50 whereas in system three it is 1.00:1.00.

6) TURN ON all operators and listen to the sound once again. When we strike notes sharply on the keyboard, we hear only the CHIME, but when we hold a key down, we hear the ORCH fade in as well. Why is this? Obviously the EGs are at play, since we are hearing an aperiodic change over time. R1 must be very fast for operator 3 (the CHIME carrier) and very slow for operators 1 and 5 (the ORCH carriers). Press edit switch 21 in order to VIEW this and NOTE that R1 for operator 3 = 80 whereas for operators 1 and 5 it is 34 and 41, respectively. Another of life's great mysteries solved!

7) The first thing we need to do is to see if keyboard level scaling is already occurring as an intrinsic part of this sound. We can determine this by examining the SCALE DEPTHs of our 12 curves (2 curves for each of our six operators). Press edit switch 25 (DEPTH parameter) and VIEW each of the 12 curves in turn, pressing the switch repeatedly to cycle between the left and right curves, and using the operator select switch to VIEW each of the six operators. OBSERVE that all 12 curves currently have a value of 0. This means that no keyboard scaling whatever is currently occurring, regardless of where the break points may be and what type of curves may have been assigned.

8) Let's begin by scaling the CHIME part of the sound, which is being contributed by system two. TURN OFF operators 1, 2, 5, and 6 ("001100"). VIEW operator 3 (the carrier) and press edit switch 23 (BREAK POINT parameter). CHANGE this from its current value of C1 (there for no particular reason, since all operator SCALE DEPTHs are currently at 0) to a new value of F3.

9) Since we wish to **lessen** the volume of our CHIME (hence the output level of operator 3) to the left of F3, we will require a negative left curve. Because linear curves are the most useful in accomplishing keyboard splits, that's what we'll choose - a -LIN curve. Press edit switch 24 (CURVE parameter) and OBSERVE that this type of curve has already been assigned to the left of the break point. Our right curve will be irrelevant, since we are looking to make **no** change to the volume of our CHIME to the right of F3.

10) Press edit switch 25 (DEPTH parameter) and OBSERVE that the right depth for operator 3 currently has a value of 0 - in other words, there is currently no right curve, which is exactly what we need. However, press the switch again and CHANGE the left SCALE DEPTH to the maximum value of 99.

11) Now for the moment of truth! Play a chromatic scale on the keyboard, starting at C6 and going down to C1, and LISTEN (AUDIO CUE 75E). NOTE that the volume of the chime is unchanged until F3 and that it then begins decreasing, until it is completely gone by about G1. However, this isn't exactly what we had in mind. Ideally, what we'd like is full volume at F3 and no volume at E3, but since the DX7 cannot give us hard splits, we know that isn't possible. What we'll settle for is a "gray area" centered around F3 of about a half-octave, in which the volume of the CHIME is noticeably decreasing, while the volume of the ORCH is noticeably increasing: **(See Figure 12-49.)**

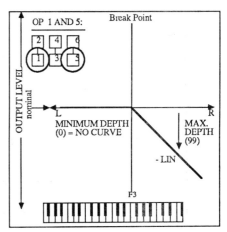

Figure 12-48

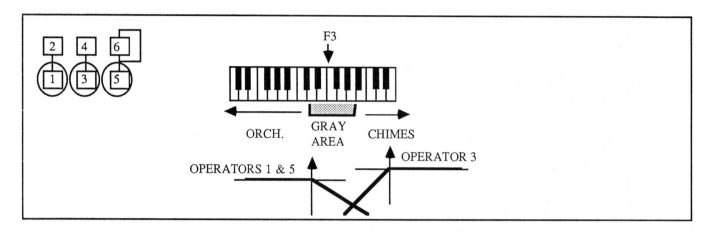

Figure 12-49

In order to accomplish this, we'll have to compromise. The method I recommend is as follows: pick a note, say A#2 in this instance, and tell yourself that no matter what, you don't want to hear any CHIME by the time you reach this note. With this in mind, call up the BREAK POINT parameter (edit switch 23) and tap A#2 repeatedly (remember, since keyboard level scaling affects output level, it won't change in real time) while pressing the "yes" button in order to raise the break point: **(See Figure 12-50.)**

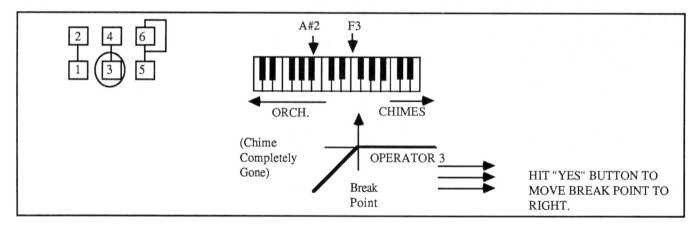

Figure 12-50

Eventually, the break point will be high enough that the output of operator 3 will be completely gone! Try it and LISTEN carefully as you do so (AUDIO CUE 75F). You should find that you'll have to raise the break point for operator 3 to about A4 in order to best accomplish this split. Remember - this is a compromise! Yes, the volume of the CHIME starts decreasing all the way up at A4, but this decrease is relatively slight at first and it isn't until you reach D4 or so that it starts to become very noticeable. In any event, you've got most of the upper two octaves of the keyboard to work with and play the CHIME part of the sound. The sound is now completely gone from the lower part of the keyboard, however, and that was our goal, so pat yourself on the back (if you can reach that far!).

12)   Okay, the CHIME part of the sound is done, so TURN OFF operators 3 and 4. We will need to scale both operators 1 and 5 the same way, but you'll probably find it easier to just work with one at a time, so, for now, just TURN ON operators 1 and 2 (you'll want to keep operator 2 on even though we're not scaling it so that our system will sound like a string, not just a sine wave). ("110000")

13) Make sure you're VIEWing operator 1, press edit switch 23 (BREAK POINT parameter) and CHANGE this value for operator 1 to F3.

14) What we're looking for, of course, is a decrease in operator 1's output level above F3, and no change below it. Therefore, we want to ensure that there is no keyboard level scaling for the left curve. To accomplish that, press edit switch 25 (DEPTH parameter) and OBSERVE that the left SCALE DEPTH is currently at 0. In order to set the right curve, press edit switch 24 (CURVE parameter) and CHANGE this from its current value of -EXP to a -LIN curve. Press edit switch 25 (DEPTH parameter) and enter the maximum value of 99 for the right curve of operator 1 only.

15) Play a chromatic scale on the keyboard from C1 to C6 and LISTEN (AUDIO CUE 75G). NOTE that our half of the ORCH sound undergoes no change in volume from C1 to F3 and then, above that point, begins decreasing in volume. Once again, we will need to select a note and decide that the sound must be completely gone by that point. Let's pick D4 for this example. Press edit switch 23 again in order to call up the BREAK POINT parameter for operator 1, and play D4 repeatedly on the keyboard while pressing the "no" data entry button (since this time we'll have to lower the break point), and LISTEN (AUDIO CUE 75H). NOTE that in order to accomplish this, the break point will have to be around G2. Now, we've got our sound cleanly over the bottom 2 1/2 octaves of our keyboard, with a "gray area" of half an octave or so, overlapping the "gray area" of operator 3: **(See Figure 12-51.)**

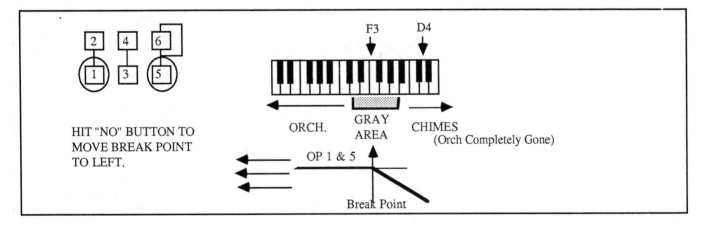

Figure 12-51

16) TURN ON operator 5 and TURN OFF operator 2 ("100010"). We'll need to enter the same scaling effect for operator 5 as we currently have for operator 1, and this is the fastest way of doing it. Simply call up each of the five keyboard level scaling parameters (BREAK POINT, the two CURVEs, and the two DEPTHs) for operator 1 and CHANGE each of these values for operator 5 so they are the same as those for operator 1. When you've done that, TURN ON our ORCH modulators (operators 2 and 6) and LISTEN. You should now be hearing the ORCH sound "split" and full strength on the lower part of the keyboard only.

17) TURN ON operators 3 and 4 ("111111"), play a few licks and LISTEN (AUDIO CUE 75I). Eureka! ORCH in the left hand, CHIMES in the right! There is a "gray area", from approximately G3 to D4, that you will want to avoid, but with that one qualification, we can call this a successful and usable keyboard split. **(See Figure 12-52.)**

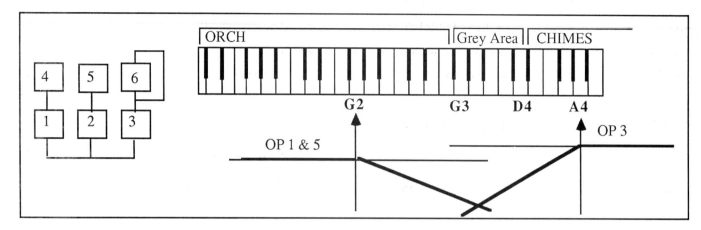

Figure 12-52

18) EXPERIMENT by swapping the split; put the CHIMES on the lower part of the keyboard and ORCH on the upper. Try setting up a "gray area" that is lower down, or higher up, on the keyboard. EXPERIMENT further by altering the pitch of either the ORCH or CHIME (remember Cardinal Rule Three!). EXPERIMENT by calling up the "TRAIN" preset mentioned above (ROM 1A-31 or 3A-30) and put your DX7 into edit mode - you should now be able to see clearly how the splits were accomplished (this sound also uses algorithm #5 - a real favorite among programmers!). Try modifying this sound so that the bell is at the bottom of the keyboard and the whistle at the top. EXPERIMENT further by splitting other dual-sound ROM presets, as cataloged above. With a little practice, this whole procedure will take only a minute or so, and will greatly enhance the performance capabilities of the DX7.

Bear in mind, again, that in order to do a keyboard split, you will need a sound composed of two or more carriers, with significant differences between the different systems involved.

We are now at the magic moment where I can happily inform you that we have covered ALL of the edit parameters on the DX7. So pour yourself a beer, light a cigar (or, for the more esoteric of you, eat some lentils and light a joss stick), and congratulations!

Seriously, before moving on to the next chapter, which covers the remaining Function Controls, take a little time out to examine the 32 edit parameters - the blue ones - and make sure you have a fair idea of what each one is supposed to do and how altering it will alter the sound you are creating or modifying. Modifying a preset, as we have stated earlier, is a fairly analytical procedure, and only a clear understanding of all the different edit parameters will aid you in this endeavour. Take your time; go back to the earlier chapters, if necessary, and be certain you have that clear understanding before moving ahead.

SWITCHES AND CONTROLS COVERED IN CHAPTER TWELVE:

SWITCH	PARAMETER	COMMENTS
Edit 23	Break Point	Operator-specific; Range A-1 - C8.
Edit 24	Key Scale Curve	Operator-specific; -LIN, -EXP, +EXP, or +LIN.
Edit 24	Key Curve Depth	Operator-specific; Range 0 - 99.

CHAPTER THIRTEEN:
THE FUNCTION CONTROLS

As discussed in Chapter Two, the function controls on the DX7 are *global commands*; that is, they affect any sound called up in the DX7's edit buffer. The reason for this is that there is only one function control memory, as opposed to the thirty-two edit parameter memories (or *internal memory* slots) in this instrument. This single function control memory is protected by the back-up battery, so changes made to function controls are remembered by the DX7 even after the instrument is turned off. Furthermore, these function controls are never reset, even upon voice initialization. The voice initialization procedure only resets *edit* parameters, and there is in fact no way on the DX7 to reset function controls.

We've mentioned from time to time that the DX7 was the first in this family of machines, and so is somewhat more limited than subsequent Yamaha digital FM synthesizers. Regarding the function controls, this is true yet again. In most of these later machines, including the TX MIDI rack, there is a function control memory for **each** of the thirty-two voice memories, so that function controls become voice-linked. You can add this capability to your DX7 by adding on a Yamaha device called the TX7 - which adds thirty-two extra voice memories and **sixty-four** extra function memories (32 for the 32 TX7 voices and 32 for the DX7 voices), but we'll talk more about this device in Chapter Sixteen (Other Digital FM Instruments).

Fortunately, for the most part, the function controls do not involve critical parameters. They concern themselves with various "house-keeping" jobs such as the mass transfer of data to or from cartridges, or they have to do with non-critical voice controls, such as portamento and pitch-bending.

In Chapter Two you were not only introduced to one of these function parameters - Master Tune Adjust (function switch 1) - but we also discussed the fact that the data entry slider remains active for the last function control viewed even after you exit function mode and return to play mode. If you don't remember about this, or if you've skipped ahead to this point, I strongly advise you to go back and review this section . We pointed out the problems inherent in this design, but somewhat sneakily didn't tell you that there was a way around it. And the solution is simple - take a look at how your back-up battery is doing!

Function switch 14: Battery Check

This parameter allows you to see how much voltage is currently in your DX7's back-up battery, allowing you to instantly know the strength of the battery. This important component ensures that the sounds you store in your internal memory remain there even if you turn the machine off or unplug it. The battery also protects the contents of the *edit recall buffer* as well as the function control memory. When you buy a new DX7, the battery should output 3.4 - 3.5 volts. As the machine gets older, this voltage will drop. When it gets down to 2.2 volts, you will need to have the battery replaced at your local Authorized Service Center. Since the battery is meant to have an approximate life of five years, and since, at the time of this writing, DX7's haven't been around for five years, very few people have had to deal with this so far. (Those that have have

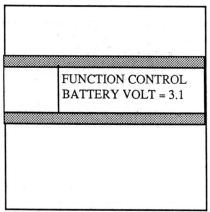

Figure 13-1

undoubtedly had a defective battery or a defective DX7). The battery is recharged by the power being on, just as a car battery is recharged by the engine running, so if you don't use your DX7 for an extended period of time, the battery will run down sooner than another one living in a frequently used instrument. To this end, if you find yourself owning a DX7 and not using it too often (shame on you!) you should at least plug it in and turn it on for a few hours once a week or so.

Put your DX7 into *function mode* and press switch 14. Your LCD should say: **(See Figure 13-1.)**

with a voltage reading somewhere in the 2.2 - 3.5 range. Try moving the data entry slider. Obviously, nothing happens - we can't enter a voltage setting. The point here is that we have effectively DISABLED the data entry slider. If you now return your DX7 to play mode, you'll find that jiggling the data entry slider has no effect whatsoever on anything. And that's probably just the way you'll want things most of the time. So, my advice (and Yamaha's) is: ALWAYS CHECK YOUR BATTERY BEFORE LEAVING FUNCTION MODE AND RETURNING TO PLAY MODE. This will ensure that the data entry slider can't affect the sound. Of course, if you're leaving function mode and returning to edit mode, you don't have to worry, since obviously the data entry slider will now become active for the first edit parameter you call up. The problem of having a potentially active data entry slider in play mode doesn't exist when you go to play mode from edit mode, only when you are coming directly from function mode to play mode.

As proof positive that this actually works, go all the way back to Exercise 4 in Chapter Two and **redo** it. This time, however, before returning to play mode (step 7), press function switch 14 in order to check your battery. Now go to step 7, call up some different presets and OBSERVE that the data entry slider now DOES NOT alter their tuning. If you don't check the battery, you'll find that the slider alters the tuning of any sound you call up. Since this is a digital synthesizer, with absolutely no drifting problems, you will have no need to quickly want to slightly alter the tunings of different sounds, as you might well need to with an analog synthesizer.

Function switch 2: Poly/Mono Mode

This switch allows us to use our DX7 as either a *polyphonic* synthesizer or as a *monophonic* synthesizer. The "yes" - "no" buttons or the data entry slider will allow you to choose either of these two modes. In polyphonic mode ("POLY" mode) - which is the way we've been using the DX7 throughout this book - we can play up to 16 notes at a time and the internal *multiplexing* system sorts out all the complex voice assignments. In monophonic mode, there is no multiplexing and we can only play one note at a time as our stupid computer gets even more stupid and can only handle one equation at a time. Why would you ever want to take a 16-voice polyphonic synthesizer and use it as a single-voice monophonic synth?

There are actually two potential reasons why. The first of these has to do with the fact that (don't get insulted now!) your keyboard technique may not be absolutely perfect. If you are, for example, trying to simulate a naturally monophonic instrument (and there are many acoustic instruments which can only ever play one note at a time - like all wind instruments) on your DX7, then playing in polyphonic mode will tend to highlight your flaws in technique. Putting the DX7 into monophonic mode, however, will allow the computer to compensate for your own human shortcomings and will ensure that only one note at a time is ever heard:

EXERCISE 76

Poly/Mono mode with "FLUTE 1":

1) Put your DX7 into *cartridge play* mode and call up ROM 1A-24 or ROM 3A-1: the "FLUTE 1" preset.

2) Your DX7 should currently be in POLY mode. Use the function mode select switch in order to put it into function mode, and press switch 2 to confirm. Your LCD should look like this: **(See Figure 13-2.)**

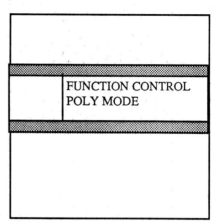

Figure 13-2

Of course, alternatively, you could just play a chord on your DX7 and OBSERVE whether all the notes have sounded. If they did, you know you're in POLY mode!

3) Since this is a flute sound, play a flute-like pattern on the keyboard, and try to play it sloppily - pretend that your keyboard technique is less than perfect even if it is perfect! LISTEN (AUDIO CUE 76A).

4) Now put your DX7 into MONO mode by pressing function switch 2 and the "yes" button. Play the same lick again, and do it just as sloppily as before. LISTEN (AUDIO CUE 76B). NOTE that it doesn't sound sloppy at all! Even though you may have pressed more than one note at a given time, the microprocessor only played one of those notes for us.

The second reason for perhaps wanting to work in MONO mode has to do with function switch 5, PORTAMENTO MODE, which we will be discussing shortly.

Bear in mind that putting your DX7 into MONO mode makes it monophonic for all sounds you call up, and that it will now stay that way until you restore it back to POLY mode.

Function switches 3 and 4: Pitch bend wheel controls:

We learned in Chapter Eleven that the use of EG bias modulation allows us real-time control over the volume and/or timbre of a sound. At that time we also mentioned that real-time control over the pitch was possible elsewhere and this is precisely the purpose of a device known as the *pitch-bend wheel*.

The pitch-bend wheel dates back to one of the earliest commercially available voltage-controlled analog synthesizers, the MiniMoog. Some fifteen years later, most synth manufacturers still wouldn't dream of making an instrument without one! In an analog synthesizer, the pitch bend wheel is a device which sends either positive or negative control voltage to the audio oscillators, depending upon whether the wheel is moved up or down from its indented center position. This will have the effect of causing the oscillators to raise or lower the speed of their oscillations, thereby "bending" the pitch, just as a guitarist can raise or lower the pitch of a string by physically bending it.

Our DX7, being a digital synthesizer, wouldn't know what to do with a control voltage if it came up and bit it! But we do observe a pitch bend wheel on this instrument, nonetheless. In this instance, the positive and negative voltages generated by our pitch bend wheel are converted by a built in *ADC* (analog-to-digital converter; see Chapter One if this concept is unfamiliar to you) into digital data - positive or negative numbers - which are fed to the pitch inputs of our six operators, causing yet another form of *pitch modulation*. As with EG- or LFO-induced pitch modulations, this is non-operator specific, for the same reasons. Therefore, the action of the pitch bend wheel will always affect all six operators simultaneously, and will thus always have the effect of causing a real-time pitch change only.

We are provided with two different pitch bend wheel controls: RANGE and STEP, function switches 3 and 4, respectively.

Let's start with function switch 3, the pitch bend RANGE control. Using our data entry slider, we can enter in any number from 0 to 12, and this number represents the RANGE of our pitch bend wheel, in **semitones** (that is, half-steps). Therefore, entering a value of 1 means that our pitch bend wheel will only cause a pitch change of one semitone (one half-step) in each direction.

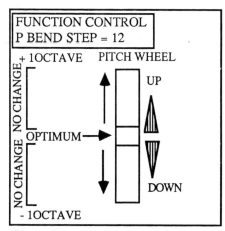

Figure 13-3

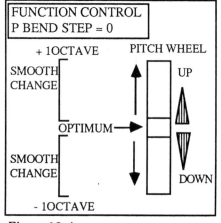

Figure 13-4

Put your DX7 into function mode, press switch 3, and try it! Similarly, entering a value of 2 will allow it to bend the pitch a full tone (full step) in each direction. Entering the maximum value of 12 will allow it the maximum range of a full octave (12 semitones, or half-steps) in each direction, and entering the minimum value of 0 will cause it to not work at all!

If we decide to enter a pitch bend RANGE value of 12, then we have the option to use function switch 4, the STEP control. This switch will determine how the pitch bend wheel changes pitch over its full octave range. Again, we can enter any value from 0 to 12, corresponding to semitones. Entering a value of 1 here, for example, will cause the pitch wheel to change in quantized semi-tone steps; entering a value of 2 will cause a change in full-tone steps. Similarly, entering the maximum value of 12 will cause the pitch bend wheel to jump the pitch from your starting pitch straight up to the octave, with no notes in-between: **(See Figure 13-3.)**

as entering the minimum value of 0 will allow for a **smooth** pitch change that is not quantized at all: **(See Figure 13-4.)**

Remember that the STEP control only works if the RANGE control is set at the maximum value of 12. The converse is unfortunately also true: if the STEP control is anything **other** than 0, the RANGE control will "freeze" at 12. You won't be able to change it at all until you go back and restore the STEP to 0. Let's run an Exercise and try and "fool" the computer:

EXERCISE 77

Pitch bend wheel controls:

1) Put your DX7 into cartridge play mode and call up "E.PIANO 1" (ROM 1A-11 or 3A-8).

2) Put your DX7 into function mode and press function switch 3 (P WHEEL RANGE control). Use the data entry section to enter a value of 2. Play a note and bend the pitch wheel up and down to its maximum and minimum settings and NOTE that our sound now "bends" in pitch over a range of a full tone in each direction (AUDIO CUE 77A).

3) Now press function switch 4 (P WHEEL STEP control) and use the data entry slider to enter a value of 4. NOTE that this value is accepted with no problem. But how can this be? First of all, we just learned that the STEP control only works if the RANGE control is at its maximum value of 12, and we know that we just entered in a value of **2**. Second of all, how can we possibly bend our pitch a tone in each direction with a STEP of two tones?? The answer lies in the fact that, like Mother Nature, you can't fool your DX7:

4) Press function switch 3 once again and OBSERVE that the RANGE control has been automatically reset to its maximum value of 12. Any time you enter any STEP value greater than 0, no matter what the current RANGE value is, the DX7 will reset it to 12. Play a note whilst moving the pitch bend wheel and LISTEN (AUDIO CUE 77B). NOTE that our pitch wheel now bends the pitch up and down over a range of a full octave, with three two-tone incremental STEPs. (i.e. if you play a C3, the wheel will bend to E3, G#3, and C4 only, with no in-between notes).

5) Because the STEP value is currently greater than 0 (4, in fact), we have learned that the RANGE control should now be frozen at 12. Try CHANGING the RANGE value and OBSERVE that it can't be done! In order to "un-freeze" this control, we'll have to go back to the STEP control and enter a value of 0. Let's do just that: Press function switch 4 (STEP) and enter a value of 0. Now go back to function switch 3 (RANGE) and OBSERVE that it works normally and that you are once again free to enter any value between 0 and 12.

Function switches 5, 6, and 7: Portamento controls

These controls all have to do with the *portamento* and *glissando* effects we can generate on the DX7. *Portamento* is a smooth glide between notes, and *glissando* is a glide between notes which is **quantized** in semitones (half-step intervals). In both instances, we can control the **speed** of this glide with function switch 7, PORTAMENTO TIME.

The range of this control is 0 to 99, and whoever designed this was obviously not the person who wrote the EG software for the DX7. In our EG rates, you may remember, 0 represented the **slowest** rate and 99 the **fastest**. With our PORTAMENTO TIME control, however, things are exactly the opposite: a PORTAMENTO TIME of 0 is the **fastest** time and effectively means no portamento. A PORTAMENTO TIME of 99, on the other hand, is the **slowest** portamento time.

The DX7 portamento time does not exhibit what is called *constant velocity*; that is, the absolute **speed** of the portamento is determined solely by the distance that must be traveled. If you play a C1, for example, and then play a C6, any given PORTAMENTO TIME value will take far longer than if you play a C5, followed by a C6. Some other synthesizers have a so-called "constant velocity" control in which the portamento time is **absolute**, no matter how great the distance. In that event, even though C1 to C6 is a far greater **distance** than C5 to C6, the glide would take the same absolute amount of time since the microprocessor would simply compensate and make the C1 to C6 **rate** a faster one. Again, our DX7 does not have this control, so don't worry about it too much.

It's pretty simple to figure out whether the DX7 will glide **up** to or **down** to a particular note if you're only playing one note at a time. The voice assignment system will simply remember whether the previous note was higher or lower than the new note and will glide equivalently: **(See Figure 13-5A and B.)**

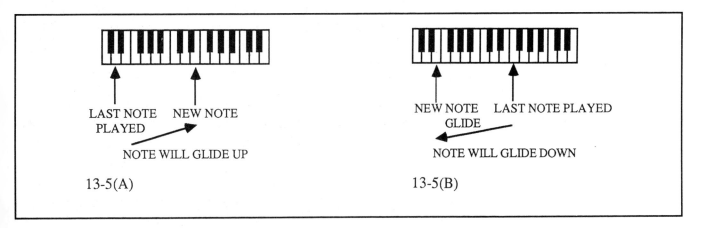

13-5(A)

13-5(B)

Figure 13-5

Where things get tricky, however, is when we use the glide control **polyphonically**. Polyphonic glide is a feature not always found on polyphonic synthesizers, and the main reason for this is that the instrument's voice assignment circuitry has to do some pretty fancy footwork in order to decide which notes to glide up to and which to glide down to.

I must confess that, even after many thousands of hours spent with this instrument, I have still not completely deciphered the portamento logic being used. There are a couple of basic rules, however, that seem to always be followed, and these may help enlighten you:

    1) Even though our DX7 thinks there are notes above C6 and below C1 (see Chapter 12), it will nonetheless always glide up to C6 and down to C1.

2) If there are notes currently being held down and you add new notes, the glide will be from the old notes, but only the first time you add these new notes. After that, it's pretty unpredictable. **(See Figure 13-6.)**

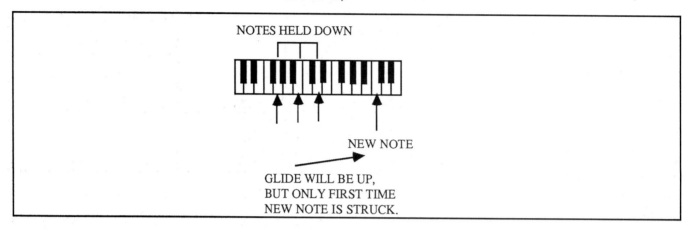

Figure 13-6

3) If you simply strike a single key repeatedly, it won't glide at all (i.e. it glides from itself) after the initial key depression. However, if you play a chord repeatedly, the glides will be unpredictable and will almost certainly not be the same every time: **(See Figure 13-7.)**

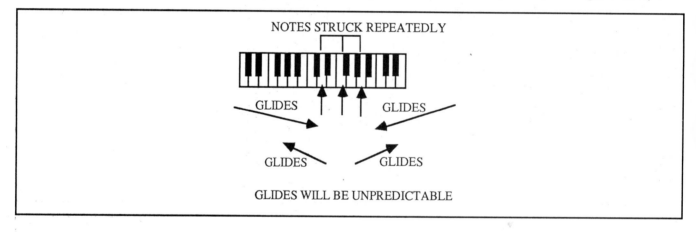

Figure 13-7

Of course, it's entirely possible that the complete portamento process is illogical in places, and that a random "seed" has been planted by the Yamaha programmers in order to keep us honest. Even if this isn't the case, for the sake of your sanity, I advise you to regard portamento that way. If you try to predict whether a given glide will be up or down, I venture that you will be right 50% of the time and wrong the other 50%, over the long haul. So my advice is - don't bother trying.

Function switch 7, then, determines our relative PORTAMENTO TIME and also allows us to not use any portamento effects, by simply entering a value of 0 (since the fastest portamento time is faster than we mere humans can detect). Function switch 6 (labeled GLISSANDO) determines whether we will have a portamento or a glissando effect. This is a simple on-off control: **(See Figure 13-8.)**

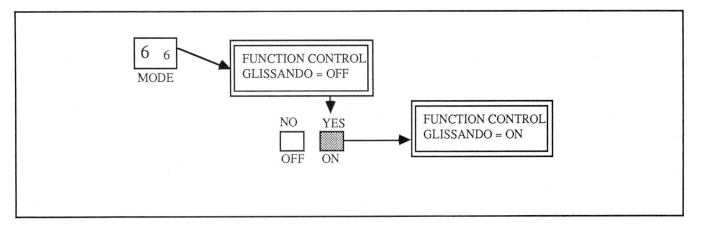

Figure 13-8

and turning "GLISSANDO = ON" (with either the "yes" data entry button or by moving the data entry slider) will cause us to have a quantized portamento, or glissando effect. Again, whatever value was entered into the PORTAMENTO TIME control will also determine the relative (non-constant) glissando time. If "GLISSANDO = OFF", then we will have a non-quantized smooth portamento, as before.

I think that this switch might have been easier to deal with if it simply toggled between a display that read "PORTAMENTO" and one that read "GLIS-SANDO" instead of giving us an on-off switch, but that's another one for the Yamaha suggestion box...

Finally, we come to the last (or, actually, first) of our PORTAMENTO controls, function switch 5, labeled MODE. This switch determines the action of the **sustain pedal** when using portamento effects in POLY mode, or the action of KEY ON/OFF flags, when in MONO mode.

This control will yield the following two LCD displays (you can toggle between them with the "yes" - "no" buttons or the data entry slider) when using the DX7 **polyphonically: (See Figure 13-9.)**

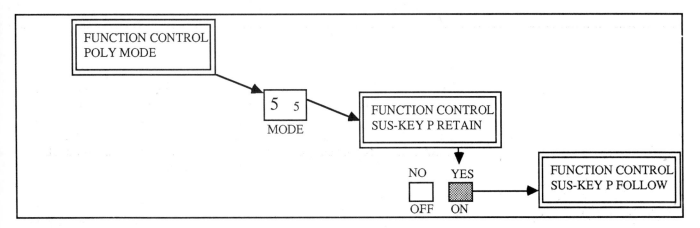

Figure 13-9

and the following two LCD displays when working **monophonically: (See Figure 13-10.)**

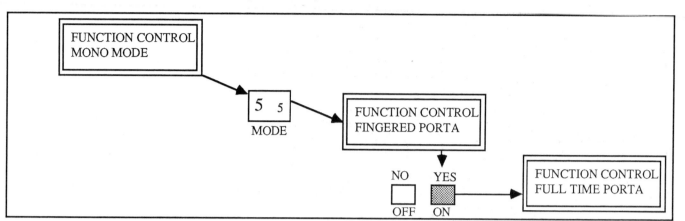

Figure 13-10

Figure 13-11

Let's discuss the polyphonic options first, since that's the way you'll probably use your DX7 most of the time. First of all, your sustain pedal can be used two different ways, depending upon which jack you plug it into on the back of your machine: **(See Figure 13-11.)**

If it's plugged into the "portamento" input, then it will act as a portamento on-off switch. When your foot is actually on the pedal, you will get whatever PORTAMENTO TIME you preset with function switch 7. When your foot is off the pedal, the portamento time will be equivalent to 0 (that is, no portamento) regardless of the value entered in the PORTAMENTO TIME control.

That's a valid use of the pedal, and will allow you to bring portamento and glissando effects in and out very quickly and in real time. But the MODE switch (function switch 5) only has to do with the actions of the pedal if it is plugged into the "sustain" jack and is truly being used for its **sustain** function, as outlined in Chapter Nine. If this is the way that you are currently using this pedal, then your PORTAMENTO MODE options (as shown in the LCD) are "SUS-KEY P RETAIN" and "SUS-KEY P FOLLOW". In this instance, "SUS" stands for sustain, "KEY" stands for **keyboard**, and "P" stands for pitch. So what are LCD is really saying is: "Sustain keyboard pitch retain" and "Sustain keyboard pitch follow". The difference between these two modes is quite simple, and can best be demonstrated with an exercise:

EXERCISE 78

Polyphonic portamento modes:

1) Put your DX7 into cartridge play mode and call up the "PIPES 1" preset (ROM 1A-18 or 3A-10). Make sure your DX7 is in polyphonic mode (function switch 2) and make sure your sustain pedal is plugged into the "sustain" jack on the back of your machine.
2) Press function switch 7 (PORTAMENTO TIME control) and enter a value of 85.
3) Press function switch 6 (GLISSANDO) and turn this ON. This will give us a quantized, glissando effect.
4) Press function switch 5 (MODE) and use the appropriate data entry control to enter "SUS-KEY P RETAIN".
5) Play a three- or four-note chord in the bottom octave of your keyboard and LISTEN (AUDIO CUE 78A). NOTE that some notes may glide up to their pitch and others may glide down (but that they all glide in half-steps, or semitones, since we have set GLISSANDO = ON). Keep the chord held down and depress the sustain pedal. NOTE that the sound continues at the same volume - this is because L3 in all the carrier's EGs is quite high.

6) While keeping your foot on the sustain pedal, and while still hearing the previous chord, play another three- or four-note chord, this time in the top octave of the keyboard and LISTEN (AUDIO CUE 78B). NOTE that we continue to hear the old chord even as the new chord glides up to its pitches and sustains . The "SUS-KEY P RE-TAIN" option, then, ensures that we will always hear the 16 most recent notes played, regardless of any portamento or glissando effects.

7) Release the sustain pedal. Press function switch 5 again and this time press the "yes" button in order to change this to "SUS-KEY P FOLLOW".

8) Repeat steps 5 and 6 above and LISTEN (AUDIO CUE 78C). NOTE that this time, the new chord follows from the old one, and that previous notes are not retained. With this setting, we will only ever hear the most recent note or notes (if they are played simultaneously) that are played, and we can be certain that they will always glide from the previous note or notes played.

Note that the PORTAMENTO MODE controls in polyphonic mode ("SUS-KEY P RETAIN" and "SUS-KEY P FOLLOW") have no effect whatsoever if you are not stepping on the sustain pedal or if it isn't plugged into the "sustain" jack.

Now let's discuss the portamento MODE options available to us in MONO mode. Here we have a choice of either "FULL TIME PORTA" or "FIN-GERED PORTA". The difference between these has to do essentially with whether the DX7 microprocessor senses a new KEY ON flag (see Chapter Nine if this doesn't sound familiar) before it senses a KEY OFF flag - in other words, are you still holding down a key when you play another key, or not? In FULL TIME PORTA, it won't matter. You'll get whatever portamento or glissando time you preset with function switch 7. In FINGERED PORTA, however, it matters a lot. If a KEY OFF is detected between KEY ONs (in other words, if you play notes stacatto), then the portamento or glissando time is assumed to be 0, or no portamento. On the other hand, if two KEY ON flags are detected without a KEY OFF in-between (in other words, if you play notes legato), then the PORTA TIME is whatever you preset it to be. This is one of these things that's easier to hear than to explain, so let's just run an exercise and try it:

EXERCISE 79

Monophonic portamento modes:

1) As before, put your DX7 into cartridge play mode and call up the "PIPES 1" preset (ROM 1A-18 or ROM 3A-10).

2) Press function switch 7 (PORTAMENTO TIME control) and enter a value of 85. Press function switch 6 (GLISSANDO) and turn this OFF. This will give us a smooth, non-quantized portamento effect.

3) Press function switch 2 (POLY/MONO) and press the "yes" button to make your DX7 MONOphonic. Press function switch 5 and OBSERVE the two different options now available to us: "FULL TIME PORTA" or "FINGERED PORTA". Use the appropriate data entry switch to CHANGE this to "FULL TIME PORTA". Play a few notes on the keyboard and LISTEN (AUDIO CUE 79A). NOTE that regardless of which notes you play, and whether they are played sharply (stacatto) or slowly (legato), we always hear the same GLIS-SANDO time.

4) Press the "no" button in order to change the PORTAMENTO MODE (function switch 5) to "FINGERED PORTA". Now play several different notes on the keyboard sharply, taking care to release each before you play the next one, and LISTEN (AUDIO CUE 79B). NOTE that we now have no glissando whatever. Play the same series of notes but this time don't release a key before playing the next key - in other words, play this series of notes **legato**. LISTEN (AUDIO CUE 79C). NOTE that we now hear the glissando effect we heard in

step 9 above. In **monophonic** mode, then, the PORTAMENTO MODE control allows us to get portamento or glissando effects, but only if we play notes legato. This will allow you to bring these effects in and out solely by your keyboard technique. With a little practice, you'll find that you can bring this in and out at will (AUDIO CUE 79D).

The use of the "FINGERED PORTA" control with function switch 5, then, is the **other** reason why you might want to occasionally play your DX7 in MONO mode, since this control is not available when working polyphonically.

Finally, be aware that, as for any other function control, the data entry slider will remain active for the last PORTAMENTO control you were viewing (MODE, GLISSANDO, or TIME) when you return to play mode, if you don't check your battery (function switch 14) in-between.

Function switch 8, which is unlabeled, is the DX7 MIDI switch, and its actions will be covered in great detail in the next chapter. Function switches 9 (EDIT RECALL) and 10 (VOICE INIT) have already been discussed in preceding chapters (see Chapter Eight for EDIT RECALL and Chapter Four for VOICE INIT), so we won't go into them here.

All of which brings us to function switches 11, 12, and 13, which are all unlabeled and which all do the same thing: CARTRIDGE FORMATTING.

For all practical purposes, these switches are probably reserved for future use since you won't need to ever use them if you work with most **Yamaha** RAM cartridges. However, if you buy third-party RAM cartridges, or if you somehow manage to get one of the very earliest batch of Yamaha RAMs (which is extremely unlikely), you may well have to use one of these controls to format, or organize the memory logic of these cartridges, before you can use them to store DX7 data. Also, if a RAM cartridge seems to be severely screwing up (giving you weird characters or changing voice data), this may be a last-resort act of desperation which might get it working OK again. But be careful - the act of formatting with this switch will cause all 32 cartridge memory slots to INITIALIZE. That means that any data stored in the cartridge will be erased and replaced with the initialization defaults, and you'll end up with a RAM cartridge full of sine waves, all named "INIT VOICE". This isn't a particularly desirable thing to do by accident to a RAM cartridge containing 32 of your favorite sounds! Fortunately, even if you accidentally hit this switch, you'd still have to accidentally answer "yes" to the "CARTRIDGE FORMAT?" question, and both the software and hardware cartridge memory protections would have to accidentally be "off" for this to happen. So I wouldn't lose any sleep over it. More than likely, you won't need to use these controls much.

Function switch 14 (BATTERY CHECK) was covered earlier in this chapter; again, pressing this switch has the action of **deactivating** the data entry slider when you return to play mode. So check your battery often!

And, finally, we come to:

Function switches 15 and 16: Cartridge Save and Cartridge Load:

These switches are used for *bulk data transfers*, and allow you to move voice data (edit parameters only, remember!) regarding 32 voices **at a time** to or from a cartridge.

In Chapter Eight we learned the storage procedure for the DX7 and this allowed us to save any one voice to any one memory slot, either in the internal or RAM cartridge memory. These two switches, on the other hand, allow us to save any **thirty-two** voices, en masse, to either the internal or cartridge memory. Of course, doing so will **always** erase the current contents of the receiving memory, so you have to approach these switches with caution.

Function switch 15 (CARTRIDGE SAVE) will take the thirty-two voices currently in your machine's **internal memory** and copy them to a RAM cartridge currently in the slot. Of course, the cartridge memory protection, both in hardware (the switch on the cartridge itself) and software (the MEMORY PROTECT switch on the DX7), must be OFF for this transfer to be allowed. In the process, the entire RAM cartridge memory will be erased and replaced by a copy of what's currently in your internal memory. This procedure will not affect the data in your DX7's internal memory in any way. So this would be a useful thing to do if, say, you have a recording session tomorrow morning and you know that the studio has their own DX7. Instead of schlepping yours to the gig, all you have to do is program the sounds you think you'll need into your machine's internal memory, put a blank (or expendable) RAM in the slot, and press function switch 15. The LCD will ask you "SAVE MEMORY - ALL OF MEMORY?" and you'll have the chance to say "no" if you want to bail out. If you say "yes", then in a matter of a second or two, your RAM will be loaded with all thirty-two sounds, and you just slip it in your back pocket the next day and take it to the gig. When you pop it into the studio's DX7, all of your sounds will come up exactly as you had programmed them the night before on your own machine.

Function switch 16, CARTRIDGE LOAD, does exactly the opposite - it will copy the contents of any cartridge - RAM or ROM - that is currently in the slot and put that data into your machine's internal memory. Again, this will only work if your DX7's internal memory protection is OFF. Again, this will completely erase the contents of your internal memory and replace them with the cartridge voice data. And again, this procedure will in no way affect the cartridge itself. This procedure may be useful if, for example, you have a gig where you know you'll need thirty-two original sounds but also a couple of ROM presets as well. In order to save yourself popping cartridges in and out of the machine all night, you simply LOAD the contents of your RAM cartridge containing the original sounds, and keep a ROM in the slot. This is also the procedure used by Yamaha just before each DX7 leaves the factory in order to load what are called the *master group* of presets (ROM 1A for international machines and ROM 3A for American machines) into the internal memory. The reason they do this is so that brand-new DX7 owners everywhere can pull their machine out of the box and hear some sounds right away, without having to read the manual or - gulp! - this book!

The entire lower row of function controls - switches 17 through 32 - were discussed fully in Chapters Ten and Eleven, so, once again, we have no need to cover them here.

And, in the immortal words of P-P-P-Porky the P-P-P-Pig, that's all, folks! We have now covered every single switch and control on the DX7. In the next chapter, we will be talking about ways that our DX7 can communicate with other synthesizers, and with computers. Here we are, at the end of a long and hopefully pleasant journey, so, good luck, good programming, and keep those good sounds coming!!

SWITCHES AND CONTROLS COVERED IN CHAPTER THIRTEEN:

SWITCH	PARAMETER	COMMENTS
Function 14	Battery Check	Disables data entry slider.
Function 2	Poly/Mono	POLY (16 voice) or MONO (1 voice)
Function 3	Pitch Wheel Range	0 to 12 semitones
Function 4	Pitch Wheel Stop	0 to 12 semitones
Function 5	Portamento Mode	"SUS-KEY P RETAIN" or "SUS-KEY P FOLLOW" in POLY mode; "FULL TIME PORTA" or "FINGERED PORTA" in MONO mode.
Function 6	Glissando	"On" or "Off".
Function 7	Portamento Time	Range 0 - 99; also affects Glissando
Function 11, 12, 13	Cartridge Format	Reformats RAM cartridge
Function 15	Cartridge Save	Bulk data transfer, Internal-to-RAM
Function 16	Cartridge Load	Bulk data transfer, Cartridge-to-Internal

CHAPTER FOURTEEN: MIDI

Lack of standardization has been a problem which has plagued every consumer industry almost since the day the first consumer appeared on this earth - one sometimes wonders if the Neanderthals had trouble getting spare parts for their clubs! In no industry, however, has this created more headaches and gray hairs than in the computer industry.

MIDI was born in a valiant attempt to solve this problem, at least in so far as computerized synthesizers were concerned. To a large degree it has succeeded. But one could make a good case that MIDI has caused as many problems as it has solved. Confused? Let's start at the beginning:

First of all, the word MIDI is an acronym for the Musical Instrument Digital Interface. The term "interface" is common computerese for any hardware or software device that allows two pieces of equipment to work together. For example, between a computer and a printer, one needs an interface, which may consist of anything from a simple cable to a complex logic circuit board. In a similar manner, the interface between a record player and your ears is a complicated system of equipment, including an amplifier, loudspeakers, and several interconnecting wires (see Chapter One for a thorough description of this process). In the instance of MIDI, the "interface" is two things: a standardized type of required hardware (here we are talking about the MIDI transmitter, receiver, and connecting cables), and a common software language which will allow synthesizers of all varieties, even those made by different manufacturers, to communicate and work with one another.

Quite simply, the key to understanding MIDI is to think of it as being a **language**. Assuming you are currently reading the original English version of this book, the reason you are able to understand these words and work with the information contained in these pages is because these words are written in the English language, and because you understand the English language.

Similarly, if we take two synthesizers which both have been programmed to "speak" and "understand" MIDI, they will be able to communicate with one another. How does this work?

Well, we have discussed the fact that today, all synthesizers of all types have one very important thing in common: they all contain *microprocessors*. In the case of the DX7, this wonderful circuit is actually responsible for creating the ultimate sounds we hear. In the case of analog synthesizers, the microprocessor will be performing much simpler "housekeeping" tasks, like calling up different voltage settings and storing them in memory slots, or keeping track of which notes are depressed on the keyboard and when (again, refer to Chapter One for a detailed discussion of this). The point is, no matter what different tasks the digital circuitry is responsible for, the important fact remains that a microprocessor is present in all these different machines.

Another thing we have learned is that microprocessors "think" only in terms of numbers - specifically, ones and zeroes. It is this feature which allows data stored in computer memories to be transferred to other computers. We've all encountered this when we've gone to our bank and the teller has turned to a computer in order to find out our balance. What the teller is actually doing is

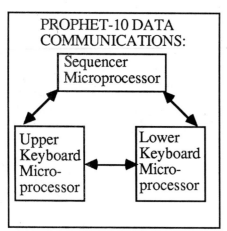

Figure 14-1

quite interesting: He or she is using a computer terminal to telephone (via a device called a *modem*) a large central computer in which all the bank's customers current balances are stored. Similarly, when you go to a travel agent and their computer is able to instantly determine if a seat is available on a flight you wish to take, a central computer is also being "interrogated" via standard telephone lines. This central computer contains up-to-the-minute data regarding all major airline flight bookings. The modem (which is short for "MOdulator-DEModulator") takes the digital commands sent out by the computer terminal and routes them through a DAC, converting them to electrical signal, which is then *modulated* (sound familiar?) by a steady audio tone. This modulated audio signal is then passed down standard telephone wiring where it is de-modulated at the other end: the steady audio signal is filtered out and the changing electrical signal is fed to an ADC, which converts it back into the original ones and zeroes!

Ah, the wonders of modern technology! All this so they can still screw up your bank statement at the end of the month! Anyway, I digress...

The point here is that computer data is very highly standardized: when you get down to it, all it consists of is a stream of ones and zeroes. Therefore, in order to use this data, we need to pre-program the different microprocessors (the logic circuits) within different computers so that they can consistently make sense of all these ones and zeroes. In order to do that, we need a language. If the microprocessor in synthesizer A can send out its stored data in a particular format that the microprocessor in synthesizer B can understand, and vice versa - well, then, we have COMMUNICATION. And that's precisely what MIDI is - a standardized format for communicating synthesizer data, which allows all these different instruments to **interface** (work with) one another.

The concept of MIDI was actually born in a large polyphonic analog synthesizer called the Prophet-10, made by Sequential Circuits. This cumbersome machine (originally introduced in 1981 and manufactured until 1983) was essentially two Prophet-5s in one box. Each had its own keyboard, and the instrument also contained a polyphonic digital *sequencer* whieh could act as a master controller. A sequencer is a device which acts something like a tape recorder (even though it doesn't use tape, but digital memory instead) in order to remember notes played and timing values between the notes played. In any event, the interesting idea behind the Prophet-10 was that each of the two independent synthesizers in it, as well as the sequencer, could interact with one another in various different ways. What this instrument contained, then, were three independent microprocessors that needed to COMMUNICATE with one another and be able to send data stored in each of the three independent memories back and forth to one another: **(See Figure 14-1.)**

Since at that time there was no standardized means of accomplishing this, the software engineers at Sequential simply went ahead and invented their own *protocol* (a set of rules for doing things) for achieving these internal data transfers. Every language has its own particular protocol - for example, in the English language we know that every sentence must begin with a capital letter and must end with either a period, question mark, or exclamation point. In the spoken English language, it is understood that when asking a question, one raises pitch at the end of sentence, and when making a statement, one lowers pitch at the end of a sentence (try it - you'll find that you sound awful funny if you consciously break these rules). Similarly, the Sequential engineers had to not only organize the internal synthesizer data in such a way that all three microprocessors could use it, but also had to invent rules for transmitting and receiving such data. For example, there had to be a particular number which meant "beginning of statement" and a different number which meant "end of statement". There had to be identification numbers which, for example, let microprocessor 1 know that it was hearing from microprocessor 2 and not microprocessor 3. There had to be numbers which signified requests for specific data, and others which signified acknowledgements of data or data errors received. In short, an entire new language had to be invented from scratch!

At the time when all this was being developed (the early '80s), it was becoming apparent that soon all synthesizers of all types would have microprocessors onboard - and there were hints that the affordable digital synthesizers of today were just around the corner. The forward-thinking executives of Sequential realized that this provided the potential for some kind of universal interface which would allow all these disparate instruments to communicate data back and forth, and, perhaps more importantly, to allow them all to communicate with standard personal computers. The rise of the computer industry in the last two decades has unquestionably been the most dramatic of any industry in human history - and one that has had perhaps the greatest impact on our everyday lives. Several different synthesizer manufacturers - Sequential, Oberheim, and Roland, among others - saw the great opportunity being presented: that of tying in the relatively small synthesizer industry with the massively greater computer industry - and, to their credit, they did not keep the idea to themselves.

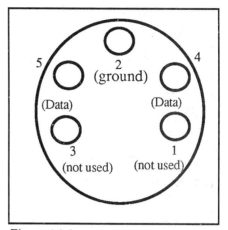

Figure 14-2

Instead, at the 1981 Audio Engineering Society convention in New York, the president of Sequential Circuits, Dave Smith, presented a paper outlining Sequential's work with the Prophet-10 and proposing a universal standard interface (at that time, actually called the USI!) that could be adopted by all synthesizer manufacturers. This original proposal was then passed on to the large Japanese synthesizer manufacturers - Roland, Yamaha, and Kawai. After nearly two years of back-and-forth, what became the final MIDI 1.0 specification was finally born. Within a year of its inception, every major synthesizer manufacturer in the world - even those who had originally voiced the most strenuous objections - put MIDI in their instruments.

And that's a curious statement unto itself - how do you "put" MIDI in an instrument? Well, this means two things. Number one, it means that a digital transmitter/receiver circuit (called a *UART*, for Universal Asynchronous Receiver Transmitter) which can "understand" the MIDI protocol (and send and receive MIDI data to and from the instrument's own microprocessor) is installed and, secondly, that the appropriate hardware connections - the MIDI jacks - are provided. These jacks are standardized, as are the cables which are meant to interconnect different machines. For some obscure reason, the MIDI spec calls for 5-pin DIN connectors to be used, even though only three of the five pins are actually wired up: **(See Figure 14-2.)**

A synthesizer that speaks MIDI will typically have three such jacks, labeled "MIDI IN", "MIDI OUT", and "MIDI THRU", as you will find on the back of your DX7: **(See Figure 14-3.)**

Figure 14-3

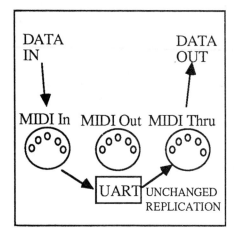

Figure 14-4

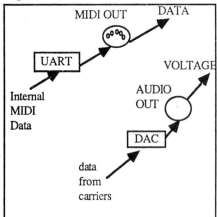

Figure 14-5

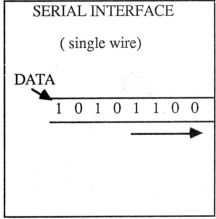

Figure 14-6

The purpose of the "MIDI IN" and "MIDI OUT" jacks is pretty much self-explanatory: this is where MIDI data enters and leaves the machine. The "MIDI THRU" jack is an **output** out of which is instantaneously sent an exact copy of the data coming into the "MIDI IN" jack. In effect, the UART replicates the incoming MIDI signal and passes a copy of it right back out of the MIDI THRU port* while the original goes on its merry way to the receiving instrument's own microprocessor: **(See Figure 14-4.)**

Therefore, the data leaving the "MIDI THRU" jack does not contain any data generated by the host machine - but only that original data sent to the host machine. We'll talk more about uses for "MIDI THRU" later in this chapter.

First, let's talk a bit more about the way that MIDI data is organized, and how the interface itself is set up. The very first point which must be clearly understood is that only digital data, in the form of ones and zeroes, travels down the MIDI cables - NO AUDIO SIGNAL IS SENT. So what goes into the MIDI cable via the "MIDI OUT" port is entirely different from what goes into the audio cable you plug into the instrument's OUTPUT jack: **(See Figure 14-5.)**

Secondly, it's important to understand what kind of interface MIDI is. In the computer industry, there are two different ways of transmitting and receiving data - via a *serial* interface and via a *parallel* interface. The difference between them is as follows: in a serial interface, the ones and zeroes all travel down a single wire, one after another, like soldiers in a single file: **(See Figure 14-6.)**

On the other hand, in a parallel interface, the stream of ones and zeroes are sent down several wires simultaneously, usually eight at a time: **(See Figure 14-7.)**

The parallel interface, then, would appear to be the interface of choice. However, MIDI is a serial interface.

Surprised? When this was announced, a lot of people were. The arguments against using a parallel interface were twofold: firstly, the parallel connectors and cables themselves were far more expensive and fragile than serial hardware; and secondly, data being transmitted via a parallel interface can only reliably travel ten feet or so before bits of information start dropping by the wayside. Serially transmitted data can travel further since it is typically sent at much greater speeds. So, in the interest of consumer cost and reliability, the serial interface was chosen for the MIDI standard.

Of course, speed is of paramount importance with MIDI since we will want events to be transmitted pretty much as they occur, in *realtime*. If we are playing a Cm chord on our DX7, for example, we want another synthesizer to which we are transmitting MIDI data to be aware of that Cm chord **as we play it**. Consequently, a lot of thought and debate went into the question of how fast the MIDI transmission rate was to be. In the end, the manufacturers settled on a rate of 31.25 kBaud. A Baud is a unit of measurement which indi-

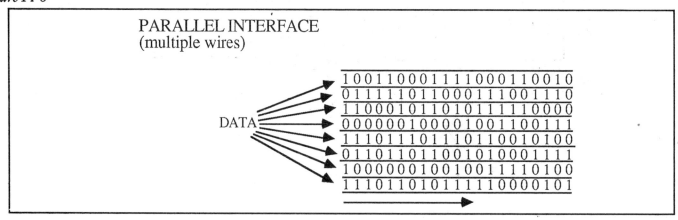

Figure 14-7

* "port" is computerese for any physical device - like a jack - which allows data to enter or leave a computer.

cates one bit of information (that is, one one or one zero) being transmitted each second. Therefore, our MIDI transmission rate of 31.25 kBaud tells us that we will be transmitting data at the incredible rate of 31,250 bits of information per second!

If that doesn't seem sufficient to you, consider this: the standard rate at which your bank teller or travel agent sends and receives data is 1200 Baud - nearly 1/30 the speed of MIDI. It all seems instantaneous to us mere human beings, but bear in mind that far more information is sent via MIDI than from your travel agent to an airline. In fact, there is a body of dissenters who argue that the MIDI transmission rate is too slow! It is possible that a future version of MIDI will have a considerably higher transmission rate, but in any event, this won't negate the effectiveness of current synthesizers which work at the "slow" 31.25 kBaud rate. It also should be noted that the current computer technology is far advanced from what it was in 1983, when 31.25 kBaud was considered extremely fast. Today, the Apple MacIntosh computer, for example, can actually transmit data at a rate of a **million** bits per second!

So now we know how MIDI data is sent, and at what speed, but the real question is, what **is** MIDI data? Exactly what is one synthesizer telling another? The answer to this question is actually quite complex. There could, in fact, be many things that our DX7, for example, could be telling the world. It could be passing along commands it's receiving from its own keyboard, such as KEY ON and KEY OFF flags, which key(s) are being depressed, velocity sensitivities, etc. Or it could be passing along data it is receiving from its controllers - the current status of the pitch bend wheel, mod wheel, breath controller, etc. Or it could be telling the world which program number is currently being used, and when we call up a different program, it could divulge that information too. Or, it could actually be sending specific information about the sound currently in its edit buffer - information about the operator EGs, frequency ratios, LFO settings, etc.

In fact, at any given time, we might require all of the above information. At other times, we'd need only small portions of it. For example, if you "MIDI up" a DX7 and a Prophet (by hooking up MIDI OUT of one to MIDI IN of the other, and vice versa), and our DX7 starts telling the Prophet about its operator output levels, the Prophet will, in computer terms, shrug its digital shoulders and, in effect, say "Huh?" **(See Figure 14-8.)**

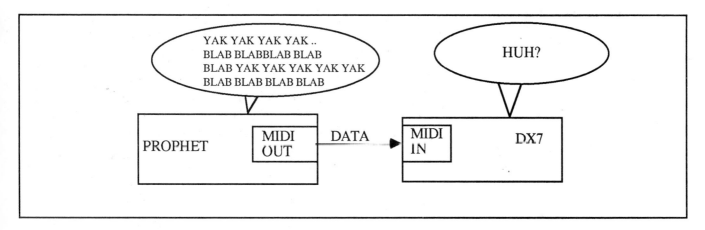

Figure 14-8

since it doesn't have any operators. Similarly, if the Prophet starts gabbing to the DX7 about its filter resonance setting, the DX7 will scratch its digital forehead and a blank expression will prevail. **(See Figure 14-9.)**

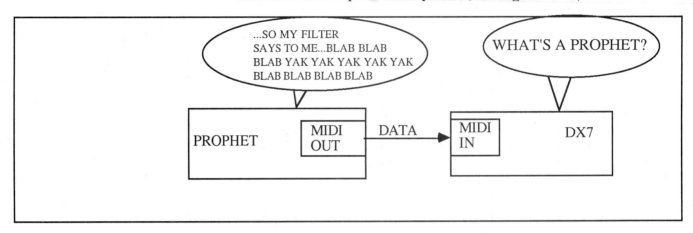

Figure 14-9

since it wouldn't know a filter if it came up and bit it! In fact, when one instrument tells a dissimilar instrument information which is exclusive to that brand and model only, the receiving instrument simply ignores that data. For this reason, you cannot possibly use MIDI to, say, store Prophet sounds in your DX7, or DX7 sounds in your Prophet.

Since speed is of paramount importance here, and since MIDI data travels only one bit at a time, we really won't want to gum up the lines with lots of useless information. For this reason, MIDI data has been divided up into four major categories:

1) CHANNEL MESSAGES: These include:
a) Common keyboard information, such as which note is being played, key on and key off flags, and velocity sensitivities.
b) Controller information, including pitch bend, mod wheel, after touch, breath controller, and any foot pedals or switches that may be attached.
c) Program information, specifically the number of the program that is currently in use - NOT any information about the sound.

When a synthesizer receives MIDI *channel messages*, it will normally respond by playing the same notes at the same times. This was in fact the original concept of MIDI - an interface that would allow for instantaneous "layering" of sounds - and this is by far the most common use of MIDI. Bear in mind that the receiving synthesizer does NOT have to have the same sound in order for this to occur, nor does it have to be tuned the same as the transmitting synthesizer. This can create some unique and interesting effects. If set properly, the receiving synthesizer may also apply the same controller information - pitch bends, velocity, etc., and may even call up the same program number. IT IS IMPORTANT TO REALIZE THAT THE RECEPTION OF MIDI CHANNEL DATA CAN IN NO WAY ALLOW THE RECEIVING SYNTHESIZER TO PERFORM BEYOND ITS OWN LIMITS. For example, sending a ten-note chord to an eight-voice polyphonic synthesizer cannot magically cause it to play any more than eight of those notes. Similarly, sending velocity sensitivities to a non-velocity-sensitive instrument cannot cause it to suddenly develop that characteristic.

Channel messages sent to a sequencer or computer sequencer program will simply be stored for later recall and playback.

2) SYSTEM EXCLUSIVE DATA: This is the information about the sound currently in use, or about all the sounds in the instrument's in-

ternal memory. By performing "data dumps" - that is, sending system-exclusive data to another synthesizer of the same model (or to a computer programmed to work with that data) - we can cause that synthesizer (or computer) to load voice parameters (in the case of a DX7, the *edit parameters*) into its own edit buffer or internal memory. Every major synthesizer manufacturer has been given a specific MIDI ID number, and many have created sub-IDs for specific models they make as well. In this way, a DX7 (which has a MIDI ID number of 67) can only recognize system exclusive messages from another DX7.

3) SYSTEM REAL-TIME DATA: Timing information (sometimes called the MIDI clock), which is normally only transmitted and used by MIDI sequencers. The MIDI clock is a standardized 24-digital-flags (or "pulses")-per-quarter-note timing signal, which obviously changes with any sequencer tempo changes. This data is normally only transmitted and received by MIDI sequencers.

4) SYSTEM COMMON DATA: A kind of catch-all "housekeeping" category which includes such minor things as an auto-tuning command for those machines whose microprocessors can perform this task.

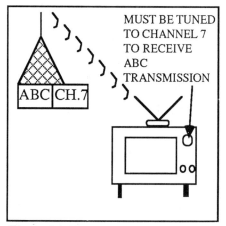

Figure 14-10

By breaking down all of the possible MIDI data into these smaller sub-categories, we are able to ensure that we aren't sending or receiving any more information than we can actually use. For example, *system exclusive* data leaving a Kurzweil is only going to be comprehensible to another Kurzweil or to a computer which has been programmed to understand and perhaps store this information - so there's no point in sending this data to an Emulator. *System real-time* data is only usable by a dedicated sequencer or computer which has been programmed with sequencing capabilities (see Appendix C for a listing of currently available sequencing programs as well as dedicated MIDI sequencers) - so there's no point in sending this information to a DX7.

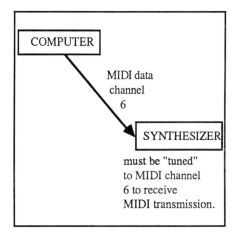

Figure 14-11

On the other hand, channel information is usable by virtually every synthesizer ever manufactured - as long as the instrument can recognize a keyboard, it can utilize most if not all of this data. Why is this then referred to as "channel" data? The answer lies in the fact that MIDI has been structured as a multi-channel system. The MIDI protocol actually allows for up to **sixteen** independent sets of channel messages - each containing up to sixteen notes at a time - to be simultaneously transmitted.

How can we send sixteen separate sets of data at once down a single wire? We can't. But at the high-speed transmission rate of 31,250 bits of information each second, we can do it fast enough that most humans in most situations will never hear the fact that it **isn't** simultaneous. Of course, in order to separate out the sixteen different sets of information, we'll have to mark each batch with identifying flags. And that's precisely the way MIDI channel information is sent. A special number - called an "address" flag - identifies a particular set of MIDI data as belonging to a particular MIDI channel. A good way to understand the concept of MIDI channels is to hold in your mind the now-familiar picture of various TV stations transmitting the 7 o'clock news, and your TV set at home being able to receive any of these stations. If you want to watch Dan Rather's sweaters at 7, you will have to tune your TV set to receive CBS. On the other hand, if Peter Jennings' ties are more to your liking, you'll have to tune to ABC. In no event could you hear Dan Rather by tuning to any channel other than CBS; nor could you see Peter Jennings if you're tuned to anything other than ABC. Each TV station **transmits** on a particular channel, and if you want to tune in that program, your set will have to be receiving that particular channel. **(See Figure 14-10.)**

MIDI works in a very similar manner. Instead of getting the 7 o'clock news, however, our synthesizer or computer can get the latest MIDI data - but it will have to be "tuned" to the appropriate channel in order to receive the channel messages. **(See Figure 14-11.)**

How do we determine which channel our synthesizer or computer is "tuned" to? Again, we have to give a fairly complex answer to a fairly simple question: first, we must know our instrument's **reception** mode.

Originally, there were three different ways that MIDI data could be received: Omni, Poly, and Mono. *Omni mode* is a kind of "super-reception" whereby a receiving instrument accepts MIDI data coming in on all MIDI channels - the TV equivalent of you somehow being able to tune in CBS, ABC, and (heavens, no!) NBC, not to mention all other local stations, all at the same time (very important, if you want to see how Peter Jennings' ties match with Dan Rather's sweaters). What you'd see on your screen would be a mess, but you'd be getting all the information at once.* *Poly mode* is the mode whereby the receiving machine simply "listens" to only one MIDI channel at a time. And *mono mode* was intended for multi-timbral synthesizers (those synthesizers, which, unlike the DX7, can produce more than one sound at a time - see Chapter Twelve, "Keyboard Splits" for an explanation) whereby they could listen to several specified MIDI channels at once, and then internally assign the incoming data to various different voices within the machine.

Unfortunately, so the story goes, someone at a major synthesizer manufacturer (who will remain unnamed but the first initial is a "Y"), misinterpreted the original concept of "Mono" mode, and so today we have to live with the following **four** MIDI reception modes:

MODE 1: Omni-on poly

In this mode, the receiving machine listens and responds to all incoming MIDI channel data, and plays its own notes in response polyphonically, according to its own limits.

MODE 2: Omni-on mono

In this mode, the receiving machine again listens and responds to all incoming MIDI channel data, but will play only the last note received, no matter what channel it is on.

MODE 3: Omni-off poly

NOTE: THIS IS THE MIDI RECEPTION MODE THAT THE STANDARD (UNMODIFIED) DX7 IS PERMANENTLY SET TO. In this, the most "normal" of all modes, the receiving instrument listens and responds to only one MIDI channel at a time, and plays its own notes in response, polyphonically. Remember that each MIDI channel can be sending up to sixteen notes simultaneously. It's a handy "coincidence", therefore, that the DX7 is itself capable of playing up to 16 notes at a time!

MODE 4: Omni-off mono

In this mode, the receiving instrument again only listens and responds to one MIDI channel at a time, but will play only the last note heard on that channel, monophonically. Although the DX7 cannot be specifically put into this mode, use of the DX7 in its own Mono mode via function switch 2 (see Chapter Thirteen) can simulate this effect when the DX7 is listening to MIDI data input.

Note that system information (system exclusive, system real-time, and system common) is not marked with an identifying channel address flag, and so is received by all devices regardless of the receive mode they are in.

* Why would we ever want to listen to all sixteen MIDI channels at once? One reason might be for quick scannings of complicated multi-timbral sequences. Rather than having to set up ten, twelve, or sixteen different synthesizers in order to hear all the different musical passages, you could simply plug in one machine, set it to omni mode, and hear all the different parts at once. Of course, that one instrument could only give you one timbre, but at least you'll be able to quickly hear the works.

So far, we have explored why MIDI exists, how MIDI data is transmitted and received, and **what kind** of information is actually sent. The obvious remaining question is, what kind of things can we actually do with MIDI?

MIDI Applications:

1) First and foremost, as mentioned earlier, is the simple hook-up of two synthesizers via a MIDI cable in order for the "slave" to receive channel messages from the "master" and to respond in kind: **(See Figure 14-12.)**

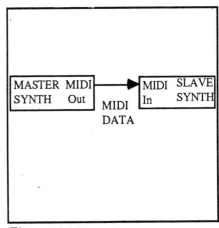

Figure 14-12

In this instance, any notes played on the keyboard of our master will result in the same notes being played simultaneously on the slave, regardless of the current sound in the slave, allowing for layered, multi-timbral effects. Although the slave will play the same keys on its own keyboard, bear in mind once again that its keyboard need not be tuned to the same notes. For example, playing A3 on a Prophet (tuned to A440) being used as a master will result in a DX7 slave playing A3 on its keyboard - but if the DX7's keyboard has been transposed (using edit switch 31 - see Chapter Two) so that C3 = G3, then the DX7's A3 will in fact be playing an E4 (since we have transposed up a musical fifth)! **(See Figure 14-13.)**

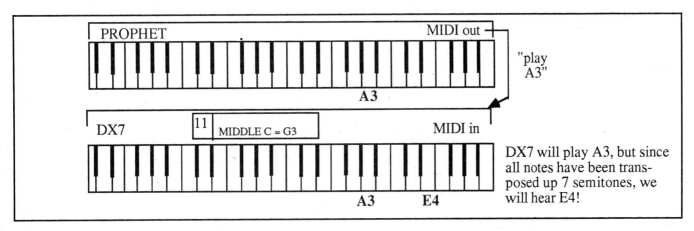

Figure 14-13

2) The use of a dedicated sequencer or computer programmed to act as a sequencer allows for the **storage** of channel messages. This information can then be retrieved - "played back" - at a later time, and the original performance recreated exactly, with all expressive controls as well as the original note and timing values. Additionally, the data can be edited to various degrees, allowing you to change note values, timing values, controller changes, or even program numbers! Moreover, the speed of the playback can be adjusted without affecting the pitch (unlike the simple act of speeding up or slowing down a tape, where pitch changes as a function of speed), or the pitch can be transposed by some fixed interval without altering the speed. Because MIDI is a multi-channel system, one central computer sequencer can output up to sixteen different sets of data at once! Each channel can be playing up to sixteen-note chords simultaneously, and, of course, any number of synthesizers can be listening and responding at any given time to any (in poly mode) or all (in omni mode) of the sixteen channels. This allows for complete orchestrations: **(See Figure 14-14.)**

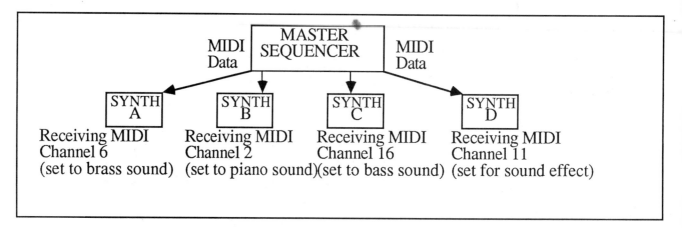

Figure 14-14

and also to a large degree eliminates the need for multi-track tape recorders, since each receiving synthesizer can have its audio output processed independently: **(See Figure 14-15.)**

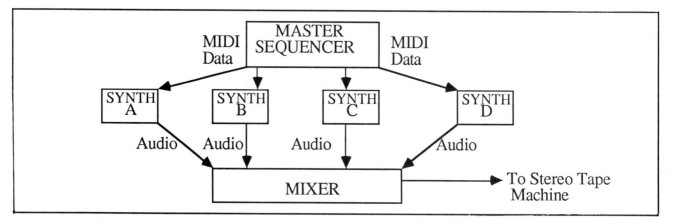

Figure 14-15

In this manner, if you physically have enough synthesizers in the room at once (and the new concept of modular synthesizer systems is making this more of an affordable reality), there is really no need to ever do multi-tracking on tape! Just set the sequencer going, get all the different machines sounding the way you want, and go straight to your stereo mixdown machine! Synchronization of all the different instruments is accomplished by the MIDI clock. Because the MIDI clock flags are tied to the overall tempo, MIDI sequencers can easily adjust to any tempo changes within a song. Moreover, they can readily be synchronized to other standard sync tones, such as FSK (Frequency Shift Keying - an analog pulse tone), or SMPTE time code (used extensively in video applications, as a means of numbering individual video frames).

Of course, the fact that MIDI is a serial interface means that the more data you send down that one wire, the longer will be the time delays between an event being transmitted and it being received. In point of fact, MIDI is fast enough to permit more than 65 16-note chords each second! But delays - more often than not engendered by the transmitting and receiving instrument's own internal microprocessors - do build up. If these delays exceed a thousandth of a second or so, they can begin to become perceptible to us mere mortals. One way of minimizing these delays, however, is to use the MIDI THRU port.

The data leaving this port, remember, is exactly the same data received by the MIDI IN port - but it doesn't have to go through the receiving instrument's microprocessor first. By setting up a MIDI "chain" like this, the original data sent out by the master sequencer is simply passed on to all the other receiving instruments in bucket-brigade fashion without each synth in the chain having to wait for the preceding one to have scanned and processed that data: **(See Figure 14-16.)**

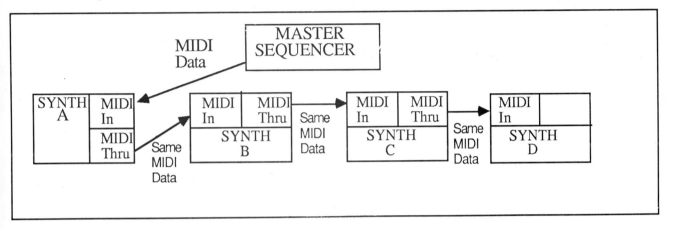

Figure 14-16

An even better method of distributing the data is to use a device called a "MIDI THRU box" - which is pretty much like an analog signal splitter. A typical MIDI THRU box will contain one MIDI INput and four or more MIDI THRU ports. A good way of setting up a multi-instrument MIDI sequencing system would be to use a MIDI thru box like this: **(See Figure 14-17.)**

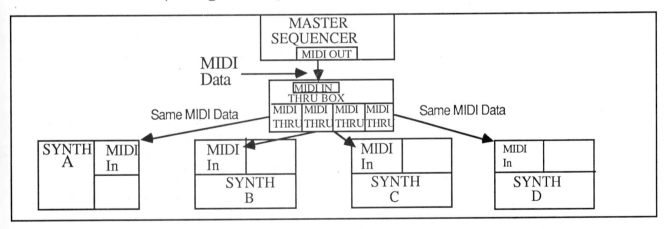

Figure 14-17

As if all this wasn't enough, some of the newer generation of computer sequencing programs, combined with the newer high-speed, graphics-oriented personal computers (such as the MacIntosh and Amiga), even allow note transcriptions of the sequencer data! This allows musicians who normally work with "dots on a line" instant access to work which need only be performed correctly once - and even then quite possibly in sections - by someone hooked up via MIDI into a computer. Appendix C lists some of the current MIDI sequencing programs and dedicated MIDI sequencers (that is, devices which can only perform sequencing tasks - and not also play Space Invaders) available as of this writing.

3) Many synthesizers, like the DX7, exhibit only rudimentary data displays. Two lines of sixteen characters each on a small LCD does not exactly allow for scintillating conversations with your instrument. However, sending system exclusive data via MIDI to a computer hooked into a video display (like your TV) will allow for simultaneous display of a great deal of data at once. Several commercial computer programs even allow graphic display of this data. The DX-PRO software package*, for example, will actually draw your envelopes on the screen for you, draw diagrams of the algorithms, and even show you the various keyboard level scalings for each sound in your DX7. Moreover, you can make changes to this data directly from the computer (or from the DX7's own data entry section) and watch the diagrams change in real time! This is an exciting educational concept which really helps to explain the inner workings of a synthesizer, and also acts as a real time-saver when editing voices. Once again, refer to Appendix C for a current listing of these so-called "voice editor" programs for the DX7.

4) Of course, once you've got the system exclusive data into your computer, it's a simple matter for the computer to store that data via its own internal data storage routines. This typically involves a disk drive of some type, and floppy disks are extremely inexpensive, especially when compared with something like the DX7 RAM cartridge, at $125 a shot! Using such "off-line" data storage allows you to inexpensively build huge libraries of sounds for your DX7. As the need presents itself, you simply download voices into either your DX7 internal memory or a RAM cartridge, and you can always have your most-needed voices at your fingertips. Most data display programs, and several sequencing programs, allow for this "librarian" function. Appendix C lists these kind of programs as well as the aforementioned sequencing and voice editor software packages for the DX7.

5) It's not only synthesizers and computers that can use MIDI data. Many other devices exist which contain microprocessors, and, as we've seen, virtually anything that has a microprocessor can theoretically "speak" MIDI. Digital drum machines capable of sending out MIDI system real-time data (in the form of the "MIDI clock") and/or MIDI channel messages ("hey, I'm playing the bass drum on 1 and 3, and the snare on 2 and 4, guys!") can be used as MIDI controllers or sequencers. Most digital audio signal processing devices, such as digital delay lines and digital reverb units have the potential for being "MIDI'd" to synthesizers. Several of these units are already available, allowing the synthesist to directly control variables such as delay time, feedback, output filtering, etc, as well as the ability to change preprogrammed settings in the outboard device's own memory. Performance accessories such as lighting rigs can be microprocessor-controlled and issued instructions via MIDI commands, directly from the synthesizer or from a master computer. If no one has done it yet, you should soon be able to turn your microprocessor-controlled dishwasher and microwave on and off from your synthesizer keyboard! (Why? Why not??) **(See Figure 14-18.)**

* currently available only for the Apple IIe or II+ computer. See Appendix C for a listing of other such programs.

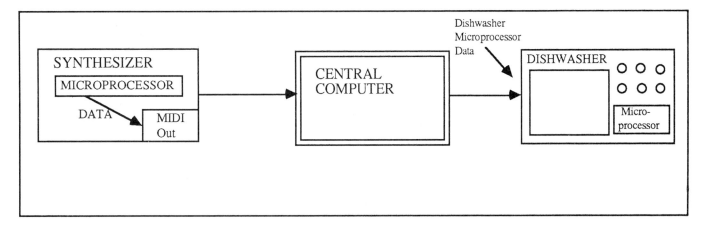

Figure 14-18

The really exciting thing about MIDI is that it is software-based and therefore open-ended. This means that the potential is literally limitless. Just as we could theoretically use the English language (or Swahili, or whatever) to communicate any idea to anyone you understands it, so too can we use MIDI to theoretically send controlling information to any device of any kind - by using that device's own microprocessor, or (if it doesn't have one) by inserting one before it. Because virtually any analog signal can be converted to digital code (via our old friend, the ADC), there is virtually no limit to what can be accomplished with MIDI.

If I sound excited, you read me correctly. Yes, MIDI has caused nearly as many problems as it has solved. But these problems are mostly those of misunderstanding and misinterpreting what the MIDI protocol allows us to do. It has forced musicians everywhere to perhaps learn more about computers than they ever wanted to. But that in itself certainly isn't a bad thing, given the increasing influence computers are having on our everyday lives. In summary, there probably isn't a creative musician anywhere who doesn't feel that the advantages presented by MIDI far outweigh any potential disadvantages. It's a powerful creative tool - learn how to use it!

For further, and much more detailed information on MIDI, I would refer you to the January 1986 issue of KEYBOARD magazine, and also suggest you contact the International MIDI Association, 11857 Hartsook St., North Hollywood, CA 91607.

Accessing the DX7 MIDI controls:

The DX7, being one of the earliest synthesizers to implement MIDI, actually only provides us with rudimentary MIDI controls. All the DX7 MIDI parameters are accessed by pressing function switch 8, which, for some unknown reason, is unlabeled. **(See Figure 14-19.)**

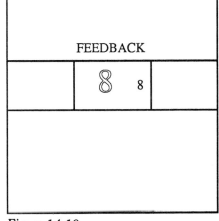

Figure 14-19

First of all, as mentioned earlier, the only MIDI reception mode the DX7 operates in is Mode 3, Omni-off poly. This means that our DX7 cannot listen to all 16 MIDI channels at once, but only one at a time. To set the DX7 **receive channel**, press function switch 8 once. The LCD will read: **(See Figure 14-20.)**

By using the "yes" - "no" buttons or the data entry slider, you can change this to any channel from 1 to 16. This value can be changed at any time. Bear in mind that this control, like all MIDI parameters, is a global function mode control, and so it will affect any and all sounds you call up in the edit buffer. Furthermore, the MIDI receive channel you set will remain in force, even after you turn the machine off, since function controls are battery-protected (see Chapter Thirteen).

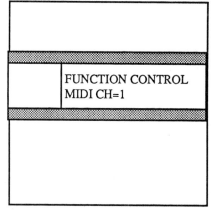

Figure 14-20

The DX7 has been set at the factory so that IT ONLY EVER TRANSMITS ON MIDI CHANNEL ONE. Within the DX7 itself, there is nothing you can do to change that fact. However, there are several companies, including Roland and J.L. Cooper Electronics, who manufacture devices called MIDI *channelizers*. What these "black boxes" do is to strip incoming channel messages of their identifying address flags and replace them with any other channel address flag that you specify. In this way, you can easily take the channel data being sent by your DX7 over MIDI channel 1, and turn it into, say, channel 14: **(See Figure 14-21.)**

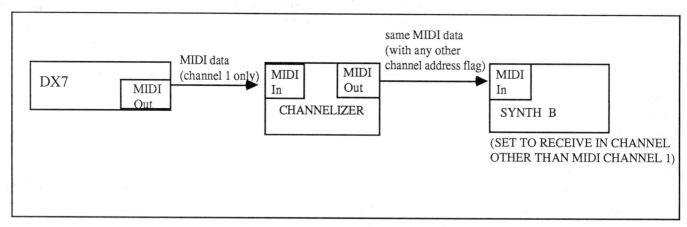

Figure 14-21

These devices are inexpensive and probably quite necessary if you are incorporating your DX7 into a MIDI system of more than one synthesizer plus a sequencer or computer. It is probable that future DX7 updates will allow MIDI transmission over any channel, and also reception in omni mode.

As you might have suspected, the DX7 is not normally transmitting *system-exclusive* data, since this data is useless to anything other than another DX7 or computer which has been programmed to utilize it. Pressing function switch 8 a second time will confirm this, showing the LCD display: **(See Figure 14-22.)**

WHENEVER YOU POWER THE DX7 UP, THE SYSTEM EXCLUSIVE INFORMATION IS MADE UNAVAILABLE. This is one of only two parameters on the DX7 that reset themselves whenever you turn the machine on - the other one being, of course, the memory protections (see Chapter Eight and also Appendix B). This is logical since in most instances you do not need and will not want to be sending system exclusive data. If you did so all the time, the lines would be "clogged" with all this mass of information pertaining to the voice currently being used - information generally useless to the receiving instrument on the other end of the MIDI line.

You can easily make the SYS INFO available, by simply pressing the "yes" button, or by moving the data entry slider. When the SYS INFO is AVAILABLE, putting your DX7 into play mode and pressing a main switch will have the effect of not only calling up that sound into the edit buffer, but will also cause a transmission of all of the system exclusive data pertaining to that one sound: **(See Figure 14-23.)**

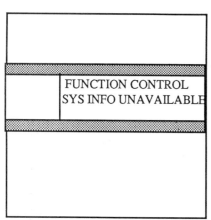

FUNCTION CONTROL
SYS INFO UNAVAILABLE

Figure 14-22

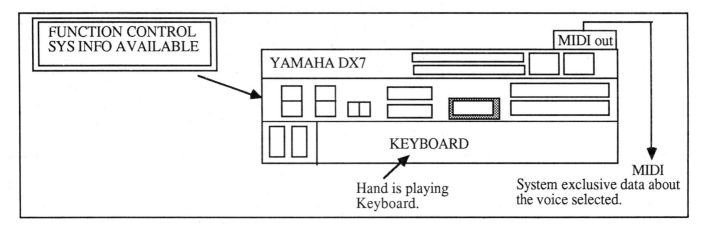

Figure 14-23

Having made the SYS INFO available, you also have the option of doing a bulk "data dump"; that is, transmitting all of the system exclusive data about ALL 32 sounds currently in the internal memory. This procedure normally takes about two seconds, and the command is accessed by pressing function switch 8 a third time. The LCD will ask: **(See Figure 14-24.)**

If you answer "yes" with the data entry button, the LCD will go blank for a couple of seconds, and when it comes back, you will know that the data dump is complete. At the other end of the MIDI cable, of course, should be either another DX7 or a computer which has been programmed to accept and store this data. If you try sending DX7 system exclusive data anywhere else, it will be ignored.

If your DX7 is at the receiving end of system exclusive information, either from another DX7 or from a computer, it will need to have its internal memory protection OFF in order to temporarily store that data in its edit buffer if the data for only one voice has been sent. If a complete "data dump" of all 32 voices has been sent, however, BE CAREFUL as your entire internal memory will be overwritten by these new sounds if your internal memory protection is OFF: **(See Figure 14-25.)**

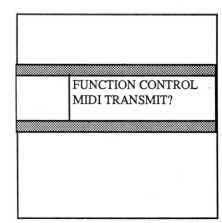

Figure 14-24

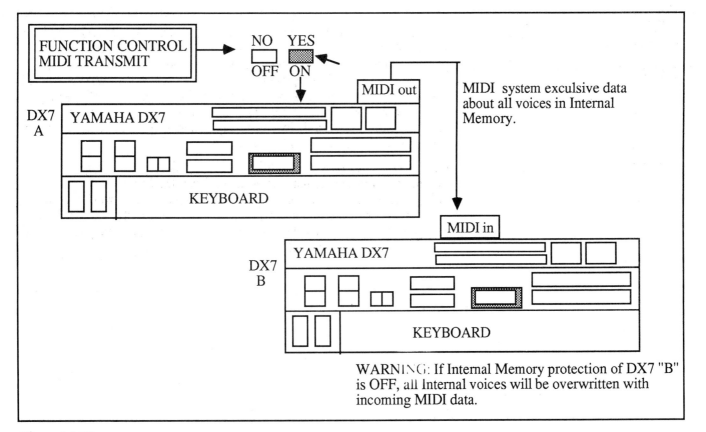

WARNING: If Internal Memory protection of DX7 "B" is OFF, all Internal voices will be overwritten with incoming MIDI data.

Figure 14-25

Of course, you can bail out of transmitting a "data dump" by answering "no" to the "MIDI TRANSMIT?" prompt, in which case you'll be returned to the "SYS INFO AVAILABLE" display. Note that you cannot get to the "MIDI TRANSMIT?" question if your SYS INFO is UNAVAILABLE - that makes sense. In any event, pressing function switch 8 yet again will cycle you back to the original "MIDI = " receive channel display. And that's all there is to the DX7 MIDI parameters. Those of you with experience on newer synthesizers may well be surprised at this "no-frills" approach, but, again, bear in mind that the DX7 was the first of a new generation of instruments.

For all of you hackers out there, a complete listing of the way the DX7 encodes its system exclusive data is provided in Appendix D.

SWITCHES AND CONTROLS COVERED IN CHAPTER FOURTEEN:

SWITCH	PARAMETER	COMMENTS
Function 8 (once)	MIDI <u>receive</u> channel*	Range 1 - 16
Function 8 (twice)	MIDI System Exclusive data enable	AVAILABLE or UNAVAILABLE; power-up resets to UNAVAILABLE.
Function 8 (three times)	MIDI TRANSMIT (bulk data dump)	Only if SYS INFO is made AVAILABLE.

*NOTE: DX7 transmission channel default is channel 1. There is no means of changing this on an unmodified DX7.

CHAPTER FIFTEEN: ADVANCED PROGRAMMING TECHNIQUES

Putting it all together - some helpful hints:

Now that we have discussed in detail all of the various controls and parameters available to us on the DX7, the time of reckoning is at hand. How can we actually make use of all this information in order to create the sounds we want to get from our instrument?

Working randomly with a DX7 may sometimes yield interesting results (as the proverbial billion monkeys in front of a billion typewriters may eventually yield "Hamlet"), but more usually will result in a waste of time. This book has attempted to clarify the inner workings of digital FM in order to point you logically in the direction you need to go in order to create any particular sound. Let's review some of those directions:

1) We'll start with that old bugaboo, *selecting the right algorithm*: First of all, you should remember that the decision you make is not irreversible and that you can change your algorithm at any time without losing any of the data you have previously entered. Of course, it's entirely possible that a carrier you were working with is now a modulator, or vice versa, but nonetheless, the changes you made remain. If you are in doubt as to what you had been doing, *compare mode* will instantly recall your past work, IF IT HAD BEEN STORED somewhere in memory. Remember that compare mode can only compare back to the original sound **stored in memory**, whether internal or RAM cartridge.

In terms of selecting an algorithm, we have given you several questions that you will need to ask yourself in order to eliminate obviously unsuitable ones. The first and most important of these questions is: how many sound sources (carriers) do I need? The second question is, how many modulators do I need to plug into those carriers? If I only require that one or more of these carriers be simple sine waves, then I won't need modulators at all for those particular carriers. On the other hand, if I am trying to create a sound or part of a sound that must be harmonically very rich, overbright, or even distorted, then I will require at least one stack of modulators. Algorithms 16, 17, and 18, which only contain one carrier, will be useful only if you are attempting to create a single, non-chorused, non-detuned, harmonically rich sound - for example the sound of a **single** bowed violin or single trumpet. They will not usually be a good choice for most ensemble sounds, where interharmonic beatings caused by physical resonances are integral (these kinds of movements can most successfully be simulated on the DX7 with detuned carriers beating against one another). On the other hand, algorithms 5 and 6, with three modulator-carrier systems, seem to provide the most scope for creating rich sounds, and it is not surprising that they are the most popular algorithms amongst the ROM presets.

Algorithm 32, with no modulators, will probably be of very limited use to you unless you are looking to create organ sounds or are otherwise heavily into sine waves. In fact, algorithms 23 through 32 all contain at least one unmodulated carrier and will only be of value to you if a sine wave is needed somewhere in the sound (one tip: bass sounds are often helped greatly by the addition of a low-pitched sine wave, since they carry the greatest low frequency content. In fact, I have often produced quite useable - and recordable - bass lines from just a single unmodulated carrier, given the appropriate EG settings).

Algorithms 1, 2, and 18 also provide limited service since they each have stacks of **three** modulators - something you won't need too often unless you are creating either highly complex waveshapes, white noise, or intricate keyboard scaling patterns. Algorithms 5, 6, 12, 13, 20, 21, and 22 are all somewhat similar in that they provide no unmodulated carriers, but no stacks either. Each has varying numbers of carriers, and their feedback loops are in different places, so you should be able to choose between them fairly easily. Apart from these seven, all the algorithms with numbers lower than 23 have stacks in them and will be of use when creating harmonically complex sounds (that is, sounds which are unusually bright).

Furthermore, algorithms 7 through 27 all contain systems of either two or more modulators into one carrier, or one modulator into two or more carriers. These are useful for setting up interesting animation techniques, or for setting up complex keyboard scalings where the timbre changes over the keyboard: **(See Figure 15-1.)**

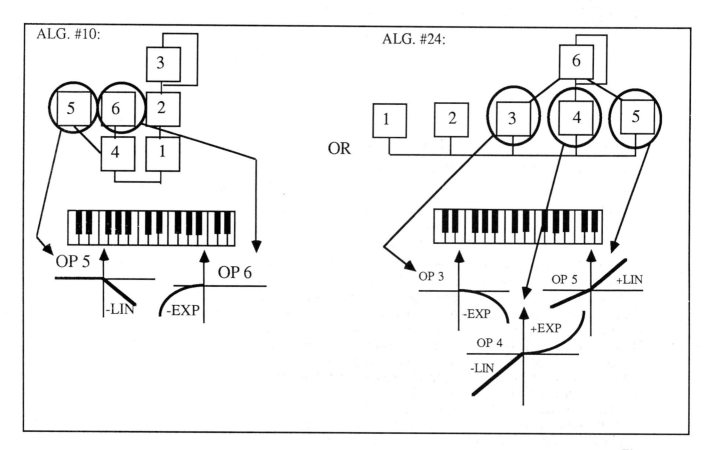

Figure 15-1

They're also useful for setting up complex timbral changes over time, using the EGs: **(See Figure 15-2.)**

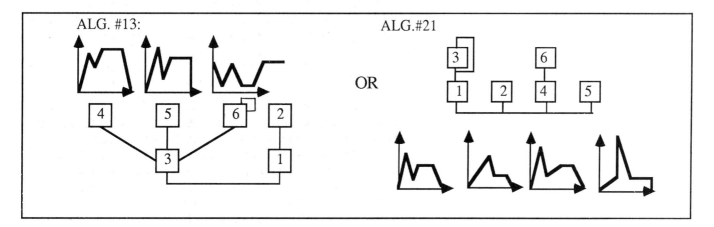

Figure 15-2

Here's a quick reference chart which may be of some use to you in selecting algorithms:

Algorithms with one carrier	Algorithms with two carriers	Algorithms with three carriers	Algorithms with more than three
16, 17, 18	1 - 4, 7 - 15	5, 6, 19, 20, 26, 27, 28	20 - 25, 29 - 32

Algorithms with unmodulated carriers	Algorithms with modulator stacks	Algorithms with one-into-two or two-into-one systems
23-32*	1 - 4, 7 - 11, 14 - 19, 28, 30	7 - 27

2) The EGs: Probably the most important tool on the DX7, and also probably the most misunderstood. THE EGS AFFECT OPERATOR OUTPUT LEVEL. Keep this sentence firmly implanted in your mind, along with Cardinal Rules One and Two, and a lot of the mystery will disappear. EGs exist solely to allow us aperiodic volume, timbral, or (if you use the pitch EG) pitch change **over time**. Remember that the timbre of almost every sound in existence changes over that sound's duration, and also that it rarely changes precisely the same way as the volume. Translation: use the EGs in the modulators, but don't just copy the carrier EG over and expect that you'll end up with a realistic sound. Think of the EG levels as a road map, on which you are plotting how the sound should change, and think of the EG rates as the amount of time it takes to get from point to point. Remember that the EG rates are relative rates and not absolute times: an R2 of 50 will mean different things, depending on where L1 is and where L2 is, and also on what the nominal output level of the operator is. The ability to set L4 anywhere we want allows us, among other things, to

* don't forget that you can always set a modulator's output level to 0 if you need an unmodulated carrier in a different algorithm!

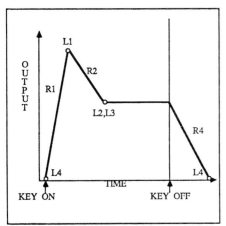

Figure 15-3

simulate a "hold" or "drone" switch. Finally, keep in mind that the good folks at Yamaha have provided us with an envelope generator that can do far more than an analog ADSR: take advantage of that fact - you're not limited to just a simple how-quickly-does-it-die-away-and-maybe-release-time EG, as you are on analog machines. Many beginning students of the DX7 create EGs that always look something like this: **(See Figure 15-3.)**

A sure giveaway of a DX7 novice! Become an Expert in the Privacy of Your Own Home: use the capabilities of the DX7 envelope generators to their fullest extent - and be thankful you don't own a Kurzweil, with its 255-stage EGs!

3) *Brightness or lack thereof*: Remember the relationship of modulators to carriers - **modulator output level** is your **quantitative** timbral control and *frequency ratio* is your *quantitative* timbral control. Translation: if you want a brighter sound, a modulator somewhere will have to somehow increase its output level. This will not always be as simple as just turning to edit switch 27. Remember that there are often many factors controlling the output level of a particular operator - the operator's EG, keyboard velocity sensitivity (which, you'll remember, is a negative sensitivity control: reducing a modulator's sensitivity will increase the softly-struck key's brightness), keyboard level scaling, and EG bias sensitivity. Adjusting these parameters will often have a more natural effect than simply cranking up the nominal output level with edit switch 27. If you're seeking a more subtle change in brightness, you might think about changing the frequency ratio instead. Introducing higher harmonics or disharmonics (don't forget Frequency Fine!) into the sound will usually create the illusion of a sharper edge - and this may well be all you need to do.

4) *Movement in a sound*: The LFO provides periodic volume, pitch, or timbral changes but is generally unsuitable for generating subtle movements within a sound, because there is only one LFO. The changes it induces, therefore, are always very regular, easy to spot, and often quite boring. String sounds created on the DX7 which rely solely on a delayed vibrato effect from the LFO for animation are usually ineffective, because the regularity of movement is a dead giveaway. For the same reason, putting a modulated carrier into a subaudio fixed frequency also creates a movement which is unchanging in speed. Usually, the best choice for creating the most natural movements is use of the detuning control, which adds a very natural beating effect to the sound, and one whose speed changes per note. Detuning is one of the most powerful tools on the DX7 because it really helps negate the digital perfection of the machine, and adds a "human" quality to the sounds generated. Be careful of overusing it, though - like anything else, it can backfire on you in large quantities and just make the sound a muddy mess. In general, I recommend that you always at least try to add detuning to any sound you create, but do it as a last step, and in small and careful doses. Keep in mind the extraordinary effects that can be generated by applying detuning within a two (or more)-into-one or one-into-two (or more) system: **(See Figure 15-4.)**

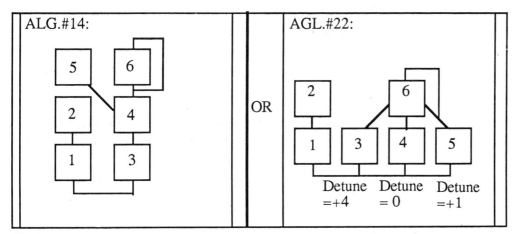

Figure 15-4

Conversely, if you are trying to remove a movement from a preset sound, don't always look to the LFO as the culprit. If you set both the pitch and amplitude modulation sensitivities to 0 and you still hear it, look to the Frequency Fine or Detune controls as the most likely source.

5) *Keyboard scalings*: One of the most amazing things we can do on the DX7 is actually scale the keyboard so that operator output levels change (the Keyboard Level Scaling controls) or that EG rates change (the Keyboard Rate Scaling controls). Remember that real sounds rarely maintain the same volume or timbre as they change pitch, and that in most acoustic instruments, higher notes undergo their changes over shorter periods of time than do lower notes. The abovementioned controls allow us to simulate these naturally occurring acoustic phenomena on our DX7. Don't overlook them! Once again, they serve to hide the digital precision of this instrument and impart a more "real" quality to the sounds we create. On the other hand, using these controls in unconventional ways allows you to set up unbelievably "unreal" sounds - and to generate audio effects that acoustic sounds could never accomplish. Either way, they're worth devoting time to!

6) *Changing pitch*: There are several ways of accomplishing this if you are trying to affect the whole keyboard. For slight pitch changes, you can use the Master Tune Adjust, but remember that since it's a global function control, it will throw out the pitch of any sound you call up. Therefore, if you're looking for a slight voice-linked pitch change, you can use the pitch EG (a level of 50 is the nominal pitch, therefore setting all four levels to, say, 48, will slightly flatten the overall sound) or you could even use the LFO! Sync the LFO to the keyboard, select a square wave, and set the LFO speed to 0. Now set the PMD to some value greater than 0. Surprise! Since the square wave will always start at the bottom of its cycle whenever you press a key down, the overall pitch will drop down and will stay down for a good minute or so. Since every time you strike another note, the whole thing starts all over again, this will work fine as long as you don't need to hold a note or chord down for longer than a minute. Adjusting the PMD will give you control over just how low you go. Of course, for semitone-quantized pitch changes you can always use Key Transpose, or even the pitch bend wheel.

But, if you're looking to change the pitch of only part of a total sound (i.e. one system within a multi-system algorithm), you will absolutely need to invoke Cardinal Rule Three, and remember that whatever you do to alter the frequency of a carrier must also be done to its associated modulators in order to keep the frequency ratio, and hence the timbre, intact.

7) Last but not least, expressiveness: The DX7 provides us with an inordinate number of expressive controls: the keyboard velocity and after-touch, the sustain footswitch, the various real-time controllers, even the data entry slider, in particular situations! These allow you fingertip control over volume, brightness, vibrato, tremolo, or any one of dozens of other periodic effects. One of the hallmarks of conventional acoustic instrumentation is that they can be played expressively. Up until very recently, the lack of expressiveness was the hallmark of synthesizers. This is certainly not true of the DX7. DON'T ALLOW a piano purist to accuse you of just pressing keys down on a "toy". Dazzle them with expressiveness! Shut them up for another day longer!!

One final observation: many DX7 users seem to become inordinately fascinated with the numbers being constantly presented in the LCD by the microprocessor. It is an easy trap to fall into: DON'T get wrapped up in the numbers. The most sage words of wisdom I can possibly impart to you regarding the DX7 can be summed up in just three words: USE YOUR EARS! If it sounds good to you, it's good, no matter what the number in the LCD says. Conversely, if you just sit at the machine and enter in numbers without constantly LISTENING to the effect they engender, you won't really have a clue as to how those numbers are changing the sound. USE YOUR EARS!!

Some generic sounds:

Having said all that, let's now run a short series of exercises and see just how we can apply these principles to creating a generic brass sound, a generic string sound, and a generic vox humana sound on the DX7.

Each of the sounds presented here is actually a severe modification of a factory preset (two points for honesty, OK?) but we'll create each of them here from scratch and explain at each step the rationale for doing what we're doing. Following each exercise is something called a "voice data chart" of the patch. These charts are useful as alternative records of the sounds you create - just in case your machine's back-up battery ups and dies in the middle of the night. It's probably a good idea to get in the habit of filling out charts like those for voices that are exceptionally important to you - Murphy's Law assures us that accidents can and do happen.

Let's start with a generic, all-purpose brass sound. This started out as an attempt to create a life-like solo trumpet but to my surprise this also works pretty well as a brass ensemble sound, if you intonate chords on the keyboard in realistic manner. Treat this sound, and the two others that follow it, not as an end product, but as a means to an end - in other words, use it as a stepping-stone to your own customized brass sound. What my ears subjectively tell me sounds "good", your ears may say "expletive deleted", so let your own ears be the final judge of any sound you synthesize.

PLEASE NOTE: IF YOU HAVE SKIPPED AHEAD TO THIS POINT WITHOUT READING THE PRECEDING 200-ODD PAGES, WELCOME ABOARD! PLEASE BE AWARE THAT A CONVENTION IN DOING THESE EXERCISES HAS BEEN SOMEWHAT PAINSTAKINGLY ESTABLISHED, SO IF THE INSTRUCTIONS BELOW CONFUSE YOU AT ALL, YOU'LL PROBABLY HAVE TO GO BACK AND READ MANY OF THOSE 200-ODD PAGES! SORRY, BUT I NEVER PROMISED YOU A ROSE GARDEN...

EXERCISE 80

Creating a generic brass sound:

NOTE: In this exercise and all succeeding ones, wherever a parameter is not specifically mentioned, it is meant to be left at its initialized default settings.

1) INITIALIZE your DX7 and select algorithm #18. Because we are setting out to create a highly complex sound (a trumpet is overbright and contains many harmonic and disharmonic overtones), and because this was originally meant to be a solo sound, algorithm #18, with its single carrier and stack of three modulators, was the obvious choice. **(See Figure 15-5.)**

2) TURN OFF operators 2, 4, 5, and 6 ("101000") and CHANGE operator 3's output level to 78, leaving the default frequency ratio of 1.00 : 1.00. Since most brass sounds have characteristic sawtooth-like waveshapes, we'll start with this ratio. Because we'll be using four other modulators to induce more overtones, we'll start with a relatively subdued sound, hence the lowered output level. Enter the following EG data for operators 1 and 3

	Op 1	Op3
L4	0	0
R1	59	46
L1	99	99
R2	24	35
L2	86	86
R3	99	99
L3	86	86
R4	55	50

Play a note and LISTEN (AUDIO CUE 80A). It's starting to sound distinctly brass-like, as the modulator envelope: **(See Figure 15-6.)**

is giving the distinctive "wah" sound to the timbre. But it's still not quite bright enough. Fortunately, in this algorithm, you will note that the feedback loop is on operator 3. CHANGE the feedback value to 7, play a note and LISTEN (AUDIO CUE 80B). NOTE that even though feedback is now at maximum, we're not hearing appreciable distortion or white noise since the output level of operator 3 is still quite low (at a value of 78 - see step 2 above). EXPERIMENT by increasing the output level of operator 3 and NOTE that you hear the distinctive distortion and white noise. When you're done, restore operator 3's output level back to 78.

3) TURN OFF operator 3 and TURN ON operator 2 ("110000"). We're going to use operator 2 only for a gentle addition of a few upper harmonics, so CHANGE it's default frequency to a new value of 23.00 and just raise it's output level to a value of 10. This will ensure that these upper harmonics don't cut through too much - we just want to add a little edge to the sound. Enter the following EG values for operator 2: L1 = 80, L2, L3, and L4 = 0; R1 = 41, R2 = 34, R4 = 70, and, of course, R3 is irrelevant and can be left at the default of 99. This gives us a very simple envelope which looks like this: **(See Figure 15-7.)**

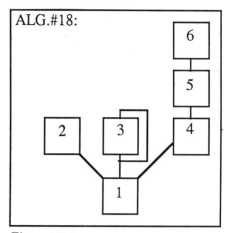

Figure 15-5

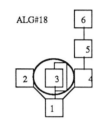

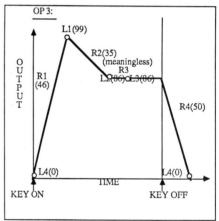

Figure 15-6

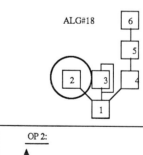

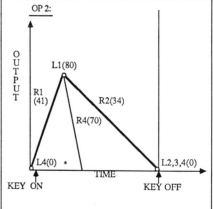

Figure 15-7

Play a note on the keyboard and LISTEN (AUDIO CUE 80C). This will be the total contribution of operator 2 to this sound - a small one, but an important one.

4) TURN OFF operator 2 and TURN ON the stack of operators 4, 5, and 6 ("100111"). Let's leave the bottom modulator, operator 4, at the default frequency, and set its output level to 79, so that we are once again working with a quasi-sawtooth wave. We're going to use the stack above it to modify it and add in the characteristic distortions and disharmonics that come from blowing hard into a brass tube like a trumpet. Therefore, change operator 5's frequency value to 4.76, and operator 6's to 7.63, and set their output levels to 75 and 47 respectively. Detune operator 5 a little, to a value of -1. This will give us a very slow beating effect which will only be audible on held notes. Enter the following EG data for operators 4, 5, and 6:

	Op4	Op5	Op6
L4	0	0	0
R1	66	48	77
L1	53	98	99
R2	92	55	56
L2	61	61	0
R3	22	22	99
L3	62	62	0
R4	50	50	70

Play a note and LISTEN (AUDIO CUE 80D). This will be the total contribution of the stack. Now TURN ON operators 2 and 3 ("111111") and LISTEN (AUDIO CUE 80E). We're getting there!

5) One thing that may be apparent as you try this sound over the keyboard is that it's a little unrealistically overbright at this point. We can start to deal with that by adding some keyboard velocity sensitivity so that only keys which are struck unrealistically hard will have this characteristic - after all, when a horn player really blows hard, these kinds of distortions make their presence known. Therefore, set the velocity sensitivities for operators 2 and 3 to a value of 1. Also, when a horn player blows hard, the volume increases somewhat. In order to simulate that, set the velocity sensitivity for operator 1 to a value of 2. So far, so good, but it's still a little overbright, particularly in the highest notes. This calls for some keyboard level scaling. Set a break point for operator 3 of A#4, and set a -LIN curve to the right of that break point. A right scale depth of 10 will do nicely, just enough to roll off some of those unpleasant distortions at the upper end of the keyboard: **(See Figure 15-8.)**

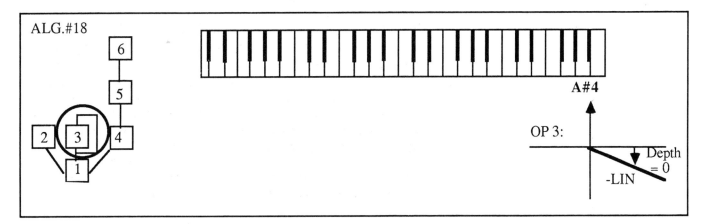

Figure 15-8

6) While a horn player can theoretically sustain a high note just as long as a low note, the timbral changes that occur within that high note happen somewhat faster than in lower ones. Therefore, set the keyboard rate scalings for some of our modulators as follows: operator 2 = 2; operator 3 = 1; and operator 6 = 7. This will accurately simulate this effect. Because we have a fair amount of release time in our carrier (operator 1 R4 = 55), we'll also have to scale the carrier a bit so it doesn't hang on unnaturally at the top end of the keyboard, so set the keyboard rate scaling for operator 1 to a value of 2. Play a note and LISTEN (AUDIO CUE 80F).

7) Finally, let's set up our LFO so we can access a nice slow vibrato from any of our real-time controllers. Change the waveshape to a SINE wave, set the LFO speed to a value of 26, and turn the LFO key sync OFF. Now set the pitch modulation sensitivity to a very slight 1, and, by turning any of your real-time controllers ON for the pitch destination (with a range greater than 0, of course), you'll be able to bring a realistic slow vibrato effect in and out at will.

8) That's all there is to it! Play a note and LISTEN (AUDIO CUE 80G). Instant generic brass... try a few well-intonated chords and I think you'll find that this sound works well as a brass ensemble also.

GENERIC BRASS

ALG. #18:

SINE	26	0	0	0	OFF	1
WAVE	SPEED	DELAY	PMD	AMD	SYNC	PMS

R1 99	R2 99	R3 99	R4 99
L1 50	L2 50	L3 50	L4 50

PITCH ENVELOPE

C3
KEY TRANPOSITION

ON
OSC SYNC

FUNCTIONS

POLY	S	0	FOLLOW OFF	12
POLY/MONO	RANGE	STEP	MODE	GLISSANDO	TIME
	PITCH BEND			PORTAMENTO	

(CONTORLLER)	RANGE	PITCH	AMPLITUDE	EG BIAS
MOD WHEEL	45	ON	OFF	OFF
FOOT CONT.	0	OFF	OFF	OFF
BREATH CONT.	0	OFF	OFF	OFF
AFTER TOUCH	0	OFF	OFF	OFF

OP 6

FREQUENCY 7.63	DETUNE 0	AMS 0

ENVELOPE DATA

R1 77	R2 56	R3 99	R4 70	RS
L1 99	L2 0	L3 0	L4 0	7

KEYBOARD SCALING

CURVE	BREAKPOINT	DEPTH		
L	-L	A-1	L	0
R	-L		R	0

OP# 6	OUTPUT LEVEL 47	VELOCITY 0

OP 5

FREQUENCY 4.74	DETUNE -1	AMS 0

ENVELOPE DATA

R1 48	R2 55	R3 22	R4 50	RS
L1 98	L2 61	L3 62	L4 0	0

KEYBOARD SCALING

CURVE	BREAKPOINT	DEPTH		
L	-L	A-1	L	0
R	-L		R	0

OP# 5	OUTPUT LEVEL 75	VELOCITY 0

OP 2

FREQUENCY 23.00	DETUNE 0	AMS 0

ENVELOPE DATA

R1 41	R2 34	R3 15	R4 70	RS
L1 80	L2 0	L3 0	L4 0	2

KEYBOARD SCALING

CURVE	BREAKPOINT	DEPTH		
L	-L	A-1	L	0
R	-L		R	0

OP# 2	OUTPUT LEVEL 10	VELOCITY 1

OP 3

FREQUENCY 1.00	DETUNE 0	AMS 0

ENVELOPE DATA

R1 46	R2 35	R3 22	R4 50	RS
L1 99	L2 86	L3 86	L4 0	1

KEYBOARD SCALING

CURVE	BREAKPOINT	DEPTH		
L	-L	A#4	L	0
R	-L		R	10

OP# 3	OUTPUT LEVEL 78	VELOCITY 1

OP 4

FREQUENCY 1.00	DETUNE 0	AMS 0

ENVELOPE DATA

R1 66	52 92	R3 22	R4 50	R5
L1 98	L2 61	L3 62	L4 0	0

KEYBOARD SCALING

CURVE	BREAKPOINT	DEPTH		
L	-L	A-1'	L	0
R	-L		R	0

OP# 4	OUTPUT LEVEL 79	VELOCITY 0

OP 1

FREQUENCY 1.00	DETUNE 0	AMS 0

ENVELOPE DATA

R1 59	R2 24	R3 99	R4 55	RS
L1 89	L2 86	L3 86	L4 0	2

KEYBOARD SCALING

CURVE	BREAKPOINT	DEPTH		
L	-L	A-1	L	0
R	-L		R	0

OP# 1	OUTPUT LEVEL 99	VELOCITY 2

Now let's take a look at a generic string sound. While this is admittedly not one of the DX7's strengths, we can simulate a fairly good bowed violin/viola/cello/bass sound. One of the problems, of course, is that each of these sound somewhat similar but are nonetheless different instruments, and synthesists have become accustomed to having all four at their fingertips over the whole keyboard. Fortunately, the sophisticated keyboard level scaling on the DX7 helps us get around that particular problem:

EXERCISE 81

Creating a generic string sound:

1)   INITIALIZE your DX7 and select algorithm #2. We've selected this algorithm because the complex harmonics induced by bowing a stringed instrument will require a stack of three modulators, and the complex beating and detuning effects we need point us in the direction of two carriers. Since both carriers will need to have overtones (a pure sine wave being of very little use here), we are essentially given the choice of algorithm #1: **(See Figure 15-9.)**

or algorithm #2: **(See Figure 15-10.)**

The sole difference between these two is in their feedback loop. Because we're going to need the feedback loop on the single modulator-carrier system, rather than on the stack, we've selected for this sound algorithm #2.

2)   We'll start as usual by working with the individual systems inside our algorithm. We're going to use the stack for the real "bowing" part of the sound, and then blend it with a smoother string sound we'll create with the other system. Let's start with the simpler system first. TURN OFF operators 3 through 6 ("110000"). Because stringed instruments produce a characteristic pulse-waveish shape, we'll begin by changing the frequency of operator 2 to 2.00, and by setting its output level to 76 (thereby giving us slightly greater amplitude of the odd-numbered harmonics which are normally present in a square wave). This still isn't nearly bright enough, so we'll also use the feedback loop that's conveniently on operator 2 and change it to the maximum value of 7. Play a note on the keyboard and LISTEN (AUDIO CUE 81A). NOTE the characteristically overbright overtones. As with the generic brass sound, even though the feedback loop is all the way open, we're still not hearing distortion or white noise since the output level of operator 2 is fairly low.

3)   In a string section, of course, there is always a great deal of movement. As a first step in animating the sound further, let's detune operator 1 to a value of -1, and operator 2 to -7. Play a note and LISTEN (AUDIO CUE 81B). That's better, but we'll need to animate the sound even more. Therefore, CHANGE operator 1 to a fixed frequency, and set that frequency at 1.259 Hz. Play a note and LISTEN (AUDIO CUE 81C). There's plenty of movement, alright, but it still doesn't sound much like a string section. Obviously, this is because our EGs are still at their static default states. Enter the following EG values for operators 1 and 2:

	Op1	Op2
L4	0	0
R1	44	99
L1	99	99
R2	25	0

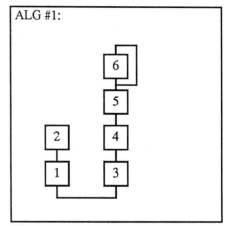

ALG #1:

Figure 15-9

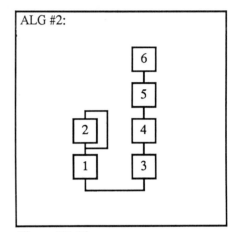

ALG #2:

Figure 15-10

L2	97	96
R3	16	0
L3	0	97
R4	45	30

ALG#2

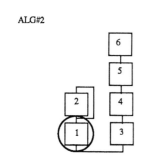

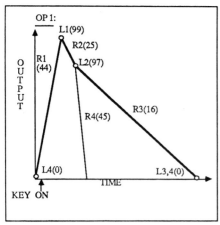

Figure 15-11

ALG#2

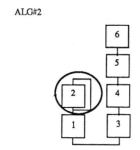

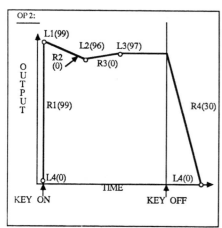

Figure 15-12

Play a note and LISTEN (AUDIO CUE 81D). Our carrier is now rising to maximum volume at a moderate rate, dropping slowly to a slightly lesser volume, and then very slowly dying back to 0: **(See Figure 15-11.)**

Whereas operator 2 is in full force right away, but then very slowly drops to a slightly lesser output, and then very slowly increases output slightly: **(See Figure 15-12.)**

4) Okay, that's enough manipulation of system one for the time being - now let's work with system two. TURN OFF operators 1 and 2 and TURN ON operators 3 through 6 ("001111"). Start by setting maximum output (99) for operator 3 (our carrier). Let's begin with a sawtooth waveshape this time, but raise it up an octave, so set the frequency of both operator 3 and operator 4 to 2.00, and set operator 4's output level to 87. Now let's use operator 5 to change operator 4 into a complex waveshape with much higher overtones. Set operator 5's frequency to 8.00 and change its output level to 77. Finally, we're going to use the top modulator - operator 6 - to induce some disharmonics, but we want these disharmonics to change for each note on the keyboard. How do we accomplish this? Simple - we put it into an audible range fixed frequency* - let's set it at 2042 Hz, give it just a bit of output level (44), and see what happens.

5) If you have a strong stomach and a good imagination, play a note and LISTEN (AUDIO CUE 81E). Of course, this weird timbre doesn't sound much like a string section, but again, our EGs are all still at their square default settings. Therefore, enter the following EG values for operators 3, 4, 5, and 6:

	Op3	Op4	Op5	Op6
L4	0	0	0	0
R1	53	92	99	97
L1	99	99	99	99
R2	18	30	49	99
L2	95	98	90	99
R3	17	0	55	99
L3	0	90	80	99
R4	56	35	46	59

* this will have the effect of giving us a different frequency ratio for each note on the keyboard. See Chapter Six (pages 77 - 78) if you don't remember this trick.

Play a note and LISTEN (AUDIO CUE 81F). The carrier in this system is behaving similarly to the carrier in system one (operator 1) but with enough slight differences that they are offsetting one another. The modulators are also following somewhat similar, offsetting patterns, with operator 6 actually pretty much remaining with the default square envelope. It is the quick attack of operators 4, 5, and 6 that is primarily responsible for the bowing sound that we hear. TURN ON operators 1 and 2 again ("111111") in order to hear the total effect. Two other "bonuses" are derived from the EGs we've set up here. First of all, the moderate R4s in all the operators imparts a sort of digital reverb effect to the total sound. Secondly, the L3 values for our carriers are both 0, and the R3 values for these same operators are slow - meaning that our sound will simulate a sustaining sound but will also do a nice, natural "fadeout" (like a violinist's arm getting tired!) if we hold the keys down. Try holding a chord for some time and LISTEN (AUDIO CUE 81G). NOTE the natural fadeout that occurs, similar to, but a bit longer than, the one which occurs by playing notes staccato.

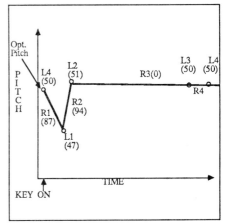

Figure 15-13

6) Of course, we'll need to add some movement into this system too, so detune operator 5 to +3 and operator 6 to +5; then, let's do something fairly unusual and detune this system's carrier also: set operator 3 to the same detune value as operator 1, that is, -1. We wouldn't ordinarily detune both carriers in a sound, since that will have the effect of making the overall sound slightly out in pitch, but the reason here is to allow us to somewhat offset an effect we're going to set up with the Pitch EG:

7) Studies of string instruments show that they undergo a subtle pitch change through their duration, as well as the more apparent volume and timbral changes. We can use the Pitch EG to simulate this. TURN ON operators 1 and 2 ("111111") and CHANGE the following Pitch EG values from their initialized defaults: L1 = 47, L2 = 51, R1 = 87, R2 = 94, and R3 = 0, yielding a Pitch EG shape like this: **(See Figure 15-13.)**

In other words, our pitch will quickly (R1 = 87) drop down nearly a quarter tone upon KEY ON (L4 = 50 but L1 = 47) and will even more quickly (R2 = 94) rise up just a bit sharp (L2 = 51) and then ever so slowly (R3 = 0) drop back to the initial pitch (L3 = 50). This extremely subtle use of the Pitch EG really helps to add realism to the sound. Play a note and LISTEN (AUDIO CUE 81H).

8) We're starting to get there! However, our sound is still unpleasantly overbright. Bearing in mind that a string section uses a great deal of dynamic range and also is capable of undergoing a great deal of timbral change (depending on how the instruments are played), we will want some kind of real-time control over both volume and timbre. Keyboard velocity sensitivity, being a negative sensitivity control, is the answer, as it will also serve to compensate for the current overbrightness of our sound, and make it far more realistic than it currently is. Therefore, enter the following keyboard velocity sensitivity values: operator 1 = 2; operator 3 = 7; operator 5 = 2. The reason we have assigned so much sensitivity to operator 3 (the carrier in the second system) is so we will hear much more of the bowing sound when we strike our keys harder. Play a few notes at various different velocities and LISTEN (AUDIO CUE 81I). Since the keyboard is currently transposed at a range in which the highest violin sounds will be too high, and the lowest bass notes not low enough, use the Key Transpose parameter to drop the keyboard down one octave (so that Middle C = C2).

9) Now for our scalings. First of all, violins and violas undergo both volume and timbral changes somewhat more quickly than cellos or basses, so we'll need to do a certain amount of keyboard rate scaling. Enter the following values: operators 1 and 2 = 1; operators 3 through 6 = 2. Play a note and LISTEN (AUDIO CUE 81J). Secondly, we'll need to adjust the relative levels of the various modulators over the keyboard in order, as mentioned earlier, to simulate the fact that we are attempting to recreate three or four different instruments over our keyboard. Therefore, enter the following keyboard level scaling values for operators 2, 4, 5, and 6:

Operator 6	Operator 2	Operator 4	Operator 5
Break point F# 2	B1	G3	B2
Right curve - LIN	- EXP	- LIN	-LIN
Right depth 45	35	47	22
Left curve		+ LIN	
Left depth		4	

As you can see, operator 2 is being gently rolled off from about F3 on up (since the exponential curve has virtually no effect for an octave and a half), with the most drastic decrease in the upper, violin range notes. Operator 4, whose output is actually determining the effects of operators 5 and 6, is having its effect slightly increased below G3 and more drastically decreased above that point (again, affecting the violin sounds). This is the reason why the bowing is most prominent in the bass and cello range notes. Finally, the effects of operators 5 and 6 are pretty much being attenuated over the upper three octaves. These complicated keyboard level scalings are actually vital to our being able to somewhat accurately simulate the differences between each of these instruments. Play several notes and chords through the full range of the keyboard and LISTEN (AUDIO CUE 81K). NOTE how the timbre of our sound now changes realistically as we play in the different ranges.

10) All that's left to do now is to set up our LFO for a subtle vibrato effect which can be added to by any of our real-time controllers. Leave the LFO waveshape at its default TRIANGLE setting, and change the speed value to 24. Set the PMD to a very subtle 17, and change the P MOD SENS. value to 1. Now set up any of your real-time controllers up to route pitch modulation, and LISTEN (AUDIO CUE 81L). Instant generic strings! Once again, treat these as a building block from which to program your own customized string sounds.

GENERIC STRING

ALG. #2:

TR	24	0	17	0	ON	1
WAVE	SPEED	DELAY	PMD	AMD	SYNC	PMS

	R1	R2	R3	R4
	87	94	99	99
	L1	L2	L3	L4
	47	51	50	50

PITCH ENVELOPE

C2
KEY TRANPOSITION

OFF
OSC SYNC

FUNCTIONS

POLY	5	0	---	OFF	0
POLY/MONO	RANGE	STEP	MODE	GLISSANDO	TIME
	PITCH BEND			PORTAMENTO	

(CONTORLLER)	RANGE	PITCH	AMPLITUDE	EG BIAS
MOD WHEEL	45	ON	OFF	OFF
FOOT CONT.	0	OFF	OFF	OFF
BREATH CONT	0	OFF	OFF	OFF
AFTER TOUCH	0	OFF	OFF	OFF

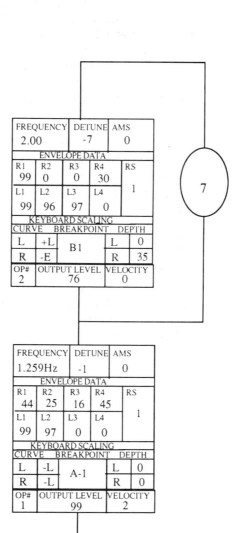

OP 6

FREQUENCY	DETUNE	AMS
2042 Hz	+5	0

ENVELOPE DATA

R1	R2	R3	R4	RS
99	99	99	59	
L1	L2	L3	L4	2
99	99	99	0	

KEYBOARD SCALING

CURVE	BREAKPOINT	DEPTH	
L	-L	F#2	L	0
R	-L		R	45

OP#	OUTPUT LEVEL	VELOCITY
6	44	0

OP 5

FREQUENCY	DETUNE	AMS
8.00	+3	0

ENVELOPE DATA

R1	R2	R3	R4	RS
99	49	55	46	
L1	L2	L3	L4	2
99	99	99	0	

KEYBOARD SCALING

CURVE	BREAKPOINT	DEPTH	
L	-L	B2	L	0
R	-L		R	22

OP#	OUTPUT LEVEL	VELOCITY
5	77	2

OP 2

FREQUENCY	DETUNE	AMS
2.00	-7	0

ENVELOPE DATA

R1	R2	R3	R4	RS
99	0	0	30	
L1	L2	L3	L4	1
99	96	97	0	

KEYBOARD SCALING

CURVE	BREAKPOINT	DEPTH	
L	+L	B1	L	0
R	-E		R	35

OP#	OUTPUT LEVEL	VELOCITY
2	76	0

OP 4

FREQUENCY	DETUNE	AMS
2.00	0	0

ENVELOPE DATA

R1	R2	R3	R4	RS
92	30	0	35	
L1	L2	L3	L4	2
99	98	90	0	

KEYBOARD SCALING

CURVE	BREAKPOINT	DEPTH	
L	-L	G3	L	4
R	-L		R	47

OP#	OUTPUT LEVEL	VELOCITY
4	87	0

7

OP 1

FREQUENCY	DETUNE	AMS
1.259Hz	-1	0

ENVELOPE DATA

R1	R2	R3	R4	RS
44	25	16	45	
L1	L2	L3	L4	1
99	97	0	0	

KEYBOARD SCALING

CURVE	BREAKPOINT	DEPTH	
L	-L	A-1	L	0
R	-L		R	0

OP#	OUTPUT LEVEL	VELOCITY
1	99	2

OP 3

FREQUENCY	DETUNE	AMS
2.00	-1	0

ENVELOPE DATA

R1	R2	R3	R4	RS
53	18	17	56	
L1	L2	L3	L4	2
99	95	0	0	

KEYBOARD SCALING

CURVE	BREAKPOINT	DEPTH	
L	-L	A-1	L	0
R	-L		R	0

OP#	OUTPUT LEVEL	VELOCITY
3	99	7

ALG.#14:

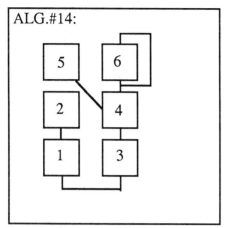

Figure 15-14

Finally, let's generate a generic human voice sound - the trickiest assignment we have so far. The only natural acoustic sound known which is believed to be timbrally more complex than the human voice is the acoustic piano - and I have yet to create or hear a DX7 do a convincing imitation of an acoustic piano. This is, more than anything, a limitation of the number of operators available to us in the DX7 - an instrument like the Yamaha TX816, with it's forty-eight (!) operators, can actually do a pretty good job of it. However, with that disclaimer in hand, let's get ourselves at least into the ballpark of vox humana sounds (in this instance with the sound of a choir voicing the syllable "ah") with the following exercise:

EXERCISE 82

Creating a generic human voice sound:

1) INITIALIZE your DX7 and select algorithm # 14. We have selected this algorithm: **(See Figure 15-14.)**

for much the same reasons as we had for selecting algorithm #2 in the last exercise. We know that we'll need a stack, but since the human voice is far less bright than a bowed cello, we won't need three modulators in the stack. However, we want the option of having different timbres over the keyboard in order to simulate some of the differences between soprano, alto, tenor, and bass voices, and the two-into-one system of operators 6, 5, and 4 in this algorithm will lend itself nicely to that. Algorithms 14 and 15 vary only in the placement of their feedback loop, but this time we'll need that feedback loop in the stacked system.

2) As usual, let's work with one system at a time. TURN OFF operators 3 through 6 ("110000") and set up a frequency ratio in this system of 1.00:2.00. This rather unusual ratio will have the effect of raising the pitch an octave and will also yield a very unusual, slightly nasal, gently harmonic timbre. (Tip: whenever the carrier is moving faster than the modulator, this type of resonance will occur). Raise the output level of operator 2 to 99. We will shortly be using the EG in operator 2 to attenuate this output level, by having none of the levels anywhere near 99, so if you listen to the sound at this point, it will have many more overtones than we're going to end up with. Remember that the rates in the EGs vary slightly as a function of the operator output level (as discussed in Chapter Nine), and so this is a valid alternative to simply always setting whatever nominal output level you need (with switch 27) and then setting at least one of the EG levels at 99. The technique we are proposing here will accomplish much the same effect, but the EG rates will be scaled slightly differently.

3) Once again, the fact that the EGs are currently at their square defaults is keeping us from hearing this sound at anything close to reality. Therefore, enter the following EG values for operators 1 and 2:

	Op1	Op2
L4	0	51
R1	37	99
L1	99	51
R2	20	26
L2	94	45

R3	53	53
L3	97	36
R4	62	25

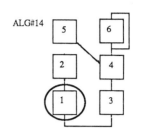

Play a note and LISTEN (AUDIO CUE 82A). Our carrier is undergoing a slow series of movements, fading in rather gently, then dropping a bit in volume, and then somewhat more quickly rising again in volume: **(See Figure 15-15.)**

whilst our modulator, as promised, is never getting beyond about a quarter of its nominal output level (remember that all DX7 controls are exponential and not linear; that means that an EG level of 51 translates to about a quarter of what a level of 99 would yield). The fact that L4 is the same as L1, also 51, means that the first timbral change we hear is a slight drop to L2 (45), followed by a faster drop again (to L3). After KEY OFF, as the carrier is moderately fading away, operator 2 will actually increase its output level back to the starting point of L4. **(See Figure 15-16.)**

If you listen carefully to just a single note (AUDIO CUE 82B) you should just about be able to hear that slight timbral increase after KEY OFF.

4) System one is only going to be contributing a very slight upper edge to our total sound: the meat of it will come from the stack provided by system two. TURN OFF operators 1 and 2 and TURN ON operators 3 through 6 ("001111"). Begin by giving our carrier (operator 3) maximum output level (=99). Then set operator 4's output level also to 99. As with the first system, we'll be using operator 4's EG to greatly attenuate this output level. Set up a frequency ratio between operators 4 and 3 of 1.01 : 1.00, which gives us a rapid detuning effect. Now open operator 5's output level to a value of 53, and leave it at its default frequency of 1.00. Raise operator 6's output level to a value of 45, and set its frequency to 5.10. We'll be using operator 6 to provide the highest harmonics found in the singing voice, and also the slight upper disharmonics which are inevitably present as a result of breathiness. In order to add a little more "edge" to the sound, open the feedback loop (which in this algorithm is on operator 6) to a value of 4. Now enter the following EG values for operators 3, 4, 5, and 6:

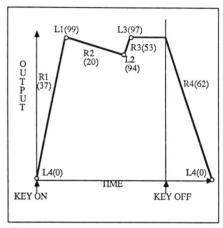

Figure 15-15

	Op3	Op4	Op5	Op6
L4	0	56	0	0
R1	42	72	35	99
L1	99	48	99	99
R2	20	19	21	99
L2	32	58	90	99
R3	53	41	36	99
L3	97	20	85	99
R4	53	12	63	17

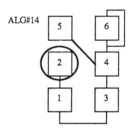

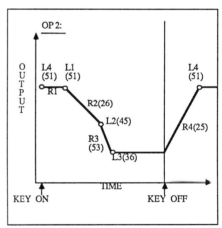

Figure 15-16

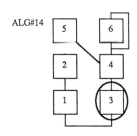

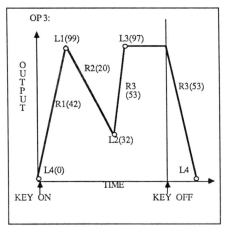

Figure 15-17

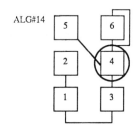

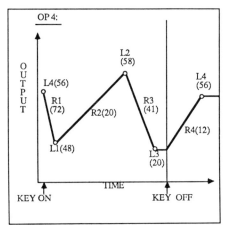

Figure 15-18

Play a note and LISTEN (AUDIO CUE 82C). The carrier in this system is undergoing a moderate attack, followed by a slow (R2) decrease in volume (L2), followed by a more rapid increase back up to nearly maximum (L3). This "roller-coaster" effect is meant to simulate the characteristic change in volume that choral singers typically exhibit when holding a single note: **(See Figure 15-17.)**

(NOTE once again that although the human voice is capable of generating literally millions of complex sounds, but that we are here attempting only one of the simplest of them - the choir "ah".)

As promised, the EG of operator 4 is serving to attenuate its output level in much the same way that operator 2 was affected by its EG. This time, however, we have a slight increase in output level, followed by a decrease, as opposed to the reverse effect engendered by operator 2's EG: **(See Figure 15-18.)**

Operator 5 is only undergoing a very slight decrease in output level throughout its duration, while operator 6 is almost entirely at its default settings, adding only a very slow R4. The fact that R4 is so slow for both operator 6 and operator 4 simply means that the overtone content they are causing to be present in our carrier will remain virtually unchanged even after KEY OFF: **(See Figure 15-19.)**

5)   TURN ON operators 1 and 2 ("111111") in order to hear our total sound and LISTEN (AUDIO CUE 82D). The human voice is potentially capable of extreme dynamics, but we won't need to incorporate a whole lot of dynamic range into the simple "ah" sound we're attempting here. Therefore, set keyboard velocity sensitivity values as follows: operator 2 = 2; operator 3 = 3; operators 5 and 6 = 1. This will give us slight timbral changes as we play keys harder, and also a slight volume increase coming from system two.

6)   Because both operator 4 and operator 6 are generating disharmonics with a fast beating effect, we won't need to use detuning to add more movement to this sound. However, in this instance we'll use the regularity of the LFO to add a bit of delayed vibrato, so change the LFO waveshape to a SINE, turn the LFO key sync OFF, leave the speed at the default of 35, but add in a delay time of 35. Now change the PMD to 3 and the P. MOD SENS. to 4, and LISTEN (AUDIO CUE 82E). Now change the AMD value to 3 and enter the following A. MOD SENS. values: operator 2 = 3; operator 4 = 1. This will induce a very slight "wah-wah" to the overall sound since we are affecting modulators only, and will also allow us, by using EG BIAS modulation, to use any of our real-time controllers as a subtle brightness control. Turn on one of your controllers for the EG BIAS destination, set a range of about 50, and try it out (AUDIO CUE 82F). It's very subtle, but it works!

7)   We only have to do a very small amount of scaling in this sound. Because human vocal chords don't quite react the same as inanimate strings, keyboard rate scaling appears to be inappropriate, so for this particular sound, leave it out (it's already defaulted to 0 for all operators anyway). In terms of keyboard level scaling, you've probably found that our sound is a bit dull at the lower end of the keyboard. Therefore, enter a break point for operator 5 of C#6, enter a +EXP curve to the left of that break point, and enter a left curve depth of 99. This will serve to make notes below A#4 brighter and brighter, with the strongest effect at the very lowest notes.

8)   Finally, to complete the picture, let's add in a slight pitch shift that's also characteristic of choir sounds. Enter in the following Pitch EG values: L1 = 48; L2 = 51; R1 = 18; R2 = 60; R3 = 95. This will give us a Pitch EG that looks something like this: **(See Figure 15-20.)**

and yields a very slight wavering in pitch, all of which helps to "humanize" the sound. And there we have a human audio choir sound (audio cue 82G), which, once again, you are encouraged to use as a starting point to build your own customized sounds.

Let's conclude now with examinations of three original sounds, which you are welcome to use as you see fit. Rather than run these as exercises, I'm going to go easy on you and just include the parameters here on a voice data chart. For each of these, initialize your DX7 and enter in each of the parameters. Boxes left blank contain the default settings and these obviously need not be entered. As you are entering in the data, THINK about how each new value is changing your starting sine wave, and LISTEN periodically. The first of these sounds, called "REPEATTT", uses a fairly ordinary timbre but uses the LFO to generate a very convincing digital-delay-with-feedback or echo loop effect:

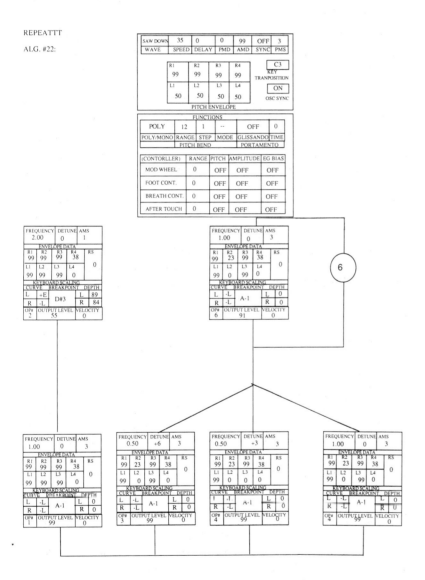

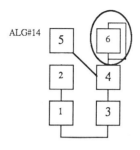

ALG#14

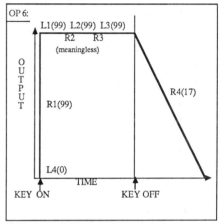

Figure 15-19

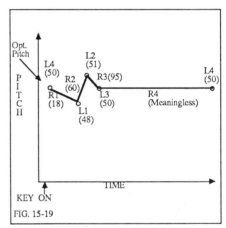

Figure 15-20

GENERIC VOICE

ALG. # 14

SINE	35	35	3	3	OFF	4
WAVE	SPEED	DELAY	PMD	AMD	SYNC	PMS

	R1	R2	R3	R4		C3
	18	60	99	99		KEY TRANPOSITION
	L1	L2	L3	L4		OFF
	48	51	50	50		OSC SYNC

PITCH ENVELOPE

FUNCTIONS

POLY	1	0	---	OFF	0
POLY/MONO	RANGE	STEP	MODE	GLISSANDO	TIME
PITCH BEND				PORTAMENTO	

(CONTORLLER)	RANGE	PITCH	AMPLITUDE	EG BIAS
MOD WHEEL	50	ON	OFF	OFF
FOOT CONT.	0	OFF	OFF	OFF
BREATH CONT.	0	OFF	OFF	OFF
AFTER TOUCH	50	OFF	OFF	OFF

OP 5

FREQUENCY	DETUNE	AMS
1.00	0	0

ENVELOPE DATA

R1	R2	R3	R4	RS
35	21	36	63	0
L1	L2	L3	L4	
99	90	85	0	

KEYBOARD SCALING

CURVE		BREAKPOINT	DEPTH	
L	-L	C#6	L	99
R	-L		R	0
OP#	OUTPUT LEVEL		VELOCITY	
5	53		1	

OP 6

FREQUENCY	DETUNE	AMS
5.10	0	0

ENVELOPE DATA

R1	R2	R3	R4	RS
99	72	48	17	0
L1	L2	L3	L4	
99	99	99	0	

KEYBOARD SCALING

CURVE		BREAKPOINT	DEPTH	
L	-L	A-1	L	0
R	-L		R	0
OP#	OUTPUT LEVEL		VELOCITY	
6	45		1	

4

OP 2

FREQUENCY	DETUNE	AMS
1.00	0	3

ENVELOPE DATA

R1	R2	R3	R4	RS
19	26	53	25	0
L1	L2	L3	L4	
51	45	36	51	

KEYBOARD SCALING

CURVE		BREAKPOINT	DEPTH	
L	-L	A-1	L	0
R	-L		R	0
OP#	OUTPUT LEVEL		VELOCITY	
2	99		2	

OP 4

FREQUENCY	DETUNE	AMS
1.01	0	1

ENVELOPE DATA

R1	R2	R3	R4	RS
72	19	41	12	0
L1	L2	L3	L4	
48	58	20	56	

KEYBOARD SCALING

CURVE		BREAKPOINT	DEPTH	
L	-L	A-1	L	0
R	-L		R	0
OP#	OUTPUT LEVEL		VELOCITY	
4	99		0	

OP 1

FREQUENCY	DETUNE	AMS
2.00	0	0

ENVELOPE DATA

R1	R2	R3	R4	RS
37	20	53	62	0
L1	L2	L3	L4	
99	94	97	0	

KEYBOARD SCALING

CURVE		BREAKPOINT	DEPTH	
L	-L	A-1	L	O
R	-L		R	0
OP#	OUTPUT LEVEL		VELOCITY	
1	99		0	

OP 3

FREQUENCY	DETUNE	AMS
1.00	0	0

ENVELOPE DATA

R1	R2	R3	R4	RS
42	20	53	53	0
L1	L2	L3	L4	
99	32	97	0	

KEYBOARD SCALING

CURVE		BREAKPOINT	DEPTH	
L	-L	A-1	L	0
R	-L		R	0
OP#	OUTPUT LEVEL		VELOCITY	
3	99		3	

Secondly, here's a sound to demonstrate creative use of keyboard level scaling to initiate a very radical keyboard split. This one's called "S-H ORGAN" and provides a rhythmic bright bass for the left hand with a pretty convincing organ for the right hand. Note that the carrier responsible for the bass accompaniment is also used as part of the organ sound: only its associated modulator is scaled off the upper end of the keyboard. This is a good way to get around the fact that we "only" have six operators (back in Chapter Two, that was an astonishing amount. Here in Chapter Fifteen, it's "only". Knowledge is power!)

S/H ORGAN

ALG. #5:

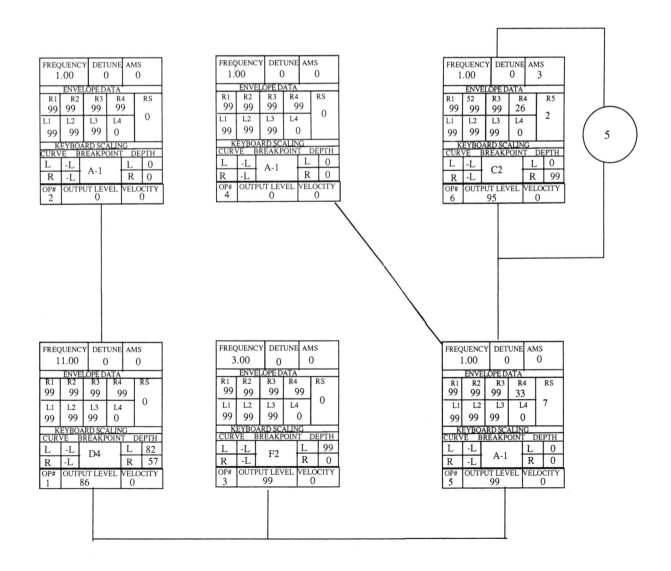

S/H	43	0	0	70	OFF	3
WAVE	SPEED	DELAY	PMD	AMD	SYNC	PMS

R1	R2	R3	R4
99	99	99	99

L1	L2	L3	L4
50	50	50	50

C2
KEY TRANPOSITION

ON
OSC SYNC

PITCH ENVELOPE

FUNCTIONS

POLY	5	0	--	OFF	0
POLY/MONO	RANGE	STEP	MODE	GLISSANDO	TIME
	PITCH BEND			PORTAMENTO	

(CONTORLLER)	RANGE	PITCH	AMPLITUDE	EG BIAS
MOD WHEEL	55	ON	OFF	OFF
FOOT CONT.	0	OFF	OFF	OFF
BREATH CONT.	0	OFF	OFF	OFF
AFTER TOUCH	0	OFF	OFF	OFF

Operator 2

FREQUENCY	DETUNE	AMS
1.00	0	0

ENVELOPE DATA

R1	R2	R3	R4	RS
99	99	99	99	0
L1	L2	L3	L4	
99	99	99	0	

KEYBOARD SCALING

CURVE		BREAKPOINT	DEPTH	
L	-L	A-1	L	0
R	-L		R	0

OP#	OUTPUT LEVEL	VELOCITY
2	0	0

Operator 4

FREQUENCY	DETUNE	AMS
1.00	0	0

ENVELOPE DATA

R1	R2	R3	R4	RS
99	99	99	99	0
L1	L2	L3	L4	
99	99	99	0	

KEYBOARD SCALING

CURVE		BREAKPOINT	DEPTH	
L	-L	A-1	L	0
R	-L		R	0

OP#	OUTPUT LEVEL	VELOCITY
4	0	0

Operator 6

FREQUENCY	DETUNE	AMS
1.00	0	3

ENVELOPE DATA

R1	52	R3	R4	R5
99		99	26	2
L1	L2	L3	L4	
99	99	99	0	

KEYBOARD SCALING

CURVE		BREAKPOINT	DEPTH	
L	-L	C2	L	0
R	-L		R	99

OP#	OUTPUT LEVEL	VELOCITY
6	95	0

5

Operator 1

FREQUENCY	DETUNE	AMS
11.00	0	0

ENVELOPE DATA

R1	R2	R3	R4	RS
99	99	99	99	0
L1	L2	L3	L4	
99	99	99	0	

KEYBOARD SCALING

CURVE		BREAKPOINT	DEPTH	
L	-L	D4	L	82
R	-L		R	57

OP#	OUTPUT LEVEL	VELOCITY
1	86	0

Operator 3

FREQUENCY	DETUNE	AMS
3.00	0	0

ENVELOPE DATA

R1	R2	R3	R4	RS
99	99	99	99	0
L1	L2	L3	L4	
99	99	99	0	

KEYBOARD SCALING

CURVE		BREAKPOINT	DEPTH	
L	-L	F2	L	99
R	-L		R	0

OP#	OUTPUT LEVEL	VELOCITY
3	99	0

Operator 5

FREQUENCY	DETUNE	AMS
1.00	0	0

ENVELOPE DATA

R1	R2	R3	R4	RS
99	99	99	33	7
L1	L2	L3	L4	
99	99	99	0	

KEYBOARD SCALING

CURVE		BREAKPOINT	DEPTH	
L	-L	A-1	L	0
R	-L		R	0

OP#	OUTPUT LEVEL	VELOCITY
5	99	0

Finally, here's one called "HOLDMEDOWN". This is one of the longest-developing sounds I have ever heard on the DX7, taking nearly two full minutes to complete all of its various transformations. HOLDMEDOWN also undergoes a final alteration after you release the key you are playing. This patch may not have a lot of musical applications, but I think it's a good example of the types of complex changes the EGs in the DX7 can induce. Just be patient with this one... and happy programming!!

HOLDMEDOWN

ALG. #12

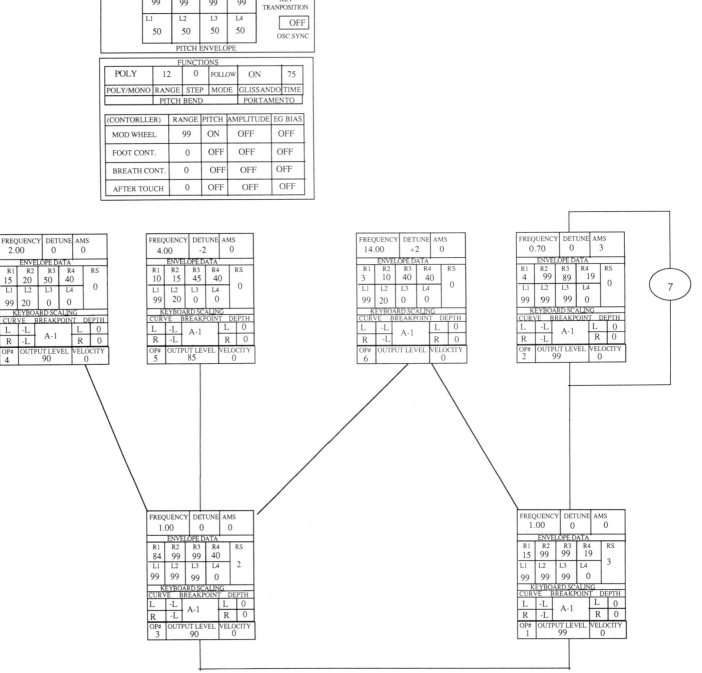

CHAPTER SIXTEEN: OTHER DIGITAL FM INSTRUMENTS

The unparalleled success of the DX7 has spawned a whole new generation of digital FM synthesizers, most of which, because of proprietary and patent considerations, are manufactured by Yamaha (as of this writing, in fact, the only exception is the Synclavier, which primarily uses additive and not FM techniques in order to generate its sounds; therefore, we will not be including it here). This chapter will present a current (as of June 1986) listing of all other commercially available digital FM instruments, with a brief outline of their features as compared with the DX7.

While many of these newer instruments boast powerful performance and programming features, it should be noted that none of them have as yet attained anywhere near the general acceptance of the synthesizer that started it all - the Yamaha DX7.

Yamaha DX9:

As new as digital FM technology is, this is an instrument which is already out of production by Yamaha and has been so since mid-1985. The primary reason for this is the original list price: nearly $1400. In other words, for only $600 more than the price of the very limited DX9, you could buy a full DX7. It was this disparity, more than anything, that contributed to the commercial downfall of this instrument. Nonetheless, it uses the same digital FM system as the DX7, but with far fewer features, and it boasts the same robust construction as is found on all Yamaha instruments.

The DX9 has four operators, instead of six, and offers only eight algorithms instead of thirty-two. There are only 20 internal memory slots, and it cannot access ROM or RAM cartridge sounds - instead, data is off-loaded onto standard audio cassette. This means of data storage is very inexpensive, but very slow and not nearly as reliable as cartridge storage. In lieu of ROM cartridges, Yamaha provided the DX9 with an audio cassette containing 420 presets, but with only four operators at your disposal, these sounds are generally quite inferior to the DX7 presets.

On the other hand, the keyboard is a full five octaves - the same size as the DX7 - although it is not velocity-sensitive; nor does it have after-touch. As with the DX7, you can play up to 16 notes at a time. The keyboard rate scaling is somewhat more limited than what is available on the DX7, but the operator and pitch EGs are exactly the same. Two other minor things: there is a pitch bend wheel range control but no pitch bend step; and the LFO cannot be synchronized to the keyboard.

There are still many DX9s in circulation but most seem to have been bought by people frustrated at the time they spent on the waiting list for a DX7. Once DX7s became readily available, the demand for DX9s virtually disappeared overnight! One can only speculate that this instrument might have done much better if it had carried a lower list price.

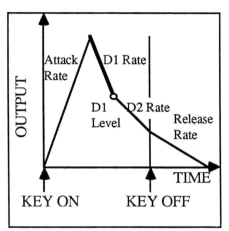

Figure 16-1

Yamaha DX21:

This is one of the newer Yamaha DX instruments, and the one that has essentially supplanted the DX9, albeit at a much lower list price: $ 795. At just over half the price of a DX9, in fact, you could pretty much categorize this instrument as being two DX9s in one package!

Yes, you heard me correctly. Inside the DX21 are two completely separate 4-operator, 8-algorithm digital FM synthesizers, labeled "A" and "B". The two share the same keyboard (the same, five-octave non-velocity-sensitive keyboard as on the DX9) but can interact with one another in a variety of ways. Different keyboard modes allow for the different interactions: "Split" puts each synthesizer over a different part of the keyboard, with the user able to designate hard split points; "Dual" stacks them together over the entire keyboard and allows you to use all eight operators for a single sound; and "Single" just puts one of the two synths over the entire keyboard. Because synth "A" and synth "B" have separate audio outputs, you can get great stereo effects in "Split" or "Layer" mode, plus Yamaha has added a stereo chorusing effect to the output which can be switched in or out. The overall polyphony of this instrument is eight voices (not the sixteen on the DX7 and DX9), but in "Dual" mode, of course, that means only a total of four since each note you play is robbing a voice from synth A and a voice from synth B (a bit like going into a Chinese restaurant...).

There are 128 onboard internal memory slots, but, as with the DX9, you cannot access data cartridges and instead must store data on audio cassette tape only. In edit mode, you can only hear one of the two synths at a time, and this can really be a pain when you're trying to program "Dual" mode sounds. Also, several of the edit parameters offer far less range than equivalent ones on the DX7. Three examples: the keyboard level scaling is less comprehensive than on the DX7; there are usually only two Frequency Fine settings between each Frequency Coarse value; and the operator and pitch EGs are much less complex than those on the DX7, containing only one user-definable level and four user-definable rates with less increments per value available.
(See Figure 16-1.)

That said, there are quite a few improvements here over the original DX7 design. For one thing, there is a separate EG bias sensitivity control. For another, most but not all function controls can be voice-linked, as something called "Performance Memories". Actually, it's the other way around: voices are linked to these sets of function controls. No matter how they do it, it's an obvious plus - and one that DX7 owners will find very attractive.

The two available real-time controllers - the pitch bend wheel and modulation wheel - are somewhat unfortunately mounted on the front panel rather than to the side of the keyboard. Even though, as with the DX9, there is no pitch bend step control, Yamaha has added a couple of snazzy new modes to the pitch bend wheel, allowing you to bend all notes played, or just the highest note, or just the lowest note. One really nice feature that's been added - pitch bias, which allows you to do pitch bends from the breath controller! The MIDI implementation is also quite improved - the DX21 can transmit and receive on any MIDI channel and can also listen in Omni mode.

Finally, even though the DX21 keyboard is itself not velocity sensitive, the voice generating circuitry is, so if you play this instrument from an external MIDI'ed velocity-sensitive keyboard, the DX21 voices will respond accordingly. Unfortunately, that isn't the case with after-touch, which is non-existent on this instrument.

All in all, though, the DX21 is a very impressive instrument in its own right and a particularly good value in terms of its low price. I suspect that DX7 owners would eventually become frustrated at some of its limitations, but for someone first approaching digital FM synthesis, it's really the ideal instrument, with some great performance features to boot.

Yamaha DX5:

This is another two-synthesizers-in-a-box instrument, but this time, it's much more like two deluxe DX7s in a box. Just like the DX21, we have the same three keyboard modes and the same stereo audio outputs, but each of our two synthesizers has the full six operators and the same thirty-two algorithms that we have come to know and love on the DX7. All this gives this instrument a whopping thirty-two note polyphony (in "Single" or "Split" mode), and, as with the DX21, in "Split" mode you can specify hard splits on the keyboard.

Ah, the keyboard. A larger keyboard, for one thing, ranging from E0 to F7 (that's nearly an octave and a half extra, for those of you who aren't counting), and it's got full velocity and after-touch sensitivities. It's also got a nicer feel to it than the DX7 keyboard, which can sometimes be a little on the spongy side.

The actual switches on the DX5 are also much nicer than those on the DX7; not membrane switches, but real honest-to-goodness, light-up-under-your-fingertips switches. And there are a lot more of them, by gum! Instead of an "operator select" switch, there are six operator select switches, so instead of cycling through, you just press the one corresponding to the operator you wish to select. Each Rate and Level for the operator and pitch EGs has its own switch (and the DX5 EGs are exactly the same as the DX7 EGs). Each of the five keyboard level scaling controls (break point, right curve, right depth, left curve, and left depth) has its own switch. Voice initialization has its own switch, as does battery check. In fact, this is switch heaven!

But where's the separate EG bias sensitivity switch??

I shouldn't be complaining - this really is a beautiful instrument. Among other improvements is the fact that there are 64 internal memory slots, and two cartridge slots, one for each synthesizer. The LCD display is quite a bit larger, too - 40 characters - allowing you to view quite a bit more editing data at a time. As with the DX21, Yamaha again gives us "Performance Memory" slots, which are essentially sets of function control data, to which specific combinations of voices can be linked.

Last but not least is a separate headphone preamplifier with its own volume control - something that I'm sure many performing DX7 owners have wished for. And the price: $3495. A bit less than two DX7s for the convenience of two DX7s in one nicely packaged unit. There's nothing revolutionary about the DX5, but it's certainly the first-class way to travel!

Yamaha DX1:

The Yamaha DX1, although still in production as of this writing, was essentially the super-duper deluxe rock star precursor to the DX5, basically containing two complete DX7s in one very large chassis. The list price of this beast, however, is an astronomical $10,900!! Improvements over the DX5? Not $7500 worth, that's for sure. The keyboard on the DX1 is a weighted-action, wooden-key piano-type keyboard, very similar to that used on the old Yamaha CS80 analog synthesizer. The keyboard after-touch, like the old CS80 (and unlike the DX7) is polyphonic. In fact, the whole instrument has the feel (and nearly the bulk) of a CS80, even including the really wonderful CS80 pitch bend strip - a black velvet strip that you sensuously slid your fingers over in order to bend pitch. Among other things, you could do terrific manual vibratos on this strip by simply dropping down a finger and shaking it slowly. Ah, I miss the CS80!

But not $10,900 worth.

Yamaha DX100 and DX27:

Only recently unveiled in the U.S., these machines represent Yamaha's bid to dominate the lower end of the synthesizer market (look out, Casio!). They are precisely the same, except for the fact that the DX27 has a full-size five-octave keyboard while the DX100 has a miniature four-octave keyboard a la the

Casio CZ101. The voice circuitry inside both the DX27 and DX100 is essentially half of a DX21, that is, a single four-operator, eight-algorithm configuration, with no keyboard splits and no stereo audio output. Both these instruments come with 192 preset sounds in ROM memory (and several of these presets are startlingly good!), and both are capable of storing 96 additional user-created sounds. But probably the most amazing thing of all about the DX27 and DX100 is their price: $ 645 for the DX27 and an almost unbelievable $ 445 for the DX100. It's expected that Yamaha will make these machines available through non-music store outlets, such as department stores and general electronic stores; that means it's more than likely that these instruments will eventually be as widely available and as ubiquitous as the Casio synthesizers already are. Another blow for digital FM!

Yamaha TX7 FM Expander:

This is a little add-on box for the DX7 that cannot do very much on its own, but is meant instead to add the sound capabilities of a second DX7 to your existing one. For a start, it has no keyboard, and no cartridge slot, though it does have thirty-two internal voice memory slots. As with the DX7, the TX7 can play up to 16 notes at a time, and each voice is composed of exactly the same parameters as a DX7's (i.e. six operators, thirty-two algorithms, the same EGs, etc.). Additionally, there are sixty-four function memory slots. Thirty-two are used by the TX7 for linking sets of function controls to its own internal voices, and the other thirty-two are available for a DX7 to use to link to its internal voices.

The only editing capabilities on the TX7, however, are for function controls - to change edit parameters, you have to dump the TX7 voice into the DX7, and then back again - a procedure that's not nearly as time-consuming or complicated as it sounds, thanks to the wonders of MIDI. The only data storage the TX7 can access is to an audio cassette, but one nice feature is that it allows you to also store DX7 voices onto cassette, by dumping the DX7 voices into the TX7 memory first. The MIDI implementation here is essentially the same as that of a DX7, with the additional ability of being able to receive in Omni mode.

There is a programmable voice-linked volume control, which will save you having to balance the relative volumes of TX7 and DX7 voices when you're using them together; and, of course, the TX7 has its own audio output, so you can run them in stereo. You can specify hard splits on the DX7 keyboard for each instrument, so for all intents and purposes, this nice little unit (list price: $845) pretty much gives you a second DX7, playable from your existing instrument. The real selling point for me is the ability to voice-link function controls. That feature alone makes this a very attractive add-on to your DX7.

Yamaha TX816 and TX216 MIDI rack:

Now this is a synthesizer! In this section, you'll have to forgive my unqualified ravings, because the TX816 is the instrument I'd Most Like To Be Stranded On A Desert Island With.

If you take a DX7, strip away the keyboard, displays, switches, and chassis, you end up with a circuit card about 4 inches by 6 inches. Take eight of these cards, mount them in a standard 19-inch rack with a common power supply and MIDI buss, add a couple of programming improvements (including voice-linking of all function controls), and you've got a TX816.

The TX816, therefore, gives you forty-eight, I repeat FORTY-EIGHT beautiful Yamaha digital FM operators, complete with forty-eight, I repeat, FORTY-EIGHT beautiful Yamaha digital FM envelopes, and all the bells and whistles you're used to on the DX7, plus a few more (like hard keyboard splits, programmable voice attenuation, and even a reference A440 tuning tone). Each module, being essentially a DX7, has thirty-two internal memory slots, and, of course, can be playing up to sixteen notes at a time, via its own audio output (one drawback is that there is no common audio output) so you can process and pan each module's sound separately in your mixer. The price for this modern-day wonder? $4995, which is considerably less than you'd pay for eight DX7s. If that's a little too steep, you can buy just the power supply box with two of these modules (this is the TX216) for $2095, and you can add on the individual TF1 modules (at $545 a shot) as you need them.

Each module can receive on any or all MIDI channels, and each module can be listening at any given time to either its own individual MIDI input, or via a common MIDI input. This gives you lots of flexibility in terms of complex MIDI setups. Remember that there is no keyboard with this beauty, so you'll need to control it from some external MIDI keyboard (a DX7 will do fine) and you'll also need either a DX7 or a computer programmed to work with DX7 data (see Appendix C) in order to program the modules. There are no cartridge slots in the TX MIDI rack but you can upload or download voice data either directly from a DX7 or from a computer data storage device.

There are really three different ways to utilize the vast sound capabilities of the TX816. One is to actually treat it as a forty-eight operator digital FM synthesizer. This approach will allow you to create sounds of far greater complexity than on a single DX7. A second technique is that of using it as a multi-timbral instrument, with each section of a MIDI keyboard playing different sounds, or with a sequencer addressing each module over a different MIDI channel. A third way is to think of it as a DX7 expander: since you can easily dump DX7 voices directly into the TX816's edit buffer, you can do wonderful things like creating incredible stereo chorusing effects by simply invoking slight detunings between the TF1 modules.

I can't possibly say enough good things about the TX816. I love the design, I love the concept, but most of all I love the sound. You owe it to yourself to at least hear this instrument. In the words of KEYBOARD magazine (October 1985 issue):

"...If you liked the sound of the DX7, you're going to think you died and went to heaven when you hear the TX816"

Yamaha CX5M computer:

This isn't strictly a synthesizer, but since this computer, manufactured by Yamaha, contains a digital FM sound chip (essentially the same one that was used in the DX9), it's worth a brief mention here.

The only keyboard the CX5M comes supplied with is a typewriter-like computer keyboard, so in order to "play" this instrument, you'll need some kind of MIDI keyboard (again, the DX7 will do fine). The digital FM circuitry here can produce up to eight voices simultaneously, but what is interesting is that each voice can be accessed independently via MIDI - in other words, like the much larger TX816, this can be used as a multi timbral instrument. Of course, whereas the TX816 could output up to 128 notes (16 x 8) simultaneously, the CX5M is also limited to 8 notes at a time. But don't let that put you off, because at a list price of $469 (plus $50 for each software cartridge), this is a very interesting little computer - remember, when you're done making sounds with it, you can also balance your checkbook in it!

As the CX5M possesses what was basically the DX9 voice chip, each of its voices has only four operators within eight possible algorithms, so the sounds themselves aren't particularly amazing. There's an onboard memory of 46 preset sounds, and at any one time you can play up to two voices at a time from a MIDI keyboard. Optional software packages allow you to store DX7 data in the CX5M memory (up to 48 sounds at a time) and offload them onto audio cassette or microdisk - Yamaha has recently answered the prayers of CX5M owners everywhere and made available a 3 1/2" microdisk drive for this computer. This same software package (called the DX7 Voicing Program) also provides for data display so you can see most of the DX7 edit parameter data on your monitor or TV screen. The quality of these graphics is fairly low, so don't expect miracles, but as we've observed before, most anything's better than the two-line DX7 LCD display.

Another software package allows for rudimentary sequencer functions - you can store up to 2,000 notes (not a lot), but each of the sequencer's eight tracks can be outputted to a separate MIDI channel, which compensates somewhat for the very small memory capacity.

The CX5M has been primarily oriented towards a non-professional consumer market, and if it helps spread the word about digital FM, then it's providing a valuable service. As a synthesizer, it's quite limited, and as a computer, its lack of memory and disk drive, along with a non-standardized operating system, have made it something less than a smash hit so far.

Still, it's a step in the right direction. Any fusing of synthesizer technology and computer technology is inevitably productive - witness MIDI. And witness Chowning's work and its end product - the DX7.

A final word:

Some of you reading this book may be amazed to know that the sum total of the information presented here was actually the curriculum of an 18-hour course I initiated at the Public Access Synthesizer Studio in New York. They were eighteen of the most data-intensive hours you can imagine, but somehow my students all got through it, none the worse for wear.

I sincerely hope the same has been true for you.

APPENDIX A:

APPENDIX A: QUICK REFERENCE GUIDE TO THE DX7 SWITCHES AND CONTROLS

SWITCHES	PARAMETER	RANGE	CHAPTER #
Data entry section		-	Two
Store (also as EG copy)		- -	Eight Nine
Internal memory protect		on-off	Eight
Cartridge memory protect	on-off	Eight	
Operator select		-	Four
Edit mode (as Compare mode) (as Character key)	 - -	- Eight Eight	Two
Internal memory select		-	Two
Cartridge memory select	-	Two	
Function mode		-	Two
LED/LCD display		-	Two
Cartridge slot		-	Two
ROM cartridges		-	Two
RAM cartridges		-	Two, Thirteen
Edit 1 - 6	Operator on-off	-	Four
Edit 7	Algorithm select	1-32	Four
Edit 8	Feedback	1-7	Seven
Edit 9	LFO wave	Triangle; Saw down; Saw up; Square; Sine; Sample/hold	Ten
Edit 10	LFO speed	0-99	Ten
Edit 11	LFO delay	0-99	Ten
Edit 12	PMD	0-99	Ten

SWITCHES	PARAMETER	RANGE	CHAPTER #
Edit 13	AMD	0-99	Ten
Edit 14	LFO key sync	on-off	Ten
Edit 15	P mod sens.	0-7	Ten
Edit 16	A mod sens.	0-3	Ten
Edit 17 (once)	Oscillator mode	Frequency (Ratio) or Fixed Frequency	Five
Edit 17 (twice)	Oscillator sync	on-off	Five
Edit 18	Frequency coarse	0.50-31.00	Five
Edit 19	Frequency fine	0.50-61.69 (range depends on Freq. Coarse)	Five
Edit 20	Detune	-7 to +7	Five
Edit 21	EG Rate	0-99 for all rates	Nine
Edit 22	EG Level	0-99 for all levels	Nine
Edit 23	Break Point	A-1 to C8	Twelve
Edit 24	Curve	-LIN, -EXP, +EXP, or +LIN	Twelve
Edit 25	Depth	0-99 for both curves	Twelve
Edit 26	Keyboard rate scaling	0-7	Nine
Edit 27	Operator output level	0-99	Four
Edit 28	Keyboard velocity sensitivity	0-7	Eleven
Edit 29	Pitch EG rate	0-99 for all rates	Nine
Edit 30	Pitch EG level	0-99 for all levels	Nine
Edit 31	Key transpose	C1 to C5	Two

SWITCHES	PARAMETER	RANGE	CHAPTER #
Edit 32	Voice name	(use with character keys)	Eight
Function 1	Master tune adjust	(approx. one semitone)	Two
Function 2	Poly/mono	poly or mono	Thirteen
Function 3	Pitch bend wheel range	0-12	Thirteen
Function 4	Pitch bend wheel step	0-12	Thirteen
Function 5	Portamento mode	SUS-KEY P RETAIN or SUS-KEY P FOLLOW in Poly mode; FULLTIME PORTA or FINGERED PORTA in Mono mode	Thirteen
Function 6	Glissando	on-off	Thirteen
Function 7	Portamento time	0-99	Thirteen
Function 8	MIDI	Receive channel 1-16; SYS INFO AVAILABLE or UNAVAILABLE; MIDI TRANSMIT yes or no	Fourteen
Function 9	Edit recall	yes-no	Eight
Function 10	Voice initialization	yes-no	Four
Function 11-13	Cartridge formatting	yes-no	Thirteen
Function 14	Battery check	-	Thirteen
Function 15	Cartridge save	yes-no	Thirteen
Function 16	Cartridge load	yes-no	Thirteen
Function 17	Mod wheel range	0-99	Ten
Function 18	Mod wheel pitch	on-off	Ten
Function 19	Mod wheel amp	on-off	Ten
Function 20	Mod wheel EG bias	on-off	Eleven

SWITCHES	PARAMETER	RANGE	CHAPTER #
Function 21	Foot control range	0-99	Ten
Function 22	Foot control pitch	on-off	Ten
Function 23	Foot control amp	on-off	Ten
Function 24	Foot control EG bias	on-off	Eleven
Function 25	Breath control range	0-99	Ten
Function 26	Breath control pitch	on-off	Ten
Function 27	Breath control amp	on-off	Ten
Function 28	Breath control EG bias	on-off	Eleven
Function 29	After touch range	0-99	Ten
Function 30	After touch pitch	on-off	Ten
Function 31	After touch amp	on-off	Ten
Function 32	After touch EG bias	on-off	Eleven

N.B. information regarding the DX7 controllers and footswitches can be found in the following Chapters:

Pitch bend wheel: Chapter Thirteen
Modulation wheel: Chapter Ten
Foot controller: Chapter Ten
Volume pedal: Chapter Ten
Breath controller: Chapter Ten
Keyboard after-touch: Chapter Ten
Sustain footswitch: Chapter Nine
Portamento footswitch: Chapter Thirteen

APPENDIX B:

APPENDIX B: VOICE INITIALIZATION DEFAULTS FOR THE DX7

The following is a complete summary of all the DX7 default values that are inserted upon entering the voice intialization procedure (see Chapter Four for more details):

Main Mode: The DX7 defaults to edit mode.

SWITCH #	PARAMETER	DEFAULT VALUE
Edit 1 - 6	Operator on-off	All operators <u>on</u>
Edit 7	Algorithm select	Algorithm #1
Edit 8	Feedback	Feedback = 0
Edit 9	LFO wave	Triangle
Edit 10	LFO speed	LFO speed = 35
Edit 11	LFO delay	LFO delay = 0
Edit 12	PMD	PMD = 0
Edit 13	AMD	AMD = 0
Edit 14	LFO key sync	On
Edit 15	Pitch modulation sensitivity	Sensitivity = 3
Edit 16	Amplitude modulation sensitivity	Sensitivity = 0 for all operators
Edit 17	Oscillator mode	Frequency(ratio) for all operators
	Oscillator sync	Osc key sync = on
Edit 18	Frequency coarse	1.00 for all operators
Edit 19	Frequency fine	1.00 for all operators
Edit 20	Detune	Detune = 0 for all operators
Edit 21	EG rate	Rate 1 = 99 for all operators Rate 2 = 99 for all operators Rate 3 = 99 for all operators Rate 4 = 99 for all operators
Edit 22	EG level	Level 1=99 for all operators Level 2=99 for all operators Level 3=99 for all operators Level 4= 0 for all operators

SWITCH #	PARAMETER	DEFAULT VALUE
Edit 23	Break point	A-1 for all operators
Edit 24	Keyboard level scaling curve	- LIN for both curves, all operators
Edit 25	Keyboard level scaling depth	Depth = 0 for both curves, all operators
Edit 26	Keyboard rate scaling	Rate scaling = 0 for all operators
Edit 27	Operator output level	Output level = 99 for operator 1; Output level = 0 for all other operators.
Edit 28	Keyboard velocity sensitivity	Velocity sensitivity = 0 for all operators.
Edit 29	Pitch EG rate	Rate 1 = 99 for all operators Rate 2 = 99 for all operators Rate 3 = 99 for all operators Rate 4 = 99 for all operators
Edit 30	Pitch EG level	Level 1=50 for all operators Level 2=50 for all operators Level 3=50 for all operators Level 4=50 for all operators
Edit 31	Key transpose	Middle C = C3
Edit 32	Voice name	INIT VOICE

NOTE that no function controls are issued defaults upon voice initialization; they simply remain at their current settings (see Chapter 13).

The following is a summary of power-up defaults on the DX7; those few parameters that reset themselves whenever turning the DX7 on:

SWITCH	PARAMETER	DEFAULT
n/a	Internal memory protection	ON
n/a	Cartridge memory protection	ON
Function 8	MIDI system exclusive info available/unavailable	UNAVAILABLE

APPENDIX C:

**APPENDIX C: MIDI COMPUTER PROGRAMS AND DEDICATED
SEQUENCERS FOR THE DX7**

The following is a partial listing of MIDI computer programs compatible with the Yamaha DX7,
current as of this writing (June 1986). These programs are of three different varieties: data
display, data storage, and sequencing. Refer to Chapter Fourteen (MIDI) for an explanation of the
difference between each category; also note that several programs listed below incorporate more
than one feature and are marked as such. Some data storage programs have the added capability of
voice-linking function controls; consult the manufacturer for details. For a more complete listing,
the reader is referred to KEYBOARD magazine, January '86 issue (MIDI Mania!). The author is
grateful to Dominic Milano and Ted Greenwald of that publication for their dedicated research
which has made the presentation of this appendix so much easier!

Key to different program types:
d/d = data display; d/s = data storage; seq = sequencer

PROGRAM NAME	TYPE	FOR	MANUFACTURER	PRICE
DX Pro	d/d; d/s	Apple II	Digital Music Services 23010 Lake Forest Drive Suite D334 Laguna Hills, CA 92653	$149.00
Patch Librarian	d/d; d/s	Commodore 64	Doctor T's Music Software 24 Lexington St. Watertown, MA 02972	$ 75.00
Data 7	d/d; d/s	Apple II; Commodore 64; IBM PC	Mimetics Corporation Box 60238 Station A Palo Alto, CA 94306	$125.00
Performance7	d/s	Apple II; Commodore 64; IBM PC	Mimetics Corporation address same as above	$125.00
MIDI Patch	d/s	Atari; Commodore; IBM PC	Hybrid Arts, Inc. 11920 W. Olympic Blvd. Los Angeles, CA 90064	$ 79.00
FM Drawing Board	d/d; d/s	Apple II	Nexus Computer Consultants 212 Main Street Toronto, Ontario M4E 2W1 Canada	$200.00
DX-TX Master	d/d; d/s	Commodore 64	Syntech Corporation 23958 Craftsman Road Calabasas, CA 91302	$149.95
DX-TX EZ Voice	d/d; d/s	IBM PC	Syntech Corporation address same as above	$399.00
MIDIlib	d/s	IBM PC	Club MIDI Software Box 93895 Hollywood, CA 90093	$ 49.95

MegaTrack	seq	MacIntosh	Musicworks 18 Haviland Boston, MA 02116	$150.00

PROGRAM NAME	TYPE	FOR	MANUFACTURER	PRICE
Midimac	seq	MacIntosh	Opcode Systems 1040 Ramona Palo Alto, CA 94301	$150.00
Total Music	seq; d/s	MacIntosh	Southworth Music Systems Box 275, RD 1 Harvard, MA 01451	$489.00

The following is an incomplete listing of dedicated MIDI sequencers which will work with the DX7. Each of these consists of hardware as well as software, and does not require an external computer:

PRODUCT NAME	MANUFACTURER	PRICE
QX1*	Yamaha Box 6600 Buena Park, CA 90622	$2,795.00
QX7	Yamaha same address as above	$ 475.00
MSQ-700	RolandCorp. 7200 Dominion Circle Los Angeles, CA 90040	$1,195.00
MSQ-100	RolandCorp. same address as above	$ 625.00
SZ1	Casio 15 Gardner Road Fairfield, NJ 07006	$ 399.00
SQD1	Korg/Unicord 89 Frost Street Westbury, NY 11590	$ 695.00

*can also be used for DX7 data storage.

PROGRAM NAME	TYPE	FOR	MANUFACTURER	PRICE
Voice Librarian	d/s	Apple II; IBM PC	Computers and Music 1989 Junipero Serra Blvd. Daly City, CA 94014	$ 49.95
DXLib	d/d; d/s	IBM PC	Noteworthy Systems 3065 24th Street Boulder, CO 80302	$ 49.00
MidiMac Patch Editor	d/d; d/s	MacIntosh	Opcode Systems 1040 Ramona Palo Alto, CA 94301	$ 99.00
MidiMac Patch Librarian	d/s	MacIntosh	Opcode Systems address same as above	$ 50.00
MacMIDI Voicepatch Librarian	d/s	MacIntosh	Musicworks 18 Haviland Boston, MA 02116	$150.00
Texture/ Texture II	seq	Apple II	Magnetic Music PO Box 328 Rhinebeck, NY 12572	$199.00
Texture/ Texture II	seq	IBM PC	Magnetic Music address same as above	$299.00
Meta Track	seq	Apple II	Mimetics Corporation Box 60238, Station A Palo Alto, CA 94306	$125.00
Keyboard Controlled Sequencer	seq	Apple II; Commodore	Doctor T's Music Software 24 Lexington Street Watertown, MA 02972	$125.00
KSQ 800	seq	Apple II; Commodore	Korg/Unicord 89 Frost Street Westbury, NY 11590	$ 99.50
MIDI Sequencer II	seq	Apple II; Commodore	Music Data, Inc. 8444 Wilshire Blvd. Beverly Hills, CA 90211	n/a
Master Tracks	seq	Apple II; Commodore	Passport Designs 625 Miramontes St. Half Moon Bay, CA 94019	n/a
MUSE	seq	Apple II; Commodore	RolandCorp. 7200 Dominion Circle Los Angeles, CA 90040	$150.00
Studio 1, 2	seq	Apple II; Commodore	Syntech Corporation 23958 Craftsman Road Calabasas, CA 91302	$225.95

PROGRAM NAME	TYPE	FOR	MANUFACTURER	PRICE
Song Producer	seq	Commodore	Moog Music & Electronics 2500 Walden Avenue Buffalo, NY 14225	$295.00
MIDI 8 Plus	seq	Commodore	Passport Designs 625 Miramontes St. Half Moon Bay, CA 94019	$149.95
Music Shop	seq	Commodore	Passport Designs address same as above	$ 99.95
964	seq	Commodore	Sequential 3051 N. 1st St. San Jose, CA 95134	$ 99.00
Sequencer Plus	seq	IBM PC	Octave Plateau Electronics 51 Main Street Yonkers, NY 10701	$495.00
MPS	seq	IBM PC	RolandCorp. 7200 Dominion Circle Los Angeles, CA 90040	$495.00
Personal Composer	seq; d/s	IBM PC	Standard Productions 1314 34th Avenue San Francisco, CA 94122	$495.00
MIDI Composer	seq	MacIntosh	Assimilation 485 Alberto Way Los Gatos, CA 95030	$ 29.00
Studio Mac	seq	MacIntosh	Creative Solutions 4701 Randolph St., Ste. 12 Rockville, MD 20852	$125.00
Deluxe Music Construction Set	seq	MacIntosh	Electronic Arts 2755 Campus Drive San Mateo, CA 94403	$ 49.95
Concertware Plus	seq	MacIntosh	Passport Designs 625 Miramontes St. Half Moon Bay, CA 94019	$139.0
Musicworks	seq	MacIntosh	MacroMind, Inc. 1028 W. Wolfram Chicago, IL 60657	$ 79.95
Performer	seq	MacIntosh	Mark of the Unicorn 222 3rd Street Cambridge, MA 02142	$295.00

APPENDIX D:

APPENDIX D: THE DX7 MIDI DATA FORMAT

The following is a complete listing of the current DX7 MIDI data format, as originally published in the IMA Bulletin (official publication of the International MIDI Association, 11857 Hartsook St., North Hollywood, CA 91607), January 1984 issue:

1. TRANSMISSION DATA

1-1. Channel Information

1001nnnn	Key ON & Channel number (n = 0; ch1)
Okkkkkkk	Key number (k = 36; C_1 — k = 96; C_6)
Ovvvvvvv	Key velocity (v = 0; Key OFF, v = 1; ppp — v = 127; fff)
1011nnnn	Control change & Channel number (n = 0; ch1)
Occccccc	Control number
Ovvvvvvv	Control value

C	Parameter	V
1	Modulation wheel	0 ~ 127
2	Breath controller	0 ~ 127
DØ	After touch	0 ~ 127
4	Foot controller	0 ~ 127
6	Data entry knob	0 ~ 127
64	Sustain foot switch	0 ; OFF, 127 ; ON
65	Portamento foot switch	0 ; OFF, 127 ; ON
96	Data entry +1	127 ; ON only
97	Data entry −1	127 ; ON only

1100nnnn	Program change & Channel number (n = 0; ch1)
Oppppppp	Program number (p = 0; Voice 1 — p = 31; Voice 32)

1110nnnn	Pitch bender & Channel number (n = 0; ch1)
Ovvvvvvv	Pitch bender value LS byte
Ovvvvvvv	Pitch bender value MS byte (O—64—127)

MS byte	LS byte
0 ~ 64	0
65 ~ 127	2 (MS byte−64)

1-2. System exclusive information

1-2-1. MIDI Active Clock

11110000	Status byte
Oiiiiiii	Identification number (i = 67; YAMAHA)

MIDI active clock is continuously output at 80 ms intervals, except during bulk dump data transmission and reception.

1-2-2. Bulk Data for One Voice

11110000	Status byte
Oiiiiiii	Identification number (i = 67; YAMAHA)
	Sub status (s = 0) & Channel number
Osssnnnn	(n = 0; ch1)
Offfffff	Format number (f = 0; 1 voice)
Obbbbbbb	Byte count MS byte
Obbbbbbb	Byte count LS byte
Oddddddd	Data 1st byte
Oddddddd	Data 155th byte
Oeeeeeee	Check Sum (2's complement of the sum of 155 bytes)

1-2-3. Bulk Data for 32 Voices

11110000	Status byte
Oiiiiiii	Identification number (i = 67; YAMAHA)
Osssnnnn	Sub status (s = 0) & Channel number (n = 0; ch1)
Offffffff	Format number (f = 9; 32 voices)
Obbbbbbb	Byte count MS byte
Obbbbbbb	Byte count LS byte (b = 4;96; 32 voices)
Oddddddd	Data 1st byte
Oddddddd	Data 4096th byte
Oeeeeeee	Check Sum (2's complement of the sum of 4096 bytes)

1-2-4. Parameter Change

11110000	Status byte
Oiiiiiii	Identification number (i = 67; YAMAHA)
Osssnnnn	Sub status (s = 1) & Channel number (n = 0; ch1)
Oggggggpp	Parameter group number (g = 0; Common DX Voice parameter, g = 2; DX7 Function parameter)
Oppppppp	Parameter number
Oppppppp	Parameter number
Oddddddd	Data

DX7s manufactured before August '83 use BOO3 for after touch.

YAMAHA DX7 MIDI DATA FORMAT

■ **g=0 : Common DX Voice parameter**

P	Parameter	d
0	OP6 EG RATE 1	0 ~ 99
1	" RATE 2	"
2	" RATE 3	"
3	" RATE 4	"
4	" LEVEL 1	"
5	" LEVEL 2	"
6	" LEVEL 3	"
7	" LEVEL 4	"
8	OP6 KEY BOARD LEVEL SCALE BREAK POINT	"
9	" LEFT DEPTH	"
10	" RIGHT DEPTH	"
11	" LEFT CURVE	0 ~ 3
12	" RIGHT CURVE	"
13	OP6 KEY BOARD RATE SCALLING	0 ~ 7
14	OP6 MOD SENSITIVITY AMPLITUDE	0 ~ 3
15	OP6 OPERATOR KEY VELOCITY SENSITIVITY	0 ~ 7
16	OP6 OPERATOR OUTPUT LEVEL	0 ~ 99
17	OP6 OSCILLATOR MODE	0 ~ 1
18	OP6 OSCILLATOR FREQUENCY COARSE	0 ~ 31
19	" FINE	0 ~ 99
20	DETUNE	0 ~ 14
21		
~	OP5 ~ OP1	~
125		
126	PITCH EG RATE 1	0 ~ 99
127	" RATE 2	"
128	" RATE 3	"
129	" RATE 4	"
130	" LEVEL 1	"
131	" LEVEL 2	"
132	" LEVEL 3	"
133	" LEVEL 4	"
134	ALGORITHM SELECT	0 ~ 31
135	FEED BACK	0 ~ 7
136	OSCILLATOR SYNC	0 ~ 1
137	LFO SPEED	0 ~ 99
138	" DELAY	"
139	" PMD	"
140	" AMD	"

P	Parameter	d							
141	LFO SYNC	0 ~ 1							
142	" WAVE	0 ~ 4							
143	MOD SENSITIVITY PITCH	0 ~ 7							
144	TRANSPOSE	0 ~ 48							
145	VOICE NAME 1	ASCII							
~	~	~							
154	VOICE NAME 10	ASCII							
155	OPERATOR ON/OFF	D6	D5	D4	D3	D2	D1	D0	
	0=OFF, 1=ON	0	OP1	OP2	OP3	OP4	OP5	OP6	

g=2 ; DX7 Function parameter

P	Parameter	d
64	MONO/POLY MODE CHANGE	0 ~ 1
65	PITCH BEND RANGE	0 ~ 12
66	" STEP	0 ~ 12
67	PORTAMENT MODE	0 ~ 1
68	" GLISSAND	0 ~ 1
69	" TIME	0 ~ 99
70	MODULATION WHEEL RANGE	0 ~ 99
71	" ASSIGN	0 ~ 7
72	FOOT CONTROLLER RANGE	0 ~ 99
73	" ASSIGN	0 ~ 7
74	BREATH CONTROLLER RANGE	0 ~ 99
75	" ASSIGN	0 ~ 7
76	AFTER TOUCH RANGE	0 ~ 99
77	" ASSIGN	0 ~ 7

YAMAHA DX7 MIDI DATA FORMAT

2. RECEPTION DATA

2-1. Channel Information

Reception is possible when the channel number of the received data matches the channel number set up at the DX7.

1000nnnn	Key OFF & Channel number
	(n = 0; ch1 — n = 15; ch16)
0kkkkkkk	Key number (k = 0,1; $C^{\#}_{-2}$—k = 127; G_8)
0vvvvvvv	Key velocity (v; Ignored)
1001nnnn	Key ON & Channel number
	(n = 0; ch1—n = 15; ch16)
0kkkkkkk	Key number (k = 0,1; $C^{\#}_{-2}$—k = 127; G_8)
0vvvvvvv	Key velocity
	(v = 0; Key OFF, v = 1; ppp—v = 127; fff)
1011nnnn	Control change & channel number
	(n = 0; ch1 — n = 15; ch16)
0ccccccc	Control number
0vvvvvvv	Control value

c	Parameter	v
1	Modulation wheel	0 ~ 127
2	Breath controller	0 ~ 127
DØ	After touch	0 ~ 127
4	Foot controller	0 ~ 127
5	Portamento time	0 ~ 127
6	Data entry knob (MASTER TUNE only)	0 ~ 127
7	Volume (Lowest 4 bits ignored)	0 ~ 127
64	Sustain foot switch	0 ; OFF, 127 ; ON
65	Portamento foot switch	0 : OFF, 127 ; ON
96	Data entry +1	127 ; ON only
97	Data entry −1	127 ; ON only
125	OMNI all key off	Ignored
126	MONO all key off	Ignored
127	POLY all key off	Ignored

1100nnnn	Program change & Channel number
	(n = 0; ch1—n = 15; ch16)
0ppppppp	Program number (p = 0; Voice 1—
	p = 31; Voice 32)
1110nnnn	Pitch bender & Channel number
	(n = 0; ch1—n = 15; ch16)
0vvvvvvv	Pitch bender value LS byte (Ignored)
0vvvvvvv	Pitch bender value MS byte (0—64—127)

2-2. System Exclusive Information

2-2-1. MIDI Active Clock
MIDI active clock is received regardless of channel number. If the clock is interrupted for more than 666 ms at any time other than during reception of bulk data, the DX7 assumes that transmitter power is off or the line has been disconnected, and stops note output.

2-2-2. Bulk Data for One Voice
1-voice bulk data is received in the same format as the transmission data when the MIDI channel numbers match in the "System Information Available" mode.

2-2-3. Bulk Data for 32 Voices
32-voice bulk data is received in the same format as the transmitted data when the MIDI channel numbers match in the "System Information Available" mode, and when Memory Protect is OFF.

2-2-4. Parameter Change
Voice and function parameters are received in the same format as the transmitted data when the MIDI channel numbers match in the "System Information Available" mode.